FREEING YOUR CHILD FROM OBSESSIVE-COMPULSIVE DISORDER

A Powerful, Practical Program for Parents of Children and Adolescents

TAMAR E. CHANSKY, PH.D.

*Director, Children's Center
for OCD and Anxiety*

Illustrations by Phillip Stern

THREE RIVERS PRESS

NEW YORK

Published by Three Rivers Press, New York, New York. Member of the Crown Publishing Group.

Originally published in hardcover in 2000 by Crown Publishers.

Random House, Inc. New York, Toronto, London, Sydney, Auckland
www.randomhouse.com

THREE RIVERS PRESS is a trademark and the Three Rivers Press colophon is a registered trademark of Random House, Inc.

Grateful acknowledgment is made to the following for permission to reprint previously published material:

American Medical Association: Slide from L.R. Baxter, Jr., M.E. Phelps, and J.C. Mazziotta (1987). Local cerebral glucose metabolic rates in obsessive-compulsive disorder: A comparison with rations in unipolar depression and in normal controls. *Archives of General Psychiatry,* March, 1987, Volume 44, pp. 211–218, Figure 6. Copyright © 1987. American Medical Association. Reprinted by permission of the Americal Medical Association.

American Medical Association: Slide from J.M. Schwartz, P.W. Stoessel, and L.R. Baxter, Jr. (1996). Systemic changes in cerebral glucose metabolic rate after successful behavior modification of obsessive-compulsive disorder. *Archives of General Psychiatry,* February 1996, Volume 53, pp. 109–113, Figure 1. Copyright © 1996. American Medical Association. Reprinted by permission of the Americal Medical Association.

Wayne K. Goodman, M.D.: Children's Yale-Brown Obsessive Compulsive Scale. Copyright © 1986 Wayne K. Goodman. Reprinted by permission of Wayne K. Goodman, M.D.

Guilford Press: Excerpts from *OCD in Children and Adolescents: A Cognitive-Behavioral Treatment Manual* by John S. March and Karen Mulle. Copyright © 1998 by John S. March and Karen Mulle. Reprinted by permission of Guilford Publications, Inc.

Emily Perl Kingsley: Welcome to Holland. Copyright © 1987 by Emily Perl Kingsley. Reprinted by permission of Emily Perl Kingsley.

Lippincott Williams & Wilkins: Leyton Obsessional Inventory: C.Z. Berg, A. Whitaker, M. Davies, M.F. Flament, and J.L. Rapoport (1988). *Journal of the American Academy of Child and Adolescent Psychiatry,* 27(6), 759–763, Appendix. Reprinted by permission of Lippincott Williams & Wilkins, A Wolters Kluwer Company.

Printed in the United States of America

Library of Congress Cataloging-in-Publication Data is available.

ISBN 0-8129-3117-3

18 17 16 15 14 13

First Paperback Edition

To my patients and their families for all you have taught me.

PREFACE

For more than a decade, I have been working with children and adolescents who have anxiety and obsessive-compulsive disorder. Many of my patients have been generous enough to share their stories with me for this book. I have included them here but have disguised their and their families' names and identifying characteristics to protect their privacy. I am extremely grateful to them for their candor. They shared their own experiences out of a desire to help others free themselves from the prison of OCD.

No book, including this one, can ever replace the experience of individualized care from a qualified health professional. As I emphasize here, it is essential to find a therapist who specializes in treating OCD to help you help your child. I have written this book to help you work more effectively with that therapist, to give you the tools to be effective on the home front, and to help you work with your child's school to make sure that he or she gets needed support there.

TAMAR CHANSKY

ACKNOWLEDGMENTS

I could not have started or finished this book without the inspiration, generosity, and encouragement of my patients and their families. It is to them that I give my deepest thanks and respect. They courageously let me into their lives and shared their stories with me for the cause of changing the face of OCD. From the 4-year-olds to the college students, each child has given me an opportunity to learn about life, OCD, and above all taking risks. My agent Gareth Esersky and my editor Betsy Rapoport at Crown believed in this book from the start, and were committed to bringing it to fruition. Patty Romanowski Bashe, also at Crown, contributed not only her editing expertise, but brought many important issues to my attention. Thanks to Nancy Marcus Land at Publications Development Company for bringing it all together.

Because this is a dynamic time in the study of neurobiological disorders, I was energized by the work of many colleagues. In using John March's innovative treatment manual, I saw how to engage children's natural creativity and sense of healthy entitlement to win the battle against OCD. Jeffrey Schwartz inspired the idea of helping parents disengage from their children's symptoms as he encouraged patients to do for themselves. The work of Russell Barkley and Ross Greene modeled the essential operation of teaching parents how to help their kids. John Ratey and Catherine Johnson brought to life the concept of being educated consumers when it comes to the brain. In addition, I am grateful to the many OCD experts whose commitment to the field has made a difference for millions and who directly or indirectly taught me so much especially: John Greist, Edna Foa, Lee Baer, Judith Rapoport, Jon Grayson, Fred Penzel, Herbert Gravitz, Susan Swedo, and Ian Osborn. A very special thanks to my colleagues who gave generously of their time, reading parts of the manuscript or helping me clarify my ideas: Michael Jenike, Gail Adams, Xavier Castellanos, William Hewlett, Jay Fruehling, and Matthew Cohen. Bette Hartley at the Obsessive Compulsive Information Center was truly a godsend. She not only lent her sharp eyes to the manuscript, she located and sent me every article I needed, and her unequivocal enthusiasm for the book kept me going through many a long haul. What good fortune to have as friends and colleagues, Jodi Mindell who has mentored me through the book-writing process, and D'Arcy Lyness, who read the manuscript and shares a vision. The OC Foundation has supported my work and the importance of the parents' role. Thank you, OCF webmaster Al Willen. I appreciate the many local psychologists, psychiatrists, pediatricians, and school personnel with whom I've had the opportunity to collaborate in the process of helping our children. The staff at the Anxiety and Agoraphobia Treatment Center gave me the freedom to grow. I thank Jeanne Marecek for encouraging me to go to graduate school and Philip Kendall for giving me so many opportunities while I was there. Mary Poovey, Donald Rackin, Jay Efran, and Michael Levine encouraged me to write.

I thank my friends who have encouraged me over the years, especially Lisa Dorothea Gillim, Nell Stoddard-Hunt, Juliet Sternberg, Margaret Horn, and Tamar Doron. Great appreciation to Shirley Brown, Sonia Voynow, Taka Suzuki, David Stoddard-Hunt, Amy Verstappen, and some guardian angels who all extended themselves with food, childcare, book runs, good wishes, and carpooling when I needed it most. Maxine Baylor's loving care of Meredith was paramount in enabling me to finish my degree without too much guilt! Lee Miller is a steadfast voice of reason, and Jen Pomykcaz was heroic in her commitment to bringing me back to health. Remembering the spirit of my friend Gael Mathews steadies me.

My parents, Elissa and Norman Chansky, have been there for all of us through thick and thin. Their willingness to help in any way has been a great source of comfort. They have taught me to help others, and not to be afraid of being practical about it—an important guidepost in my professional life. Each of my siblings has rallied for me: Linda Janidlo, James Chansky, Keren Chansky Suberri, and Matthew Chansky.

To my core: Meredith and Phil, thank you for believing in me and this project so much that you let it take over our house and my thoughts for a long while. Meredith, you have taught me to use metaphor to make things understandable, and have helped me remember how to play. Phil, the kindest iconoclast—you have encouraged me to live out on a limb and have surrounded us with a whirl of color, creativity, and inspiration. You have immeasurably transformed this book: your command of language and image, along with your willingness to spend hours sitting next to me as I reach for clarity, has been critical to the evolution and completion of this book.

This book reflects my understanding of OCD. I hope that my colleagues can forbear any omissions I may have made in my attempt to get information to those who urgently need it.

CONTENTS

PART FOUR

APPENDICES

INTRODUCTION

As one of the few psychologists in this country specializing in childhood obsessive-compulsive disorder (OCD), I have been immersed in this parallel universe for many years. I spend most of my working hours treating children and their parents, educating school personnel, providing expert advice on-line for the Obsessive Compulsive Foundation, and giving workshops locally and nationally. This is a new era in the history of OCD. We now have potent tools for fighting OCD—behavior therapy and medications—but these treatments do not implement themselves, and that is where you as parents come in. The message of this book is that children can truly break free from OCD if they have their parents' help and support.

I have seen how essential parents can be in the process of recovery. As director of the Children's Program at a suburban anxiety clinic, armed with the powerful treatment manual from Dr. John March, Duke University child psychiatrist and national authority on OCD, I have watched the power struggles and fireworks that emerge when parents attempt to apply the behavioral principles for fighting OCD in their homes. These difficulties occur, in part, because OCD simply makes no sense to parents—it is so illusive—and kids get frustrated when their parents try to make changes without understanding what is wrong. For you to lead your child out of the land of OCD, you need to be a good tour guide. You need to know the territory well yourself. My emphasis is on addressing the emotional and practical needs of parents, identifying the barriers OCD creates to their essential role of raising their child. My strategy is to translate the rules and prescriptions of OCD—to unlock and demystify the bizarre customs of this foreign land—into knowable concepts and provide a language and steps that can help your child work his or her way out of OCD. My mission has been to create a parent's "travel companion" to OCD, a sort of road map detailing the twists and turns in the terrain and how to navigate them. Road maps should make the landscape recognizable and less intimidating; therefore, with the generous words of my patients as illustrations, I have highlighted the emotional landmarks, making connections between OCD and other, more familiar experiences we face as parents. When parents are surefooted guides, their children are more likely to follow in the same direction.

In session with my young patients each day, I go on journeys navigating the tumultuous land of OCD. I try to end each session at a higher elevation, with children more convinced of their right to boss back OCD and equipped with a new technique or experiment to test their muster each week. Parents acquire scripted lines to support their child's current challenges. And children get better.

The changes I witness in these families are nothing short of miraculous. These are not miracles that come from waving a magic wand or using a breakthrough overnight procedure. Rather, they arise from families courageously taking clear, strategic steps to wrestle free from this disorder that disrupts daily life with senseless rules and demands for perfection, cleanliness, and order. The life of a child is simply transformed when he or she emerges victorious from under the oppressive spell of the OCD monster, no longer taken in by the tricks that his or her brain is playing. For example, Haley (you will meet her later on), who used to hold back tears in school all day thinking that she was schizophrenic because of her intrusive thoughts about the devil, was able to turn OCD on its head within a few months of treatment. She recently e-mailed me, triumphant that she is off to college and is not taking OCD with her. I have learned from the heroic journeys of people like Haley and her parents, and it is their stories of triumph that have urged themselves onto these pages.

Because I have specialized in the treatment of anxious children since the beginning of my graduate school career, my emphasis on OCD is a natural progression. But the passion and commitment I feel for my patients and the OCD cause is a personal one. What pulled me in was that I could identify with the terror of parents who feel that they are losing their child but do not know how to stop it. About five years ago, my husband and I experienced a medical scare with our daughter. After she spent a week in intensive care, we endured the next year reeling from that experience and fearing for her future. We lived in that very frightening place you inhabit only when worrying about your child. Watching my daughter struggle through invasive medical procedures, I realized that though I could not spare her from these trials, my presence and support were gifts that only I could give. It was out of these lessons learned and the feelings I had of being a misunderstood, fearful parent that I began to make notes for this book.

Although all parents may get upset when their children fret needlessly about things, for the most part they can relate to their child's worries as similar in kind but more pronounced than their own. As a parent of a child with OCD, you have a different story. You are not just concerned—you are alarmed. You child's bizarre behavior frightens you; your son or daughter has become unrecognizable—licking door-knobs, tapping furniture, scrubbing his or her skin, flipping out at the mere mention of an innocuous, ordinary word. In your shock and effort to save your child, you get pulled into OCD's web, too. You get stuck trying to protect your child from distress. This is a natural response, although many therapists attempt to exclude parents, saying they are "undermining" the treatment or "enabling" the disorder. The despair I see in the parents of my patients is piercing, and yet familiar to me as a parent and as a therapist.

The impact of these families on me has been immeasurable. Each child's journey is unique and yet all are saddled with the common burden of this misunderstood disorder. I have coached and watched these kids become self-possessed and assertive OCD detectors. They have learned how to "sort their brain mail," disposing of OCD junk mail while holding onto the valid thoughts in their mind. While all of them wish that OCD had never been part of their lives, many of them have taken the challenge as an opportunity to galvanize their conviction in themselves and approach life with even greater determination. These children are some of the strongest people I have ever met. My immense respect and admiration for them inspire me to work hard to fight the stigma associated with OCD. In 1999, as a step toward making treatment for OCD and anxiety as common and unremarkable as going to the pediatrician or the allergist, I opened the Children's Center for OCD and Anxiety, in suburban Philadelphia. In addition to providing treatment, the mission of that clinic includes doing outreach to schools, physicians, and community groups. Increasing awareness of OCD and anxiety, in turn, may encourage early intervention and prevent years of unnecessary suffering for affected children.

I hope this book provides not only information and clear steps to follow in your daily life, but a place to garner new hope when yours is waning. My goal is to present a reflection of your life that you can't get from chatting in the supermarket line or at the bus stop—a reference point to help you look at your experience and say, "Yes, others have been here before, that's 'OCD-normal.'" Most of all, I want to return to you the confidence and the knowledge that you can help your child break free from OCD. To the children who coached me to make sure I tell the parents "We really don't want to be doing these things, we can't help it," I hope I have made good on my promise.

PART ONE

DEFINING THE
PROBLEM

What Is OCD?
And What Can Be Done?

It is morning, and here I sit in tears while my daughter Kathy struggles to get dressed for school. My heart sinks as I watch her—once so carefree, personable, honor roll student, soccer star—trapped by this invisible demon that is robbing her of a normal life. Getting ready for school is supposed to be an easy part of the day, yet it is torture for both of us. Kathy insists I can't touch her clothes; I will contaminate them. I gave birth to her, but now I am one of many sources of her ruin that she must avoid at all costs. I can accept that she won't let me touch her or hug her, but she needs to be able to function. To her, the world is full of contaminants. She opens her dresser drawer with a tissue—furniture is contaminated too—and carefully lifts out her clothes making sure that neither her hand nor the clothes touch the dresser. And if her shirt or pant legs touch the floor while she's getting dressed, she picks them up with her toes and flings them into the pile of "untouchables"—it is another day where she misses the school bus and the mountain of laundry builds. She gets so upset and I feel so helpless watching, that I want to pick her up and save her, but I know that the source of the evil is somewhere within her. She is trapped and the worst thing is, *I feel like a prisoner too.* It is a shameful secret—she tries to hide it from her friends, hide that she can't touch money, keys, the remote control—anything if they have held it first. Kathy won't let me talk to her, she gets furious and says I don't understand. At first I challenged her, but now I am afraid—maybe I should just do what she wants—I don't want her to crack, but how is she going to make it to high school—when will this go away? I want to help her, but I know she won't let me. I am afraid I have lost her. . . . What do I do?

—*Mother of an eleven-year-old with OCD*

OCD: Common and Treatable

In the United States alone, over a million children suffer from obsessive-compulsive disorder (OCD). Striking children as young as 4 years old, OCD is a neurobiological condition that disrupts home life, social relationships, and academic functioning for 1 in every 100 young people. OCD is more prevalent than diabetes, but much less talked about. Until recently, OCD was poorly understood and the prognosis was grim. We live in a time when advances in our understanding of the brain and its effects on behavior are something we can actually see happening. Today, we have a revolution in how we look at OCD. We can successfully treat and manage OCD through cognitive-behavior therapy (CBT) and medications. Children with OCD can gain control over their symptoms and lead normal lives. The following statements from OCD experts reflect this new attitude:

> For the first time ever for any psychiatric condition or any psychotherapy technique, **we have scientific evidence that cognitive-behavioral therapy alone actually causes chemical changes in the brains of people with OCD.** We have demonstrated that by changing your behavior, you can free yourself from Brain Lock, change your brain chemistry, and get relief from OCD's terrible symptoms.
> —*Jeffrey Schwartz, M.D.,* Brain Lock

> Cognitive-behavioral therapy (CBT) is the psychotherapeutic treatment of choice for children, adolescents, and adults with OCD. CBT helps the patient internalize a strategy for resisting OCD that will be of lifelong benefit. While periodic "booster" sessions may be required, those who are successfully treated with CBT tend to stay well.
> —*John March, M.D., and Karen Mulle,* OCD in Children and Adolescents: A Cognitive-Behavioral Treatment Manual

> . . . The outlook for OCD sufferers has improved dramatically in recent years with the development of proven behavior therapy and medication treatments for OCD. As a result, we now can successfully treat the vast majority of our patients with OCD.
> —*Lee Baer, Ph.D.,* Getting Control: Overcoming Your Obsessions and Compulsions

The starting assumption in this book is that your child can markedly improve from OCD and be armed with lifelong strategies to combat any recurrences. A second assumption is that a parent's understanding of OCD is an essential piece of the treatment puzzle. So quickly do you and your child become entangled with each other as you try to make your way through your day, trapped in a labyrinth of fear and ritual, that you feel the walls are closing in—blocking out what is familiar and safe to you and your child. The strange and unsettling OCD symptoms leave you disoriented. You start to doubt yourself, "Are my efforts to help my child setting him free or ensnaring him further?"

As parents, you are on the front line. You can successfully combat the enemy OCD, but you need a battle plan. This book is your acting commander in chief. Just as you taught the lessons of not talking to strangers, and choosing clothes for cold weather, you can be your child's essential guide in learning to deal with OCD. First, however, you need to be oriented to the actual enemy and the strategies that work.

We're Not in Kansas Anymore

Living in the land of OCD changes everything. The once tried-and-true parental tricks to soothe or redirect no longer work. Your power has been zapped. The mysterious force of OCD has picked you up out of your known way of life and plunked you down in a foreign land. The rules of daily life that you took for granted don't seem to apply here. Safe isn't safe enough, clean isn't clean enough, and loving reassurance— once a simple parental pleasure—is now an endless prospect. As much as you feel disoriented, your child is lost too—her region of safety shrinking with each passing day as doubt erodes any beliefs about what is. Commensurate with this erosion is your loss in confidence as a parent. The new daily "musts" of your child's life seem bizarre and unnecessary. You watch with amazement as the natural order of things is turned on its head. Your child is now in charge, running your household with his moods, moments, rituals, rages. Frightened and desperate, he leads the way, setting the rules. As parents, you race around after your child trying to put out fires before they start. However precarious, you take any risk to try to make things right, although you know that peace won't last.

You Are Here!

You have lost your bearings; OCD has taken you down so many blind alleys. What you will learn from reading this book is that while the change of scenery is jarring, perplexing, and frightening, your parental instincts *do* have jurisdiction in this new land. You don't have to start over, or trade in your old tricks for new ones. Armed with the right information, you can sort through the confusion of OCD and see it for what it is—a brain hiccup, a misfiring, a mechanical glitch. It is not the last word; it only acts that way. It can be fought and defeated. With the OCD demystified and demoted from brain demon to brain hiccup, you will be able to reclaim your parental authority and stand firm in your belief that your child can break free from OCD.

Where Do I Turn: I Want to Run Away

There is no worse feeling for a parent than helplessness. Your child is miserable with a fever, having a temper tantrum, refusing to do homework, or having her heart broken. Our instinct says "help them," but our hands are empty. And it doesn't end there. What we do with that uncomfortable feeling of helplessness can spawn new problems. We get angry and blame, we get unreasonable, or we lie. As parents, we want to know what to do. And although our children never admit it, insisting just the opposite, they want us to be in charge too—to set limits, to know what's what, to maintain order. If your toddler is exploring electrical outlets or your adolescent is experimenting with your car, it is easy to say no and to enforce an inflexible rule; next you teach what you want the child to learn from the situation that will lead to better decisions next time. But turning to the OCD predicament: your 7-year-old is repeatedly asking to check that his pants aren't ripped and that they aren't going to rip, or your teenager is going through three bottles of soap in a week, and making a lake on the bathroom floor. What do you do? If saying "stop" worked, there would be no OCD. And what should kids learn from that situation? That it doesn't "make sense" to do that? Probably they already know. OCD can wreak havoc on a family. The parents are in charge, but it doesn't look that way. The danger isn't external like an oncoming car at a crosswalk, nor is it exactly coming from your child. You can get angry, or you can accommodate the nonsensical demands, but either way, it's a lose-lose situation. You need a third party and it is the OCD.

What Is OCD: A New Understanding and a New Direction

Until recently, OCD was misunderstood as a neurotic condition. Adults and kids who had it were suffering from conflicts and guilt that led to repetition, superstition, and overcontrolling behaviors. As the theory went, parents were not immune from responsibility or scrutiny. Accused of being either overcontrolling or overindulgent, parents were the culprits. Many people suffered the consequences of our limited understanding.

There is no one to blame for OCD: "It's nobody's fault," as summed up in Dr. Harold Koplewicz' popular book by that title. The key to freeing your child from OCD is learning not to be afraid of it. That is easier said than done. Like the man behind the curtain in the *Wizard of Oz,* OCD talks a good game of frightening you and your child with its disturbing symptoms, but underneath it all OCD is no great wizard of truth and holds no special powers; it is simply a mechanical glitch of an extraordinary piece of machinery—the brain.

In OCD, the part of the brain that filters information is not functioning properly, causing certain thoughts to get stuck which should just be forgotten. OCD is described as an attention-surplus disorder by Dr. John Ratey and Dr. Catherine Johnson, authors of *Shadow Syndromes.* Fear and dread hold attention in a "death grip," according to Drs. Ratey and Johnson, and will not let it go. The take-home message for you and your child is that OCD is a problem to be tackled, not an aspect of your child's personality that must be changed. The shift is from "I *am* a problem" to "I *have* a problem." This essential distinction is the first step in Dr. Jeffrey Schwartz' *Brain Lock* solution—"It's not me, it's OCD."

OCD is a condition about control, but not in the way that many think. From the outside, children with OCD seem to control their environments by placing unreasonable demands on themselves and others for cleanliness, order, and symmetry

till parents begin adopting a language of being controlled—
"She won't let me eat without telling her what's in the food; we are not allowed to touch her after she has showered. I have to shower before he'll let me cook his food." When we look at the situation only from the outside, we think, this child is *choosing* to be rigid, difficult, impossible. This leads down a path of blame.

But OCD from the inside is different. It is as if the child is trapped by an unrelenting heckler who throws out jabs of worry, fear, and uncertainty, making it impossible to take things for granted. At bedtime, the OCD urges, *what if the pool was dirty and you got AIDS?* During a test at school, *what if your house is on fire, are you sure you unplugged the curling iron?* Children have no idea what is going on when they start to experience intrusive thoughts and compulsions. Looking from the outside, we don't see their anguish. When we look from the inside out, we see that kids are being controlled by these intrusive thoughts—the invisible demons who seize on a topic as microscopic as a plaguing speck of invisible dirt or as large as a cataclysmic end of the world. These thoughts barge into the children's thought world and refuse to leave, making them desperate to get rid of the torment at any cost. The child may think that if she wears certain clothes, those thoughts won't come back, or at least the danger won't come true. But day after day, the thoughts *do* come back with a vengeance, and the compulsion expands. Perhaps she did not complete the ritual exactly right; she lost count when saying 10 Hail Marys, so she starts over, but then she had a bad thought during the middle of the 10th, so now she has to do it again without having any bad thoughts. *Start over again.* Then she thinks, *I've been in here for 15 minutes, this is ridiculous, I am a jerk. But no, what if it is true and if I do it wrong, my parents will get in an accident. Uh-oh, that's another bad thought, start over.* Who is being controlled?

OCD is an intrusion, a brain hiccup. It is different from your child's voluntary thoughts. But he doesn't know that. All thoughts are created equal, so we all think, unless we are told otherwise. While thoughts of the mind are welcome messages, OCD brain hiccups are junk mail, but because they happen in English, we think we need to listen to them, understand them. The more we try to figure out what they are saying and why, the more we are being pulled into their trap.

Buyer Beware

Consider how you teach children that what you see is not what you get when it comes to freebies: you teach them about the "catch"; you teach them about quality. OCD says, look I've got a deal for you, your family can be safe *if and only if* you make sure that every time you hear a word like danger, bad, fire, hurt, cancer, AIDS, crash (and the list grows daily—that is the fine print), you fix it by washing your hands. This is no bargain. When you understand the difference between mind and brain, then you can help your child who has been led astray. This OCD brain trick and others are described in Chapter 2. Your job as parent is to keep your eye squarely on your child and his goal to be free of the acrobatics required by OCD. Tell your child, "That's the OCD talking; of course you want us to be safe. But there's no way you have to sacrifice your whole life spending all of your time in the bathroom or worrying in order to do it. Your job is not to do OCD, it's to live your life like you are in charge, do what you want to do." The problem for parents is that your child is not likely to say, "Mom, the OCD has my brain again, get me out of this mess"; what he might say at 2:00 A.M. is, "I've got to clean my room or something bad will happen." That is why as a parent you need to know what OCD is about so you can override the specific words of the situation and listen to the message from your child—*"I'm stuck, help."* Your new template for help is about labeling the OCD and helping your child out of it, instead of simply telling him it is too late to clean.

When I first worked with children with OCD, I approached them as worriers like other worrier children I had helped. Much like many well-meaning parents, I thought these kids needed help evaluating the reality of their fears because they were catastrophizing, exaggerating, and distorting. The more I applied logic, the faster I got nowhere. The more I listened, I saw that these children already knew the "right answers"; they knew how excessive their rituals were, but they were stuck with having to do them to make sure. They did not need information of likelihood or probabilities. This was about needing to be 100 percent certain. I began to focus on process and stopped listening to the confusing content. It is this same process that needs to happen for parents and kids. As Dr. Jeffrey Schwartz says, don't take OCD thoughts at face value.

What You Already Know Will Help You

What throws parents off their game in OCD is the jarring change of scenery in their own homes. So perplexed are they by the behavior of their children, that they find themselves suddenly empty-handed. Legendary pediatrician, Dr. Spock, said to parents, "You know more than you think." This applies to OCD as well. The challenge is to not panic and let the contagion of anxiety envelop you. Flash on any OCD situation, push the mute button, and what you see is children asking you the same thing as they might when struggling with homework—help, mom, what do I do? Reading this book is one of the steps you are taking to be able to answer that question. Why is it so much easier to help your child with homework? Well, for one thing, homework is a known quantity: you went through it yourself and can draw from your experience. Second, the homework problem is defined as *outside* both of you. It is a problem between you, not within one of you. OCD looks like it is coming from your child; after all, isn't your child in control, voluntarily doing these actions? What psychiatrist Dr. John March recommends is seeing the OCD as a biologically based brain problem. Then you can externalize the OCD and make it an entity—a bully out there who is bossing your child around. The goal of treatment is for parent and child to join together to boss back the bully who is controlling everybody's life. The treatment is straightforward in theory, but by the time you approach the challenge of OCD, you don't know what end is up.

[handwritten margin note: OCD is a bully bossing your child around]

Pulling Against the Vortex: How Parents Get Sucked into OCD

What parent in her right mind would follow her child around, vacuuming the floor, shoes, chairs, and light switches because invisible specks of dust torment her son? The answer: any parent who watches the trauma unfold—and the child disintegrates, writhing on the floor: "I can't stand it, get if off me." It is not the child who is crazy, nor the parent, but the OCD thoughts themselves. The junk mail that overwhelms this previously reasonable, generally solid, thoughtful child, is insisting that mother help him clean his hands with alcohol—and then throw out the bottle that she just opened to afford cleanliness at the moment. Right-minded parents go out on a limb when their children have OCD for two reasons: first we all have an instinctual wired-in parental response to our children's plea for help from their pain; and second, these children have generally been trustworthy and reasonable when they have asked for help in the past. So, this *parent trap* is completely understandable when you take a closer look.

Parents fall into traps all the time. Cutting the sandwich in triangles, not squares, opening up a dozen jars of baby food to find one that pleases, or waiting while your teenager tries on 15 pairs of what seem like identical jeans until she is happy with the fit—we have all been caught in the spotlight doing the ridiculous for our children. What makes those moments safer than when you are dealing with OCD is that you know you are *choosing* to indulge a whim at that moment to avoid a scene. That is a major safety net. When parents first confront OCD, they do not realize that their child can cope, because they don't know what they are contending with. Likewise, kids don't know that this is a survivable moment. And that's where things get really precarious.

Balancing on the head of a pin. You are cornered. Your child is teetering on the edge of the tiniest sliver of "just right" or "safe." With OCD, the world shrinks, safety is precarious, and each moment and movement counts in a way that is unnatural and urgent. You feel constantly pressured to have the right answer—or over the precipice your child goes. At any moment, it could be the end of the world as you know it. The OCD demands that your child know for sure—is the fork clean, is the shirt folded right, is the pencil sharp enough, how do you know Saddam Hussein won't attack, how do you know the entire water supply won't be contaminated by pollution? What do you do? How do you certify the uncertain? If you stick with your child's perspective, you are stuck. There is either a yes or a no, and neither will suffice. You could keep trying to achieve the impossible single point of satisfaction. Perhaps you are a parent who has been trying to console, comfort, and satisfy, and you have the gray hairs to prove it! Soon you will feel that you have lost solid ground and are teetering on the edge. You are pulled into the balancing act— the myopia—the all-consuming OCD moment.

What happens when parents follow their kids around is not good. First of all, how long can you keep that up before you yourself crack? This is OCD taking control. You are trying to meet your child where he is, but that is life under a microscope.

Meanwhile, you know that the rest of the world is out there. It is this knowledge—a foot out of the tiny, boxed room of OCD—that can save you and your child. It is not having one foot in the land of logic that counts. Logic on OCD is like air freshener on an oil spill. It might be nice, but it is not what the problem is about. What matters is that you know there is life out there and that your child wants to live it. You can engage the importance of friends, sports, fun, and living free. You can help him distinguish OCD land from his land—one of choice and confidence—and encourage him in being satisfied with it instead of being certain. Add to that what you will learn in this book—that OCD moments *are* survivable—and the empowerment has begun. Parents armed with the knowledge that their child can survive these moments can communicate that confidence to their child and help him live through it.

The Slippery Slope of Parental Helplessness

Why do parents need a book on childhood OCD; why not just have kids follow a treatment manual? The answer is that parents are the landscape where the drama of children's lives takes place. When parents are unclear, it pulls the rug out from under children who are already on shaky ground. By learning about OCD, you can translate this confusing experience into concepts and metaphors that are accessible and positive.

You may want to tackle OCD on your own strength and experience as a parent; however, some of your parental instincts work in OCD land, and others do not. For example, reassuring your child will not work, and punishment definitely will not work. Setting limits is important, but it is not easy to know how to go about it. You need strategies to set limits on the OCD rather than on your child.

I'm Losing My Child

It is frightening to watch your child slip out of your reach. When the bad guy was the bogeyman, you understood what that meant. The fear was common and expectable; you could immediately connect with that experience and intervene. What if the bad guy is all the odd numbers or perfect corners or a relentless indefatigable thought—*I am going to kill myself?* What weapon can you hold up against those elusive intruders? Suddenly, you feel ill equipped to deal with what is becoming an emergency situation in your own home. With such a narrow margin between managing and combustion, many parents are afraid they might make things worse for their child if they were to insist on stopping the excessive washing, counting, or checking. Many parents feel isolated and helpless in this situation. It is difficult to reach out to others because their failure to understand is one more letdown. Parents are not willing to risk telling their friends that their 15-year-old can't be left alone because he has an obsession that he will kill himself. As one parent described it, "It's impossible to explain OCD to people; maybe if I said Jeff was *possessed* that would capture the experience—but then I would seem crazy—I feel very alone."

Living in the Land of OCD

Though OCD was not on your life's itinerary, here you are (as suggested by Kingsley's piece, p. 14). It is a place that you will learn to master. After a few rounds of symptoms, and they do change frequently, you will start to predict the sequence of events. You will begin to recognize the road signs and the weather patterns. Then as the learning curve flattens out, knowledge, information, and solutions will replace anxiety and fear; and you will be on your way to helping your child get back to familiar territory.

A Top-Down Approach: Parenting in the Power Seat

Our children will never tell us that they rely on us to show them the way. So it is very dangerous for parents to be in the dark. Although you want to help and researchers tell us that constructive parental involvement accelerates the recovery process, you know that unwittingly you have become accomplices, woven into the problem. Remember—your kids don't want to be doing this! They just don't know what else to do! This is your leverage with your child. They want out, but they don't know how. You must be the advocate who points to

WELCOME TO HOLLAND
Emily Perl Kingsley

I am often asked to describe the experience of raising a child with a disability—to try to help people who have not shared that unique experience to understand it, to imagine how it would feel. It's like this. . . .

When you're going to have a baby, it's like planning a fabulous vacation trip—to Italy. You buy a bunch of guidebooks and make wonderful plans. The Coliseum. The Michelangelo David. The gondolas in Venice. You may learn some handy phrases in Italian. It's all very exciting.

After months of eager anticipation, the day finally arrives. You pack your bags and off you go. Several hours later, the plane lands. The stewardess comes in and says, "Welcome to Holland."

"Holland?!?" you say. "What do you mean Holland?? I signed up for Italy! I'm supposed to be in Italy. All my life I've dreamed of going to Italy."

But there's been a change in the flight plan. They've landed in Holland and there you must stay.

The important thing is that they haven't taken you to a horrible, disgusting, filthy place full of pestilence, famine and disease. It's just a different place.

So you must go out and buy new guidebooks. And you must learn a whole new language. And you will meet a whole new group of people you would never have met.

It's just a *different* place. It's slower-paced than Italy, less flashy than Italy. But after you've been there for a while and you catch your breath, you look around . . . and you begin to notice Holland has windmills . . . and Holland has tulips. Holland even has Rembrandts.

But everyone you know is busy coming and going from Italy . . . and they're all bragging about what a wonderful time they had there. And for the rest of your life, you will say, "Yes, that's where I was supposed to go. That's what I had planned."

And the pain of that will never, ever, ever, ever go away . . . because the loss of that dream is a very very significant loss.

But . . . if you spend your life mourning the fact that you didn't get to Italy, you may never be free to enjoy the very special, the very lovely things . . . about Holland.

the fork in the road that shows them there's a way to get out of the problem.

Is There Another Choice? Creating the Fork in the Road

Creating the fork in the road means teaching your children that OCD is a misfiring in their brain; then they can start to see they have a choice: *I don't have to listen to this message— it's not real—it's a brain trick, I can fight this.* But before we can expect children to make a choice, they need to know that they *have* a choice. Once they understand this, they can begin treatment in earnest, step-by-step reclaiming their authority and control over their time and actions. As 10-year-old Laurence who was fast on the way to mastering his OCD told his father who was struggling with his own OCD, "You see Dad, it's not you, it's these bad cells in your brain, and they're eating up the good cells, but you can fight back!" What Laurence understands is that the goal is not to make the OCD disappear, but instead to change your response to it. For example, if you have a fear of bees, your goal can't be to make bees disappear: you will end up a prisoner in your home. Instead you want to be able to cope with that fear.

What Do Kids Want?

In the film *As Good As It Gets,* the character played by Jack Nicholson, fed up with his OCD, barges into his therapist's office and shouts "Help!" In a word, he wants out. If parents could only wave a magic wand and get rid of this problem, that would be number one on kids' wish lists. Short of that, kids want to be accepted, understood, and not blamed. We live in a world where great stigma is attached to psychiatric conditions. OCD is embarrassing, it would be shameful to be caught doing blinking, counting, washing, tapping, so children work super hard to keep their symptoms private. Children tease each other for a new haircut, for stumbling over an answer, or for wearing the wrong jeans. For doing an OCD symptom, the scrutiny and humiliation could be devastating. At home, kids need space, support, and understanding. What a family can give is tremendous. If children had to fight for survival on the home front as well, the stress might become unbearable.

This book will provide the information you need to put you back in the power seat—doing what you need to do—living your lives and helping your child to do the same. Armed with information, you can resist the contagion of stuckness, and provide direction for your child—helping her develop a different way out of the situation she is in.

Once you grasp the subject, you will be able to recognize the early signs of trouble with your child. You can help your child early on with operating instructions for the vulnerabilities of his brain. Freeing is a process. By educating your child about what is going on, he will begin to see more and more opportunities to fight back and break free—*you mean I don't have to do this stuff, I won't die?* The reassurance they really need is your unbending belief that this is OCD, that they are not crazy and that they definitely do not have to do this "stuff."

Diving into the Wreck

By the time parents begin to talk about their child's symptoms or seek help for them, there is no one clear center or crux of the problem; instead, it is a tangle of strange, frightening traps overlapping ordinary daily activities. Working with a behavior therapist, your child will begin to sort the various symptoms and rank them by severity. Then step-by-step, he will begin to tackle them, learning how to fight the OCD logic. Both you and your child will come to know the patterns of OCD and can spot the order in what looked like chaos. No longer foundering in the morass of fear, you have the courage to dive in head first with a mission.

Who Should Read This Book

Whether you are a veteran of the battle with OCD—struggling to get through—or you are not sure whether your chid has the diagnosis, this book will provide you with a clear understanding of the disorder, show you new ways to help your child, and help you cope as well.

This book is not intended to be a substitute for professional treatment, as the majority of children with OCD will require in-person therapy to get their OCD under control.

Rather, this book is an insider's guide to help you understand how OCD works and how you can support your child's recovery on the home front.

Putting Together the Pieces of the OCD Puzzle

This book will help you take the following steps to deal with OCD:

1. Get the information—what is OCD and what is the way out?
2. Redefine your role as a parent—what constitutes coaching and how do you unhook yourself from the emotions this disorder evokes in order to be a good coach.
3. Evaluate your child—consider the factors that will affect implementation of your strategies, such as age, temperament, personality, strengths, and vulnerabilities.
4. Acquire the language you need to construct and reinforce "Operating Instructions" for your child's brain—educate your child about how his brain works.
5. Think creatively about how to respond to your child's problems by reading the examples in the book.

The challenge of OCD requires a pioneering spirit. One of the staples of parenting is thinking about what it was like for us to be a kid. As parents, we know how to respond because usually we have gone through whatever our kids bring up. By contrast, it can be very jarring when you have no reference point to relate to the ordeal your child is going through. By reading this book and gaining knowledge about the ways of OCD, you will be able to get past the intensity and connect with your child's experience.

In reading the stories in this book, I hope you will be as struck and inspired as I have been by the extraordinary courage, warmth, and resilience shown by these children and their families in the face of OCD.

CHAPTER 1

Understanding OCD

What Is OCD?

You see your child putting on her socks for the tenth time, screaming that the seams aren't straight. The blood is pulsing through your veins and your temperature's rising; late for work, you're furious and you feel helpless. The temptation to shout, "Stop this and just get over it," is gaining on you. Watching your child melt down before your eyes leaves you desperate, as if you're running in place. Unfortunately, your basic assumption about your child's behavior—that she is doing everything of her free will—does not apply here. To understand OCD, obsessive-compulsive disorder, you must accept the *involuntary* nature of the condition. Your child isn't doing this to annoy you, or even because she wants to. She derives no pleasure or satisfaction from OCD; in fact, she hates it. Children with OCD endure scrutiny, pain, and embarrassment because they are victims of a brain condition that turns the simple task of surviving each day into an all-consuming battle between what she knows to be true and the irrational fears OCD unleashes.

Understanding OCD requires a shift in perception, from seeing your child controlling you to seeing your child being controlled by the commands of the invisible enemy in her brain. The Greek word *sciamachy* means "a battle with an invisible foe." This is the essence of OCD. The brain gets stuck in gear not allowing the mind to be rational, to be free, to believe what makes sense, for example, that washing forty times a day will not ensure that no one dies. There's no connection. Instead, the frightening .0001 percent chance that a rogue germ will kill someone becomes the message—the only message—blasting over your child's internal PA system. From the outside, OCD looks so stoppable, so easy to walk away from, but it is the invisible internal grip of anxiety that keeps the fires fueled.

Children don't like to be bossed around by anyone. So how does OCD get them to pour time and energy into doing jumping jacks for it?

OCD plays dirty; it doesn't play fair. It raises the stakes as high as they can go—safety, survival, and health. There are some things you would never do under ordinary circumstances, but you would do it in a heart-beat if you thought it would save your child. OCD takes this basic in-stinct and twists it by distorting the true possibility of danger and grossly exaggerating our personal responsibilities and ability to control them. Similarly, OCD holds your child hostage; its propaganda quickly takes over. Your child knows it's not likely that washing hands and preventing cancer are connected. Yet OCD forces her to think: *You don't know 100 percent that it won't, so don't be selfish, you better wash to be sure.*

Wouldn't you check the locks ten times to avert a disaster befalling your family? When faced with the threat of the unbearable enormity of worst fears come true, children with OCD decide not to take a chance. Because, despite plenty of adults telling them, "Just stop it—don't recheck," they are not free enough to think beyond, *There's no way I could do that.* OCD is not about the inability to think rationally; it's about the anxiety that results from the inability to believe what you know to be true in a given situation. OCD acts as agitator, insisting that you be certain beyond a shadow of a doubt, which is impossible. It makes its sufferers believe that a remote possibility is a clear and pres-ent danger requiring our most urgent attention.

What Are Obsessions?

Obsessions are intrusive, unwanted, distressing thoughts or pictures that barge squarely into your mind's eye, refuse to budge, and keep re-playing themselves. Obsessions are involuntary, occurring sponta-neously whether the child wants to think about them or not. When obsessions hit, they create an uneasy, anxious, or dreadful feeling. You try to get rid of it, ignore it, pray for it to leave you alone, but it won't. It sits there, occupying your territory, clogging the information super-highway in your brain, preventing you from moving on. In fact, the word *obsession* comes from the Latin for "to besiege or to occupy." Think of how you feel when you realize you made a big mistake, you forgot an important message for someone at work, or you have a near-miss while driving. That realization triggers the fight-or-flight re-sponse; your heart races and you get sweaty. You also try to quickly put it out of your mind and get back to business, because you are compelled to rid yourself of the anxiety brought on by the thought. The actual danger has passed, an internal "all clear" has sounded. When a child with OCD experiences an obsession, it creates an uncomfortable feel-ing that doesn't go away. The all-clear signal doesn't come. The brain has called "911" and there's no turning back. There are three main reasons why obsessions make kids feel uncomfortable. First, the content itself is typically unpleasant; like the most ruthless enemy, the obsessions fire off "what ifs?" such as: "What if someone dies because you didn't rub the table when you bumped into it? What if that doorknob gives you AIDS, it looked dirty?" Second, kids are distressed because they know that there really is no interrogator, no enemy, that the voice they hear is coming from inside of them. In an instantaneous flash this sends waves of dread: *Why am I thinking this? What's wrong with me? Am I going crazy?* The obsession attacks and won't relent. Third, obsessions are troubling because they take so much mental energy and time to listen to them and work through them. If you're in the middle of biology class when Mr. Franklin is giving study tips for one of his killer tests and you've missed the whole thing because you keep picturing the cafeteria

Common Obsessions

Contamination	Fear of touching shoes, doorknobs, spots on clothing or furniture, pencils on the floor, for fear of germs, illness, or death.
Harm to self or others	Fear of causing harm: stepping on bugs, stabbing with a kitchen knife, poisoning from cleaning chemicals, running over children or animals on bike or in car Fear of being harmed: illness, burglars, throwing up.
Symmetry urges	Needing objects lined up or body movements even on right and left sides in order to feel "just right" or to avoid harm.
Doubting	Being unsure whether you've completed common actions—locked the door, put homework in backpack, are the lights really off, is the door shut, is the water off, is the match out?
Numbers	Thinking that you need to do something a certain number of times to avoid harm or to feel right, avoiding "bad luck" numbers, e.g., unable to watch a certain TV channel.
Scrupulosity/religiosity	Fear that you have sinned, are guilty, a bad person, needing to confess all bad thoughts. Fear that you are praying to the devil, or are praying wrong, or need to pray continuously; intrusive doubts about lack of faith.
Hoarding	Fear of throwing out useless objects because you may need them later, need to buy or accumulate objects to not miss a chance.
Sexual themes	Intrusive thoughts, images or doubts about sexual orientation, or fears of being perverted; intrusive sexual images; thoughts of incest, fear of bumping or touching "private parts."

worker rubbing her nose—Did she then touch your hamburger?—now you also have to contend with how to pass the test.

Sometimes the obsessions are relatively harmless; but it's the repetition of the mundane—a word, a thought, a picture, or a tune—that is as maddening as a dripping faucet.

OBSESSIONS ARE THOUGHTS THAT ARE:
- *Intrusive:* They come into your mind without you wanting them there.
- *Irrational:* They concern things that make no sense.
- *Recurrent:* They keep replaying so you can't shake them in your mind.
- *Disturbing:* Their content is frightening because you know it's not "normal."
- *Anxiety producing:* As you try and fail to get rid of them you feel out of control.

What Are Compulsions?

Obsessions are thoughts; compulsions are actions. When Carly has to put on her shoes, she wiggles into them, never touching them with her hands. Nevertheless, she's not *sure* she didn't touch her shoes, and the mere thought of layers of dirt, germs, and contaminants on them leaves her with such a feeling of disgust that she has to wash her hands *just in case.* So when a fear about contamination hits, kids wash to reduce the dread. It is a commonly held notion that compulsions "control" anxiety, making it appear that a child is deciding to employ a compulsion—as if there is a choice: "I could do something else, but I'm choosing to do these crazy things." Compulsions only reduce temporarily the anxiety created by obsessions. Very soon after a ritual is completed, the nagging feelings of doubt and dread resurface, setting off the whole cycle again.

When OCD starts, children don't think, *I'm deciding to do this.* It doesn't feel like a choice at all. Instead, rituals feel like necessary tools for survival. That's where treatment comes in. Treatment is about making OCD moments into a choice between two worlds. In the OCD world, your focus narrows into a small moment where life itself hinges on getting rid of the obsession, putting the need to be certain and safe over the need simply to be. Through effective treatment, you learn to take a step back and recognize that the obsession is an intrusive thought. Not only is the thought trespassing on your private property, it has the nerve to demand that you do things that waste your time.

Common Compulsions

Washing and Cleaning	Repeated hand washing, showering, using alcohol or detergents to wash; avoiding touching shoes, keys, money, doorknobs, chalk; not bringing school items home, not allowing others to touch things in room or to touch self.
Checking	Rechecking door and window locks; turning off oven and water; unplugging appliances.
Symmetry	Exiting a room the same way as entered; if bump right hand, bump left; blinking right eye if blink left; pulling up socks so they are the same height; retying shoes till loops are exactly the same.
Counting	Counting to a certain number while putting on clothes, brushing hair or teeth; needing to arrive at a certain time; turning TV or radio to certain numbers; fixing "bad luck" numbers by writing or counting to "good luck" numbers; having to count doors, floor tiles, windowpanes.
Repeating/Redoing	Turning lights on and off, opening and closing doors or dresser drawers; rebuttoning clothes till just right; rewriting, erasing, rereading till perfect.
Hoarding	Being unable to throw out objects, school papers, old crayons, sorting useless objects in categories.
Praying	Continuous praying, confessing every bad thought, apologizing incessantly, needing to pray for everyone to avoid being responsible for harm, repeatedly questioning proof of existence of God.

The obsession is so strong that kids would do anything to get rid of it, even if it means missing their favorite TV show, leaving a ballgame early, walking up and down stairs until the bad feeling goes away, counting, scrubbing in the bathroom, or asking their parents the same questions even though they know they'll get in trouble. OCD requires major sacrifices from your child, with little return. It's that inequity—the lack of fair play—that needs to be brought to kids' attention so they can begin to fight for what is rightfully theirs: their time, their freedom, their fun.

Some compulsions are invisible; these are called *mental rituals*. A child may have a disturbing thought of death and then will count or pray, spell out the word *life* in his mind ten times, repeat a word until the bad thought is fixed. These invisible rituals are especially difficult for children because, while on the one hand no one can see you doing it (as opposed to handwashing), it is occurring completely within your mind, and so no one sees how you are suffering. As one child described it, "If I had a physical handicap, it would be right out there, and people would understand. But I look perfectly normal so they think, *Well, what's wrong with her? Get over it.*"

To what degree can children control their symptoms? Many parents ask: How can my child be fine at school, but lose it as soon as he walks in the door? Why can she kiss her boyfriend but think we are dirty and not even hug us? Why is she fine in a hotel room when our house is riddled with rituals? Children have some ability to *delay* rituals, but that doesn't mean the moment is forgotten. A seventh grader in the bathroom can quickly interrupt her scrubbing when a classmate walks in, or make a "deal" not to wash even though she just touched the blackboard chalk that everyone else has touched. But "payment" will come due. A child might think, *I will be careful not to touch any of my things, and I will scrub with alcohol when I get home.* Children can sometimes manage not to ritualize, but the compulsions are still going to happen; they just pay the penalty later. This is why some experts refer to compulsions as *unvoluntary* in the sense that breathing is not voluntary. We can hold our breath, but eventually we've got to breathe.

Obsessions are more difficult to control, because just as quickly as you tell your mind to stop thinking about something, it insists that you listen. The brain plays that record whether you want to hear it or not. Sometimes children can exhibit compulsions without having any precipitating obsession. This is more often the case with younger children who may report needing to check, tap, or do things a certain way without having any fear associated with refraining from doing the compulsion.

COMPULSIONS ARE ACTIONS THAT:
- Involve repetitive behaviors (hand washing, ordering, checking, redoing, asking for reassurance) or mental actions (prayer, counting, repeating words) to reduce anxiety brought on by obsessions.
- Reduce anxiety temporarily.
- Create an urge to do the compulsion that gets stronger over time.
- Grow less effective over time, requiring the addition of other compulsions.
- Require compulsive avoidance of feared situations (won't shake hands, touch doorknobs, step on cracks).

The Trap of OCD: Vicious Cycles

Sometimes there is a meaningful connection between obsession and compulsion; for instance, washing when you feel contaminated.

Sometimes there is no logical connection between them; for example, wearing certain clothes or avoiding certain others to prevent the fear of the house catching on fire or a flood. Whether it makes logical sense or not, compulsions will reduce anxiety for a brief amount of time; that's the "perk" that locks in the cycle of OCD. A child with OCD believes that unless he does things a certain way, something bad will happen. Not only that, but over time his brain builds up a "tolerance" to the rituals and he then has to develop more and more elaborate rituals to get relief from the obsession. He thinks, *Maybe the ritual worked this time because I had my eyes closed—I better do it with my eyes closed all the time, I better hold my breath, I better not have a bad thought while I'm doing the ritual or I'll have to start all over again.* It creates a vicious cycle. This is the trap of OCD.

For many children, this innocent pact to get relief from a bad thought quickly becomes a life sentence. Caroline, age eleven, whose OCD began six months ago with checking page numbers, making sure she ended on even numbers only because odd numbers were bad luck, confessed at our first meeting that she couldn't believe she had let it go so far. Soon she was counting letters making sure that each word could result in an even number. Her spoken words had to have an even number as did hockey drills or hair brushing. Avoiding odd numbers in any form became her focus. She likened this shame of "letting" it get out of control to eating one candy, and ending up finishing up everything in the box. This pattern is very common; children don't know how much it will cost them when they buy into this process of escaping bad thoughts. They don't know that it's a black hole into which they keep falling.

A Learned Connection: Of Compulsions and Swimming Pools

When children engage in compulsions, it's not because they want to. In fact, they really don't want to, but it's the only way they've figured out to get away from the dreadful feeling of the obsession. However, each time a child engages in a compulsion, it reinforces the idea that doing the compulsion is the *only* way out. Fortunately, when kids learn that it's a false message from their brain, that nothing bad will happen if they don't do these weird tricks, they can see that the anxiety that the obsession brings on *will actually go away on its own.* Why? Because the human body is built in such a way that it will "reset" to baseline within a certain period of time. Anxiety goes away on its own, especially if, instead of fanning the fires with worry talk, you get involved in something else. It's a safety mechanism for the human species. (See Chapter 2 for how to explain this and other anxiety mechanisms to your child.) This is the epiphany of behavior therapy. The OCD brain hiccup misleads us into thinking it's something more urgent because it's speaking in our language. Children can begin to fight compulsions when they label OCD as a brain hiccup not worthy of their attention.

What do OCD and swimming pools have in common? Behavior therapy is like jumping into cold water. If you jump into a pool and the water is cold, you have two choices. You could get out and avoid the cold water or stay in and see what happens. If you get out, then your experience of a swimming pool is that the only way to deal with it is to avoid it. If, on the other hand, you stay in, you'd see that the uncomfortable cold feeling passes after a time. This occurs not because the water "warms up" but because the brain stops paying attention to the message "it's cold, it's cold" and we habituate to the water. Similarly, with OCD, kids learn that the only way to avoid or escape the bad feeling of an obsession is to do a compulsion. In behavior therapy, they get to see that the bad feeling passes on its own—the brain stops sending out the "danger, danger" message; they can be free from compulsions and that feels much better.

> OTHER SYMPTOMS OF OCD:
> - *Stress.* OCD is time consuming. With so much anxiety and time eaten up by OCD, children are rushed to complete their daily tasks.
> - *Sleep deprivation.* Often children with OCD stay up late ritualizing or worrying about how they are going to manage the next day; they may get up hours early in the morning to get their rituals done.
> - *Depression/Shame.* Kids feel demoralized because they are "different" and feel "crazy."
> - *Agitation.* When children are unable to get the ritual right, or someone interrupts the ritual, they become angry and irritable.
> - *Slowness.* Kids may slow down to get things right, and may do things more slowly because of how time-consuming rituals are.
> - *Need to keep busy.* Many children with OCD keep themselves on the move all the time as a way to avoid the OCD. If they keep busy, they won't be able to "hear" the OCD as well and can get out from under its spell temporarily.
> - *Academic difficulties.* Rituals and/or distraction of obsessions can interfere with learning.
> - *Neuropsychological differences.* Children with OCD may have stronger verbal skills, relatively weaker nonverbal skills, difficulty

writing, reduced processing speed and efficiency, and impairment in expressive written language skills.

- *Behavioral difficulties.* A subset of children may exhibit hyperactivity, inattentiveness, impulsivity, and disinhibition similar to symptoms of Attention Deficit Hyperactivity Disorder, without having the disorder.
- *Social difficulties.* Children may withdraw because they don't have time to socialize because of their time-consuming rituals; they may be embarrassed or awkward because the OCD fear of contamination precludes getting close to others. OCD fears may prevent them from participating in sleepovers or watching scary movies.
- *Family conflict.* Having a child with OCD is very stressful; it is a confusing disorder with an unpredictable course. Under these circumstances, tensions run high, and family conflicts over how to handle the OCD are inevitable.

Where Do These Symptoms Come From?

OCD has been around in some form for centuries. One can find writings from the Middle Ages describing religious compulsions and related behavior so clearly different from religious devotion (though the words may have been similar) that thinkers in those times recognized the anomaly. Currently, you will find the phenomenon of OCD almost everywhere in the world. Australia, Japan, Israel, as well as less developed countries have individuals riddled with doubt about cleanliness or order.

OCD was at one time explained as the work of the devil, and its sufferers were believed to be individuals possessed by Satan. Next came the early medical explanations that posited fevers and illnesses as the cause of these fits of symptomatology. Psychoanalysis was the prevailing movement in the third cycle. The argument went that overly rigorous toilet training and intrusive parenting practices during the anal stage of development fueled obsessions about cleanliness. Despite the fact that Freud himself acknowledged the limits of psychoanalytic explanations of OCD and left the problem to "biological research," for decades therapists persisted in exploring childhood conflicts to explain why someone would "need" their OCD to bind anxiety. The notion that OCD symptoms are an attempt on the part of the child to control or bind anxiety prevails among many mental health professionals today. Framed this way, OCD sounds like the child's calculated maneuver to control anxiety. As OCD expert Dr. Ian Osborn points out in his book *Tormenting Thoughts and Secret Rituals,* for sufferers of OCD, symptoms feel much more like "enemy attacks than defensive maneuvers."

As we will see in the next chapter, the source of OCD is nothing so personal as blasphemous thinking or early sexual conflicts; rather, it is biologically-driven—as impersonal as the exquisite machinery of the brain. Simply stated, OCD comes from a biochemical mishap in the brain. Part of the brain sends out a false message of danger and rather than going through the proper "screening process" to evaluate the thought, the brain gets stuck in *danger gear* and cannot move out of it. The emergency message circuit keeps repeating and is "immune" to logical thought.

Although we know where OCD comes from in the brain, it does not mean we understand why some children are checkers and some washers, or why children's symptoms change form over time. Sometimes there is a specific stressor that sets off a specific fear; for example, a fear of meningitis following the death of someone at school, fear of rabies when a rabid dog is reported in the neighborhood. However, that still doesn't explain why all people with OCD in that neighborhood don't react the same way. What we know is that the disorder is characterized by variability. What is inherited is a tendency for OCD, not a blueprint for a particular symptom.

Causes of OCD

Research in the past 20 years has effected a monumental shift from seeing OCD as a neurotic condition to understanding its biological basis in the structure and operations of the brain. The next section highlights many of these important discoveries.

Neurochemistry: PET Scan Research: A Picture's Worth a Thousand Words

One of the most compelling findings of the last decade is in the work of UCLA researcher Dr. Jeffrey Schwartz author of *Brain Lock*. Dr. Schwartz coined the term *brain lock* to describe how brain structures get in a "traffic jam" during OCD. The brain "sending false messages, is stuck in an inappropriate groove." How do you unlock this situation? Dr. Schwartz states unequivocally that OCD is associated with a biochemical imbalance and can be treated effectively by behavior therapy. His groundbreaking PET (positron emission tomography) scan studies demonstrate the changes in brain chemistry that result from successful treatment (behavior therapy or medication). With behavior therapy,

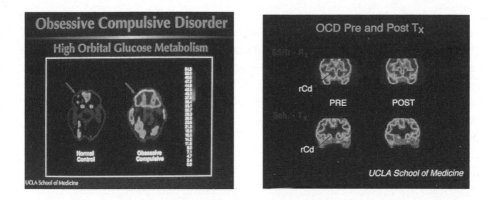

you can change how your brain responds to the thoughts and over time you can "retrain your brain" to shift more smoothly.

At UCLA, Dr. Schwartz and Dr. Lewis Baxter made these discoveries by comparing PET scans—which measure metabolic activity of the brain—of people with OCD to those of people without OCD. They identified the areas of the brain that are overactive in people with OCD. The *basal ganglia, caudate nucleus* and the *orbital frontal* regions light up differently on the PET scans of adults with OCD, compared with those of adults who do not have OCD. The slide on the left, shows these differences between a normal "control" subject and an individual with OCD. The arrow points to heightened activity representing the areas of the brain affected by OCD. The groundbreaking news is that, after successful treatment with *either medications or behavior therapy,* these abnormalities in brain activity in these areas are markedly diminished and in some cases disappear, as shown in the slide on the right. The brain can be retrained, and as we know from many other disorders, brain responsiveness is much more rapid in children than in adults.

The Serotonin Hypothesis

Serotonin is a neurotransmitter, a brain chemical whose job it is to carry information from one nerve cell to the next. If there isn't enough serotonin available, message circuits do not function properly and the message won't stop. One receptor site for serotonin is in the part of the brain called the basal ganglia, the region which contains the thought filtering station. Consistent with this, a person who suffers an injury to the basal ganglia will develop OCD symptoms. The medications (Prozac, Zoloft, Paxil) used to treat OCD affect serotonin levels, the selective serotonin reuptake inhibitors (SSRIs) target the receptor sites in the basal ganglia keeping more serotonin available to direct messages properly. The strongest evidence for the role of serotonin in OCD comes from the numerous medication studies that have found that OCD symptoms decrease in response to SSRI treatment. Researchers studying the function of serotonin have theorized that one important purpose it serves is helping people tolerate the experience of wanting to do something, and not doing it. In fact when children begin to respond to SSRI medication, they will describe how they have the obsessive thought, but the urge to respond to it isn't as strong.

Genetic Links in OCD

The fact that OCD runs in families provides further evidence for the biological roots of OCD. Many studies have documented the greater prevalence of these disorders in families where one member has either OCD or Tourette's Syndrome (TS). If one parent has OCD, children have roughly a 2 percent to 8 percent chance of developing the disorder. If that parent developed OCD in childhood or if there are other relatives with OCD, TS, or tics, the chances of the child developing OCD increase.

Some studies have found a higher correlation between child and parent OCD. For example, Marge Lenane and her NIMH colleagues in a study published in 1990 found that of 46 children and adolescents with severe OCD, 17 percent of the parents and 5 percent of their siblings met diagnostic criteria for OCD as well. The authors note that this estimate may be low considering they used very strict guidelines for diagnosing OCD, and suggest that closer to 30 percent of patients have a family member with OCD. One might be tempted to explain these high rates as a result of modeling, or "learning by example." However, in all cases where both the parent and child had OCD, the symptoms were dissimilar, for example, a parent who compulsively cleaned, had a child with prayer rituals. It is important to note that some people develop OCD without any family history of OCD or TS. Researchers at Rockefeller University are working to identify the gene associated with OCD. For further information about participating in this study, see the resource section.

Pediatric Autoimmune Neuropsychiatric Disorders Associated with Strep (PANDAS)

Another factor in the OCD puzzle is the role of strep infections. A critical discovery was made over a decade ago by NIMH researchers—an association between sudden onset OCD and a common childhood illness, strep throat. For an estimated 25 percent to 30 percent of children with OCD, the episode is thought to be triggered or exacerbated by the body's own immune cells that rather than attacking the strep, begin to attack the basal ganglia. This subtype of OCD is referred to as Pediatric Autoimmune Neuropsychiatric Diseases Associated with Strep (PANDAS). When OCD presents with a sudden onset, with tics, and/or in young children, PANDAS should be ruled out.

This groundbreaking discovery may change the course of treatment for a subset of children with OCD. Before you run out and have your child tested for strep or quarantine the neighbor's child with a sore throat, there are several points to clarify. Children do not "catch" OCD from strep. Children who have a genetic predisposition for this disorder may have either a first episode or recurrences triggered by a strep infection. Medical researchers at NIMH Susan Swedo, Susan Perlmutter, and Henrietta Leonard identified this link between OCD and strep throat. This connection arose from two lines of inquiry; first, the observation that a majority of children with Sydenham's Chorea (a variant of rheumatic fever) also exhibited OCD symptoms and second, the clinical observation of the presence of strep in childhood onset OCD and TS. What mechanism accounts for this link? Researchers took the example of Sydenham's Chorea or Saint Vitus' Dance and Rheumatic Fever; these conditions are brought on by the antibody attack on the basal ganglia, characterized by a sudden onset of neurological symptoms—clumsiness, frequent jerky movements usually of the extremities and less frequently the facial muscles. Inspired by "residents" of the nearby zoo, Dr. Swedo and her colleagues coined the acronym PANDAS to describe this subset of children with OCD. NIMH has been conducting studies to assess the effectiveness of various treatments for PANDAS including the use of preventative antibiotics and a process to clear the blood of antibodies called plasmapheresis. See Chapter 3 for guidelines for diagnosing and treating PANDAS and the Resource Guide for information on the NIMH program.

Stressful Events

Is OCD triggered by a traumatic event or prolonged stress? The answer is not clear. It seems that for many adult OCD sufferers, onset of the illness is associated with increased family responsibilities or change in health or a job. Many research studies have described precipitating stressors associated with the onset of OCD in children. For example, one study reported an association between the onset of OCD and illness or death of a relative or change in school. A 1992 study conducted by David Rettew and colleagues at NIMH, reported that 38 percent of patients or their family members believed a specific event precipitated their OCD behavior. Some examples included events such as divorce, illness, moving, or unemployment; however, many children identified more personally meaningful triggers such as seeing *The Wizard of Oz* or *The Exorcist,* hearing news items about war, getting poison ivy or fleas, watching Mom clean, seeing leaking battery acid. This was a retrospective study, meaning that children and parents were relying on memory (on average a 3.9-year period between onset and time of the study) to recreate the sequence of events. While there may be a tendency to see a connection after the fact, one would imagine that the child's particular symptoms would in that case be related to the stressful event (for example, fire leading to checking behavior or touching a needle fear of AIDS). In many cases, the symptoms bore no resemblance to the reported triggering event, for example, a child who had witnessed a fire had handwashing symptoms.

In my own practice, many children have described how they were already experiencing "low-grade" OCD symptoms when a major stressful event took place (for example, a death in the family, learning of someone's cancer, seeing someone throw up, news of a terrorist act, the challenge of sleep away camp, hearing about a poison scare). Then the symptoms flared into full-blown OCD. It is as if the brain is already primed for OCD and these events tip the scales.

How Common Is OCD in Children?

Once considered a rare condition, OCD may affect as many as 1 in 100 children, according to current estimates. Approximately 1.9 percent of children and adolescents will develop OCD. In other countries, comparable or higher rates have been reported (for example, in Israel 2.3 percent, New Zealand, 3.9 percent, Denmark, 4.1 percent). Despite these high prevalence rates, OCD remains a "hidden epidemic," as described by Dr. Michael Jenike of Massachusetts General Hospital. The conclusion about OCD and children is that it is not rare, but that it is rarely diagnosed. OCD lacks household recognition; in sharp contrast to attention deficit hyperactivity disorder (ADHD) with a 2 percent prevalence rate, OCD is not generally discussed in supermarket lines or at PTA meetings. The reason for OCD's hidden nature is twofold. First, children with OCD try to hide the symptoms so they may not appear to the adults around them as a problem. Second, many professionals are ill-equipped to diagnose OCD. Because children don't jump up and say, "I have these weird thoughts and rituals," many children with OCD may go undiagnosed—even in a mental health professional's office. For example, in a epidemiological survey conducted in the late 1980s, where researchers calculated prevalence rates for different conditions within a community sample, Dr. Martine Flament and colleagues at the National Institute of Mental Health (NIMH) found that of 5,000 New Jersey adolescents, only 4 out of 18 students whose symptoms significantly interfere with daily life thus meeting criteria for a diagnosis of OCD were actually receiving treatment. However, *none* of those students had been identified correctly as having OCD.

The average age of onset for children with OCD (combining results from multiple researchers) is approximately 10.2 years old. Of the estimated five million to six million adults in the United States with OCD, nearly half identify the onset of symptoms in childhood. However, according to a national survey completed in 1993, led by Dr. Eric Hollander, the majority of adults with OCD were too ashamed to get treatment or treatment was not available, and this put a gap of as much as 17 years between the onset of the condition and obtaining appropriate treatment.

For most children with OCD, symptoms will wax and wane throughout their life. However, in a 1998 article in *The Harvard Review of Psychiatry,* Dr. Daniel Geller and colleagues speculate that some children may outgrow their OCD. Dr. Geller bases this argument on the fact that prevalence rates in children and adults are comparable, and we would expect that if all the childhood cases continued into adulthood, the prevalence rate in adults would rise as children reached adulthood and were added to the adult population. It is not yet understood why for some this is solely a disorder in childhood, while others carry it into adult life.

There is also speculation that there may be more than one type of OCD. For example, from epidemiological data it was observed that the most common age of onset of OCD was 7 and the mean or average age was 10.2, suggesting an early-onset group and a late-onset group. Other research has found that children with early-onset OCD are more likely to have blood relatives with OCD or Tourette syndrome than those with adult-onset OCD. Tourette's syndrome is a neurobiological disorder, like OCD, but which is characterized by involuntary movements such as eye-blinking or neck rolling or sounds such as squeaking, coughing, or swearing. Some experts hypothesize that genetic vulnerability may play a greater role in early-onset OCD than in later-onset OCD. OCD and subthreshold OCD (those who show some symptoms but not the full-blown disorder) are very prevalent in the first-degree relatives (parent or sibling) of children with OCD at a rate of 18 percent to 30 percent. There is an increased rate of OCD in people with tic disorders and vice versa. This suggests that they may be manifestations of the same underlying gene.

OCD does run in families. However, genes are only partially responsible for causing OCD. Some people develop OCD without any family history of OCD or Tourette's, and in contrast, even in twin studies there is a 13 percent chance that the other twin will *not* be affected. If one parent has OCD, children have roughly a 2 percent to 8 percent chance of developing the disorder. If that parent developed OCD in childhood or if there are other relatives with OCD and/or tics, the chances are higher.

Many parents are troubled by the thought of "passing on" OCD to their children. The short answer to this is of course that we pass on the good with the bad in the genetic roulette of growing a family. This important issue is addressed at length in Chapter 9.

The Characteristics of OCD

There are some gender differences in the onset and presentation of OCD. Boys tend to develop OCD earlier than girls; in childhood there are more boys with OCD than girls by a ratio of 3 to 2. Girls tend to show OCD symptoms beginning in adolescence, at which time there are no gender differences in prevalence of OCD. There are no clear relationships between age or gender and severity or type of OCD symptoms, though it has been observed that boys may exhibit more checking behavior and tics, and girls more washing symptoms.

The Changing Course of OCD

Typically OCD symptoms wax and wane over time. Sometimes this may occur with identifiable reasons: for instance, if your child is sick or sleep-deprived, you're more likely to see symptoms. In these cases, it's important to make the connection between the trigger and the reaction so that all parties can be prepared the next time. Sometimes OCD feels like a shell game: Just when you have tracked down one symptom, know its patterns, and have it under control, suddenly a new symptom crops up in a totally unexpected place. The tough news is that this changing course in symptoms is to be expected. The majority of children will exhibit multiple OCD symptoms, a lifetime average of approximately 4 obsessions and 4.8 compulsions, according to researcher Dr. Gregory Hanna. While symptoms may change, the mechanism behind them and the approach to controlling them remains the same. The good news is that you and your child will become experts at bringing symptoms under control quickly: The words may have changed, but the dance steps remain the same. When new symptoms emerge or old ones resurface, you will be "seasoned" and able to draw on your previous experience. Developing a game plan for managing setbacks in OCD is addressed in Chapter 4.

Most Frequently Asked Questions

Does Every Case of OCD Require Treatment?

The answer is no. However, most individuals with OCD will require treatment at some time, and generally it is advisable to get early intervention so that children and parents can learn how *not* to let OCD take over. Becoming knowledgeable about the symptoms and avoidances of OCD, especially if your family has a history of OCD, is just good preventive medicine. You may be able to weave discussions of "brain choices" and other techniques into the natural flow of your parenting. This way your child can learn from you about how to manage fearful situations, just as he learns from you about how to look both ways before he crosses the street, or what to do when he has the hiccups.

Why Can't Kids Stop?

Children may know that what they are thinking or doing makes no sense, but two factors get in the way of their stopping. First, they have come to associate rituals with relief and safety—a learned association that gets reinforced every time they ritualize. And second, if their brain says, "Okay, so this may be stupid, but since you don't know for sure that it's unnecessary, don't take a chance," then they'd rather be safe than sorry. But that's no way to live.

What Constitutes a Diagnosis of OCD?

A little information can be a dangerous thing. When you begin to read about these conditions, you will begin to see OCD everywhere—your daughter insisting on having her hair perfectly even, your son refusing to let anyone touch his baseball card collection and dusting it nightly. However, there is much perfectionism, rigidity, and strong willedness that is *not* OCD. To meet diagnostic criteria for OCD, the key factor is the presence of obsessions and/or compulsions that:

- Are time-consuming (for example, take more than one hour a day).
- Cause significant distress.

- Interfere with daily functioning (academic, social activities, normal routine, family relationships).

If your child has these signs of distress or dysfunction; he's likely to get a diagnosis of OCD. In Chapter 3, I will discuss in detail how OCD is diagnosed.

What's a Habit? What's a Trap?

Kids love habits, and that's a good thing, because habits are a wired-in building block for learning. As a species, we thrive on structure and routine—whether it is the peanut butter and jelly sandwich cut in triangles *not* squares, the lucky shirt, the favorite cup, the good-luck pencil, and so on. Therein lies the difference between OCD and ordinary quirky behaviors and habits. Ordinary habits help us to organize, free up time, and allow us to feel in charge. However, when you see a child unpacking and repacking her book bag for fifteen minutes before she can leave the house or spraying all her books with Lysol as soon as she gets home from school, it is clear how OCD routines actually prevent children from thriving.

Magical Thinking and Superstitious Behaviors

Five-year-old Sara always puts her right shoe on first—her right foot is her favorite one she explains, because it's "right." She likes to put on her shoes herself and enjoys the feeling of control of being in charge of her shoes. This is an example of the mastery-building rituals that all children experience in one form or another. Young children's insistence on the way things should be is an integral part of their learning about rules. Three-year-olds may be less rule-bound, since they are less aware of the rules. A four- or five-year-old knows pretty well what the limits are and therefore challenges them and then also practices establishing rules for himself or his peers.

In grade school, superstitions abound. Step on a crack, break your mother's back. Don't look in the mirror or Bloody Mary will get you. Hold your breath going past a graveyard or you'll let the spirits in. Say "rabbit" the first day of every month and you'll have good luck for the next thirty. All children have superstitions and rituals, and children with OCD have more. However, it is unclear whether this surplus is subthreshold OCD or a marker of a vulnerability that may emerge later.

All children can have unpleasant thoughts: *I miss my mom, I'm going to fail the test, I made a fool of myself at the party.* These are real, willful, organic products of an active mind. Obsessions are different. Think of a muscle spasm in your brain, a brain hiccup, a mechanical glitch in which the wrong message is getting sent over and over again because the brain can't move on to the next groove. Like a skip in a record, the words playing over and over are not doing so because they are more important or because they need to be heeded urgently, but because the machine is stuck.

From the Inside Out: Children Speak

One of the major roadblocks to helping children with OCD is their fear and shame about their experiences. Most children do not know they have a brain miswiring, they take it as a personal failing and will go to great lengths to hide their symptoms. Adding shame to the pain of having OCD only compounds their struggle. When children feel safe to speak, they poignantly describe OCD better than any psychiatric manual could. When parents hear how children suffer with this, it helps melt away the barriers of their own anger, resentment, and fear. Now they are ready to help.

> I walk through the hallways at school and all I can think is how dirty I feel knowing that the doorknob to every door has been touched by thousands of kids just today. I can feel the germs on my hands and it's unbearable. I sneak to the bathroom whenever I can to wash, and it helps a little, but kids are starting to look at me funny because I hog the sink. I'm tired of making excuses for this stupid problem.
>
> —*Sixteen-year-old girl*

> I feel so stupid when I have to make my footsteps perfectly even and count each one. I can't hold a conversation with my friends, and if I mess up counting, I have to go back and start over. I hate having to pretend I dropped something or make up a lie about why I need to go back to that tree and start walking again—but if I don't go back, somebody could get hurt in my family and that would be the worst.
>
> —*Eight-year-old boy*

> My parents keep yelling at me to stop playing around at night asking them to say good night again 'cause I didn't hear it the right way. I wish they knew that I'm doing it for them, [that] if I don't hear it right, I'll be up for hours trying to get that okay feeling, 'cause if I don't, we might not wake up tomorrow.
>
> —*Twelve-year-old girl*

I do have OCD, but I'm not really a nervous person otherwise, but my OCD makes me tap rhythms and do things evenly. A lot of people tell me to chill out because I'm biting my nails, but I'm not nervous. It's just that my OCD tells me I have to make my nails perfectly even or it doesn't feel right. Same with my feet. I have to shake my legs evenly on both sides; if I don't do it evenly or if I lose count, I have to start all over. I could spend a whole class period shaking my legs, and it's not because I'm scared of a test or something. It's just that it won't feel right unless it's even.

—Fifteen-year-old boy

I try to dodge it when I'm going to sleep at night, I try to trick it that I'm asleep, but I just crack my eyes, it's there waiting for me: "You have to deal with me—think about horror, think about Bosnia." And then it's over. I'm up for hours.

—Sixteen-year-old girl

It gives me these choices all the time, it's like every minute I have to decide. Which is worse—do you want to be healthy or do you want to be able to get through the school today? Do you want to do well on the test or not get cancer? Just ridiculous things, like I really have a choice—but I'm afraid. I feel like I better make the right choice.

—Sixteen-year-old girl

What's Happening to My Mind?

How do children explain these magic games and bothersome thoughts to themselves? Children go for the least common denominator; in the absence of other explanations, they begin to attribute these thoughts to themselves and think, *I must be crazy, no one else cares about sharing art supplies or using the bathrooms or counting the steps.* This may convince them to hide their symptoms, withdraw, and not risk the humiliation of being found out.

Prior to entering treatment, kids with OCD are convinced that there is something terribly wrong with them, they are abnormal, freaks, bizarre, perverts, bad. They have taken the OCD as a given of their personality, seen it as part of themselves and assume that these strange thoughts—unwelcome as they are—are a reflection of their internal workings. When I explained to thirteen-year-old Henry—who was up until 6:00 A.M. every day with a plethora of rituals about moving right, seeing things right, washing right—that he had OCD, he realized that his rituals, which he had come to think of as his own creations, were very similar to those of the million other children with OCD. This changed everything for him. "I thought I was so weird, but I guess you're telling me that all this stuff is kind of ordinary. I guess everybody's OCD is like this; this is just run-of-the-mill OCD." This realization helped Henry to begin to look at OCD as a mechanical glitch and to cultivate the attitude of detachment. *Brain Lock* author Dr. Jeffrey Schwartz advocates detachment to break the cycle of OCD—to step back and *evaluate* the brain message rather than *react* to it by heeding its demands. Kids can learn that their obsessions and compulsions are not true, just a glitch—a brain loop out of whack, not worthy of their attention.

In Chapter 2, we take a behind-the-scenes look at explanations for the phenomena involved in OCD and offer some metaphors to help you understand the mechanics of OCD and how to explain them to your child.

Cracking the Code

Visualizing the Secret Mechanisms
of OCD

"Knowledge is power: when you know how your brain works, you can take whatever steps you need to anticipate problems and to play to strengths."
—*John J. Ratey, M.D. and Catherine Johnson, Ph.D.,*
authors of Shadow Syndromes

The Specter of OCD

"This behavior makes no sense!" Such is the refrain heard from parents, teachers, and even kids with OCD around the world every day. What stymies us is the strange and disturbing ways that OCD presents itself. As human beings, we are always trying to make sense of our environment, being drawn to what is familiar and logical and being fascinated, repelled, and even offended by the strange. As bystanders to OCD, we find ourselves needing to defend against the excesses of the normal activities, too much washing, checking, and asking for reassurance with thoughts of *What's wrong with you? Just stop it!* Our discomfort is piqued because children are digging up and worrying about what we *could* relate to—cleanliness and safety—but have put to rest in our own mind, and don't want to think about. We cringe even more from the fright of the bizarre—children's sexual or violent thoughts. These normal reactions sit right next to our acute concern for our child's well-being. This is not something you can get away from; you are not a bystander to OCD.

A natural response to OCD is to try to decipher the meaning or purpose of these strange behaviors. In fact, there is none. Rather than approaching OCD from the "why would my child do that" angle, it is more appropriate to think about OCD as a brain hiccup, as Dr. Judith Rapoport author of *The Boy Who Couldn't Stop Washing* describes it. When someone is hiccuping, we don't ask why, but we say, "Hold your breath and it will pass." That's because we've come to expect hiccups; know that they are meaning-free and we have techniques to combat them. We know how they work. We know they're purely physical. We know they can't hurt us. Unlike an actual hiccup, OCD brain hiccups mislead us into thinking they are urgent because there's a message attached—a warning spoken in our language. While our understanding of the exact causes and mechanisms of OCD continues to evolve, the past two decades of brain research have revealed connections between the bizarre manifestations of OCD and a few central identifiable mechanical glitches. Thus, the specter of OCD has narrowed.

Making Sense of OCD: What Science Tells Us

The discoveries of the past twenty years have given us a new place to look at OCD—in the brain structure and function itself, as opposed to the psyche or the personality. Why does this distinction matter? First, it takes the blame away from your child, which allows him to be available for recovery. Second, it has spawned the development of highly effective treatment interventions. Consider the millions of adults who lived and died, hating themselves and thinking they were to blame for the bizarre things they thought and did. Imagine instead that we tell children with OCD, "Look, here are some tricks that your brain is going to play on you. It's just a mechanical slip up, but when that happens, here's what you do." This is the approach we would use with children coping with diabetes, asthma, or any other chronic medical problem. There is no shame, and we focus on preventive strategies. This approach is possible now with OCD. Years ago, the prognosis for OCD was poor; people were not getting better, and OCD was a life sentence. Today, however, highly effective treatments are available. An OCD sufferer can reduce his symptoms by 50 percent to 80 percent and go on to live a full life.

Outsmarting the Brain Traps: Lessons on Why We Get Stuck and How We Get Out

When parents understand that their child is stuck in a brain trap, they can dispense with the "why" questions and take up with the "how." If

your child were stuck inside a machine, you wouldn't start reasoning with the machine: *That makes no sense.* What follows are descriptions and pictures to give you a creative, imaginative rendering of OCD, a sort of x-ray vision of what's happening under the stormy surface of "stuck" moments, and what can you do to help. Consider them operating instructions for your child's brain.

Lesson One: OCD Thoughts Are Junk Mail from the Brain

Everyone has strange thoughts—bizarre, impulsive, and unacceptable. In a classic study conducted by Dr. Stanley Rachman in 1992, experts could not tell the difference between the intrusive unacceptable thoughts of normal subjects and the obsessions of OCD patients. Children with OCD are terrified that the awful thoughts, like "I hate God, poke her eyes, I want to lie, that drink could be poison," are a true reflection of their personality, and indicate that they are bad or crazy. Imagine the relief when your child learns that other kids have the very same thoughts and that they are nothing personal and not real!

Step one is sorting out the messages in the brain into two categories—the child's own thoughts and OCD junk mail. OCD thoughts are like junk mail from the brain. Junk mail looks official, sounds important: "You may have won, mail before midnight tonight, you can't live without this service, we guarantee results" and on and on with empty threats and promises. Obsessions are junk mail because they claim that terrible things *will* happen, though kids know it's not likely. Compulsions fit in the junk mail slot because they falsely purport to be able to protect you from anything.

If a child fluffs his pillow at night, sorting his brain mail means asking: Are you fluffing because you want to do it (a preference), or because OCD is telling you that if you don't fluff it five times in a row something bad will happen (an ultimatum). If it's the child's idea, keep it, if it's a tricky promise from OCD—that's junk mail—don't waste your time on it, rip it up!

Just as we have learned to recognize junk mail by sight, rip it up, and throw it away, kids can learn to do the same thing with their OCD thoughts. By age 7, children can distinguish a commercial on television from a program, at which point they are consumers and can be taught to identify a scam. You can use the model of false advertising to illustrate the point about OCD: Let's say OCD sent you a letter saying, "I can guarantee safety for your whole family if everyday for 3, 4, 5 hours a day you just do a few things for me, checking and washing." Would you agree to the deal, or say, "no way—first of all you can't guarantee that, and second of all I don't have 5 hours to give to you—I don't even want to give you a minute!" Children under the age of 7 can understand OCD junk mail as the "brain trickster," a tricky little creature, who whispers lies into your ears to get you to do silly things.

Since all people think "bad thoughts," why is it that they seem to stick for some and not others? The research of English psychologist Dr. Paul Salkovskis describes how people with OCD tend to be excessively responsible. When a potentially distressing thought or picture flashes in the mind's eye, rather than letting that thought float by with the caption "hmm, weird," or "forget it," you give it a "danger" label. "This is a clear danger—better do something to prevent it," or, "why did I think that someone was going to get hurt—it must be true, I must want it to happen." The passing thought, labeled as something that belongs to you, is now your responsibility, and you have a mission to prevent it from becoming a reality. So an adult with OCD who has a flash of stepping on the accelerator instead of the brake, begins to fear driving. Or a child with OCD who has an intrusive image of stabbing his mother with a knife instead of cutting a piece of cake avoids touching knives.

What a weight it puts on a child, knowing that at any time she could be accosted by a thought that would carry with it godlike responsibility! This is where "relabeling" thoughts becomes essential. We need to correct the tag to these pictures: "This isn't real, this is junk mail from my brain, return to sender!" Thoughts and pictures come to

FAR OUT THOUGHTS

us neutrally. It's the tag we put on them that seals our fate. The question is, how is your child going to label the thought?

That catastrophic thought is not important incoming information; it's brain junk mail. Your child's brain—like a net—catches some junk thoughts that other people's brains might let through. How does the brain come up with such thoughts? When you've got OCD, your net is of a finer mesh on a longer pole. It dredges up all sorts of thoughts other people's nets miss. You have not chosen those thoughts so you are not

NON-O.C.D. BRAIN   O.C.D. BRAIN

THOUGHTS GET
STUCK

THOUGHTS FALL
THROUGH

responsible for them. They just happen. Or, another way to describe it is that your child's amazing ability to imagine things makes OCD even more vivid. According to Dr. Edward Hallowell, author of *Worry*, "Toxic worry is a disease of the imagination." Your child has "good crayons," so to speak, but the fact that he can visualize and draw a catastrophe does not mean it's going to happen. When you are writing an English assignment or painting a picture or playing with blocks, it's great to be so creative. It's that great creative mind that can take you where you want to go, but sometimes it takes you where you don't want to go. What you need is traffic signals (in the form of relabeling and redirecting) to get yourself out of the places you don't want to be.

HOW TO TALK TO YOUR CHILD ABOUT THIS:
- Don't own that thought.
- It's not you, it's OCD.

- Don't talk to that thought, it doesn't deserve your time.
- Just because you *can* imagine it, doesn't mean it will happen.
- Label it junk mail—don't be tricked.
- Don't get pulled into a dead end—refuse to go down that road.

Lesson Two: OCD Is a Loop, the More You Do It, the More You Need To

Another OCD brain trick is making you think that you can do a ritual one time and be done, when in fact it never stops there. Immediately after, the discomfort and doubt creep back in: "Did I do it right, did I do it enough, I better make sure." Eleanor, thirteen-years-old, has developed an elaborate nighttime ritual to protect her family from bad luck. Lining up all her stuffed animals in her room, she has to say good night to each one, give each one a kiss, make sure they don't fall over, and look them in the eyes. When that is done, she starts with her prayers, which must include every family member, friend, animal, and child she has seen on the news or heard about; if she forgets someone, she has to start over because it wasn't a good prayer, it had a mistake in it. On a good night, she can get the ritual done in 45 minutes; on bad nights, she is up most of the night, alternating between trying to get the ritual right and worrying about the terrible harm she may have done by not doing it perfectly. The ritual didn't start out as an hour long endeavor; it took just a few minutes, lining up her animals, but each night it grew. In response to an odd thought—maybe her stuffed animals could suffocate—Eleanor would have to develop a new twist in the ritual. Even though she knew the stuffed animals weren't alive, OCD

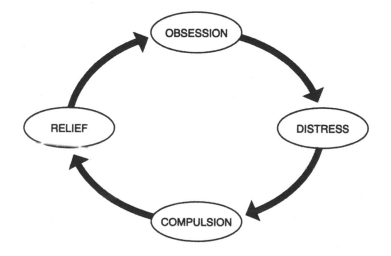

convinced her that she couldn't know with 100 percent certainty and she didn't want to take the risk that someone would suffer because she took a chance.

Four ingredients go into the OCD loop; these are obsessions, distress, compulsions, and relief/negative reinforcement—and they emerge in a clear sequential pattern. First comes the obsessive thought—intrusive, unwanted, recurrent—*What if that vitamin is contaminated and I get poisoned.* Your child reacts to this with anxiety. The anxiety delivers a two-part punch, especially for older children. The first anxiety comes from the thought itself, in this case being poisoned, which is scary! Anxiety's second punch comes from knowing intellectually while you're worrying that it makes no sense to worry about it, because it's probably not true. It's all the more terrifying to watch yourself do something that's unnecessary or makes no sense. Despite this, the child's need to get rid of the powerful and uncomfortable anxiety produces the compulsion. This action or thought that your child feels forced to carry out will (magically!) rid him of the anxiety—but only temporarily. *I have to keep asking my mom if the vitamin is safe till it feels right.* So in the short-run the compulsion brings relief from the anxiety brought on by the obsession. But the power of the rituals doesn't last long. Soon enough, the obsessions sneak back in and your child has to repeat the compulsions again. Even though the compulsions seem silly (and kids may know this when they are tapping, counting, or washing), the obsessions are so dreadful that doing compulsions feels like a matter of life or death.

Relieving the anxiety in this way is a form of *negative reinforcement.* We are drawn to that which rescues us. It is the taking away of the anxiety that reinforces the compulsion. Obsessions bring on anxiety, and compulsions reduce it. The cycle reinforces the idea that in order to get out of an obsession you have to do a compulsion. But it doesn't stop there. You have a mosquito bite and you itch; you know you shouldn't scratch it, and you think, "I'll scratch it just one more time," but then it's even harder to resist. The brain with OCD will continue to provide obsessive thoughts that your child feels he must undo with compulsions.

The idea that we do more of whatever rescues us is much like having to rely on a neighbor you don't particularly like. Imagine your car breaking down in the middle of the highway, and who should stop to help you but that obnoxious neighbor you always avoid? After that, you have to think well of him and feel that you owe him something because he rescued you. Unfortunately, *he* feels like you owe him, too. Once you start being nice to him, he asks for more and more: Can he borrow the

"You can't do just one compulsion!"

lawnmower? Can you babysit his kids and his dog? The rescuer—just like a compulsion—wants more from you all the time.

HOW TO TALK TO YOUR CHILD ABOUT THIS:
- Compulsions are a brain trick—OCD makes you think you have to do them or something bad will happen.
- You don't have to do compulsions to get rid of the bad feeling.
- Doing the compulsions just makes the obsessions stronger—to break the cycle, you've got to break the compulsions.
- The anxiety will pass without doing the compulsion.
- OCD is greedy. It won't let you stop at one compulsion; it wants all of your time.
- You are learning a new route out of the brainlock.
- Fighting OCD makes you stronger; doing OCD makes the OCD stronger.

Lesson Three: If You Think Something, Then It Must Be True (NOT!)

OCD often connects things that are totally unrelated. It's like a superstition gone way out of control. For example, you may have the thought, "if I wear red I will have a bad day, because red is the color of blood, and that means I'll get sick, so I better not wear red, or, if I blink when I say goodnight to my parents, the house will burn down, so I have to keep saying goodnight without blinking, or thinking of blinking, to protect them." Blinking and fires, clothes and illness—what do they have to do with each other? Nothing, it's another brain trick. One way to explain this is that it's the work of the OCD Wizard, connecting things with Super Glue that have nothing to do with each other. Like junk mail, the OCD Wizard is false advertising making you believe something that isn't true. Another way to explain it to older children is that the circuits got crossed accidentally in the brain and the brain is putting the apples where the oranges should go. By being clear that the two issues aren't related, your child can eventually "uncross" the wires in the brain.

HOW TO TALK TO YOUR CHILD ABOUT THIS:
- It's not true—this is like a superstition.
- Just because you think it, doesn't mean it's true.
- It sounds like that OCD Wizard is working his tricks sticking things together that don't belong.
- What do you think is true; let's turn up the volume on that thought!

Lesson Four: You Can't Go by Your Thoughts and Feelings in OCD; They Will Steer You Wrong

> We have a feeling that the stove has been left on, we check the stove, then we have a feeling that the stove has been turned off and all is well. We do not simply know these things, we feel them. . . . It is this feeling that people with severe obsessive-compulsive disorder cannot capture—and it is the inability to achieve this feeling that contributes to their anguish, to the torture that is their entire existence. They are *compelled* to wash, for many hours on end, until their hands are cracked and bleeding, not because they enjoy washing, but because their brains continue to broadcast the choked and panic-stricken bulletin that something is wrong!
>
> —*John J. Ratey, M.D. and Catherine Johnson, Ph.D.*
> from Shadow Syndromes *(reprinted by permission)*

In an obsession, your senses are giving you the wrong information— you *feel* dirty touching a doorknob, you *feel* contaminated touching a health quiz on AIDS, you *feel* unlucky if you read something two times instead of four. But, feeling it doesn't make it true. The message is: You are not dirty, contaminated or unlucky—don't judge your safety by how you are feeling.

OCD Wizardry:
Connecting things
that don't belong together

Struggling in an OCD moment, your child loses the ability to know and to trust the simplest things that we take for granted. For most of us, we lock the door, get the automatic all-clear signal as our brain invisibly checks that activity off its "to do" list, and it's out of sight, out of mind. For the child with OCD, that all-clear signal does not come. Instead it is painstakingly revisited again and again. He can't trust his eyes that he saw it right: "Maybe I only think I locked it, maybe I didn't." He can't trust that after the first, second, fifth time, he is pretty sure he locked the door. Your child is looking at the lock, but it's as if there's a forcefield preventing the information "Yes, it is locked" from getting through. This moment quickly spirals into epistemological paralysis: "How do I know for sure? How do we know *anything* for sure?" Although the content or theme may vary between dirt, safety, or evenness, the process is always the same.

Obsessions trigger the human alarm system and set off a series of physiological, cognitive, and behavioral events. In response to a situational cue, the mind says *Danger* and the body responds by sending out adrenaline. This creates shortness of breath, tingling in the extremities, sweating, stomach distress, heart palpitations, and other physical symptoms associated with anxiety. The shut-down function occurs when the brain recognizes that the danger has passed. The all-clear signal is sent and the body returns to normal functioning.

In an anxiety disorder, the alarm system can't distinguish between an actual alarm and a false alarm. It keeps sending out the danger signal, no matter what we do or what we know. The more we think, "uh oh, something's wrong," the more our body sends confirmation with racing heart beat, sweating, and tingling sensations. The brain reads this also as the go-ahead to keep being on alert. Anxiety is like a "he said, she said" misunderstanding—a misreading of cues that escalates. Caught in the spiral of misread signals, we gear up more and more. Meanwhile, just as chicken little discovered, it isn't the sky falling, just a twig with a lot of "hype" attached.

Specifically, in the OCD hot spot in the brain, the orbital frontal region, the caudate nucleus—the filtering mechanism for errors or danger is stuck in the "on" position and is wired to the cingulate gyrus, what Dr. Jeffrey Schwartz calls the "dread center." So with an obsession your gut is getting the message: Something terrible will happen if you don't listen to OCD.

Dr. Lee Baer, author of *Getting Control: Overcoming Your Obsessions and Compulsions* (Penguin, 1991), offers the following statements to summarize this lesson:

1. You cannot always control your thoughts.
2. You cannot always control your feelings.
3. You *can* always control your behavior.
4. As you change your behavior, your thoughts and feelings will also change.

How to Talk to Your Child About This:
- The OCD is making you feel bad, but its not real.
- It's stuck in dread mode.

- You can feel afraid and do it anyway.
- Keep going, the bad feeling will pass.
- You will teach your brain not to respond to false alarms.
- Change your behavior first, your thoughts and feelings will change later.
- Pick up your brain—do what you want to do!

Lesson Five: Anxiety Will Reset to Normal without Doing a Compulsion

When an obsession strikes, it creates feelings of guilt, disgust, or dread and children think that the only way to stop anxiety is by doing a compulsion. With this cycle, they never get to learn that there's another choice. They can choose not to do the compulsion and the awful feeling of dread they experience when they have an obsessive thought will actually go away without having to do the weird tricks or jumping jacks of OCD. The obsession is a false alarm, but when you say, "That's OCD, I'm not fooled," you send the brain another message—in essence, "Hey, there's no fire, no emergency, shut down the sirens, send back the trucks." Then the brain stops sending out the anxiety message and resets to baseline and the anxiety passes on its own. This is another built in survival mechanism of the species. Imagine the first caveman who heard a "snap" in the bushes when it *wasn't* a wooly mammoth. If his anxiety had kept on going and going, the species would never have survived. There is a shut-off valve, that stops anxiety when the coast is clear.

HOW TO TALK TO YOUR CHILD ABOUT THIS:
- Don't fall for that, it's a brain trick—it's making you do extra work for no good reason.
- You don't have to listen to the OCD.
- OCD is bossing you around.
- The anxiety will pass—the bad feeling will go away and you'll be in charge.
- Anxiety is uncomfortable but not unbearable.
- Don't let OCD fool you!
- It's a false alarm.
- You can break this pattern.

Lesson Six: With OCD, Your Brain Doesn't Know When to Stop

It's the brain's job to sort out information and it's a good thing that we have a signal wired-in to our brains that will alert us to danger. Picture again the caveman, who needed to know which berries were poisonous. The brain's sorting and error-detection system helped the survival of the species: We learned how to tell whether food was safe, keep our bodies clean, and make primitive buildings stable by judging symmetry.

In OCD the brain's danger message is in "overdrive" and doesn't know when to stop. It keeps sending out unsettling messages: "Is it safe enough? Is it even? Is it clean?" But like having someone looking over your shoulder while you're working, cautioning you on your every move, these intrusive thoughts create anxiety and tension. Kids perform rituals to appease the relentless obsessions. Sometimes the rituals are directly related to the fear—as when fears of catching AIDS from touching a doorknob lead to washing compulsions. Other times they are more magical or superstitious, such as counting the letters of every word and making them end on an even number to prevent something bad from happening to your family.

According to psychiatrist Dr. William Hewlett, there is a part of the brain that responds to incompleteness with a negative feeling, and people with OCD have a low threshold in this area. For them, it takes less incompleteness to set off the negative feeling. At the same time, there is a center of the brain that responds to completion with a positive feeling;

people with OCD have a higher threshold in this area, which means it is harder to get that feeling of completion. Let's take Jake, who has to check and recheck his locker to make sure it's locked because each time he does so, then starts to walk away, he tries to picture the lock, and there's a shadow of a doubt. What if he was distracted, what if he only thinks he checked it; he may have been mistaken. Though he may be fairly sure it's closed, he can't shake the feeling of dread in the pit of his stomach. So Jake heads back down the hallway to his locker, and he's late for class again. If an adolescent with OCD blows out a match, he may continue to think it is not out. He will submerge it in water—his brain still not registering that it is okay—and he will then begin to start collecting matches in water to make sure they don't ignite anything. The fear will remain. The more he does compulsive behaviors to make the bad feeling go away, the stronger the "something is wrong" feelings become. So the adolescent will soon begin to dread appliance fires and will have to begin a crusade to unplug toys, computers, and lamps in order to be safe.

HOW TO TALK TO YOUR CHILD ABOUT THIS:
- It's the broken record; it only knows how to say one thing!
- Your brain is stuck in a rut.
- Your brain is like a radio playing all fear, all the time, change the station.
- It's Repeater Man, let's tell him to be quiet!
- The message isn't true, it's just a brain hiccup.
- Remember that it just feels like you need to do it again, but you really don't.

Lesson Seven: Needing Certainty: Your Brain's Radar for Doubt or Harm Is Too Sensitive

> In one way or another, every patient with OCD wants to know how to know.
> —*Dr. Judith Rapoport author of* The Boy Who Couldn't Stop Washing

Sometimes your child doesn't know for sure whether something is safe or clean, but he can borrow your grasp of what is reasonably true in any given situation. If put to the test and told that he could win a million dollars for guessing the right answer—clean or dirty, safe or un-safe—he probably would be able to overcome his uncertainty and get the answer right. This is what Dr. Schwartz calls "that small holy voice of reason," and it is this resource—this foothold in reality—that we tap into with treatment.

In France, OCD is referred to as the "doubting disease." Riddled with doubt, OCD sufferers are unable to take things for granted, unable to rely on "out of sight out of mind." We live with some uncertainty all of the time. There are no 100 percent guarantees—with our health, our jobs, and our children. Did I lock the door, will my car be there when I get back to the lot? For most of us, these thoughts are fleeting. We locked the door, we know it's locked, but we are able to function and cope with the fact that we aren't guaranteed anything.

Kids with OCD have areas where their brain radar beeps with uncertainty: *my mom and dad didn't kiss this morning—maybe they are going to get divorced—better ask to make sure—my mom looked away, maybe she didn't mean it—better ask again.*

One especially nasty trick that OCD can play on you is making you doubt that your problem is OCD at all. Many kids worry, "maybe it's not OCD this time, maybe this is how I really do feel, maybe I am a bad person." If you think it might be OCD, then it is OCD. If your child is reluctant to accept that idea, here's a quick test to give your child: "Do you want to be thinking about this, are there other things you'd rather be doing or thinking about, does it make you feel bad in the pit of your stomach? Would you recommend this thought to a friend?" If the answers are no, yes, yes and no—then it's OCD.

HOW TO TALK TO YOUR CHILD ABOUT THIS:
- Obsessions are thoughts that don't knock on your door; they barge in.
- Fight back by saying, "No trespassing obsessions, this is private property."
- The doubt has a hold on you.
- The certainty critter is getting greedy, he's bossing you around.
- You can live with "maybe"—you do that lots of times, let's do that now!
- You don't have to be sure.
- Other kids don't worry about knowing 100 percent, it's not your job.
- Knowing for sure isn't as important as living.
- I can be "pretty sure" I don't have to be 100 percent sure.
- This is a time to practice living with "maybe."

Lesson Eight: Ignoring Doesn't Work: Name It, Boss It Out

The two million children in the United States who suffer from Attention Deficit Hyperactivity Disorder (ADHD) are challenged to keep their attention from being distracted by outside stimuli. In contrast, the one million children with OCD are trying to reclaim the control of their attention away from the OCD Monster. As Drs. Ratey & Johnson describe it in *Shadow Syndromes*, with OCD, attention is "seized and bound in a death grip." The struggle in OCD is that while there are circuitry problems that keep attention locked on one moment— *"what if there are bugs in my bed?"* the person is trying to pull out of that grip and *not* think of that. Meanwhile the harder he tries, the more he can feel his skin crawl! We know that the "just ignore it" strategy for OCD doesn't work in practice, but researchers have identified why it doesn't work in theory either. Psychiatrist Dr. Ian Osborn explains that when we try to avoid something, the brain needs to focus on it more. You could call this the bubble gum phenomenon—the more you try to pull away from it, the more it gets stuck to you. In a study by psychologist Dr. Daniel Wegner on the impact of instruction on memory, one group of students heard a talk on white bears and rapidly forgot about them. A second group that heard the talk was told *not* to think about white bears, and had "bear thoughts" all day. Applying this principle to OCD, a child walking down a sidewalk trying to simply ignore thoughts of avoiding the cracks to protect his mother's back can think of little else *but* the sidewalk beneath his feet and his mother's ill-fate.

The key in winning the battle against OCD is devaluing the enemy. When you reduce OCD to a brain hiccup or junk mail from the brain, it's easier to boss it back or walk away from it. If instead you continue to think that the OCD tricks have something to offer you, OCD will have the upper hand.

How to Talk to Your Child About This:
- Face down the enemy—it doesn't deserve your time, you've got better things to do!
- You are in charge—nobody's going to tell you what to do!
- Boss it back—do what you want.
- Remember, it's just a brain hiccup—you are smarter than it is, you know better.
- Tell it off, it doesn't know anything.
- It's not your job to worry, you don't need to do extra work!

"Bossing back" OCD is the foundation of cognitive-behavior therapy for helping young patients overcome this condition. Using the "brain trick" label helps children separate themselves from the problem and fight back. The more they relabel OCD as a bossy brain bug giving them extra jobs for no good reason, the faster the brain will learn to get un-stuck and children will be back on track thinking and doing what they want.

CHAPTER 3

Diagnosing OCD

The Difference Between OCD and Normal Behavior

Is This Your Child?

Mary can barely hold a toothbrush; brushing means dividing her mouth in four parts and doing each part four times, but each tooth has four sides and each side has to be done four times. If she messes up or loses count, she has to start over. When her brother knocks on the door, she screams because it messes up everything and she has to begin again. Because odd numbers are bad luck, she can't do anything an odd number of times, so if she messes up and does it three or five times, she's got to do the whole ritual again to make it an even number. Getting dressed is no easier. Mary has to put on her clothes two times; the first time is bad luck because it's an odd number. The second time is even, so it's good. She has to button and unbutton clothes twice, open and close her drawers two times; she's always thinking of another thing she has to double on. Mary looks stressed and exhausted by the time she's done.

Or Is This Your Child?

Carol hates brushing her teeth but loves to smell the toothpaste. With vigor she sniffs the toothpaste, giggles at herself, and puts the toothpaste on the brush. She doesn't like the gummy part at the end of the tube, so she wipes it off with a tissue. Getting dressed, she likes to do the right side first, puts on socks, shoes, shirt on the right side, it has always been her favorite side. It feels good to dress this way, and Carol takes pride that this is "her system."

"My daughter smells her fingers; my son licks his lips; sometimes it looks like my daughter is staring out in space; my son won't wear any clothes with a stain or small tear. If his socks aren't just right, my son flips out—it's got a bump—and has to take a new pair." Taken sepa-rately, these habits or preferences can occur normally for a developing youngster on the road to control and mastery over his environment. They do not constitute a disorder. From toddlers to octogenarians, human beings are creatures of habit and routine. We can all point to quirks, habits, and even superstitions that we live with daily that help us live happily and successfully; for example, saying "Knock on wood," wearing the lucky golf shirt, and not walking under ladders. Children thrive on predictability, order, and even superstition; they are organiz-ing responses to an unpredictable world. However, when these behav-iors or beliefs become obstacles for your child (i.e., they are highly distressing or interfere with your child's daily functioning), seeking a professional assessment is warranted. Even if your child does not meet the diagnosis of OCD, helping him work through these "sticking points" using the steps in this book will be good preventive medicine.

OCD symptoms differ from habits in several important ways.

Distinguishing OCD from Habits of Childhood

OCD Behaviors	*Non-OCD Habits*
• Are time-consuming	• Are not overly time-consuming
• Are disruptive of normal routine	• Do not interfere with routine
• Create distress or frustration	• Create enjoyment or a sense of mastery
• Make child believe he *has* to do them	• Are habits the child *wants* to do
• Appear bizarre or unusual	• Appear ordinary
• Become more elaborate and demanding with time	• Become less important and change over time
• Must be executed precisely to prevent adverse consequences	• Can be skipped or changed without consequence

When habits become inflexible and unpleasant, we move into the realm of OCD. Parents can be instrumental in helping children accept uncertainty or a lack of uniformity. Because there is a continuum of OCD behaviors, if your child is exhibiting some of the characteristics on the left side of the chart, early intervention can teach them ways to increase their flexibility.

This section will cover the following topics:

1. The diagnostic criteria for OCD.
2. What to do if you suspect your child has OCD.
3. How OCD is diagnosed.

4. How PANDAS is diagnosed and treated.
5. The difference between OCD and other related disorders.

The Diagnostic Criteria for OCD

To meet a diagnosis of OCD, obsessions and/or compulsions are evaluated according to four key indicators:

1. *Degree of control* over the behavior (Can you walk away from it if you need to?)
2. *Degree of distress* (Do you derive pleasure or get upset from completing the behavior?)
3. *Degree of impairment or interference* (Does it get in the way of school, bedtime, family activities?)
4. *Time* (Do these behaviors take more than an hour a day?)

When this stickiness becomes a way of life and a child begins to think he or she needs to be consistently certain 100 percent of the time and to do things in a prescribed manner, you should consider that they might have OCD.

The following questions will help you determine when to go for an evaluation. If you can answer yes to any of these, it is time to seek professional help.

OBSESSIONS
- Does your child have persistent, disturbing, and inappropriate thoughts or images that he can't get out of his mind?
- Does your child repeatedly ask questions without being reassured by the answers?
- Does your child avoid certain situations or activities because of fears?

COMPULSIONS
- Is your child spending too much time doing things over and over again?
- Does your child have overly precise rituals or patterns that must be done?
- Is your child generally slow or late because of precision or repetition?

DEGREE OF INTERFERENCE
- Do the behaviors interfere with daily functioning for your child or for the people around him?

- Is your child extremely frustrated, edgy, or distressed as a result of these thoughts or behaviors?

Formal Assessment of OCD: Seek Out an OCD Expert

Many parents first consult with their child's pediatrician when they suspect a problem. Your pediatrician will then refer you to a specialist in childhood OCD. Unfortunately, not all professionals—physicians, psychologists, and psychiatrists—are proficient at diagnosing OCD.

You can locate an expert in your area by contacting the OC Foundation or other professional organizations listed in the resource section. (See chart on p. 63 for important issues in choosing a therapist.) Although your pediatrician may refer you to a psychiatrist, if this is your first stop, your child will likely get a prescription for medications. It is important to know that this may not be a necessary first step and there are alternatives. Qualified psychologists can not only diagnose OCD, but may be able to treat your child without the use of medications. In fact, according to the expert consensus guidelines published in *The Journal of Clinical Psychiatry* in 1997, the first line of defense for children with OCD is cognitive behavior therapy (CBT). CBT is conducted primarily by psychologists. Psychiatrists can diagnose OCD and evaluate your child for medications but generally do not do CBT.

Unfortunately, there is a dearth of trained child OCD specialists at this time. You can ask your pediatrician or other health care provider for references. Also contact one of the several national organizations that maintain referral lists for therapists and may know a professional in your area. Contact the Obsessive-Compulsive Foundation, the Obsessive-Compulsive Information Center, Anxiety Disorder Association of America (ADAA), or the Association for the Advancement of Behavior Therapy (AABT). See the resource section for phone numbers and websites. Another option is to contact your local medical school's departments of psychiatry or psychology to find out where research is being conducted in your area.

Ideally, you want to work with a behavior therapist who is an expert in childhood OCD. If you find a behavior therapist with whom you feel comfortable but who is expert in depression or other anxiety disorders, he or she can translate CBT skills to working with OCD following Dr. John March's treatment manual. His manual, entitled *How I Ran OCD Off My Land,* is described in detail in *OCD Children and Adolescents,* which he cowrote with Karen Mulle. Working with a child specialist is important because he or she will know how to handle OCD-related developmental, academic, and family matters. It is important that there is a good therapist-child match. If your child isn't comfortable with the therapist, and/or if you don't have confidence in him or her, make a switch. Treating OCD is often a raw, take-it-to-the-mat experience, so a good trusting alliance is essential. Also important is whether the therapist respects and listens to your concerns and values your role in the therapeutic process. If the therapist is evasive when you ask basic questions such as "How do I get him out of the car?" look elsewhere. The crux of therapy will be guiding you and your child through the day-to-day impasses which are the work-a-day world with childhood OCD.

It may be easier to find a psychiatrist who is knowledgeable about the use of SSRIs than it is to find a qualified behavior therapist. At the same time, there are not many psychiatrists who are current in their information about treatments for OCD. Many do not know about the importance of concurrent behavior therapy. This is not a matter of opinion, but rather a lack of awareness of state of the art treatment, as study after study documents the efficacy of behavior therapy.

Likewise, if the therapist expresses an approach in which he or she proposes to explore issues of family, peers, and self-esteem with the idea that by simply working on these issues you will clear up the OCD, this is another red flag. OCD is a specific problem that needs to be treated directly. The situational issues are important in their own right, but they neither create nor will they "undo" the biologically rooted OCD patterns.

If the therapist is seeing OCD as rooted in early toilet training experiences or other early developmental junctures, look elsewhere for help. According to OCD expert Dr. Michael Jenike, "We do not know precisely why OCD symptoms develop, but it is certainly not the parent's fault." It is essential that the professional not only understand the mechanisms of OCD and the twists and turns of its presentation but be able to talk about it in a way that you and your child can easily grasp and apply to daily situations. It is important to ask questions such as:

- "How do you involve parents in treatment?"
- "Can you help us do OCD homework outside of the office if necessary?"
- "Are you available to do school consultation if OCD-related difficulties are surfacing there?"
- "Can you travel to the child's home or other locations in order to observe or complete the treatment?"

At the evaluation, you and your child will both be asked questions to determine the nature of your child's difficulties. Key questions will

What to Look for in an OCD Professional

Expertise	Rapport
• OCD Treatment	• Approachable
• Behavior therapy	• Accepting and reassuring about our child's hesitations
• Exposure and response prevention (E/RP)	• Helps your child find what's in it for him
• Child and family therapy background	• Comfortable with your questions
• Willingness to collaborate with the other professionals on the team: school and other mental health providers	• Accessible by phone or e-mail
• Willingness to do exposures at home or out of the office when indicated	

concern the types of worries, avoidances, rituals, and the degree of control your child has over these symptoms. In addition, your child may complete a questionnaire such as the Leyton Obsessional Inventory or another anxiety checklist. Some practitioners use the CYBOCS, the Child version of the Yale Brown Obsessive Compulsive Survey. This measure lists multiple OCD symptoms and asks for severity ratings (see appendix for sample measures).

Because many children have multiple fear symptoms and even multiple anxiety diagnoses, one of the tasks of the practitioner is to do a *differential diagnosis*. This means determining which symptom cluster or diagnosis best fits your child's difficulties. This step is essential for determining the type of therapeutic intervention that will be most helpful for your child. Two children with the same symptoms can look similar on the surface, but the mechanisms and beliefs supporting the fear can be very different. For example, take the symptom of a child who is afraid of dogs. If the child is avoiding dogs because of a fear of being bitten by a dog, this suggests a phobia. If a child is afraid of dog germs or rabies and is avoiding dogs and other animals or objects to avoid contamination, this suggests OCD. Because the treatments for phobias and OCD are very different, differential diagnosis is an essential step in ensuring that you are attempting the appropriate treatment for your child.

This is why consulting an OCD expert is so important. Unless your child reveals the telltale signs of OCD (for example, raw, cracked hands from washing too much), practitioners may not pursue the nature of his fears and could easily miss a diagnosis of OCD. Take any common childhood fear: thunder, throwing up, dogs. Unless practitioners ask, "Do you do something to get rid of the fears or do you have to do things in a certain way?", they won't hear about the rituals or the extent of the fear. They may assess anxiety or depression but not necessarily OCD. Children may be too embarrassed to bring up the symptoms. Or they may not even realize that they are symptoms; rather, they may just think these are just quirky things that they do.

General Problems with Diagnosing OCD

While in the majority of cases, OCD is easily diagnosed by a clinician who is experienced with the disorder, even a skilled clinician can "miss" a diagnosis or be unable to determine with high certainty your child's diagnoses. This is most often the case where there are co-occurring (or co-morbid) symptoms. For example, if a child has some OCD symptoms, some tics and mood fluctuations or attentional difficulties, it may take months or years to determine a diagnosis as patterns of specific disorders emerge. This is not to say that treatment is not helpful in these situations. In these instances, practitioners are actively treating the presenting symptoms, but may only be able to give a provisional diagnosis until one or another condition becomes most pronounced.

At the end of the evaluation, the practitioner should:

- Give a diagnosis and treatment recommendations,
- Discuss the frequency of treatment sessions,
- Discuss the need for collaborating or coordinating treatment with school staff and family members,
- Refer the child for a medication consult if indicated, and
- Answer your questions.

Commonly Asked Questions

- *Should I meet alone with the doctor first?* Some parents prefer to meet with a practitioner first, without their child, to gather more information about the treatment and to determine whether the therapist is a good match for their child. An initial informational meeting for the parent alone can be helpful particularly if your child is under seven or if you suspect your child has a mild or sub-clinical level of OCD. Subclinical means that the symptoms are present but they are not interfering or distressing your child significantly. In both of these cases, parents may be able to help their children make changes based on accurate information about OCD and by changing their own behavior in response to the OCD.

- *Do we have to tell the school it's OCD?* Deciding whether to involve school in your child's treatment plan is a common question when a child is first diagnosed with OCD. The main advantage of informing the school is garnering staff cooperation in assisting and accommodating your child's limitations. Without the correct information about why your child is not completing work or is late for school, teachers are left to draw their own conclusions, which may be inaccurate as well as unfavorable. Weighing this benefit against the loss of privacy is something that each family must do for itself. It is important for parents to recognize that in a classroom situation, a child with a problem has already lost a degree of privacy simply by being different (for being late, working slowly, or repeating questions). It may be more helpful to get the school involved in restoring the child's dignity by making changes that accommodate his difficulties rather than focusing on keeping the diagnosis hidden. Sometimes families inform individual teachers as issues arise; they may refer to anxiety rather than OCD in particular. These issues are discussed comprehensively in Chapter 15.

- *Do we have to tell our child that it's OCD?* Many parents don't want to label their child. They fear that their child will begin to look at himself negatively and that this will set off a downward spiral. In my experience, children and adolescents are generally relieved to know there's a name for what they have, that it's not their fault, and that it's treatable. Telling your child that she *has* OCD, rather than that she *is* obsessive-compulsive can steer away from this risk of self-blame. Especially when OCD is placed in a biological context, a child can see himself as no different from any other child who has a medical condition such as diabetes, asthma, or arthritis. One mother wrote that her son was diagnosed by a pediatric neurologist who told them, "I have many colleagues with OCD, the difference is, theirs is managed, and yours will be too." This gave them hope that it was not "the end of the world" for their son to have OCD. With more and more celebrities going public about OCD—Roseanne Barr, Marc Summers (Nickelodeon Game Show Star), Howie Mandell, Howard Stern—children have role models, they know that they can fight OCD and be successful. At the same time, parents also fear that children will be met with scrutiny and stigma. Unfortunately, this is a realistic fear. However, you do have a point of reference from which to discuss this with your child. You choose carefully to whom you tell personal things, whether it's news that your family is moving, your uncle has cancer, or you got an A on your algebra test; you share information with people you trust. As one twelve-year-old advised, "Don't worry that friends will think you're 'crazy.' If they're true-blues, they can really help!" Alternatively, parents can use the term "brain trick" to describe their child's symptoms rather than OCD, if they prefer. What matters most is not what you call it, but what you do about it!

A Special Case of OCD

Pediatric Autoimmune Neuropsychiatric Disorders Associated with Strep (PANDAS): OCD Triggered by Strep Infection

As we saw in Chapter 1, an area of investigation with critical implications for OCD treatment is the discovery of the link between OCD and common childhood illnesses such as strep throat and viral infections. Over the past decade researchers at NIMH, under the direction of Dr. Susan Swedo, have studied children with Sydenham's chorea (a variant of rheumatic fever) and children with neuropsychiatric disorders. This research has demonstrated that A Beta-hemolytic streptococci (strep infections) can trigger initial onset or exacerbation of OCD and tics in children who are genetically predisposed to these disorders. This occurs when strep cells "disguise" themselves as regular tissue and hide out; meanwhile the antibodies that the body has produced to attack the strep attack instead the cells in the basal ganglia, a brain structure involved in the production of OCD symptoms. PANDAS, which affects children from three years old to puberty, is estimated to account for approximately one-third of the cases of OCD in children. Children typically develop their first PANDAS episode several months after an acute infection. Subsequent episodes occur generally within days to weeks of a strep infection. It is important for parents to be informed about PANDAS, because even your pediatrician may not be alert for this syndrome.

How Does PANDAS OCD Differ from Non-Autoimmune OCD?

Looking at symptoms the two conditions may be indistinguishable; it is the course that differentiates the two. Non-strep OCD has a gradual onset, with signs for months or even years before the symptoms become noticeably dysfunctional. In contrast, PANDAS episodes develop rapidly and dramatically practically overnight. Parents of children with PANDAS describe how it's as if their child went to bed as one kid and woke up as someone they barely recognize. In a flash, OCD symptoms become so severe and incapacitating that the child can barely make a move without being barraged by awful thoughts and demanding rituals. A second distinction is the course or progression of symptoms. The pattern of PANDAS children's OCD symptoms is characterized by sharp ups and downs which may correlate with the rise and fall in strep titers. For children with non-autoimmune OCD, the ups and downs are more gradual, symptoms coming and going but without acute exacerbations. A third feature of PANDAS is the symptoms associated with the episode. Children may have numerous neurological symptoms: tics, handwriting problems, choreiform movements (trembling, twitches, grimacing, clumsiness) loss of math skills, tactile or sensory defensiveness (new onset of sensitivity to clothing tags, or to touch); behavioral symptoms: fidgetiness, poor attention span, distractibility, new irritability, and impulsivity, separation anxiety or bedtime fears.

The following guidelines recommended by Dr. Swedo at NIMH will help you become knowledgeable about the signs and symptoms of PANDAS, as well as the steps to take if you suspect that your child has PANDAS:

PANDAS: What to Look For:
- Sudden onset or sharp increase in OCD symptoms.
- Presence of tics and/or hyperactivity.
- Choreiform movements: involuntary and irregular writhing movements of the legs, arms, or face.
- Irritability, temper tantrums, mood lability.
- Age regression: reverting to younger developmental stage.
- Separation anxiety.
- Nighttime difficulties.
- Severe nightmares and new bedtime fears or rituals.

What to Do If You Suspect PANDAS:
- Contact your pediatrician, who can obtain more information from NIMH.
- Have the doctor do a throat culture for group A B-hemolytic strep (this shouldn't be the rapid test, which is less accurate) rather the 24-hour test is preferable.
- Your doctor may choose to do a blood test to check elevated anti-streptococcal antibodies (Anti-DNAse B and antistreptolysin [ASO] titers).
- Contact the OC Foundation if you are having difficulty locating an OCD expert in your area (see the appendix section).

- Contact NIMH for treatment guidelines.
- Have your child retested when there is an exacerbation in OCD symptoms.

Treatments for PANDAS

There are several treatments currently under investigation at NIMH. Some children are on prophylactic antibiotics (daily doses of amoxicillin) to control the possibility and severity of strep infections, however, the effectiveness of this treatment is not yet clear. Experimental treatments include plasmapheresis and intravenous immunoglobulin (IVIG). These more invasive treatments requiring hospital stays anywhere from several days to as long as two weeks involve essentially clearing the blood of the antibodies that are triggering the neurological symptoms. The treatments appear to be effective, producing dramatic reductions in symptoms, though they are still under investigation and are not standard medical practice. It is estimated that children will have on average 1 to 8 strep infections prior to puberty; at any given time, 5 percent to 20 percent of school age children have a strep infection. Until there is a vaccine for strep—possibly three years down the pike—parents should be vigilant for early signs of strep infection. To learn more about the NIMH program, see the listing in the appendix.

Dealing with Your Child's PANDAS

1. Be watchful of strep and tic symptoms without turning daily living into life under the microscope.
2. Get throat cultures or blood titer tests if your child has a sharp increase in OCD or tic symptoms.
3. Help your child establish good sleep and eating habits to reduce stress and maintain the immune system.
4. Find an informed pediatrician or one who is willing to learn.

Sarah, mother of five-year-old Hannah, recalls the terror she felt watching her daughter disintegrate within a matter of weeks. Hannah couldn't wear her clothes because the tags bothered her, her socks felt funny, and she'd end up screaming and crying every morning and changing her clothes many times a day. She couldn't go outside because she feared stepping or sitting on insects, and she was afraid of being contaminated by going to the bathroom—that the urine or feces would get into her mouth. Turning in circles, counting to four, hoarding uneaten food and trash, reciting prayers that doubled the family's mealtime—the symptoms controlled her days. Soon thereafter she developed eye-blinking, head-jerking, and nose-rubbing tics. Sarah was fortunate that the psychiatrist they consulted recognized the possibility of PANDAS and recommended a strep test. Sarah recalls that although her daughter's pediatrician thought the theory "ridiculous," the throat culture came up positive. Hannah was treated with IVIG at NIMH and within two weeks her tics were almost gone and her OCD symptoms were subclinical.

Since then Sarah has had to get very assertive with the staff at her daughter's pediatrician's office and insist that her daughter get the tests she needs when the tics return.

Fourteen-year-old Peter had OCD for several years when he suddenly began having severe shoulder, eye, and stomach tics—involuntary movements that terrified him because he had no control over them. He had a sore throat for which he was taking over-the-counter medicine, thinking it was allergy-related. On my advice he went for throat culture and blood testing for strep. Peter's tests were negative except for the antibody titer. Peter's psychiatrist prescribed a course of antibiotics, and within days Peter's symptoms remitted significantly.

A Word About Obsessive Compulsive Personality Disorder (OCPD)

Many people are confused about the relationship between OCD and OCPD. Put simply, people with OCD feel trapped by their rituals, which are distressing and oppressive; they wouldn't wish them on their worst enemy. In contrast, people with OCPD are perfectionistic but they think their approach to the world is the right one and righteously believe the world would be a better place if everyone were more like them. While adults can meet criteria for both OCD and OCPD, according to the *DSM-IV,* personality disorders are not diagnosed until late adolescence; children may display traits of a personality disorder, but generally these will remit over time.

The Difference Between OCD and Other Anxieties

Because it can be helpful to know what you are looking at (or for) in your child, the following section describes the difference between OCD and other anxiety disorders.

The Many Faces of Worry

Anxiety disorders are very prevalent. In fact, according to the Surgeon General's recent report on Mental Health, anxiety disorders are the most common problem occurring in 13 percent of children and adolescents. There are children who are temperamentally (from birth) sensitized to danger. These children have an "it's going to hurt" orientation to the world and, as a result, have a curbed approach to exploration. Dr. Jerome Kagan, at Harvard University identified this trait, which he calls behavioral inhibition, in children as young as twenty-one months. Such children show extreme caution, avoid new people or situations, and are most comfortable with the familiar. Dr. Kagan found that they had a higher than average likelihood of developing an anxiety disorder later in life.

A fear is a fear is a fear, right? Wrong. Once it has been established that a child has an anxiety disorder, it is important to identify what "brand" of anxiety is at play. There are two key dimensions to consider: content—what's the fear about—and process—in what form or pattern the worry manifests. Though the anxiety disorders are distinct entities, it is very common for children to have symptoms of several anxiety disorders at the same time. Because different treatment strategies work for different disorders, it is crucial to identify which category best fits the child's symptoms.

SYMPTOMS OF GENERALIZED ANXIETY DISORDER (GAD)
- Excessive, unrealistic worry about ordinary issues—usually apprehension about the future.
- Worry present most of the time for at least six months.
- Worry that feels uncontrollable.
- Physical symptoms of anxiety (restlessness, sleep disturbance, irritability, difficulty concentrating, fatigue).

Children with GAD have uncontrollable worry about a variety of ordinary situations (grades, friends, health, and money). In GAD, anxiety is like a free agent, available to attach to anything. Children with GAD have at any given time a laundry list of worries. New situations—a test, a party, or a trip—invariably set off a cascade of fears and a need for information. Posing all the "what if?" questions, children with GAD tend to anticipate the negative in everything, and so they worry before, during, and after a situation. While the content varies, the process is a free-flowing waterfall of worries and questions.

Children with GAD may be real fact finders. Seven-year-old Tanya was so worried about her parents' finances—though this was unwarranted—

that she told me in our first meeting about the high cost of aluminum siding that they were considering for their house and about her aunt's health problems. You could say that the child's parents are exposing her to inappropriate information, but it's more than that. Tanya is drawn to information especially anything that sounds risky, harmful or otherwise worrisome, like a bee to pollen. Children with GAD suffer from physical signs of anxiety—most notably stomachaches, headaches, and sleep disturbances. They may go to many specialists with real pains that are diagnosed as stress-related. The problem for these children is that the spinning wheel of worry takes its toll. They will be overly conforming and unsure of themselves, quiet, tense, eager to please, and sometimes the "teacher's pet." These children often fear that someone is mad at them or that they will hurt someone's feelings. Typically, children with GAD are timid and don't take risks. They look stressed, may be fidgety, and may sound older than their grandparents.

With GAD, the chain of fear is extended far beyond the original circumstance. Less than a perfect grade on a test—no college. The consequence is highly improbable, but the path is a logical one. Compare this with a child with OCD: Worry about a test could be linked to failing, but more likely that someone will get hurt, or that she will have bad luck, or will throw up. In OCD, the path doesn't make logical sense.

SYMPTOMS OF SEPARATION ANXIETY DISORDER (SAD)
- Excessive distress on routine separations from parents or from home.
- Symptoms present for more than four weeks.
- Crying, clinging, panic behavior upon separation.
- Reluctance or refusal to go to school or activities because of fear of separation.
- Difficulty sleeping alone.
- Nightmares and/or fears about harm to loved ones.

On first seeing Kenny, an energetic, coy, five-year-old with a sprightly look in his eyes, it was hard to imagine what his mother, Marianne, described as terror when separating or trying new things. Kenny could not be apart from Mom at home, even when Marianne went to the bathroom. Kenny, who arranged his trips upstairs and downstairs based on his mother's whereabouts, would scream a bloodcurdling "M-o-o-o-m!" whenever she was out of sight and then grab onto his mother's leg when he was reunited.

The red flags for SAD in children are: overt excessive fearfulness about going to school, going to bed, going to friends' houses, or wanting to avoid school trips; clinging behavior; not wanting to be on a separate floor; shadowing around house; sleeping in parents' or sibling's bed; phone calls home, and trips to the nurse's office. While uneasiness about separating may occur occasionally in all kids, in children with SAD, the problem is present for at least four weeks and interferes significantly with the child's life and often with the parent's mobility.

Symptoms of Panic Disorder
- Recurrent, unexpected panic attacks.
- Abrupt surge of anxiety symptoms which peak within ten minutes.
- Racing heart, sweating, trembling, shaking, breathing difficulties, nausea, or stomachache.
- Feeling unreal or detached, feeling like you're going to die or have a heart attack or go crazy (start screaming or losing control).
- Feeling unreal as if in a movie or cartoon or everything in slow motion.
- Avoidance of situations for fear of having a panic attack.

A panic attack is a sudden surge of anxiety and terror with physiological symptoms—dizziness, choking, sweating, nausea, chills or hot flashes, and cognitive symptoms—feeling like you're in a movie, dying, or going crazy. Some researchers have proposed that SAD is an early manifestation of panic disorder, where there is a sudden onset of terror and a need to connect with a safe person. The two phenomena have strong parallels in the strong, sudden surge of anxiety; the feeling of imminent danger, and the need to go to the safety zone. (For people with panic disorder, this safe zone is home; for SAD kids, it's mom's lap.) In fact, 50 percent of adults with panic disorder had SAD as children.

While many children with OCD also suffer panic attacks, the experience is very different. With panic, fear is related to the meaning of a surge of physical symptoms in the moment, for example, "I'm hot, I'm hyperventilating, I'm going to die" then and there. As opposed to a child with OCD who thinks, "Am I going to get sick from touching that doorknob?" and feels anxious about that future possibility.

Jessie Anne, a ten-year-old, was sitting in Mass at her parochial school. When she looked up at the high ceiling, she got a little dizzy and suddenly scared. Feeling that she was going to throw up and that something awful was going to happen, she ran out of Mass. After this incident, Jessie Anne went to the nurse's office to avoid being in Mass for fear of experiencing the same reaction again. Rather than recognizing that the dizzy feeling came from the visual experience of looking up,

Jessie Anne believed that it was the situation itself that caused the reaction and was afraid to return to it.

SYMPTOMS OF SPECIFIC PHOBIAS
- Intense fear of a specific circumstance or object that poses no real danger.
- Avoidance of feared situations.
- Immediate, extreme distress about feared situation: crying, tantrums, freezing, clinging.

Bugs, dogs, bees, airplanes, injections, elevators, and bridges. What do these have in common? These are common childhood phobias. It would be safe to say that most children don't like bees, but when children start to restrict their activities—skipping a pool party, not joining the family's outdoor picnic, refusing to attend camp—because of the possibility of bees, it is considered a phobia. Overestimating the danger while underestimating the ability to cope, is the formula for a phobia. Often phobias will begin after a frightening incident. A child feels a bump in the elevator, doesn't like it, gets frightened, and from that point on refuses to ride in an elevator. However, just as frequently, parents are unable to recall any particular event that would account for the onset of their child's phobia. The treatment is desensitization. Phobias are different from OCD in that the fear is limited to a specific stimulus or situation, and children with phobias are generally worry-free when they avoid the feared situation, unlike a child with OCD whose intrusive thoughts continue to attack even if the object is put away.

Social Phobia

A subtype of specific phobias, social phobia describes a condition in which someone feels that life has no "backstage." Unlike occasional shyness or performance anxiety, children with social anxiety are consistently uncomfortable around people. Afraid to raise a hand in class, afraid of eye contact, kids with social phobia find going about their normal routine painful and embarrassing. Seth was terrified of talking on the phone; he could avoid talking to kids at school, but at home, if someone called, he would run mortified from the room to avoid picking up the phone.

Cheryl begged her mother to let her be home-schooled. School was a total horror to Cheryl, who was painfully shy. Hoping not to be seen, with her hair hanging in her face, she struggled until age sixteen when she was legally permitted to drop out of school.

Children with social phobia are intensely self-conscious. They anticipate scrutiny from others, expect to make dreadfully embarrassing mistakes, and avoid social contact, whether it is talking on the bus, ordering at a restaurant, or making eye contact in the school corridor. Some children with social phobia keep it hidden. On the outside they may appear comfortable, perhaps even outgoing, but internally they die a million deaths. Unlike children with OCD, those with social phobia fear looking foolish, even when there's a low risk of that. With OCD, looking foolish is a risk that kids take by engaging in their symptoms, securing safety from the OCD thought is more valuable to them than concerns about how they will appear.

Can Your Child Outgrow Fear?

Fears change over time, and most children outgrow the fears of one stage, only to meet with new fears later on. One way of looking at this is that fears normally accompany any new challenge—they are the harbingers of a new development. A fear is a crisis—an opportunity. It provides the chance to learn how to handle something new. It is important to help your child develop an outlook for new situations they meet: "Take it slow and figure it out," rather than, "uh-oh, this is going to be trouble."

How do you help your child learn a more optimistic attitude? First, don't label your child. Instead, describe what's going on for him. For example, instead of saying "you're shy," or "don't be shy," say "Meeting new people is uncomfortable at first; it takes time to warm up." Second, encourage your child to face a fearful situation gradually in small manageable steps, to allow time for a new picture or template to develop for dealing with the unknown or unpredictable. What you will be supporting is the belief that "I can manage it." Every time a child manages a new situation, she becomes more confident. Avoidance leads to limited practice with new situations, and the gap widens between the child's abilities and comfort and that of his peer group. General strategies for helping your child face his fears are found in Chapter 7.

Other Pieces of the Puzzle of Your Child

In a study of seventy children with OCD conducted at NIMH, only 26 percent had OCD alone. The majority of children had more than one diagnosis; for example, 30 percent had tic disorders, 26 percent had major depression, 10 percent had ADHD. The disorders and syndromes listed next are what child psychiatrist Dr. Harold Koplewicz, describes as "no-fault brain disorders" in his book *It's Nobody's Fault*. Sometimes these co-occur with OCD, and sometimes they are confused with OCD. The disorders and their treatments are described in this section.

Tourette's Syndrome (TS)

TS is a type of tic disorder, a relatively rare neurological condition that involves involuntary motor and vocal activity. Only 1 in 2000 school children have TS, but as many as 15 percent have tics that come and go. Motor tics can be simple (for example, blinking, grimacing, or neck rolling) or they can be complex (for example, pinching, kissing, or throwing things). Sometimes complex motor tics can resemble compulsions; some children may even experience a warning or feeling that the tic is coming on. Tics can also be phonic or vocal; examples of simple vocal tics include throat clearing, squeaking, or clicking. Complex vocal tics include involuntary words, such as saying "oh boy" or "yep, that's it" often at the beginning of a sentence. The most distressing and most well-known symptom is coprolalia, or outbursts of foul language, but it is very rare among patients with TS, occurring in 5 percent to 30 percent of cases. OCD symptoms and tics can be difficult to distinguish from each other. Many times children with tics will get a "warning" before the tic, which resembles an obsessive thought, some children with OCD, especially young children have compulsive behaviors such as tapping which are not triggered by an obsessive thought. Tics in isolation are generally not TS, it is when motor and vocal tics are both present. As Dr. Stanley Fahn describes, you establish the diagnosis of TS "by the company it keeps."

Some children have what it called Transient Tic Disorder, where tics such as palm licking, poking, nose puckering, squinting, or vocalizations last only a few weeks or months and may recur over the course of several years. In contrast, TS is diagnosed when motor and vocal tics are present for a year with no more than three consecutive months tic-free. About a third of children with OCD will also have TS, which may develop later in the course of the disorder. In one 1992 study, Dr. Henrietta Leonard and colleagues found TS in 15 percent and chronic tics in 31 percent of children with OCD two to seven years following treatment, even though children with identified TS were excluded at the beginning of the study. While TS is common in children with OCD, at least 50 percent of children with TS have obsessive-compulsive symptoms. Like OCD tics create anxiety because sufferers feel out of control and worry that this strange sensation (eye blinking or stomach turning) could happen again and aside from being alarmed, someone might notice. TS is typically treated with medication and a type of behavior therapy called habit reversal, which helps a child learn relaxation strategies and behaviors that are incompatible with the tic. For more information about TS, contact the Tourette Syndrome Association listed in the resource section.

Attention Deficit Hyperactivity Disorder (ADHD)

A condition that affects approximately two million children in the United States, ADHD is best described as a developmental disorder of self-control, according to expert Dr. Russell Barkeley. Children with ADHD have a no-fault brain disorder in which their ability to harness their attention, impulses, and behaviors is not functioning properly. As a result, these children (and their parents) struggle with a lack of inhibition, a surplus of activity, and a deficit in future-oriented cause-and-effect thinking. Some children have primarily hyperactive-impulsive symptoms, others may not be hyperactive but are primarily inattentive, other children have both aspects of the disorder. While we often think of a child with ADHD as unable to focus, actually given an activity of interest, that child may be so locked in to what he is doing, for example reading or drawing or playing Nintendo, that he may be unable to withdraw his attention when asked. ADHD is treated by a concerted effort among the adults in the child's life to provide limits, consequences, reminders, and structure to keep the child with ADHD in tune with the resources and demands around him. Stimulant medication such as Adderal or Ritalin is frequently used to treat ADHD. Many children with OCD also meet for a diagnosis of ADHD. For more information about ADHD, see the resource section or contact CHADD (Children with Attention Deficit Disorder).

OCD Spectrum Disorders: Trichotillomania, Nail Biting, Picking, Gambling

In the early 1990s, psychiatrist Dr. Eric Hollander developed the concept of the OCD spectrum, placing other disorders that share some similar characteristics with OCD. These include trichotillomania (hair pulling), nail biting or picking, and compulsive gambling. There is a similarity in the compulsive nature of these behaviors, and therefore the same treatment strategies may be useful in helping children gain control over them. Like OCD, these disorders begin with a cycle of strong urges accompanied by tension that is released through engaging in the behavior. Unlike OCD, however, some disorders in the OCD spectrum often have an enjoyable, or appetitive, dimension; there is an experience of pleasure and relief associated with performing the behaviors (albeit the pleasure is replaced with distress and disgust when the child surveys the damage done). This is a key diagnostic difference: OCD sufferers may experience some relief after completing a compulsion—similar to what one feels after a near-accident—but it is fleeting and there is nothing enjoyable about OCD. For disorders such as trichotillomania and compulsive gambling, there is a reinforcing nature other than avoidance of fear. The repercussions of these disorders are tremendous and far-reaching. Consider the embarrassment of the adolescent contending with Trichotillomania. They have no privacy with their problem—it's out there for everyone to see. Habit Reversal is effective with OCD spectrum disorders. Other disorders in the OCD spectrum include hypochondriasis, which is a belief that one has a physical illness despite medical advice to the contrary, and Body Dysmorphic Disorder (BDD), a belief, similarly unassailable, that one is disfigured, deformed, or ugly in some way. See the resource guide for web sites and reading on these topics.

Depression

Most children experience negative moods as a result of OCD, for a quarter of these children it reaches the severity of a major depressive episode. The isolation and hopelessness that children can experience with OCD can quickly evolve into depression if untreated. Though we may think of depression as signaled by sadness and crying, children often express depression through irritability and low frustration tolerance. Additional signs are loss of interest and pleasure in previously enjoyable activities (not interested in friends, too tired to play sports, doesn't care about going to the movies); unexplained physical complaints, trips to the school nurse, change in appetite and/or sleep patterns; failure to meet expected weight gains, difficulty making decisions, delinquent or oppositional behavior; desire to run away from home; drop in grades at school. If this constellation of symptoms is present for at least two weeks, reflects a marked change in your child's usual behavior, and is interfering with your child's functioning, it is time to pursue professional help.

Pervasive Developmental Disorders (PDD)

The category of PDD encompasses such disorders as autism and Asperger's disorder. Children with PDD have in most cases markedly impaired development in social skills and interaction; depending on the subtype of PDD, they may also have significant delays in language development and communication skills as well as other impairments. For children with PDD, they may show little interest in others, may be unable to engage in such social behaviors as making eye contact, facial expressions or gestures to regulate social interaction. Some children with milder forms may show interest in others but may struggle with distinguishing closeness in a relationship and may for example hug someone she has just met or consider classmates "good friends" even though she has little contact with them. Often times children with PDD will have extremely restricted interests or preoccupations, such as amassing information on baseball statistics, or meteorology. They may also perseverate on one word or repeat it frequently.

While some children with PDD have repetitive or stereotyped behaviors such as head-banging, flapping, or tapping, these behaviors may in many cases be soothing or enjoyable to the child. Generally these behaviors which some may refer to as "compulsive" are not associated with a feared consequence as occurs with OCD compulsions.

Some children with PDD also have OCD; they can benefit from cognitive-behavioral interventions, however additional care must be paid to ensure that the treatment is appropriately geared to the child's level of comprehension.

Sensory Integration Dysfunction

Some children seem unable to ignore the background music in their life. Feeling and reacting with anger and irritability to every bump in the road, whether it's the tag on their clothing, a strong food smell, or getting into the tub, it's as if every piece of sensory input is registered as a painful or aversive obstacle to overcome. When something that should light up a 60-watt bulb sensation-wise, lights up a 400-watt bulb instead, you've got oversensitivity in the nerve endings. These children are described as having sensory defensiveness, a condition first identified by Dr. Jean Ayres in the 1960s. Though adults may perceive them as "picky" and "oversensitive" their experience is not deliberate, voluntary, or a factor of their personality, but rather of the efficiency, coordination and maturity of their central nervous system. A child with sensory integration dysfunction processes and experiences sensations differently than other kids. The dripping of a faucet sounds like a crashing waterfall or nails on a chalkboard, a light touch on the skin can feel like being stuck with pins. Common place events create an assault on the senses.

Dr. Xavier Castellanos at NIMH, explains how a large amount of sensory information that should be processed automatically—without bothering our conscious experience—is not gated or screened properly in the brain. Therefore, instead of brain resources being available to process more meaningful information, it is taken up with "my underwear is tight, my socks have a seam, or this food is too crunchy." Motor coordination is typically affected and children may appear clumsy. This dysfunction can be overcome through desensitization, retraining, and providing children with an enriched sensory diet to aid in desensitization to common sensory triggers. Sensory integration dysfunction is treated by occupational therapists. For an excellent description of the problem and treatment, see *The Out of Sync Child* by Carol Stock Kranowitz.

Nonverbal Learning Disability (NVLD)

In Chapter 1 we detailed some of the cognitive differences that tend to correlate with OCD. The hallmark of NVLD is having weaker nonverbal skills than verbal skills. This is indicated by lower Performance versus Verbal scale scores on the Wechsler Intelligence Scale for Children (WISC-III). Thus, children with NVLD have strengths in rote learning and memorization and activities where there is a clear right and wrong answer; they tend to be have weaknesses in flexible problem solving, abstraction, sequencing, and nonverbal memory. NVLD interferes with learning in school, but also greatly affects social functioning as so much of interpersonal relating requires deciphering of subtle cues, and working out flexible compromises.

Temperament

Temperament is a complex term that encompasses the nature of your child's characteristic actions and reactions that are consistent across situations; temperament may be thought of as inborn personality features. To some, temperament is the word we use politely to describe a child who's losing it in some public place, and in fact that may be accurate, but it is not a willful production. Temperament is a real blueprint of wired-in tendencies that we all have from birth which shape both how we experience the world and how we participate in it. First described and classified by Dr. Stella Chess and Dr. Alexander Thomas in the 1950s, temperament is built upon nine dimensions of a child's response that are identifiable and predictable. These nine dimensions are: Intensity, Persistence, Sensitivity, Perceptiveness (noticing and being distracted by things in surroundings), Adaptability (dealing with change), Regularity (staying on their own predictable schedule), Energy, First Reaction (hold back or jump in to something new), and Mood (happy/content or serious/analytical).

Take the example of intensity where low and high on this dimension are represented respectively by at the low end a child who is easygoing and rarely gets upset and at the high end a child for whom a scream which might be reserved for torture is signalled when the cereal box is empty. Children low on persistence, another dimension, are those who will easily wrap up an activity when its time to stop—in contrast, a high persistence child locks in and won't take no for an answer. On the Energy dimension—at one end there are kids who can sit still for hours, at the other extreme are kids who need to keep moving all the time— you may feel dizzy watching them bounce around as you are trying to hold a conversation.

When parents understand their child's temperament, they can help him or her maneuver through life by predicting what situations are likely to be difficult and then helping their child with strategies to negotiate those challenges. For example, the parents of Dixon and Alexa have noticed the differences in their children's personalities from the get-go. They need to prepare six-year-old Dixon for any change in routine; a change of plan topples Dixon's footing, time and explanation help him get reoriented. At the same time, Dixon tends to be a very active child and helping him wind down is an issue. In contrast, eight-year-old Alexa is a placid child; changes in routine are no problem for her. She doesn't miss a beat and can be calm and confident when there is change of plan, for example, a substitute teacher or a delayed departure. Alexa's energy tends to run low, she prefers sedentary, indoor activities (reading, watching television), and her parents have to coax her to go outside and exercise. To learn more about temperament and how to assess your child, see Chess and Thomas in the reference section.

Summary

While you may feel daunted by this discussion of the diagnosis of OCD and the related disorders and fear that it is impossible to put all of the pieces together which make up your child, don't despair. This is not a job for you alone. One of the most important things you can do as a parent is to be informed and aware, but remember to share your observations and concerns with your child's therapist. A parent can detect nuances which fall below a therapist's radar, so by contributing your "noticings" you will be increasing the likelihood that your child will get the help she needs. We now turn to a discussion of the course of OCD and what to expect at each stage.

CHAPTER 4

The Course of OCD

What to Expect

Depending on the stage of the OCD process, the issues and expectations for your child will differ. From the moment you notice the symptoms worsening through diagnosis, you will probably feel bombarded by OCD. Whether fielding the symptoms themselves or trying to arrange treatment for their child, most parents are reeling from the present and feel overwhelmed about the future. This period ends when you begin to notice that OCD has shifted from center stage in your life. Perhaps your child has been less symptomatic, he hasn't been asking as many questions, his hands aren't as red, he's smiling more, and the cloud that has hung over your family is lifting. Finally, when your child has reached the point where most of the battles are won, and he has become himself once again, active treatment comes to a close, and you enter the maintenance phase. This chapter provides guidelines for successfully managing these four stages of life with OCD.

Stage One: Levels of Noticing: It's Not a Phase

Our five-year-old could not get dressed in the morning. The tags bothered her, her socks felt funny, and she'd end up screaming and crying every morning. When we'd go outside, she'd cry because she might step on bugs. She'd cry if her crayons got mixed up in the box. We knew this wasn't just inflexibility—something was very wrong.

* * *

The first indication that something was seriously wrong was when our sixteen-year-old son could not settle down to sleep, he became completely sleep-deprived. He actually came to us for help. We noticed some checking symptoms, but they didn't register. We thought it was school-related stress and had him tested for ADD; when the results came back negative, he was at the height of his checking lights, doors, and washing his hands a lot. I went with my intuition that whatever it was, it was not going to go away on its own.

* * *

My daughter was always a little fearful, asking questions about the weather, lingering longer about safety issues than other kids might, but nothing that jumped out at us as a red flag. But over the course of about one or two years it escalated; the turning point came when she was eleven on a trip to Disney World where she panicked at every ride or "fun" thing, she couldn't leave my side.

* * *

We saw our ten-year-old daughter doing several repetitive behaviors and patterns with her feet and her hands, when we asked her why, she said "My stomach feels empty if I don't do it. It's like my stomach is filled with cubes and one cube is missing until I do it." She voiced "bad thoughts" about her favorite stuffed animals and Santa, and we saw her pain and guilt as she talked about it. These symptoms coupled with her rising general anxiety level let us know that we needed help.

* * *

Most parents wish they'd gone for help sooner and wish they'd understood the disorder so they could have gotten the right help. Though the role of "prevention" with OCD—intervening when the symptoms are not severe enough to meet a diagnosis—has not been sufficiently investigated, early intervention is generally a good practice. Parents at this early stage of noticing may benefit from the following suggestions:

- Read up on OCD—be informed.
- Go for a parent consult with an OCD specialist to learn strategies to handle any symptoms that may already be present, when to bring your child in for help, and how to talk about symptoms with your child.

In this way you will be prepared for the changes taking place now, and have a better understanding of what to look for and perhaps prevent in the future.

Stage Two: The Beginning of Treatment: Life in Dark Times

I don't want to be on this ride. I don't need another experience where we show how well we can cope. I hate this disorder.

* * *

I feel like there's no life. It's all OCD—nothing is spontaneous, every move is calculated, we are all prisoners in our home.

* * *

I can't force her to stop asking me questions, but not answering them is like taking heroin from an addict.

Freeing Your Child One OCD Moment at a Time

Just getting through the day is an exhausting, disorienting, and disturbing ordeal when you have a child with OCD. You may still be coping with the idea of the disorder. At first you may have expressed annoyance at your child's needing to line up everything; it may have looked like a dance to you; you may have even teased your child or yelled when your patience wore thin. When you realize this isn't a phase, you begin the slow climb to treatment and recovery. It is painful to look back and hard to resist blaming yourself for not seeing what is clear to you now. But you couldn't have known. It is only with hindsight that you understand that what once baffled or annoyed you was serious and not your child's fault. Forgiving yourself is one of the more difficult tasks of parenting. But it is necessary to help you be available where you are needed most.

You are now working to free your child from OCD. It is an active, present-tense endeavor. Using the strategies presented in this book, you are helping your child untangle himself from OCD each moment it occurs, one moment at a time.

The first step in behavior therapy is the hardest one. Although children don't like their OCD, and its rules may be cruel and unfair, at least OCD is familiar. Beginning therapy is like stepping off a ledge: You don't know where (or if) you are going to land, and that is terrifying. Taking that first step requires a monumental leap of faith, but I think that writer Anne Lamott's term "lurch of faith" is more accurate. To help you understand why this is especially hard for children, imagine if someone barged into your life, ransacked all of your neatly organized filing systems, shook out all of your drawers and said,

"Okay, now put it back together *differently*." You've lost your footing with the most ordinary things in life.

Be supportive of how hard it is for your child. Remember that your child may agree to doing "OCD homework" in the safety of the therapy session, but making these changes at home may prompt a surge of anxiety.

The Initial Backlash: The Extinction Burst

There is a phenomenon in behavior known as the extinction burst, which experimental psychologists discovered when working with rats, a surge in behavior to bring back reinforcement that has been suspended. When we kick, shake, pound, and curse at a candy machine because we've put in our quarter and nothing comes out this is an example of such a surge in behavior. If you give a rat a pellet each time he presses a bar, he eventually learns the expected behavior. If you do this one hundred times, he's made a strong connection between action and reward. What happens if you change the rules the one hundred first time and there's no pellet? The rat doesn't just accept this change in the program. He presses madly at the bar to make it happen like it did before; this frenzied activity is called the "extinction burst." Eventually, if no pellet appears, the rat adjusts his expectations and stops pressing the bar. However, if instead you sometimes reward bar pressing with a pellet, the rat will learn to keep trying because it may be successful. This reward schedule called variable reinforcement is what keeps people coming back to Las Vegas even though they usually lose. They persist for that occasional blast of quarters. Now, let's say your child has a prayer ritual where he is asking you for forgiveness twenty to thirty times a day and with the help of the therapist, you and your child agree that you will not reassure him. Even though he has agreed to this plan in theory, when you start to redirect him from his rituals and the anxiety hits, he will likely try harder to get your reassurance, begging, "Just answer the question, you know what you're supposed to say. Why are you torturing me like this?" The extinction burst—a surge of behavior to get the relief the child did before—ensues. In the worst case scenario, kids cry, scream, and melt down. Some children have no noticeable extinction burst. Most bursts happen when the parent is directly involved in the ritual. When they are not involved, breaking the ritual is still hard, but may not get as interpersonally complicated.

This is one of the toughest moments parents face. While you may feel like a terrible parent when you refuse to give in to OCD, you are actually a good parent, and a brave one. You are not torturing your child by refraining from reassuring him; you are helping free him from this disorder. OCD expert, Dr. John Greist of the Madison Institute of Medicine reminds us that surgeons have to make incisions to cure a patient; likewise parents may have to create pain for their children *temporarily* to help them recover. Stay firm during this time. Say, "I know this is hard, but this is the way out. I do care. I'm not going to let the OCD get you stuck. I'm not giving you up to the OCD. I'm fighting back!" Going back to what we learned from our rat friends, if you switch gears and do concede to the ritual occasionally, your child will keep trying for reassurance, the ritual will be strengthened further, and you will have even more work cut out for you. But remember that unlike rats, kids may understand why you are changing the rules and know that it is better for them in the long run.

Think back to the night that you stopped lying in bed with your child at night or took away her pacifier. Brace yourself for a few tough days, but know that the worst of it will pass and the pattern will be broken. Then you can look forward to your child being free from that ritual. Note that if the surge lasts for more than a week for any given symptom, the goal may have been too hard; in this case, it is time to take a step back and let the therapist reassess what your child is ready to tackle.

There are things parents can do to decrease the fuel of that burst. First, have your child choose the symptom he is tackling; that way rather than it feeling like a surprise attack, he is aware that you are changing your response to symptoms. Second, explain why you are making the change, taking some of the responsibility on yourself. For months you've answered the question, "Are there bugs in my bed" and then one day you won't answer that question anymore. A child may feel it's his fault for asking, though his parents have "encouraged" him to ask by answering each night. Parents can explain, "I made a mistake (right then your child will feel better); every night I've been helping you be more scared by answering that question, I didn't mean to. Now I understand that my job is to help you fight the fear by refusing to let the OCD make you worry all the time—we need to boss it back together so that you can be strong when that fear monster comes knocking at your door." How and when to make changes is discussed further in Chapter 8.

Prioritizing Recovery

Because early intervention is so important for your child's recovery, treatment should be the top priority in your child's life. It's easier said than done when there is homework, SATs, soccer practice, and chores, but cutting back on those activities for a while to devote more time to getting the OCD under control is an investment that will show strong returns. You can't stop everything, but this may be a time to reevaluate your lives and see where you may be able to cut back, at least temporarily.

Summary of Stage Two

- Your goal for now is not stopping the OCD, but changing how you think and talk about it.
- Work on ground rules for communicating about OCD so you can label it when you see it. (See Chapter 8.)
- Remind yourself that change happens slowly, one small goal at a time.
- Expect an extinction burst—an initial increase of your child's symptoms—hold steady with your responses and it will pass.
- Remember that you won't have to battle every single symptom of OCD.
- Give your child the control of choosing what he's ready to fight.
- Limit your responses to OCD; don't rush to accommodate every symptom.
- Don't blame your child; remember that OCD is the enemy.
- Prioritize treatment: Adopt a "just say no" policy for extra commitments in your life.

Stage Three: Mid-Treatment: Change Is Good!

The following letter from a parent of a six-year-old illustrates the shift in thinking that locates OCD outside of the child's self:

Hope is really connecting with the difference between Mr. Perfect [our name for OCD] controlling her and herself. The other night she was getting very upset thinking about fires because we are renovating our home. She kept asking me questions about what would happen, and I could see the anxiety rise. So then I said, "Listen, it's okay to be scared of a fire, and we should discuss what we would do just in case. But if Mr. Perfect is playing with your thoughts, telling you, "Oh no, you'll never see your toys again, or you'll never have any of your clothes again," or, "Yes, keep crying, get scared," then I'm not going to talk with him. I left the room briefly, and about five minutes later my daughter came running downstairs. "Mom and Dad, I bossed out

Mr. Perfect. I told him to stop making me feel so scared about fires!" She ran over and hugged us, we dropped a play dollar in the reward jar! It was awesome! She's really getting it!

Change Is the Nature of OCD

The fact that OCD frequently moves from symptom to symptom is disconcerting to most parents. Once you think you've got a handle on your child's symptoms, a new one sneaks up on you unexpectedly. An important survival mechanism is to expect that this kind of change will take place; it is not a sign that the condition is worsening, but simply is the nature of the beast. Nearly all children experience symptom shifts, with an average of four obsessions and four compulsions during the course of the disorder.

A new symptom is a chance for your child to see what she's learned. *I recognize you OCD, you can't fool me, I see through your disguise; you're up to your old tricks. But I know what to do, you are bogus, you're a pain, I'm fighting you!* It is also a chance for parents to gauge how far you have come in managing this condition. Whereas before your family may have been at the mercy of a symptom for months or even years, now, with your newfound ability to spot OCD, you can mobilize and treat a symptom within weeks or, in some cases, days.

When OCD symptoms emerge initially, there may be a one-to-one correspondence of obsession to compulsion. For example, Carol started out tapping each hand whenever she would have a bad thought. As her condition progressed, the spread of doubt led to uncertainty about what was a bad thought; for example, when her friends said something bad about someone, well, that could be a bad thought, too. Carol would think, *Better tap evenly, but these were someone else's thoughts, so I have to do it differently . . . I have to hold my breath, but then what if I die, uh-oh there's another bad thought. I've got to tap again. . . .* Just as rituals may change, the theme of the OCD may switch from hand washing to counting to being plagued by evenness; we don't know why this happens, just that it does. Symptoms may remit at different speeds, and this may be independent of their severity. For example, a prayer ritual that happens only at night may be easier to break than a germ-avoiding ritual that happens 50 times a day, in 50 different settings. Change doesn't necessarily have to be bad. From a therapist's point of view, when children develop new rituals, they are often easier to get rid of because they are not so ingrained yet. Because there is less adhesive, they're easier to loosen.

Expectations for Daily Life: The Rule of Thumb

There are two patterns that emerge out of the tangle of OCD:

1. Parents feel so sad for their child's suffering that they indulge, accommodate, or let their expectations go, or
2. Parents feel so frustrated by the bite OCD takes out of life that they clamp down and hold their children "accountable" for their symptoms.

Finding the balance is every parent's quest. There are no hard-and-fast rules about what is reasonable to expect of your child in terms of chores, homework, or grades; this depends on your child's abilities, the severity of his condition, and the personal values of each family. You always want to expect the most you can from your child but be flexible about how you define "the most" at any given time. Your child will likely show or tell you what she can manage by how well she's coping. For the sake of trying to maintain a "normal" life, be flexible on the number of responsibilities your child has, rather than crossing them off the list altogether. Household jobs can provide kids with a good feeling of membership in the family and teach them responsibility as well as the satisfaction of getting things done. Also if you treat your child like an invalid, he will begin to see himself that way. You can limit the number of chores your child does, or use a chore jar: Put slips of paper listing different tasks in the jar and let your child pick. Let younger children draw the pictures for the jobs, and they'll be more invested in the process.

Many parents struggle over how much pressure to put on their child about homework and grades. While maintaining high academic standards may be a family value, there is an important life lesson to be learned about having the courage and flexibility to adjust the goals temporarily when maintaining them is doing more harm than good. There are no absolute failures in life. This might be a time for you to reevaluate that idea for yourself. What's your priority? I've worked with many high school students whose grades took a nose-dive with the appearance of their OCD. I coached their parents to focus on the goal at hand—getting the OCD under control—because without that crucial foundation, long-term goals such as graduating, going to college, and having a career and family would be jeopardized. In cases like this, you can work closely with your child's therapist and school personnel to fashion an appropriate modification of your child's performance requirements. (See Chapter 17 for more advice on school interventions.)

The optimal approach to homework and grades depends on your child's age. For younger children, you will probably need the help of the school or therapist to decide on realistic goals and gauge your child's stress level. Rule of thumb: Don't punish the child for things he can't control. Older children have more independent views about work and may be ready to actively participate in decisions and to take responsibility for their choices. Aside from the OCD issue, your child may be reacting to something else and taking a stand against working so hard getting straight A's. If the question becomes "Whose life is this anyway?" then you know you are midstream, negotiating the choppy waters of adolescence.

Situational Factors That May Affect OCD

Stress does not *cause* OCD. However, we do know that it lowers a child's coping ability, emotionally and physiologically. Checking out the stress temperature in your lives is well worth the effort.

Several stressors have been identified as exacerbating OCD symptoms. These include illness, fatigue, exams, performances, family events, divorce, a change of school or relocation, a death or illness in the family. Some of these things we can control, others we cannot. For example, we could all benefit from healthy habits such as getting enough sleep, having sufficient exercise, and eating nutritious foods. You might insist on these things even if your child did not have OCD because they make good sense. These staples of healthy living become even more important to the child with OCD, because he's already got a tremendous battle to fight; if he's going into the battle tired, overstimulated on caffeine, or lethargic, he's sunk.

Many parents have lamented with 20/20 hindsight how a weekend sleepover (arguably one of the better oxymorons) triggered an OCD setback for several days until the child regained his sleep equilibrium. Caffeine from soft drinks is a known culprit in increasing anxiety. It triggers the sympathetic nervous system (fight-or-flight response), which results in speeded-up heart rate, rapid breathing, irritability, and sweating. Remember that caffeine is found in many colas, root beer, and even non-cola drinks in addition to chocolate, coffee, tea, and some headache remedies. Exercise is an excellent stress reducer with the biochemical boost of increasing endorphin production, the body's natural high. Especially for children with OCD who run marathons in their heads, having a physical outlet for releasing tension is a stress reducer worth pursuing.

Summary of Stage Three

- Your child is working hard so be careful about adding extra demands.
- Work on lowering your family's stress temperature.
- As your child starts to feel better, he may express more annoyance and frustration about having to work so hard.
- Expect new symptoms to develop; don't fear them—they will be less "sticky" and easier to fight.
- Don't get overly ambitious and try to push your child to take on more goals than he can achieve; rushing change doesn't lead to lasting change.
- If your child reaches an impasse, take stock of the successes so far and celebrate them; this may help jump start forward movement.

Stage Four: Maintenance Phase: Words of Hope

We have our son back, he is a changed person, he smiles, he jokes, and our lives are no longer under a reign of terror.

*　　*　　*

Our lives are so pain-free now, I don't know how we managed before.

*　　*　　*

We don't have any ugly scenes anymore, I almost forgot how bad it could be. Things still take longer than I'd like to get going in the morning, but we can talk about it; no one flips out.

*　　*　　*

I thought we had been to hell and back with Kathy's obsession about rape. We were all assaulted by these thoughts that would just seize Kathy anywhere—at church, school, or the mall. She would get this look like she had just seen a ghost and then the thought, "Mom, he could rape me, I don't feel safe, I can't fight it, it's taking over." Countless times we would make a mad dash to the car before Kathy became really hysterical. We'd just hold her till she cried it out. Then we all learned in treatment how to fight these thoughts and get mad at them. I would say to OCD, "Hey, stop scaring my child with this junk, don't you see how upset she's getting, I'm not giving you my kid, you're going to have to deal with me first!" That one line would help Kathy get mad too and refuse to let the OCD ruin her time. Just when I thought the coast was clear after several crisis-free months, we were sitting in a restaurant with my parents, and all of a sudden Kathy went pale and started to cry. We ran to the bathroom; the thought had returned. I tried to brace myself against the feeling of defeat. I knew what we needed to do to fight the OCD, but in the flash of a second I felt exhausted and betrayed as we plummeted back into hell again. But not for long. Kathy was able to pull together within minutes, and we went back to the table and finished our meal. I'm learning that slips happen and we can live through them.

The Good News About Maintenance

One of the most rewarding aspects of my work is when families move into the maintenance phase. At this point, all parties have learned how to identify OCD, have the strategies to battle it, and are ready to move on. Life has been restored to normalcy, and children get fidgety about coming in for sessions. They want to play with friends on their Wednesday afternoons instead of working on OCD. When the OCD flares up again, I may get an e-mail and bring in the family for a booster—a quick review of what to do when OCD tries to trick them—but there is no way they are going to give back the freedom they've earned. Good treatment means teaching children about relapse prevention. Coping with the potential chronicity of the condition is often harder for parents to accept.

Coping for the Long Run

The million-dollar question for parents is this: Will it go away? The short answer is, no. But will you have to go through the same hell again as you did the first time? Again, no. You know too much now to be caught off guard again. Before you were scrambling to get a diagnosis, to find treatment, now you've got that information ready at hand. Like having a first aid kit—you are prepared. OCD is a chronic condition that waxes and wanes over time. Several factors are associated with setbacks. We can attempt to control or manage them. These include illness, sleep deprivation, stress, and change. While some kids appear to "outgrow" OCD, many of them will carry the predisposition throughout their lifetime. The *Diagnostic and Statistical Manual* of *Mental Disorders (DSM-IV)*, the psychiatric diagnostic manual, states that 5 percent of sufferers have an episodic course with minimal or no symptoms between episodes. This number will likely increase as effective treatments become more widely used.

This may sound like a very difficult message to deliver and receive. However, as you read this chapter, an alternative picture for accepting the chronic nature of OCD will emerge. You will discover ways to do damage control for slips and lapses and of decreasing your child's vulnerability to setbacks. You will also learn the ways that OCD changes over time, so that you can be on the lookout for potential trouble spots.

Pacing for the Marathon Called Life

The adaptive mindset for OCD is that the potential for symptoms is lifelong. You may begin thinking *Forever? I can't bear it!* However, there are many things that are a lifelong risk to your child—getting hurt, getting injured, being frustrated—and you're not going to stop your life because of them. Even some of the wonderful things in life are chronic—the possibility of love and joy and satisfaction, for instance. We prepare for these possibilities one and all, but just like getting out of the trap of OCD itself, we don't want to get stuck in perpetual "what if?" mode because that isn't living, it's waiting in fear.

So how do we live with this perpetual uncertainty? We don't spend all of our time noticing it. Let's say your child is afraid of dogs. We work on his dog phobia and he is no longer afraid. Is that because all of the dogs in the world "went away" and never came back? No, the dogs are there, but your child learned to ignore them and live his life. This is the change that happens in OCD: The thoughts may reappear from time to time, but if you don't respond to them in the way OCD tells you to, they don't constrict your life. Your child will not have to go through exactly the same things again because she will have won back territory from OCD. Recognizing its signs and armed with strategies to fight back, she can't be tricked in the same way again.

Reading this may leave you with a feeling of dread. It *is* very difficult to cope with a chronic condition. But some of that dread and anxiety comes from trying to take in and digest the rest of your child's life in one gulp, all at once. If you bear in mind that there will be good days as well as bad days, it won't all feel so frightening. Just as understanding the mechanics of OCD will help you guide your child out, understanding its course will help you help your child navigate through the bumps and curves along the way. When you work on this, you can keep your discouragement in check, and that will in turn buffer your child from getting discouraged as time goes on. Remember that much of the stress of those early episodes derived from not knowing what was really happening. You are becoming an experienced tour guide. OCD is becoming more familiar territory.

It's Normal to Have Relapses: Be Prepared for Them

When you know that symptoms will recur, you can be prepared to respond. You can use your energy to stomp out the brush fire instead of siphoning it off to deal with your distress, disappointment, or self-blame. In fact, it is common to have recurrences in OCD symptoms. Next we will discuss some possible triggers to relapse so that you can be on the lookout. Although we don't know why all relapses happen—in many cases there are no identifiable triggers—it may be possible to predict when you will be vulnerable. In fact, some adults have found that there is a seasonal component to their OCD; for example, winter may be a time when symptoms worsen. What is most important is being able to snap into action at the first sign of a lapse. The essential role you can play for your child in curtailing a relapse is illustrated by the following two cases:

> Thirteen-year-old Jennifer had been symptom-free for two years posttreatment when she began to have some nighttime fears. At first she needed her mother to lie with her in bed at night, then she needed her mother to be on the same floor with her, then she couldn't turn on the lights by herself. The fear was quickly taking over. Her mother suggested that she return for a booster session, but Jennifer said that she was afraid that the OCD would come back if she went back to my office. Had her mother not intervened at this point, Jennifer's lapse might have developed into a full-blown recurrence; fortunately, alert to the telltale magical thinking of OCD, Jennifer's mom called me for advice. I suggested that she tell Jennifer that the progress she made is hers to keep, nothing is going to take that away, certainly not going to my office—that was a trick that OCD was playing on her to boss her around again. She soon started fighting the OCD and got back on track.

* * *

> Patrick, a sixteen-year-old, had been symptom-free for about eight months when his mother's radar went off and she began noticing little things—avoidance of clothes, irritability. She approached Patrick and suggested that he call me. Patrick had new OCD symptoms: He had to turn the TV and light switch off and on five times, the TV and radio had to be set to certain numbers, and he could only wear certain clothes or, in his thinking, his girlfriend would

break up with him. We talked about OCD as offering a guarantee: Do this and nothing bad will happen. I asked Patrick if he got a package in the mail that said, "Take this potion and you will be safe for the rest of your life," would he believe it? He said, "No way. I'd throw it out. That's ridiculous." That's exactly what the compulsions are offering. We made a distinction between worrying about whether a relationship is going to work out, which is normal, and doing unrelated behaviors to "make sure" it doesn't happen. Patrick was relieved, according to his mother; he walked back in the house a new kid. The weight was lifted.

What can be confusing to parents is that sometimes a recurrence can signal a problem in the child's life, and at other times not. For example, some parents worry that when they see more symptoms, this means the child is having "more anxiety" in his life. They begin to look for what might be making him so nervous (problems at home, in school, with friends). While it is true that stress is a trigger for many "adverse reactions"—including OCD—in some cases OCD spikes occur independently of stress. It may be due to fatigue or illness rather than an identifiable life event. OCD can be so cryptic that an image flashed on the television—a mummy, a skeleton, or a passing comment, overhearing the school custodian talking about leukemia—can set off a new raft of OCD symptoms.

Keeping Your Head in a Storm

Your challenge is to keep focused on your child's present situation. The cyclone may be heading toward you, but you can do only one thing at a time. Strategically, the approach to setbacks is the same as any OCD moment (see Chapter 8), but the extra job is keeping one step ahead of your emotions. Many parents describe posttraumatic stress flashbacks about their child's setbacks. When you've lived through periods of horror with your child's OCD, seeing the familiar first sign is like sighting a shark: You see the telltale fin cutting through the surface and you panic about the ensuing attack. But remember: now you know it's a shark and you know how to contain it; before you didn't know what it was or how to commandeer the elusive OCD. If you can keep calm and address the situation at hand, your child can follow your lead, and your fear won't be fueling the fire. To be most effective, you need to distinguish between types of setbacks: a few steps of ground lost versus a catastrophic landslide.

If you suspect that your child is having a recurrence of symptoms, here are some ways to talk about it:

- *For a younger child:* It looks like the OCD monster is at it again, we're not going to let him take over, we've got to counter-attack. Can you believe he thinks he can sneak back in and start taking up your time and ruining your fun again? Let's pull out our boss-back talk and show him who's the boss!
- *For an older child:* Is there something I can help you with? It looks like it's getting tougher to fight the symptoms. I think it's time to get a booster, you've come so far and I don't want anything to get in the way of you having life the way you want it.

Your child may want a week or two to try to fight it out with the OCD on his own. Therefore, you should set a meeting time for a week later to evaluate how it's working; if it continues to be a problem, it will then be time to go in for the booster session with your child's therapist. Just as you go to the dentist or doctor regularly when you're not sick to help prevent illness, you go to your behavior therapist for booster sessions.

Categories of Slips: Lapse, Relapse, and Collapse

When you are waging a battle against OCD, every step feels like a critical one. That's why any backsliding can be alarming to a parent. Likewise, it's very hard for your child to keep perspective on a bad day. You can be helpful by reminding him that these slips are normal and beatable.

While we all want our children to be successful and moving forward every day, we tolerate exceptions to this rule in other areas of our parenting. For example, you forgive the day or two your child has less of an appetite, brings home a mediocre grade, forgets a book, doesn't make her bed, or goes blank in the school play. We also accept this in ourselves if we go back on a diet, miss an important meeting, or burn a dinner. Adopting the attitude that the vicissitudes of life are a way of life helps us keep our grounding during a "slip" and not be taken by the undertow. Dr. Alan Marlatt and his colleague Dr. Judith Gordon working in the field of alcohol addiction brought the importance of being prepared for slips or lapses to the forefront. They point out that lapses are a single mistake, a slip, which can be "nipped in the bud" by seeing them as such and differentiating them from a relapse where one loses control or a total collapse. Translating this to the realm of OCD: a lapse may be a slight struggle with an old issue. For instance, a child with a previous history of multiple reassurance-seeking rituals at night has gone to bed for months without a problem. As Halloween approaches and there is more talk of ghosts, goblins, and monsters, some questions begin making their way into her nighttime routine. She demands that the door stay open, the light on, and so on. This may last only a couple of days, particularly if you coach your child like this: "I bet the OCD is getting in there because of all this talk about monsters and ghosts. Let's not let it ruin Halloween for you, because I bet you'd miss the fun parts, like the candy and the costumes."

A relapse may occur when, for whatever reason, the early signs of a slip have been unidentified, ignored, or not relabeled as OCD. When we fail to relabel, the child may take in the OCD logic and make room for it. For example, a teenager who is beginning to drive may have thoughts of running over someone, but he doesn't tell anyone because he thinks, *Oh, this may not be OCD—it's me.* Weeks go by while his confidence quickly erodes. He begins to stop and check when he hits a bump. He is afraid to drive. Though he is symptomatic, the OCD is circumscribed, he is functioning well in other aspects of his life. Now is the time to intervene so that the relapse goes no further. The final step, a collapse, may be the culmination of significant stressors, depression, and includes an inability to function. An example of this is a child who has been highly symptomatic and has disengaged from family and social accountability—everything has been gobbled up by the OCD. In these cases, the first goal is to ensure safety and work on reestablishing stability, day-to-day functioning, eating, sleeping, showering, and getting dressed before the OCD symptoms can be tackled directly. The take-home message is this: Teach your child to fall and get back up. Just as we have fire drills at school, being prepared for relapses is a key component of behavior therapy.

Coaching to Prevent and Contain Setbacks

So how do we safeguard our kids against future OCD episodes? Should we encourage them to think that it won't happen—take that "positive thinking" angle? No. In fact, the way to inoculate your child against future episodes is to teach him to expect them and how to bounce back from setbacks. This goes against the natural grain for many parents, who complain, "My child is so negative; he already sees the negative in everything." Seeing their children's pessimism about the future, many parents feel compelled to counter with the antidote of the "power of positive thinking." Psychologist Dr. Martin Seligman has refreshed the notion of optimism in our culture. True optimism is not about positive thinking, according to Dr. Seligman. Rather, psychological optimism comes from accurate thinking about the causes of adversity—how permanent, widespread, and how much due to our own as opposed to others' actions.

Children with a pessimistic explanatory style are more vulnerable to depression, achieve less, and have worse physical health than do optimists.

Red flags of pessimistic thinking are the words *always* and *never*—for example, "I will always have trouble with OCD" or "I'll never get better." This relates to the permanence dimension of optimism. Anchors for optimistic thinking are *sometimes* and *lately*. "Sometimes this feels impossible. Lately I've had trouble with hand washing." These explanations frame problems as more manageable, because they are temporary. If a child perceives that her problems are 100 percent permanent, the only reasonable solution is to give up. When it comes to positive events, children who see the causes of good things as permanent are more optimistic than children who see them as temporary. For example, Charlie says, "I got a 90 on my test, but that's because the teacher made it easy this time" (temporary). Josh says, "I got an 85 on my test, I'm really a hard worker. I'm getting the knack of studying." Children who attribute success to their own permanent characteristics are more likely to try harder next time. If success is due only to temporary factors, children may not feel it's worth it to try; it's a gamble, so what does it matter?

The second dimension is pervasiveness—how specific as opposed to global is a child's thinking about the meaning of events? Thinking globally, a child might say, "I am such a jerk for having OCD—I can't do anything right in my life." By contrast, an optimistic style for dealing with bad events requires damage control—limiting the negativity to the domain at hand rather than letting it spill over into everything about the child: "I really lost it at that sleepover last night. I'd better go to bed early tonight." For positive events, the more global the explanation the better: "I got through that sleepover because I'm determined and I'm a fighter."

The final dimension is the personal: internal versus external, us or them, who's to blame? When a child consistently blames himself inappropriately, it leads to low self-esteem. The reverse—consistently blaming it on the other guy—isn't a viable solution either. It's more about knowing "how" to blame oneself when it is one's "fault." The object is to stay specific about what you did wrong, rather than resorting to character assassination. "I blew that exam because I didn't study. I gave in to the OCD because I was angry and didn't feel like fighting" as opposed to "I gave in because I'm a total jerk and a loser." It is equally important for children to be able to place blame on others when that is accurate. For example, fifteen-year-old Kelly says, "The boys tease me about having to line up everything on my desk. . . . What is wrong with me? . . . When will I ever stop this?" Yes, Kelly is frustrated about her OCD; however, she is blaming herself for the boys teasing her instead of holding them responsible and giving herself credit where credit is due: "Yes, I'm frustrated about having OCD, but those boys are really obnoxious for teasing me—that's really rude!" A child whose mother gets impatient may say, "My mom gets so angry when I can't tie my shoes quickly—I'm a terrible kid!" But there is a better way. Again, it is important for kids to see where the criticism is coming from: "Mom, I hate this problem too, but don't yell at me—it's not my fault!"

We can help our children build the buffer of optimism by reinforcing their accurate appraisals of the causes of relapses, for example, you could reinforce the temporary—"Yes, you're right. You were too tired to fight last night"—and focus on their errors, "Gee, it sounds like after what happened today, you feel like it's always going to be that way, that you always mess up. But remember that when you're tired and especially when you're sick, OCD takes advantage of the situation."

Looking at Lapses from Both Sides of the Table

"He has totally gone downhill. He's back to where he was three years ago." As his mother spoke, I watched Charlie's face and his spirits sink. "I don't understand, he was really tackling this thing. He'd been making a lot of strides, then he saw something on television about exorcism and now he's terrified again." Charlie said that he feels totally hurt that his mother doesn't see his progress. "Doesn't she know that now it takes me about three days to get over this stuff, but before it would go on forever? She doesn't trust me. I hate this. Now I have to argue with her over something I'm not totally sure about, and that makes me mad. It's bad enough having this problem, I don't want to have to fight with my parents over it." Sometimes children are able to compartmentalize better than we are. If you catch yourself catastrophizing over a lapse, the best thing to do is backpedal and apologize to your child for letting your own anxiety cloud the picture. At other times, our children forget the steps and need our active direction.

Coaching: Behavioral Issues

During a relapse, you may need to be a more active coach than you've been in the past, for several reasons. First, your child is out of practice and may simply have forgotten how to fight OCD because he's had it under control for a while. Second, he may have difficulty doing things because he is under stress from the relapse itself, aside from whatever other situational factors may be present. You've probably seen in your own experience that when you're stressed, you have trouble with even the little things: You turn on the coffeemaker without putting the coffee in, you can't find your keys. What you may need to do with your child is provide more scaffolding—show him the ropes, do the fighting back for him till he gets the hang of it again.

Identifying Triggers to Relapse

If a child is having a bad day, parents typically ask, "What happened?" and attempt to reconstruct the links between feelings and situations. This is important in light of our discussion of optimistic explanations for bad events needing to be specific and accurate. Some common triggers are excessive stress (e.g., exam time, family events, whether positive or negative, weddings, and death), fatigue, illness, conflict, and change in routine. Whenever possible, if you can identify the temporary or situational factors that may have precipitated the recurrence of symptoms, this will help your child in two important ways. First, it will offset your child's depressive feelings of hopelessness borne from global, pervasive explanations—"OCD is always going to be this way," or "I'm weak, I just can't handle things." Second, it will help your child make decisions in the future about whether to be involved with that situation if he has options. Should he go to that rock concert, and, if so, how can he prepare for it? Will the prom be too stressful? How can she plan to rest up before and after so she doesn't feel overwhelmed?

What about your own stress? Chances are that if you're stressed about an upcoming event, your child is getting that through osmosis from you. There may be good reason for your stress, but we can always choose to look at things differently. The New Age mantra "Don't sweat the small stuff"can apply here. When you stop and look at the modern-day demands that accost us—"Do it all, but make it all seem effortless"—it's no wonder that our children are stressed, too. The wonderful gift of being a parent is how our children help keep us honest. Many things lose urgency in the telling, so that if every once in a while we spoke to our children about the spin we are in, it might snap things back into perspective. In the scheme of things, a screw-up at work, a faux pas, or a missed deadline are fleeting and will soon be forgotten, but the quality of your family life endures.

Developmental Issues

Childhood is all about change. There are so many firsts: the first day of school, first sleepover, first real test, first date, driving for the first time. For all of us, milestone experiences are so called because they are turning points and they create a new echelon of expectations. Even if we are "ready" for these changes, they bring with them new situations and challenges, which may spur new symptoms temporarily. So, for example, when a child with OCD first loses a tooth, she may begin to have obsessions about having blood in her mouth, or swallowing a tooth, reassurance compulsions may then follow. Or the ten-year-old who is faced with superstitions at school may have difficulty setting these aside and begin nighttime reassurance rituals. Obviously the answer is not to shield a child from such experiences, but rather help her sort out her brain mail. Instead of feeling the normal discomfort that anyone would in a new situation, maybe her brain is saying it's a near certain emergency that something bad is going to happen and that she has to prevent it by doing rituals. If her best friend were in that situation, would she have the same worries? Would she tell her friend that she *should* worry about those things? If not, then OCD is sending junk mail, messages she doesn't need. Encourage her to refuse that mail, rip it up, or send it back; tell OCD not to dare to come back again. In so doing, you can prepare her to be on the lookout for times when she gets stuck with sticky thoughts or brain tricks, so that she can quickly handle the situation. Take the example of Hannah. Hannah had been managing her OCD very well until she began to drive. Then she was hit with a new wave of symptoms. She began to worry about stopping at red lights. She kept worrying that she would step on the gas instead of the brake. She worried this meant she wanted to hurt people. Fortunately, Hannah was right on top of this being OCD; she contacted me early on, so that she was able to nip this symptom in the bud and enjoy her new look from the driver's seat.

How Much Should You Ask: Dos and Don'ts

Shelly, who has been symptom-free for over a year, complains that her mother brings up OCD all the time. While it may be only once a month, to Shelly, whose OCD was so crippling that she was unable to attend school, it feels like all the time. Shelly doesn't like to look back on her days with OCD because it is unpleasant to think about how "messed up" things were. "It almost feels we're talking about a different person. I'm normal now, I fight with my friends, I get mad at my parents, I hate to do homework. I'm a normal seventh grader!" In order to honor Shelly's feelings about her OCD, as well as help her mom know that she wouldn't miss any signs of a lapse, we talked about how Shelly wants her mom to ask her about what's going on. "Can you just say, 'Is there something wrong, is there something I should know about?'" Shelly also agreed that she would let her mom know if she was struggling with OCD. Shelly's mom was worried that Shelly might try to hide her symptoms so as not to upset her parents: "No," she said. "You've seen everything, I've got nothing to hide." With that, the case was closed.

Summary of Stage Four

- You will win this battle with OCD one step at a time. Don't look ahead, don't look back, focus on now.
- Expect setbacks or recurrences and be prepared to seek help to contain them.
- OCD may be recurrent for your child, but he won't be passively suffering; he will have a repertoire of tactics to actively curtail the episode.
- Trade in the picture of your child at the whim of this disorder for one where she is poised to disarm it skillfully when it attacks.
- Establish good health habits, regular meals, and sufficient sleep to keep your child's resources well stocked.
- Help your child find accurate explanations for slips.
- Don't panic if you see signs of slippage in your child. This is the time to snap into action, not get frozen by fear.

CHAPTER 5

Treatments for OCD

At this time there is no cure for OCD; however, there are highly effective treatments. Children are able to resume happy, productive lives. Parents are able to wake up without dreading what the day will bring. Treatment for OCD is hard work, but so is having OCD. The difference is that working hard in treatment gets you free, while working hard doing rituals just gets you more stuck. For more than 90 percent of OCD patients, the available treatments offer the "realistic hope of substantial improvement," according to OCD expert Dr. John Greist of the Madison Institute of Medicine.

As parents you may have tried your own "treatments" for OCD varying from the "Just Say Stop" method to the "Reassure till you're Blue in the Face" technique to no avail. This chapter will provide the how and why of your child's recovery with an insider's look at behavior therapy and medication. In Chapter 8 we will tailor behavior therapy principles to the home front, but reading this chapter will help you be "on the same page" with your child's therapist.

The Importance of Early Intervention

You notice a slight squeaking sound on your car, but you ignore it. Weeks go by, the squeak turns into a clang, and there's smoke coming out of the hood occasionally. Finally, you're on the highway going on a family vacation and the car breaks down at the worst possible time. When we wait until problems incapacitate us, we end up having to resuscitate first, and it may be months before we are well enough to deal with the "squeak" that was causing the problem to begin with. A case in point is Danny, who had been struggling with OCD since he was eight years old. Now at fifteen he was burnt out from years of obeying the commands of the relentless Evenness Monster—clothing had to be perfectly straight, rug fringe flat, no footprints on his rug, and he would walk only on the periphery so he could smooth out the rug on his way out. He straightened books on shelves and pictures on walls. Fingerprints were washed off the display cases holding his trophies from soccer championships he'd won. Never could he have friends over—it would be too exhausting to "fix" everything they "ruined" by merely walking into his room. The summer Danny finally came for treatment, weeks before a championship game, it was all he could do to keep his appointments. Exhaustion from his grueling OCD schedule weakened him, and depression overtook him. Nothing could pique his interest. Swimming, movies, girlfriends—it all felt like work to him—and he wasn't eating or sleeping. So there he was, at one of the most important moments of his life, feeling utterly unable to perform. Danny was in no shape to tackle the OCD. Helping him dig out from under the depression was the first order of business. It was months before he could tackle the OCD in earnest.

Though you may be tempted to adopt a "wait and see" approach, and may even be advised by your pediatrician to do so, rather than leave it to your child to figure it out for himself—don't put off getting help, you can use it as little or as much as is necessary.

How to Introduce the Idea of Therapy to Your Child

After you've made the decision to bring your child to a therapist, the question then becomes how to introduce the idea to your child. Before the first visit, you can tell your young child, "You are going to meet with someone who will help you with your fears—someone who knows about fears and how they can get in your way of doing things. This person will coach you in how to outsmart the fears and get stronger and stronger at fighting them." For older children focus on what your child has to gain. It may be better to notice how things seem hard for your child, rather than discussing fears. For example, let him know that you notice that he seems frustrated a lot, seems to run out of time, and that things get him stuck. You can share that you've read that this is often a biological issue—a wiring problem that you are born with and that responds well to certain kinds of treatment. Then invite him to come check out what the therapist has to offer. You can also first ask the therapist how he or she presents the concept of therapy, so you can be accurate in your description. I have found that introducing myself as a coach to help children win against fears and rituals helps take the stigma out of the situation. Otherwise, kids draw their own conclusions, as one child put it, "If you're my shrink, then I must be nuts." Your child also needs to be reassured that he is not alone with this problem, that there are millions of people in the United States, including many others in his school, who have this problem, and that the problem is no more his fault than the freckles on his nose or his blue eyes. Just like diabetes, OCD is a chronic medical condition, and it requires treatment to get it under control. I have also found that it is helpful, especially with adolescents, to let them know it's okay if they don't believe this treatment will work, because they haven't found anything that helps them feel better, so far. But with this new biological explanation of the problem, there is hope and recovery. They just have to try it.

Approach with an Open Mind

The decision to bring your child for treatment is often fraught with trepidation and doubt. You weigh your fear of stigmatizing your child against the growing knowledge that your child's problem is not just a "phase." If your child had a medical problem or needed braces, you wouldn't hesitate to get help. And though your child may never thank you or skip merrily in to sessions, he will be relieved to work with someone who can help. You can be most helpful to your child if you present a positive attitude about the process. I have had parents ask in front of their children, "Well, how do you know this will work?" or "If this doesn't work, we'll have to try drugs." Or even "Aren't those drugs dangerous, can't they make you sick?" While these are certainly issues that warrant discussion, don't do it in front of your child. Because your child is already uncomfortable about having to talk about these private issues with a stranger, any inkling of pessimism on your part may influence your child and he may not give treatment a chance.

Because you will have questions and concerns that are better not discussed in front of your child, ask the therapist to speak privately with you before or after the initial meeting. Some professionals believe that all discussion should happen in front of the child. It is my firm conviction that it is *essential* that parents have a place to air their fears, concerns, questions, and frustrations freely without worrying about what their child is seeing or hearing. Establish a system for communication beyond the first visit; e-mails, faxes, or phone messages can help keep the therapist's "finger on the pulse."

When Is Hospitalization Necessary?

For the majority of children with OCD, outpatient therapy is adequate. However, in situations where a child's safety or the safety of those around him is in jeopardy, hospitalization is indicated. While no parent wants to see their child in a hospital, it is an intervention that must be considered in certain situations. For example, a child who is malnourished as a result of extreme food contamination obsessions, or a severely depressed and suicidal child, or one with violent behavior needs the close monitoring and protection a hospital can provide.

Though some families are contending with a highly acute situation, this is relatively rare. A more common, though still relatively infrequent occurrence, is when symptoms have become so severe that daily functioning is not just compromised, but has come to a halt. There is no quality of life: school, friends, and family have all been replaced by severe compulsions and avoidances. In these situations, a day treatment, or intensive outpatient program should be considered to help the child get back on track. With early intervention and implementation of powerful treatments, the need for hospitalization may become even less likely. There are a limited number of hospital programs specializing in OCD. Contact the OC Foundation for more information.

Treatment Options

Some people mistakenly think that because OCD is a biochemical condition, the only or best solution is medication. Psychiatrists and psychologists alike are recognizing that cognitive behavior therapy (CBT) is effective in treating OCD. Dr. John March and his colleagues at Duke University found that the majority of children who had learned the CBT framework for resisting OCD were able to maintain their gains, even after medication had been withdrawn. In 1997, *The Journal of Clinical Psychiatry* published expert treatment guidelines for OCD, having polled professionals working on the cutting edge. Their conclusion: Behavior therapy first, to be augmented with medication only if necessary. (To order the complete Consensus Guidelines, contact the OC Foundation.)

What's better—medications, behavior therapy, or both? The answer is, we don't yet know. This question has been investigated in adults with mixed results; some studies have shown an increased benefit to combining treatments, while others have not. Summarizing the research conducted with adults, Dr. John Greist wrote in a 1998 *Bulletin of the*

Meninger Clinic: "Meta-analyses have confirmed the greater efficacy of behavior therapy over pharmacology." However, we do not yet know if a combination of medication and behavior therapy would yield even better results; to date, that has not been shown. Concerning children and adolescents, these questions are just beginning to be addressed. Large scale studies are currently underway at Duke University with Dr. John March and at the University of Pennsylvania with Dr. Edna Foa to investigate the relative effectiveness of medication, cognitive behavior therapy, and a combination treatment. In several studies conducted with smaller samples of children, CBT is emerging as a strong treatment strategy. To make good decisions about your child's care, it is important to be informed about all treatment options: Research studies report on typical treatment responses; they cannot determine how a particular individual will respond.

Medication and behavior therapy both improve life for people suffering with OCD, but they work in different ways. Medication has a few specific actions:

1. To help turn down the volume and intensity of the symptoms, in effect slowing down the jump rope so you can more easily jump in,
2. To decrease the levels of distress and anxiety associated with OCD, and
3. To lift the depression that can result from OCD.

Thus, ideally, medication can take the edge off of OCD, even out the playing field so that your child can fight it. Indirectly, medication may also help parents do their job, because if your child is feeling less distress, it will be easier for you to "push" your child to fight back. Psychiatrist Dr. Jeffrey Schwartz likens medication to "waterwings." In his book *Brain Lock,* he writes, "It will help you stay afloat while you learn to swim through the rough waters of OCD." However, he states, the more behavior therapy you do, the less medication you'll need. If this is the only way to get in the water in the first place, then waterwings are essential.

Furthermore, while CBT may work for many children, there are many children who will also need medication to get control of their OCD. There are multiple, *unidentified* factors that determine which children will need medication and which will not—none of these is strength of character. Children should not feel "less than" strong or motivated because they need medication.

OCD results from a combination of brain chemistry—the mechanics that set a child up for repetitive thoughts—and learning—the child's experience contending with those thoughts. We know that the relief from an obsessive thought that a compulsion provides, albeit temporary, is very reinforcing, because the distress is so great. When kids are significantly depressed or generally anxious, they are already carrying a heavy emotional load, and may be very reluctant to engage in behavior therapy which requires energy, and withstanding temporary anxiety for the sake of doing away with compulsions. In these cases especially, medication may be an essential component of treatment to reduce distress, and therefore increase the child's readiness for taking risks with his symptoms. But medication will not educate your child about OCD; it won't help your child touch doorknobs or refrain from washing her hands. The learned aspect of OCD must be "unlearned" through behavior therapy. Behavior therapy teaches your child that OCD is a false alarm, a bully in your brain bossing you around, and the way to get rid of OCD is by "show and tell." *Show* it that you are in charge by doing what *you* want, not what it wants, then *tell* the OCD to back off and leave you alone. Behavior therapy provides planned opportunities for your child to see that he *can* control his actions.

Behavior Therapy: An Overview

In this section I will describe the OCD treatment I use at my Center. It is based on a model developed by Dr. John March to treat children with OCD and has a very high success rate. A comprehensive description of behavior therapy is beyond the scope of this book, and is available in March and Mulle's *OCD in Children and Adolescents: A Cognitive-Behavioral Treatment Manual.* I will highlight three key areas: first, the treatment strategy itself, second, how to access your child's motivation for treatment, and finally, how a behavior therapist may involve you in the treatment. The core intervention is exposure and ritual prevention—putting yourself in the OCD situation and resisting doing the compulsions. Dr. March refers to this as "bossing back OCD" or "running OCD off your land."

Behavior therapy for OCD began in 1966 when ritual or response prevention, a radical treatment, was first described by British psychiatrist Dr. Vic Meyer. He found that when patients in a hospital setting were prevented from doing their rituals, this led to a rapid and lasting reduction in their symptoms—both obsessions and compulsions. Since then, numerous studies have confirmed the efficacy of behavior therapy for treating OCD. In 1984, OCD expert Dr. Edna Foa, conducted a meta-analysis—a statistical study that pools results from many studies in many countries—which found that the majority of patients (76%) were moderately improved months to years after behavioral treatment ended.

When you talk to children about their symptoms, many describe OCD as some other voice that sounds sort of believable but has a mind of its own and tells them to think and do things they don't want to. They feel as if someone has taken over their mind. Dr. March and colleagues at Duke University have capitalized on this idea of this other voice, their treatment program is based on giving the OCD voice its own name—the bully who keeps goading you to do things that really take time and make you feel worse. Giving the OCD a name and externalizing it does three important things:

1. It reassures the child that he is not crazy, that it's not him, that there is a physiological explanation for why this is happening.
2. It frames the OCD as a neurobiological condition, not the child's fault. By giving the OCD a name, it reminds everyone of what the problem really is.
3. It gives the child and parents a common enemy so they can join forces to fight the OCD rather than fighting each other.

The beauty of this treatment is that it utilizes children's natural resources; after all, what child doesn't want to be in charge and have power? It taps into something that is abundant and desirable to children. In this treatment they can be the powerful one bossing back and refusing to listen to whoever their demon is. Giving the brain trick a nasty name—common choices are "Mr. Bossy," "Worrywart," "Brain Bug," "Mr. Clean," "Ritual Revenge," "Broken Record," "Scare Box"—helps children focus their anger and efforts at winning back power and territory from OCD so that they can resume doing what they enjoy in life.

As treatment progresses and children see that nothing bad happens when they fight the rituals, they start to talk back to the OCD: "You want me to jump through hoops, run around in circles to get to the same place I could get without doing any of that. It's a trap. No way, that's a waste of time. Get a life!" One teenager would come in and say, "You should see the places OCD went this week." Notice how she wasn't taken for that ride!

Behavior Therapy in Action: Nuts and Bolts

There are six basic components in behavior therapy to take control of OCD. I have coded them as follows:

1. Relabel the problem as a bad guy bossing you around.
2. Do the opposite of the OCD warnings (show).
3. Boss back the OCD (tell).
4. Refocus on what you want to be doing instead of having symptoms.
5. Define the motivation for treatment: What I hate about OCD.
6. Determine the parents' role in treatment.

Four Steps to Break the Brain Tricks

Step One: Relabeling

OCD is a brain hiccup, but it's a tricky one. Disguised as an important thought, OCD fools us into thinking that we must respond, ask the question, do the ritual, and avoid the contaminant. That's where relabeling comes in. The very first step in battling the disorder is distinguishing between the thoughts that belong to your child and those imposed on her by OCD's meaningless brain hiccups. Until you and your child are seasoned OCD detectives, you will both be tricked by the surface problem. "Are your hands clean?" your child asks before you make his sandwich. What do you do? Whether your answer "yes" or "no," you've been snared by OCD. "No" means you go wash (but you didn't really need to). "Yes" means reassuring your child that your hands are in fact clean, and reassuring, and reassuring and reassuring! Lasting change in OCD means reframing the problem. It's not about being clean, because it is likely your child knows that your hands are clean. No, the problem isn't about clean, it's about certainty. What you need to envision is that your child's brain is locked in a fruitless search mission for a 100 percent guarantee and getting stuck on the hook of certainty. Life isn't certain. Let him know that. "Is that your question, or is that OCD?" "Who wants to know?" "Do you want to be examining my hands or enjoying your sandwich?"

Step Two: Do the Opposite of the OCD Warnings (Show)

This is where exposure and ritual prevention comes into play. The child *shows* who's boss by breaking OCD's rules in any one of several ways:

- Doing the ritual wrong: wash the wrong number of times, say the wrong word, wash with eyes closed or without soap.
- Refraining from doing the ritual at all: walk away without washing; delay for 10 to 15 minute intervals.

- Shortening the ritual: if washing to the count of 100, count to 20 or 30 instead
- Purposely doing exactly what the OCD is warning not to do: touch the toilet seat, sink handles, doorknob.

For example, nine-year-old Mira has contamination fears and carefully avoids touching doorknobs directly, turns on the sink faucets and uses the soap dispenser with her elbow, and has to count to 250 while washing. Doing the ritual wrong would mean counting to 29, or 17 (not a multiple of 5) while washing, or whistling a song while washing instead of counting, or saying to herself, "I refuse to count while I wash, I'm going to say random numbers to make sure the OCD doesn't make me count!" Refraining from doing the ritual at all would be washing "once and done" without any counting. Purposely spiting the OCD would be to touch the doorknobs, soap dispenser, and faucets, then not washing at all. Or to top it all off, Mira could touch worse stuff like a trash can or public telephone or money and not wash before having a snack.

This component is ritual prevention, but rather than taking that in the strictest sense of *not* ritualizing, it brings to bear flexibility and multiple opportunities in order to break the OCD gridlock. Dr. Jeffrey Schwartz advises adults to use the "fifteen-minute rule" of delaying the ritual for that period of time, and trying to lengthen that period over time. I have found with children that one or two ten-minute intervals are generally sufficient time for the anxiety urges to pass. The child notes his fear temperature before, during, and after the exposure to track his level of anxiety (see page 111). It is important to "grade" the fear level because your child is going to feel nervous when he's doing response prevention, but you want him to see how nervous, and see that the numbers go down with time.

Step Three: Boss Back the OCD (Tell)

Your child tells the OCD to knock it off. Some children accomplish this by the succinct "Stop it, leave me alone!" Others use their creativity to put their own personal trademark on their battle cry.

This step is the cognitive piece of the treatment, focusing on the child's answers to these questions:

1. What do I hate about OCD?
2. Do I want to be doing this now?
3. Does most of me think this is unnecessary?
4. What would I rather be doing instead?

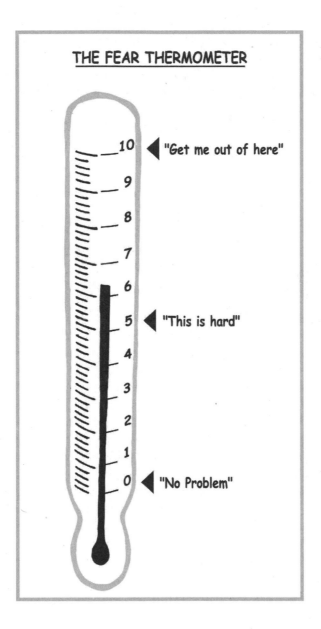

The treatment is still about refraining from engaging in the ritual and habituating to anxiety (recall from Chapter 1 how we get used to the cold water in the swimming pool). We are just adding a cognitive ingredient to the treatment when your child says to the OCD, "You are junk mail, you're not real, so stop bossing me around!" This will help him feel empowered and mad, rather than scared and trapped.

*Step Four: Refocus on What You Want to Be Doing
Instead of Having Symptoms*

Remembering the OCD formula, we know that when a child refrains from a ritual or "messes it up," he will start to experience anxiety. Kids learn from OCD that the only way to avoid or escape the bad feeling of an obsession is to do a compulsion. In behavior therapy, kids get to see that the *bad feeling passes on its own,* generally within ten to fifteen minutes, if they are not actively engaging in the symptoms. There are three main approaches to managing this anxiety time:

1. Anxiety management techniques such as:
   - *Diaphragmatic breathing* (balloon breaths). The child takes deep, slow breaths from the diaphragm (not the chest), breathing in through the nose—1-2-3—and out—1-2-3—without holding their breath, saying "relax" silently on the exhale. If your child is having difficulty finding his diaphragm, have him take a breath and say "ha ha ha." You have to engage the diaphragm for this. Place his hand on his belly below his rib cage so he can feel this muscle in action.
   - *Progressive relaxation.* Starting with the toes and working his way up to the head, have your child first tense and then relax each body part, saying to himself, "My feet feel heavy and relaxed," and so on through his entire body.
   - *Coping self-talk.* Have your child remind himself, "I can do this, the fear is a brain trick, it will pass, this is how I'll get better, I don't like this feeling but I can get through, this is a false alarm, I'm not going to fall for it."
2. Engaging in preferred activities such as:
   - Talking to a friend or family member.
   - Solving low-frustration puzzles such as word-finds, word scrambles.
   - Listening to music.
   - Doing something physical—a quick game of catch, walking, running, dancing, riding a bike.
   - Watching television; play video or computer games.
3. Monitoring the fear temperature by:
   - Label his distress at the time of the exposure on a scale from 0 to 10.
   - Record his "fear temperature" one, two, five, ten, and fifteen minutes later.

- Notice how his fear temperature goes down as he uses his coping skills and spends time doing things he likes.

The anxiety will pass, but time passes more quickly when you're having fun, it's better to do something enjoyable or mind-engaging. As Dr. Jeffrey Schwartz describes, this actually helps the brain forge a new path out of OCD mode and into normal functioning.

Step Five: Define the Motivation for Treatment: Or, What I Hate About OCD

For many, the challenge of CBT is how to get children to take the risk to agree to treatment. Though children don't like their symptoms, they prefer the devil they know to the one they don't know. Risking it by refraining from doing compulsions is a frightening prospect. That's why it's important to give children an anchor. They *are* sure that OCD is painful, upsetting, and time-consuming. Help them focus on what they want to gain from taking the risk rather than thinking about changing or stopping the rituals. They will have more conviction about doing their OCD "homework," and they will see what's "in it for them." Children can make two lists: (1) "What I hate about OCD" and (2) "On the horizon," what they want to be able to do one month, two months, and six months down the road. These lists will be helpful resources to draw on to steer a child through a rough period or to encourage them to take the lurch of faith. (See Chapter 8 for more ideas.)

Step Six: Determine the Parents' Role in Treatment

As parents, you are already involved in your child's OCD whether you want to be or not. With cognitive-behavioral therapy you have a chance to use your involvement to the greatest good. A study of exposure and response prevention conducted by Lori Knox, and Drs. Anne Marie Albano, and Dave Barlow at the State University of New York, Albany, in 1996 found that in their small sample, children did not show a decrease in rituals until their parents got involved with their treatment. Parents can play different roles:

- Active coaching and managing of your child's OCD homework.
- Being on call to help your child through OCD moments as needed.

- Supporting from "backstage," keeping a respectful distance from your child's work.
- Establishing and reinforcing "house rules" that limit the spread of OCD.

During the course of your child's treatment, you may switch back and forth among these roles. Your child's therapist can help you determine how you are needed at any particular stage. Parents of young children will be acting as co-therapists and may become less actively involved as children grow. Initially, you may need to remind your child about OCD homework time and be there as your child does an "exposure" (e.g., dips his hands into the trash or the plants, or walks away from the stairs without going back three times). As your child progresses with each symptom, or if your child is older, you will be able to pull back from active treatment. Often without your involvement in treatment, there can be no "response prevention," because parents become the compulsion when they fall into the trap of providing reassurance: "No it's not going to rain," "No, we are not going to get divorced," "Yes, I'm sure no one will have an accident." With your child choosing weekly goals under the supervision of the therapist, you will refrain from answering the reassurance questions. It's important that you don't involve yourself haphazardly—only work on the symptoms that have been agreed upon. Asking your child to stop asking for all reassurance is unrealistic. Your child will become overwhelmed and discouraged. There are many ways to refrain from reassurance. You might point to the OCD as the bad guy and say, "It's OCD making you do this. I know you don't want to be worrying about death. What do you want to do now? Let's tell that worrywart OCD to leave you alone so you can have some fun!" Avoid responses like, "I'm not going to enable you to do the OCD, I am not going to be manipulated anymore," which evoke anger and leave your child feeling to blame for asking. Remember, it's not his question, it's a mechanical problem—thoughts are getting stuck in the net.

Because so many things can go wrong in an exposure—children become overwhelmed and upset, and parents abandon the plan—it is important to predict and script out likely scenarios. The therapist may call you in at the end of a session to do a dry run of your child's OCD homework, which can help smooth out the kinks before they crop up at home. Your child can assign who will play the OCD, the parent, and the child, then switch. For example, the child: "I feel like I need to keep washing, but I know it's not true, so I'm going to show and tell: OCD, you are a brain trick, you are wasting my time, there is no 100% clean," the nasty OCD: "Come on you don't care about playing with

---

Denise's Homework Permission Slip

I permit my parents to knock on the bathroom door and ask me to turn off the sink or to turn it off for me if I can't. If I can't leave after two attempts, they can walk me out of the bathroom and remind me to take a few balloon breaths and then help me play Nintendo or watch TV.

I am doing this because I want to be able to go to dance parties, eat lunch at my friend's houses, pay attention in school, and not worry about having clean hands. My mom and dad can remind me of this if I'm having a hard time.

---

the other kids, keep washing, you have to, it's not so bad, you don't mind wasting time," and the parent: "I know you feel like you are dirty, but it's that brain trick OCD, let me help you win this battle— OCD doesn't know how much fun it is to play with your friends, but you do—let's help you get back outside." It is often very productive to have the child and parent switch roles for the roleplay. It can be an eye-opening experience for kids to see what it's like to be "pestered" for reassurance and for parents to see how frustrating and upsetting it is to be riddled with doubt. Another safeguard for homework success is to use a *Parent Permission Slip;* a contract from your child that gives you permission to help out as needed. The permission slip settles the matter during heated moments when you get home, find your child engaging in a OCD behavior, and hear him shouting, *"No, get out of here!"* You point out that you have a contract that was drawn up at a calmer moment.

The parent might say: "Mr. Clean, you are not welcome in our house. We don't have time for your worry and washing. My daughter has more important things to do. Anyway, you are a brain trick, a false alarm, and we're not going to be tricked by you anymore."

Parents' Most Frequently Asked Questions

How Long Will It Take to Get Results?

Most children with mild to moderate OCD may begin to feel relief within the first five therapy sessions. For some, learning in the very first session that they are not crazy or at fault prompts a dramatic shift. Be prepared, however, that some children appear more symptomatic initially after beginning treatment than they did prior to treatment. As you begin to make it okay to talk about the OCD and fight it, your child may feel freer to show symptoms; also she may discover that some things that she "just did" are actually OCD symptoms. While it can be discouraging to witness this, the less your child has to hide his symptoms, the greater his chances for recovery. It is when children have to go underground and hide the symptoms that you hit the danger zone.

How Frequent Are the Sessions?

You and your child's therapist will determine the frequency of sessions. The Expert Consensus Guidelines state that a gradual treatment (one time a week) of individual therapy is preferred. An intensive treatment approach (daily or three times a week) is recommended when time is of the essence, or if there is no response to gradual treatment. A rule of thumb for many behavior therapists is that if children are able to complete the OCD homework assignments, then weekly sessions are sufficient. If children are unable to complete the work at home, this suggests they need more coaching, more frequent sessions, or even a home visit to tackle the problem where it happens.

How Do I Know What Symptoms to Target?

Your therapist will help determine what your child is ready to tackle. The key to success is listing symptoms and ranking them on a "ladder" of severity. Tackle the least severe symptom first—the lowest rung on the ladder—and then advance to the next rung as a child meets his goal. There is no gain from moving too quickly; mastery is built on a foundation of small successes. Therapists build the symptom list by asking the following questions and using pie charts, for example:

1. Look at the two circles on page 117, one for day and one for night. Then divide up each circle according to how much of your day and night you control, doing what you want, and how much the OCD controls. [Using play dough circles, ask your younger child, "How much does the Worry Wart take, how much is left for you?"]
2. Now, tell me what behaviors and situations make up the part that OCD controls.
3. On a scale of 1 to 10, tell me how hard or easy is it to resist each symptom.

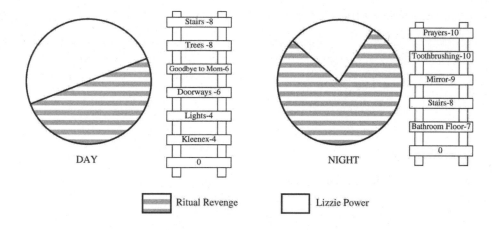

This type of dividing the territory helps children see themselves on the map from the beginning, and each week they can see how the shaded portions of their days and nights get smaller and smaller as they fight back. Some parents have told me that they use the pie charts to check in with their children (even teenagers) about how they are doing with their recovery: "How would you draw the circles today?"

Children under the age of six or seven may have difficulty establishing a hierarchy as they may not be able to distinguish between low, medium, or high fears. In this case, tackle the issues that are most pressing and that the child says he wants to get rid of.

If We Get Rid of One Symptom, Won't It Just Pop Up Somewhere Else?

Cognitive-behavior therapy does two things, it treats symptoms *and* provides an explanation for what all OCD symptoms have in common; it teaches children how to fight back against the illness that is hungrily eating up their time. Professionals and laypeople alike have raised the concern that symptoms will only go away if you treat the "underlying" conflict. Recall that this psychoanalytic view of OCD has not been borne out in the literature on OCD. Psychoanalysis has had disappointing results in improving OCD symptoms. Remember, too, that OCD symptoms change over time because that is the nature of the condition. While it may feel like you are patching up one leak in the roof only to find that the water has made its way through elsewhere, keep in mind that these roving symptoms are not a sign that the condition is worsening. The change only helps kids learn to battle OCD more thoroughly—to be prepared for symptoms that have yet to emerge.

How Will My Child Respond to Treatment?

Children are often so relieved to finally talk to someone who not only understands their private suffering but can also help them feel better, that they are very engaged in the therapy process. There are a few exceptions. Young adolescents struggling to fit in are particularly affected by being different from their peers and may reject what you have to offer, as if it was really meant for someone else. A few years ago, I sweated through an evaluation with fifteen-year-old Alex, who was brought in by his mother to work on his "habits." I struggled to make a connection with him or at least to show him what I had to offer—that he could live a different life than the hopscotch of dodging danger he was in. He flatly refused. After ninety minutes, I had done what I could do and surrendered. I told Alex that if he changed his mind, the door was always open and referred him for a medication consult, which was more palatable to him. He definitely didn't want to be in the "club" I was offering. Alex was also being pressured by his parents to "fix" his problems, and he couldn't concede to that power struggle.

There are going to be children who refuse to work in behavior therapy. Often, however, as in Alex's case, these are children who are stuck in a power struggle with a parent who is "forcing" them to get help or criticizing them. This just evokes resentment and resistance.

Some younger children are hesitant about treatment because they are afraid that the OCD monster will get mad and make things worse. I assure these children that I know the OCD monster might say that, and that's what makes him a bully—how mean to say that he would punish you for getting better! I tell these children that I'm not worried about the OCD monster, because what happens as kids boss him is he gets wimpier and smaller so that all he can do is whisper or squeak like a little mouse, and finally he gives up. If children want the OCD monster to "stay," I help them "tame" him and make rules for OCD cooperating with the child. Like the rules the child has for his friends, the OCD has to listen to the child, not be bossy and not prevent him from doing the things he wants. Using incentives such as toys, CDs, and baseball cards will help some children get to the starting gate of treatment; typically the need for rewards fade as the child enjoys the natural rewards of freedom.

How Old Does My Child Have to Be to Participate in Behavior Therapy?

Studies have documented the effectiveness of cognitive-behavioral treatments for children as young as eight years old. I have had success in using the techniques with children as young as four or five. Young children cannot necessarily describe what they are afraid of, but they know they don't like being afraid. Though there is an impression that young children are unable to participate in cognitive-behavior therapy because they have not yet developed the cognitive skills to report on, evaluate and change their thoughts, I have found that the unique strengths of young children often more than amply compensate for these shortcomings. Being unabashedly "power" hungry helps young children quickly latch on to the outrage that a braintrick is bossing them around. They know intuitively how to fix that—they boss right back! Because play is still in their natural repertoire, they immediately fall into step creatively engaging in the drama of teaching OCD a lesson. Using puppets, dolls, or even the child's own drawings, young children can act out first how Mr. Perfect, Mr. Watch-it, or Counting Man makes the child "follow rules" she doesn't like. Next she can draw or roleplay how she wants to boss back, fight back, and break the rules of OCD. Openly revelling in the victory is the icing on the cake for these young fighters. It's a team effort: Parents can quickly learn the principles of exposure and ritual prevention and are active co-therapists, and children are typically eager to try, since they want to be happy. Parents following through at home can reinforce their young children for bossing back the fear and taking bravery challenges, while preventing them from avoiding feared situations. Also, because young children look to their parents for guidance about how to respond to situations, parents are in a unique position to model courage and boss-back talk.

Medication Options for OCD

There are several medication choices for OCD. They fall into the category of serotonin reuptake inhibitors (SRIs) including Anafranil (clomipramine, a tricyclic antidepressant) and Prozac (fluoxetine), Luvox (fluvoxamine), Zoloft (setraline), and Paxil (paroxetine) (the selective serotonin reuptake inhibitors, SSRIs). Anafranil was the first medication to receive approval for use in children with OCD. In the past few years, other medications have also received FDA approval. Under current FDA guidelines: Anafranil is approved for children ten and up; Luvox eight years and up; Zoloft six years and up. How to interpret this information? FDA approval means that the pharmaceutical companies have conducted studies with children and have satisfactorily met the requirements for approval. This does not mean that medications without FDA-approved indications for children are dangerous, rather that the pharmaceutical companies have not conducted the necessary studies to get a specific FDA age-approval.

The main challenge with medication is finding the right one for your child, one that is effective but with few side effects. For many children, it may take several tries to find the optimal medication and dosage. Overall, studies suggest that about one-third of patients fail to respond to an SSRI.

How Do Medications Work?

Medications for OCD work by acting on neurotransmitters, chemical brain messengers, that communicate between brain cells. In particular, the action of the neurotransmitter serotonin is implicated in the process of OCD. The brain is made of nerve cells, or neurons, that rely on neurotransmitters to jump the groove (called a synapse) between neurons and deliver messages. Serotonin is released to help communicate a "message" and then is reabsorbed to be used again. SSRIs act to keep more serotonin in the synapse so that messages move appropriately.

Which Medication Is Best for My Child?

All of the SSRIs have demonstrated effectiveness with OCD in open trials. While they all do the same job, they each go about it in a slightly different way. Children respond differently to medications—there is no "best" for every case. Physicians take into account a child's current symptoms and family history, both for the presence of other psychiatric illnesses as well as for positive or adverse reactions to medications. Your child's unique history, current symptoms, and reaction to side effects will determine the course of medications tried. Some children have a quick and positive response, and the medication makes a world of difference for them. It is for many, however, a frustrating process, with fits and starts of hope and disappointment. It is important to have good communication with your child's physician as well as in some cases to notify school so they can monitor the impact of the medication being tried.

How Long Do Medications Take to Work?

Though children may begin to notice a change within three to four weeks, typically it takes as long as eight to ten weeks before the medication reaches its most effective level in the bloodstream and the child's obsessions begin to weaken. Staying on a medication for this period is important in order to give the medication an "adequate trial." Before that period of time, you can't really tell if your child is responding. OCD expert Dr. John March cautions against changing medications, adding a second medication, or increasing dosages until a sufficient amount of time has passed to see how your child is responding to the medication. If no response has occurred within approximately ten weeks, often tapering off and switching to another SSRI is appropriate. It is essential for your child's safety that this or any other medication changes be done under a doctor's supervision.

Sometimes psychiatrists will continue to raise the dose until a child begins to show a benefit. What is unknown in such cases is whether it is the increase in the dosage or the additional time the medication has had to reach effective levels in the bloodstream that is responsible for the decrease in symptoms. It is possible that the initial dosage overshot the optimal lowest dose; you can discuss this matter with your child's doctor to see if the dosage can be titrated or lowered once your child is responding to the medication.

How Will My Child Respond to the Medication?

Your child may initially have mild side effects such as a slight upset stomach or fatigue, these nuisance symptoms generally resolve within the first two weeks. (See below for a fuller discussion of side effects.) In a subset of children, there may be an initial worsening of their current symptoms or of irritability when they first begin taking medication and, paradoxically, this may predict a good response to the drug. If you are aware of this possibility, then you won't be taken by surprise and prematurely want to discontinue the drug. OCD expert Dr. Michael Jenike explains that this initial spiking occurs because serotonin receptors are "up-regulated" in OCD, taking too much serotonin out of the synapse; when you add more serotonin to the synapse, those receptors become even more active and thus may worsen OCD symptoms. After the first few weeks, the receptor sites are then "down-regulated"— readjusted so they don't remove serotonin from the synapse, and the initial response resolves. Therefore, when there is an initial worsening of symptoms, this may predict a good response because it indicates that the site of the problem may be the up-regulated serotonergic receptors. It is important to have realistic expectations for what medication can and can't do. Parents and kids who expect the medication to take the symptoms away may be disappointed if that does not occur. Examples of what a parent may notice when a child is having a positive response to medications is that the rituals may be less frequent or shorter, that their child's mood is brighter, less depressed, and less withdrawn. There may be fewer melt-down or explosive moments and your child may be more outgoing. Because children's medication responses vary widely, this description may or may not be reflective of your child's response.

Certainly if your child's symptoms are worsening, or new and/or dangerous behaviors develop, contact the psychiatrist immediately. In rare cases, children have developed high risk behaviors such as extreme impulsivity, disinhibition, mania, and even suicidality that have been resolved by making a medication change.

How Often Will My Child See the Psychiatrist?

After the initial evaluation, your child will have brief monthly medication check appointments. If your child's response is satisfactory, there will be a longer interval between appointments, generally six months. If after a sufficient trial period your child isn't responding to the medication or is having negative side effects, more frequent appointments may be necessary to evaluate and either switch medications or add a second medication to augment the effectiveness of the first medication, or to treat a coexisting condition such as ADHD, tics, or agitation. Because questions often arise, it is important to have a reliable system for contacting your child's psychiatrist. Ask whether e-mail is available for nonemergency questions, and make sure that you have a number for emergencies.

How Long Will My Child Stay on Medication?

If your child is on medication for OCD, the Consensus Guidelines recommend waiting one to two years after your child has reached a maintenance phase of treatment before considering tapering off the medication. Maintenance phase is defined as the point at which your child's OCD requires monthly rather than weekly behavior therapy sessions, because the gains are maintained between sessions. The tapering procedure depends on your child's response and should only be done under the direct guidance of your psychiatrist. Monthly booster behavior therapy sessions are recommended as a precaution during this time of medication discontinuation to offset the chance of relapse. *Never* discontinue your child's medication without your doctor's supervision.

Lifetime medication as a preventive measure is recommended for those who have had two to four severe relapses or three to four milder relapses.

Sometimes doctors will recommend a child take a medication vacation to see where things stand. This is a planned break to reevaluate the child's medication needs and when recommended is generally done in the summer so as not to risk interfering with the child's school experience.

What If the First Medication Doesn't Work?

If you are not seeing some reduction in your child's symptoms after ten to twelve weeks of being on an adequate dosage of a medication, most experts recommend switching to another SSRI. To quote the Guidelines, "Patients who do not respond to one SRI have about a 40 percent chance of responding to a second SRI; the response rate drops into the teens for the third drug." Anafranil is generally not tried first because of the increased side effects; however, if a patient has had two to three failed SRI trials, a trial of Anafranil is recommended as it is a different class of medication and therefore may prove more effective.

How Do These Medications Affect My Child's Development?

According to Dr. Hugh Johnson, psychiatrist and director of the Child Psychopharmocology Information Center in Wisconsin, it is not likely that SRIs have long-term effects on a child's developing brain. However, there have not been follow-up studies to investigate this. Clomipramine has been available in Europe since the 1960s, and no significant long-term harmful effects have yet been reported. There is no information on the long-term effects of Luvox, Prozac, Paxil, or Zoloft on a child's developing nervous system. However, this is an area of active research.

Are OCD Medications Addictive?

SSRIs are not addictive substances, they do not create a high, rather, they reduce unpleasant and uncomfortable feelings. If, however, your child is on a medication and wants to stop, he needs to follow his doctor's instructions for discontinuing gradually.

What If My Child Doesn't Want to Taper Off Medications and I Want Her To?

Battles over medication often take the form of the parent insisting the child take the medication, and the child refusing. Sometimes the reverse is true. Some parents are eager to have their child taper off of medication, while the child is not ready to do so. While this matter can be discussed with the prescribing physician, it is important for parents not to judge a child as "taking the easy way out" or "using meds as a crutch" for wanting to stay on medication. Only the child herself knows what she's feeling inside and what is most important is her having the confidence to take on therapeutic challenges when she is ready and to feel her parent's support in her decisions.

What If My Child Can't Swallow Pills?

Young children may have not mastered the skill of swallowing pills; older children may be unable to swallow pills due to a fear about choking. Desensitization techniques can be used by your child's behavior therapist to help him learn how to swallow in small steps. A sample desensitization program supervised by the therapist might begin by letting your child swallow mini M&M's, Mini-Chiclets, or even small cake decorations, and proceeding then to regular sized M&M's. Often the pleasant experience of eating candy overrides the fear of swallowing.

If your child has trouble swallowing or needs a lower dosage of medication than is available in pill form, ask your doctor about liquid preparations of medications. Some medications are available in liquid form, such as Prozac, while others can be made into a liquid preparation by a qualified pharmacist. Have your doctor call the International Academy of Compounding Pharmacists (800-927-4227) to locate a pharmacist who specializes in this technique.

Medication: Weighing Risks Against Benefits

When ritalin was introduced, it was hailed as a magic pill for children, parents, and teachers in controlling attention-deficit-hyperactivity disorder (ADHD). It has changed children's lives, enabling them to focus, participate, and control their temper. Many parents and children consider it a godsend. Then some studies suggested that children on stimulants suffered stunted height and weight. Later, these results were dismissed as more recent studies suggested that the effects on size were minimal and possibly reversible after the first year of treatment. Developments of this sort sound a note of caution to parents and physicians alike. Each child is different, and side effects need to be monitored carefully. While the FDA and pharmaceutical companies work conscientiously to protect consumers' health, there may be risks that do not emerge until after many years of use and collected reports of consumers and physicians.

Medication Cautions

Parents of children who also have tics or may have a predisposition for tics should raise the question with their psychiatrist of the safety of stimulant treatment that is used for ADHD (Ritalin, Adderal, Dexedrine). Some studies suggest that stimulants can seriously exacerbate tics.

Other substances can have adverse interactions with medication. This list is not exhaustive and you should consult with your doctor or pharmacist before using any medication:

- Caffeine can cause sweating nervousness and insomnia when mixed with Luvox;
- Dextromethorphan, commonly found in cough medicine, can lead to extreme anxiety and chest and abdominal discomfort; and
- Phenylpropanolamine, commonly used in cough medicines and anticongestants can lead to extreme nervousness.

What to Ask Your Doctor About Medications

- What are the immediate side effects of this medication? The long-term side effects? Which are common? Which are relatively rare?
- Are there interactions with other medications, foods or over-the-counter treatments (e.g., allergy, cold, or sinus medicines) that I need to look out for?
- What do I do if we miss a dose?
- How long will my child stay on medication?
- How often do dosages need to be adjusted and my child's response evaluated?
- Can my pediatrician prescribe the medication?
- What should the school nurse look out for? Is there an information sheet to share with her?
- How will this medication affect my child's other conditions; e.g., ADHD, tics, trichotillomania?
- Are there other periodic blood tests that need to be conducted while my child is in treatment?
- How soon should I expect a response?
- How often will my child come for appointments?
- How can you be reached in an emergency?

- In an emergency, how should we go about stopping the medication?
- What is your experience treating a child of this age with these symptoms with this medication?

For further information, I recommend *Obsessive-Compulsive Disorder in Children and Adolescents: A Guide,* by Hugh F. Johnston, M.D., Child Psychopharmacology Information Center at the University of Wisconsin, and *Drug Treatment of OCD in Children and Adolescents,* by J. Jay Fruehling, M.A., both are available from the OC Foundation.

Common Side Effects of Antidepressant Medications

Dry Mouth and Constipation

Some medications, in particular clomipramine (Anafranil), may reduce the amount of saliva in the mouth. While this is not hazardous per se, it can be annoying to children, and may in fact result in an increased rate of tooth decay. Because this result is most likely when a child has braces, it is important to inform your child's dentist of the prescription so that he or she may monitor for tooth decay more frequently. Children can get relief from dry mouth by chewing gum or increasing their water intake. If you child is in school, you can ask for permission for him to carry a water bottle or to chew gum in class.

Constipation may be minimal to significant. Maintaining a high-fiber, high-liquid diet and regular exercise can easily counteract it. Especially with younger children, parents should look out for constipation, as they may be less aware and slower at reporting changes in their bowel habits.

Irregular Heartbeats

Clomipramine has a slight potential to cause irregular heartbeat, especially in children with heart disease. Not all physicians see the need to prescreen for heart problems using an electrocardiogram (EKG) given the small percentage of cases in which this occurs. Ask your physician about your child's particular risk.

Stomach Distress

A nuisance side effect of the SSRIs (Prozac, Paxil, Zoloft, and Luvox) is upset stomach. Generally this side effect diminishes over the first few weeks as the body becomes adjusted to the medication.

Negative Behavioral Changes

In a slight few cases, SSRIs have caused children to become irritable, hostile, and defiant. This may occur because there is a predisposition toward bipolar disorder or mania—and the antidepressant is inducing a manic episode in a genetically vulnerable child. Conversely, it may be that these drugs are behaviorally "activating." In Dr. Johnston's *Guide to Childhood OCD*, he writes "all anti-OCD medications have the capacity to produce behavioral side effects (BSEs) in children." The behaviors including defiance, irritability or excessive energy are more likely to occur in younger children or when higher doses of medications are used. If a pattern of behavior is emerging that differs from the child's usual self, a BSE may be indicated. Often a reduction in medication can reduce the negative side effects. For example, in a study by Dr. Mark Riddle of John Hopkins University and colleagues in 1990, 50 percent of children experienced BSEs on Prozac. However, these negative symptoms were eliminated within two weeks for all of the children who reduced their dose by half, and they were still able to maintain their improvements in OCD symptoms at the lower dosage.

Rash

A small percentage of children have developed a rash while taking Prozac or Zoloft; this side effect should be reported to your physician, who will most likely make a change in medication.

Headache

Some SSRIs may cause headaches in children. Because these medications are relatively new to children, the side-effect profiles are still being determined. Any adverse symptoms should be reported immediately to your child's physician.

Sleepiness, Insomnia, and Fatigue

Several medications can impact the sleep-wake cycle, which can be one of their benefits, since they help a child who is not sleeping well relax and a child who is overly fatigued have more energy. These aspects must be monitored carefully by your child's physician. Some people report more vivid dreams when on an SSRI. This may be frightening to your child; you can help allay some of the fear by explaining that the medicine sometimes makes the dreams feel more real.

Children may complain of sleepiness when on an SSRI. Sometimes this can be addressed by changing the time that the medication is taken (for example, at night instead of in the morning), or reducing the dose. All decisions about medication should be made in consultation with your child's psychiatrist.

SRIs can cause fatigue. Clomipramine in particular can sometimes reduce children's physical endurance. This may be particularly unacceptable to children who participate in sports. They may not want to take their medication because they can't run as fast, or run out of energy too quickly.

What About Neurosurgery?

In very rare cases of OCD where all treatment avenues have been exhausted, a procedure called a cingulotomy may be considered. This computer-aided surgical procedure involves making a cut in a tiny bundle of nerve fibers in the part of the brain that controls feelings and actions. Though surgery carries with it significant risk, and this procedure is a last resort, some patients have been successfully helped by cingulotomy.

Special Problems: When a Child Refuses Treatment

One of the most difficult situations for parents is when a child won't agree to treatment. Parents suffer as they watch their child agonize with his symptoms while knowing they can't force him to go to therapy. There may be many reasons for a child's refusal to get help, as we discussed earlier in the chapter; a child's fears about treatment may be an obstacle. "Will I get better, will I fail at treatment, is this really my problem or maybe I really am a freak, will I be able to handle life out there without my symptoms to hide behind, will it be too humiliating to tell someone about my symptoms?" These concerns are commonly on the minds of adolescents. If parents and therapists understand that this hesitation may not be due to oppositional behavior or resistance, they can normalize these feelings for the child and help him work through his apprehensions so that he may give therapy a try. One of the most common obstacles is that the battle over OCD is embedded in larger power struggles between parent and child. No child is happy about having OCD, so when he refuses to cooperate with treatment, he may be trying to communicate something to the parent through this refusal. Common messages that kids send are, "You're pushing too hard," or "You're just embarrassed by me, you don't really care about what it's like for me," or "I'm not the only one with the problem—

you've got to get a handle on your OCD first!" Parents in these situations need to evaluate if there's a power struggle and address it.

If your child is using OCD as a weapon (or mode of communication), you must first and foremost take charge of your own lives; then, get out of the enabling role by deciding what you will and won't do for your child. Finally, kindly but firmly set new rules for behavior at home. Easier said than done! The strategies throughout this book guide families through the process of disentangling from the emotional ties that bind the family to OCD and circumventing power struggles by cultivating parent-child communication and respect.

Interim Solutions: Hot Topics/House Rules

Depending on the severity of your child's symptoms, you can reach an interim solution by making an agreement about how things need to be run at home. Approaching this challenge from the angle of family needs or house rules is much more likely to engender cooperation when children are refusing to comply with treatment. Think of this as a pretreatment phase. The goal here is not to focus on your child's OCD but rather the implications it has for your child's or your family's functioning. For example, Ari, a fifteen-year-old with mild OCD, refused to do behavior therapy, but his family was struggling with his many daily long showers because they were expensive, created morning bottlenecks at the bathroom, and produced excessive piles of laundry. We discussed this problem from a purely practical point of view without any mention of OCD and worked out a family peace plan. Ari would take one fifteen-minute shower a day and gave his parents permission to turn off the water if he went past that. He also had a two-laundry-load-a-week limit. Ari's parents agreed to say nothing about these behaviors provided that Ari could keep to the house rules.

When you make a family peace plan around a behavior, your child doesn't have to buy into how this will help him in order to do the plan. Once you as a parent have laid out the goal—for example, conserving water—giving your child ample say in how the plan will be executed often creates less defensiveness for the child who feels pressured or indignant about confronting his OCD.

When Your Child Won't Cooperate in a Family Plan

With some children, the OCD is so severe and has tied such a strong knot around them, that their ability to work on the problem or even accept that it is a problem is greatly compromised. There are extreme cases where years have passed and parents and child alike are slaves to the tyrant OCD—children not attending school, living in one room, parents slipping meals under doors, sterile scrubs for all family members. How could things get so out of hand? These scenes, distressing as they are, can be a wake up call not only for parents themselves, but also for professionals: parents must be equipped with tools to prevent OCD's erosion of family life. Because this erosion does not happen overnight, be on the lookout and take action.

Remain firm in the knowledge that life cannot continue the way it has been. Before things get to a point of no return, seek the help of an OCD therapist yourself and be coached on how to handle this situation with your child. If children in these extreme situations refuse treatment, then for the child's own good, parents may have to make a plan without him which may involve hospitalization or an intensive treatment program (see resource guide). While you cannot force your child to change, you can send a clear message about the limits you place on the OCD in your life; just as you would bring your child to a hospital if he were in a diabetic crisis, parents can make sure that treatment is available to him at the level he needs.

PART TWO

THE PARENTS' ROLE: ROOTS AND WINGS

Now that I understand what's going on with Julie, we get along much better. I used to get so angry at her when she asked me questions like, "What if Iraq attacks or there's another Holocaust, or there's a nuclear war, what are we going to do, what if it happens today?" Out of frustration I would yell at her to just stop it and she would get angry and cry. It was awful. All I could think was, *I can't take this anymore. I want her to change!* Now, even when she's spinning in an OCD moment, I'm at peace, I'm not afraid. I know I can help her get mad at the OCD and make a choice not to listen to it.

—*Mother of an eleven-year-old*

Re-Establishing an Environment of Knowing

For years, parents have been left on their own to figure out OCD, and the decks have been stacked against them. Heroically braving the challenges, parents have had to cope with a demon-disorder that reinforces their feelings of incompetence on a daily basis. Even worse, parents have been blamed for causing the symptoms in the first place. The times are changing and treatments for OCD offer new hope to children and parents that life can be different, that life can be great. But what are parents to do while waiting for these new treatment technologies to "work" on their child? Many times they are asked to stay in the waiting room, it's "easier" that way. Meanwhile, they still need to know how to get their child in the car after the session, to school the next morning, and on and on.

Parents have been an enormously underutilized resource in the treatment of OCD. The amount of time and influence they have on their children beats a psychologist's or psychiatrist's hands down. However, professionals have known that parents—like the leftover cord that doesn't quite fit in the box after you've packed up your CD player—are an important component of the child's functioning, but have not known exactly what to do with them. Slowly the field of mental health has been waking up to the benefits of including parents in treatment, and much good has come from the collaboration.

You may not be experts in OCD, but you are the experts on your child. You know your child more intimately than anyone, and it is that expert experience you will draw on while incorporating your new knowledge of OCD. OCD thwarts parenting at every turn. A parent's role has been described as providing roots and wings: a sense of internal confidence and safety and the wherewithal to make it out in the world. OCD puts up a huge roadblock on both fronts. How can a child develop confidence when his internal voice is making him doubt everything, from the most remote—nuclear disaster—to the most immediate—are you really my mother? Whether we are talking about the preschooler who can't touch the play dough because it has germs on it, or the teenager who can't drive because of the intrusive image of a fatal hit-and-run, it's easy to see how OCD sabotages the child's efforts to participate in normal activities.

As parents, you see all this happening, see your power being usurped by this illusive enemy that has inhabited your child. You feel horrified because you know your child is headed for disaster if he can't tie his shoes in less than twenty minutes and he has SATs this weekend. Your child may be worried, but kids tend to live more in the moment, so they don't see the big picture. You see it, and you don't know how to change the course of this downward spiral. It is important to address your role first, because we know that when parents get stuck, kids get stuck. Consider the wisdom of the airline safety procedure: Parents, put the oxygen mask on yourself first, so that you will be able to help your child.

Our confidence in our parenting abilities cycles with the vicissitudes of our children's development and the other stressors in our lives. Remember those anxious first days at home with a newborn? But as the days wore on, you became more confident that you could meet your child's needs reasonably well, could tolerate the crying, and had a repertoire of effective responses. Developing this fit of needs and responses, which the late child psychiatrist Dr. Donald Winnicott called being a "good-enough" parent, wasn't perfect

1-to-1 correspondence, but it got you through and allowed your child to learn to tolerate frustration in small doses.

Parents faced with OCD don't have the security of "good-enough" parenting when first faced with the condition, because they no longer know how to read their child's signals, and their repertoire of responses doesn't seem to fit current and changing demands. Faced with this revisitation of the "unknown quantity" of their child, parents don't trust their instincts. Only with time, experience, and information can you regain that comfort zone of good-enough parenting.

For example, when your five-year-old child is cranky and demanding at ten at night, you recognize that she's tired and it's late, so you're able to override the words and listen to the *process*—getting out of control—and put her to bed. There is a parallel in OCD. Your child may be saying, "Lock the doors, one more time, you have to do this for me," or "I have to keep washing." You'll want to override the specific words and listen to the process—"I'm stuck, get me out of this mess"—then help your child become free by showing her the way out—relabeling what's going on as OCD and redirecting her activities.

Part Two covers the many facets of the parent's role so that you can re-establish your footing with good-enough parenting. In Chapter 6, we'll discuss the issue of how to inspire your child's confidence by finding the balance between nurturing and launching your child as you coach her through these obstacles. Being a good coach requires a playbook; Chapter 7 describes the basic principles of anxiety management and parent effectiveness; Chapter 8 presents a new template and language for handling OCD episodes on the homefront; Chapter 9 highlights pressure points for OCD, such as mornings and evenings, and how to handle them as well as what to do if things reach the level of crisis; Chapter 10 is a place for you to see in black and white how important it is to take care of yourself and get some ideas on how to do so.

CHAPTER 6

The Parents' Role

Roots and Wings

Childhood OCD pulls in parents: This you know well, but getting out is another matter. Kids are doing the best they can to rid themselves of uncomfortable feelings, and they suck you into their symptoms. Parents need clear guidelines on how to avoid the induction process that kids may inadvertently use, without feeling like ogres. In the face of childhood OCD, your natural instincts about when to protect (roots) and when to let go (wings) get confused. Instinct tells us that when a child is in pain, we protect her; when she is disobeying, we make her accountable. But when she is crying because her hands aren't "clean"—although they've been washed to the point of bleeding—how do you protect your child when the source of the danger seems to be the child herself? Or if a child refuses to eat a meal with you unless he sees you wash your hands, how can you reprimand him when he's not trying to be disrespectful? These critical issues will be described in the following section.

Finding the balance between roots and wings is a challenge that is not unique to OCD, but it will take some extra thought and practice in this realm. There is a continuum of parental intervention. At one end is protecting and doing for your child; at the other end is encouraging and witnessing. In the middle is *scaffolding,* a term developmental psychologists use to refer to parents participating in activities with their children before they are able to do so independently. Scaffolding allows children to reach for things not quite in their grasp, to get places they don't yet know how. When you see your child struggling—in a fight with a friend or exasperated with a homework problem—do you jump in? Your child is suffering in these situations, but you may just offer a few words of guidance or a hug and then encourage your child to finish up. Because children change and grow so rapidly, we as parents must be constantly revising our ideas of what they can do for themselves and when they need our help.

Scaffolding in the realm of OCD may mean prompting your child with the lines to boss back OCD or even bossing back the OCD yourself. It may mean sitting with your child when he's doing homework to help him not erase. What's different here? You know that this situation is absolutely survivable, and you convey that confidence to your child. You are especially aware of the difference between coaching and doing for a child.

Redefining Safety in the Land of OCD

Sometimes when I have a bad day I just want a hug. I don't want to talk about OCD. I don't even want to hear those words. I want be a million miles away from my problems. I just want my mom to say, "I love you and it's going to be okay."

—*Eleven-year-old with OCD*

Nurturing the roots of your child—providing a safe "holding environment"—requires some clarification with respect to OCD. Safety has come to mean reassurance, but in the context of OCD, you are creating safety not by taking away your child's pain, but rather by creating a safe place to express it and showing your child a new path out of the pain. He is going to have to do a great deal of the hard work himself, but your steadfast belief in the possibility of recovery will help immeasurably.

OCD is actually a condition of seeking security, albeit in ways that are ultimately harmful. How can you tell which kind of protection helps children get out of OCD and which kind reinforces it? Is it okay to answer questions such as, Am I going to throw up? Are we going to get bombed? or Is someone going to break into the house? Normally these questions could be a source of parental pleasure; you get to wrap your child in your arms and make everything right with the world again. But when your child has asked the same question every night for three months, frustration and anger set in, and it's a rare parent who doesn't think of punishing instead of protecting. While the specific response to excessive questioning is addressed below, throughout this chapter you will find ideas for building a family environment of trust, so that your child will accept your help.

It is important to know that the way out of the OCD maze is facing the fear—feeling the discomfort so that your child can learn that it is survivable without performing the rituals. The goal is to convey the idea that anxiety is *uncomfortable* but not *unbearable*. If you maintain that stance, your child will be able to grab hold of that idea, too.

Redefining security for children with OCD from which solid inner strength springs consists of the following:

Creating a Safe Environment

Accepting Fears Without Asking for a Justification

A safe environment isn't one that is free from fears; rather, it is one where a child is free to express fears and has the support to manage them. Expressed fears can be addressed. Unexpressed fears pile up, fester, and emerge later in the form of depression or panic attacks.

> At age ten, Robin was quite embarrassed that she still believed in monsters. None of her friends did; only her little brother Mike did, but he was six. Every time she went into a room, she would have to step in and out twice—one time with her right foot first to let in the good, and a second time with her left foot to take out the bad. Whenever she did this, her siblings would tease about her "stuttering at the door." When Robin finally got up the nerve to tell her parents why she did this, the unfortunate response was, "Is that it? But you know there are no such things as monsters."

Kids have no choice other than to feel silly when called on the carpet about their fears. Acceptance means understanding your child's predicament of being locked into fear of something while also knowing full well that it doesn't make sense. This is where seeing your child as stuck in the maze will help. Rather than asking: Why are you afraid of that? a more accurate and strategic question is: How does the OCD get you to be afraid of touching your shoes? What is it telling you? Robin's parents could then go on to say, "Oh, I hate how that OCD scares you. It pulls the most unfair tricks, terrifying you about just walking in the door! We're going to show that OCD that it can't go bossing you around!"

Letting Your Child Set the Pace of Treatment, One Fear at a Time

"We've got to work on this every day, every chance we get." Statements like this make your child feel like you're bossing him around, that his OCD is intolerable to you, and you want it gone yesterday. What message does that send to your child? Watch out for bombardment: "You've got to watch this video about OCD—don't you want to get better?" "Look, this is our chance to work on this—I'm not going to be the only one who is serious about this treatment."

This is where OCD is like other aspects of your child's life. You didn't dictate when he learned to read or ride a bike. Your child builds confidence by doing what is in his reach. Your child knows best what is difficult for him and will actually be most successful in therapy if he starts with the least difficult challenges and works his way up. Success is a powerful motivator, building your child's confidence for future challenges. If there are situations where you need your child to change because his OCD is making things impossible for you, then an alternate plan needs to be worked out until your child is able to tackle the symptom directly (see Chapter 8 for this backstage work). If your child feels that you're in charge of his recovery, he will likely rebel; you won't get compliance in treatment, and your child will feel overwhelmed—which is not a safe way to dive into the unknown.

It can also be a relief to parents to know that they don't have to be scanning for OCD all the time. This is what Dr. Herbert Gravitz, author of *OCD: New Hope for the Family*, calls the "fallout" of living under the influence of OCD. Know that unburdening yourself of this job as the OCD police will help both you and your child. As a mother of a sixteen-year-old wrote:

> The most useful thing (and the toughest) I have found for helping my child is being given permission from Dr. Chansky to back away from Patrick's OCD. I stopped asking if he was feeling okay, I stopped offering to help (I had been doing this constantly out of worry). Once Patrick started to trust my staying out of his OCD, he seemed better able to embrace his responsibilities for controlling OCD himself and, if he needed my help he would ask for it.

Providing a Calm Home Environment

Your child is going to be taking major risks; she is trying to launch into her new life, like diving off a diving board. She is going to be able to do that more easily if you aren't shaking the board.

A house free from ridicule, teasing, and name-calling is essential for all. Think of your own vulnerabilities—your gray hair, your love handles. Teasing about these things pulls the rug out from under us and certainly doesn't help us work at them. Before you knew what was going on with your child, you may have teased or joked, "Why are you doing your dance at the door, or the shuffle at the table?" Eventually, you may even return to a point of humor, but it will be humor at OCD's expense, not your child's: "OCD, are you going to make him do that dance again, give it up!"

Providing Emotional Safety

Safety means providing an environment where your child is able to express fears and discouragement and try something new. For some children with OCD, there is very little time and space that is free from OCD attacks. The school day is full of contaminants, dodging other kids' curious looks; dealing with the unbearable weight of uncertainty—did they hear the teacher right, write down the right information? The stress of living just one day can be insupportable, so at home they need freedom. This doesn't mean giving your child an automatic pass from all family dinners, but understanding the stress he encounters and giving him a break from time to time. Also, your child may need to express total discouragement about his or her situation.

Parents feel so worried about their children in general that they get terrified on a bad day. The challenge becomes how to buffer yourself against your child's negative experiences. In some instances, parents of children with a problem give their children *less* slack; so ready to read every down moment as a setback, they tend to have higher expectations for their kids and to catastrophize setbacks. Bottom line: it's normal to have a bad day.

Making Room for Negative Feelings: Distress and Discouragement

Because we are accustomed to showing approval only for the positive, it's hard to put out the welcome mat for negative feelings. Can you imagine if we warmly invited in our children's negative feelings as well? But think about what happens when we don't. You don't want to add rejection and shame to the negative feelings your child already has.

Evolution has left us confused about signs of distress. When children cry or discharge emotion, we sense that something is wrong. While this is true some of the time, sometimes crying signals the end of a crisis, because then it's safe to cry. Think of yourself getting a call from school that your child has fallen and broken his arm; you rush to school, to the hospital, all the while keeping your composure. Only later that night, when your child is settled in, do you start to cry. That's because you know the coast is clear. Your child does the same thing: He wrestles with a problem, keeps trying to work it out, and finally—successful or not—he just lets go, surrenders the solving of the problem, and cries.

Don't get alarmed by your child's tears or discouragement; see instead that she is in surrender or recovery mode. What do you say when your child starts to turn the problem back on herself? If she starts to say, "I'm no good, I'm a spaz, I'm stupid because I have these problems or because I can't control them." Sometimes a lighthearted approach at the right moment can help point the finger back to OCD: "So, let's see—yes, this OCD is your fault, you ordered it from the catalog, that's right—you wanted that obnoxious tape in your brain telling you to wash all the time."

Empathy is easier said than done for parents. Especially with negative emotions, we may feel cornered by them, overwhelmed because our job is to "fix it" and we can't. Our parental aversion to negative emotions in our children is a protective mechanism against the helpless feeling that we can't make our children's pain go away. But that's not the goal—it's not fixing it, it's compassionate listening. Picture in your mind two jars—one is for listening and one is for doing. Often kids object to their parents jumping into "fix-it mode" when all they wanted was to be heard. Once they feel heard, they may even know how to solve the problem on their own.

Children will also discount their progress, because they are so frustrated about having to deal with OCD in the first place: "So what, other kids just do this stuff, I have to work at it—and it's just normal stuff." Here's a time when you want to empathize: "It feels like this is an extra job, a job that you don't even want. I don't blame you for being totally sick of this. It's not fair, it's not your fault, and we don't want to take any more of your freedom away than OCD already has. That's why we've got to fight it. But maybe today is not a day to fight—today it's a day to just hand over to the OCD; let it just do its thing if it wants to." Model for her other people's bad days; teach her that progress is never a smooth curve. You might say, "I don't blame you for not wanting to have a bad day after you've made so much progress, but no one can take away those good days you had—you worked hard and you earned them. Does a baseball player get penalized for the games he loses? Or do they just keep count of the wins? Is every concert stellar? No. When I have a bad day, I try to be nice to myself; after all, I'm the one who had the bad day, so I don't want to beat up on myself. And I know that I have another chance tomorrow."

Frustration and anger are a natural by-product for kids as they fight the uphill battle of OCD. Parents are going to be the punching bag from time to time when children feel safe showing those intense emotions at home. Extra emotional padding will help parents protect themselves. Holding out the bag may help, "Do you need to get mad at someone, do you need some one to blame? Today it can be all my fault, I surrender." Often just being able to say this can break the tension and children can feel the weight lift from their shoulders.

Leaving Room to Not Talk

Jill's mother was frustrated: "I have to get her to talk to me at home. She talks to her friends at school, but I can never get her to talk to me." Safety is accepting the autonomy of your child and her personal rhythms; maybe she doesn't need to talk as much as you'd like or need. If this is the case, then your approach can be to come clean with your child. Rather than saying, "You never talk to me, why don't you?" you could say, "I know I'm more chatty than you are, but I need some details here." Your child may still refuse you, but she won't feel bad about herself for not talking, nor will she be mad at you for being intrusive because you "asked first."

Making Room for Trying Something New and Making Mistakes

When you find yourself in the situation where the OCD is so frustrating for *you*—your expectations governed by the rule "We've got to get rid of this, and we will!"—that your child has no breathing room for the trial and error of recovery, something needs to change. While the prescription for behavior therapy is to do it daily and not to cheat (by doing extra rituals later), neither is it "do the behavior therapy assignments every single day *or else!*" Being in behavior therapy does not exempt you from humanity—and after all, to err is human. Children complain that if they slip on a certain day, they feel doubly bad because not only are they mad that the OCD won, but they also know that their parents are going to give them grief for the extra washing they did. What can parents do instead? One option is to say nothing. Or you can mention that it looked like today was a tougher day and ask if there's anything you can do to help. (And then accept your child's answer.) Remember that the goal as your child's coach is to focus on the wins, not the losses.

Self-Esteem: Saying No to OCD, Not to Your Child

Last Christmas Eve, eleven-year-old Melanie wasn't awake with excitement about the bounty of presents awaiting her downstairs. Instead, she was plagued by visions of flames engulfing the tree, the rug, curtains, furniture, and finally the entire house. Terrified by this picture, which seemed more and more real as the day wore on, she asked her parents every few minutes, "Are you sure the house is safe, that the lights are okay? Shouldn't we unplug them?" Dad became fed up and told her she was ruining Christmas with this dark cloud and to get that crazy question out of her head. Mom, sympathetic to her fears, would answer every time, "There's no fire, everything is safe." Meanwhile, Melanie was being taunted by the news item she saw that evening about the blazing house fire started by faulty Christmas tree wiring, trying to believe her mom, but feeling terrified.

The problem with reassurance in OCD is that it doesn't stick: You have to keep "reapplying" it. Rather than answer the question of danger with a yes or no, point to the third option—the OCD. That's the worry chip that won't leave your child alone. It's the "what if?" and "are you sure?" trick wreaking havoc with your child. Your best defense is to look at the process: Your child is stuck and the fear has dug in. Words of reassurance are not going to do it. Instead, point to the bad guy: Help your child accuse the brain: "Why are you doing this now? I don't want to be doing this! Brain you are ruining my Christmas, making me think about this—and I don't need to—buzz off!" Tell your child "You know the answer to that question. Your brain isn't letting you hear it; we need to switch gears."

OCD can turn parents and children into enemies. "Why aren't you helping me? If you loved me you would just answer the question!" Your child's plea pulls at your heart. However, parents and children are both dealing with the same force that's changing the rules on both of them. If you can keep this clearly in mind, you'll be able to help your child out of the OCD. Remember, the problem isn't your child, it's the OCD.

A mother told me of a night when her daughter was having an OCD episode, having fears of throwing up, recurrent images of a bad sleepover experience. "I was exhausted, we'd had company all weekend, I just wanted to be off duty, and my daughter kept coming down. I kept saying in my head, 'Don't engage, don't engage,' so I said, 'Evie—knock it off, enough!' Then my daughter started to cry, and our house was a disaster area. I was so mad that OCD couldn't leave us alone, but I guess I put it all on Evie—and there she was, saying she was scared. I probably scared her more."

Evie's mom should have engaged Evie, not the OCD. Rather than saying, "You're not going to throw up, I promise," she should say, "Evie, you're tired, we've had a long weekend. I think the OCD is taking advantage of your being tired—remember it's a false alarm, junk mail, it's not real. Let's boss it back—we're in charge here, we're listening to music, not to you." Now it may feel like it takes more energy to be creative and boss back than to just blast, but it's really that we're more used to getting mad, which takes energy, too. Yelling at your kid instead of bossing the OCD is like doing the dishes by throwing them out: It solves the problem for the moment, but it's going to require more time and effort later.

Creating a Safe Zone Between You and Your Child

Every night Sharon would ask her mom, "Am I going to die in my sleep?" Her mother felt frustrated that this question kept coming back to haunt her, to taunt her. Mom would answer, "No, why are you asking, you know you're not going to" and close the door. Sharon was not only stuck with the OCD, but on top of that she knew her mom was mad at her. She couldn't handle it on her own—she had too much room.

By contrast, another mother's enthusiasm frightened her daughter when she suggested an extra-intensive treatment program to fight the OCD. There is such a thing as watering a plant too much. In some cases, an intensive program makes sense, but only if you have the child's cooperation. You can have the most elegant treatment plan and expert behavior therapist, but if your child feels forced, there will be pain without gain.

Thank You for Not Being Perky!

As the popular slogan on buttons and bumper stickers suggests, when it comes to enthusiasm, more is not always better. Many children have complained about the pressure they feel from cheery questions about how they're doing. One eight-year-old refused to answer the question anymore because it put him on edge—"As if you have a deadline and people keep bugging you about it." He also came to feel that his mother cared more about tracking the OCD, that it was almost compulsive for her, and that she didn't care about him and his well-being. Another particularly acerbic adolescent put it like this: "You know, I feel like it's Thanksgiving and you're checking on me like the turkey. 'Are you done yet?' But it's not Thanksgiving, I'm not done, and this is no happy holiday." You may need to hear that your child is doing better, but patience is the key, pushing for good news may backfire.

How Can You Help When Your Child Won't Let You Talk About OCD?

We often feel uncomfortable talking about things that are close to home. Because your child needs help with a medical condition, you may think that there's nothing to hide. However, think about the issues that make you feel uncomfortable as adults—the pints of ice cream you gulp down at a single setting, your wrinkles, the spreading bald spot. Basically, the issue for everyone is, *Don't touch my Achilles heel!*

This may be the first time you encounter the experience of not being able to mention something to your child, that a mere word may send off

OCD spirals. It's difficult for many parents to accept that something so serious is something your child may not want to discuss with you. As difficult as this is to do, if you can respect the boundary that your child is setting up, it is likely that he will feel safer to share with you. Good fences make good neighbors: Knowing that there is separation and respecting it can help foster connection.

Every time you mention your child's OCD seems to be the wrong time. "My mom asks, 'How are you doing?' after school and I know what she's thinking is, 'How's your OCD?' I can't get away from it." *Ask* your child when and how she wants you to talk about her OCD. It may be that you have to adopt a hands-off position for a while if your child does not want to open up to you. You may not be able to talk about the OCD and how your child feels, but you can certainly talk about the problems that the OCD causes, for example, missing the bus every day or using up too much toilet paper or soap. Try saying something like, "I've noticed this . . ." "It's a problem because . . ." "We need to find a way that works for everybody . . ." "How can we help you to do this?" Of course, your child's first reaction will probably be anger and defensiveness: "This is not a problem, leave me alone!" Expect this reaction and keep moving forward: "Look, I know this isn't your fault, you're not trying to do this, but having you do the laundry every day is not going to work."

Seeing Your Child's Strengths

It's easy to get pulled in body and soul to the project of freeing your child from OCD and miss out on what else is there. The urgency of fixing the problem and working on it all the time can backfire as your child begins to feel that he is a broken vase in need of gluing. Make a promise to yourself to step back and look at what a great kid you have. This will help him see his strengths as well. One mother described how she feels so worried about her daughter, her OCD, and her social skills, that she forgot what a treasure she has—one who will hold up well against the vicissitudes of growing up. To help remind your child of how terrific she is, have her fill out the Resource Refill Exercise (page 147).

Parent Traps to Avoid

Blaming Each Other

"You indulge her too much!" "This is ridiculous; you give him way too much rope." In times of stress, spouses may begin to attack each other

Resource Refill

What Is Special About Me That's Not OCD

What I like about me: _____

_____

_____

_____

What people have complimented me about: _____

_____

_____

_____

What are my proudest moments: _____

_____

_____

in the midst of the fears and anger they have about the disorder themselves. Don't blame each other, but do work on being consistent on how you handle your child's OCD (and all behaviors, for that matter). If one parent is too tough and blaming, the other parent will surely be too permissive to make up for it, and your child will get nowhere fast trying to field the mixed messages about how to behave.

It's very confusing to children when parents send mixed messages. If Mom is saying, "You're working on the OCD, grades are secondary," while Dad is saying, "Don't be a quitter, you've always been a straight-A student," then your child will be stuck right in the middle not knowing what to do. Likewise, if Dad is saying, "Be a man, you can tough it out," and Mom is there comforting and protecting, a child can feel like he can't trust the "goodies" he is getting from one parent, because he's being told he shouldn't get them. There may be long-standing differences between you and your spouse; now is a time to look at them.

If you find you cannot work out your differences with your spouse, seek professional help. The extra time and effort will keep conflict out of the picture and provide a consistent message that your child will be able to learn much faster than two contradictory ones.

Overdiagnosing

> My daughter calls me the OCD police. I can't help myself. She's right. I'm on her back too much. But whenever I see her hesitate at the door or say she doesn't want a hug, I think—okay, it's OCD we've got to fight it. We spent so much time putting together the puzzle of her contamination fears that now I'm on the lookout for it to come back. She tells me, "Mom, when are you going to accept that I don't want you to hug me because I'm sixteen and you're making me worry about it more the more you watch me!"
>
> *—Mother of sixteen-year-old*

OCD has been a part of Giselle's life since she was five years old, lining up her dolls in bed each night and insisting that her parents wash their hands before they made a meal. At eighteen, Giselle has conquered many of her dragons and her OCD is a shadow rather than a monster. Like all parents, Giselle's mom and dad didn't know how to take Giselle's fears. She'd been terrified night after night of starving after she'd seen the suffering children of Africa with their swollen bellies. Bedtime was a dreaded event to Giselle, she was so afraid and couldn't get the pictures out of her head. Her parents alternated between thinking *There's something wrong with my child* and *She's got to stop acting up like this!*

Enter the diagnosis of OCD. At last, a dragon they could all slay together, right? Wrong. Before the diagnosis, Giselle felt weird for thinking these thoughts. But after the diagnosis, the pendulum swung back at her. Her parents started to see OCD as the explanation for any and all of Giselle's difficulties. If she was upset that the door was left open at night—this wasn't reasonable, it was OCD. Giselle began to feel that she couldn't win, because her parents simply thought OCD dictated her behavior all the time. Fortunately, after a few parent sessions these issues were ironed out and both Giselle and her parents are better at distinguishing between OCD and non-OCD moments.

Because you may feel you missed out on so much before you had the diagnosis for your child, you may be tempted to be hypervigilant so you don't miss an OCD symptom again. This can make your child feel like she's lost her uniqueness and identity, that everything she does is because of OCD. Because children are already at risk of feeling that OCD is their life, it is important for parents not to add to that.

Missing Out on Clues

What happens when you as a parent have your radar off? You may inadvertently fall into OCD traps; it may be weeks until you realize you've been caught in an OCD loop and the child's behavior is entrenched. For example, your child begins to ask you about germs, "Do you think it's okay to eat this?" Or he waits to eat his meal until the last ten minutes before leaving the restaurant, feigning disinterest or lack of appetite, when he is actually afraid of throwing up at the restaurant. This is avoidance behavior tied into OCD that you want to address.

Notice if your child asks a lot of questions, more than you are comfortable with: "What happens if I look up at the sun? Will I go blind?" Here's where preventive work comes in handy. Begin pointing out what he is doing: "Do you want to be thinking about this, is the Worry Monster bossing you around again? What do you want to say to him so that we can enjoy our vacation?" Or an older child begins to ask about quality control at meat packing plants with a bit more zeal and tenacity than could be explained by a passing thought. That is the time to say, "How interesting is this to you? I have a feeling this is another chore that OCD told you to do, rather than something that you want to be doing now. Gee, it is really determined to ruin things for you, what do you want to do?"

Overreacting to Your Child's Behavior

One mother described how she learned that her overreacting to her daughter's symptoms led to her daughter using them to get back at her mother. Shawna's mom was a worrier: every time Shawna had a problem, she would become alarmed and disturbed that OCD was taking over. This angered Shawna; it seemed that her mom was more concerned with her own distress than with how Shawna was doing. To "get back at" her mom, Shawna would sometimes exaggerate her symptoms or dangle a problem in front of her mother just to get her started. Since then, Shawna's mother has learned to under-respond, not get alarmed, and take it one step at a time. When, for example, Shawna said, "I'm so fat, I'm going to stop eating," her mother thought, "eating disorder!" but fought the impulse to grill her with questions, and casually commented, "Oh, really?" Within minutes Shawna was filling her plate with seconds—the bomb had been dismantled.

Making Comparisons

To help your child feel safe, don't compare him to other sufferers. Each child is different; each case is different. OCD is not something that your child is likely proud of—especially when he's in the thick of fighting it. Making him feel like he is not keeping up with his sister, or cousin, or friend with OCD, by not getting better fast enough, is adding insult to injury. Treasure your child's uniqueness.

Wings: Coaching Your Child to Face the Challenges Out There

Although none of us can be therapists for our children—by definition the parent-child relationship is neither neutral nor history-free—we can step into a coaching role with our children. Coaching means teaching a new strategy and encouraging its use. But often it means encouraging forward motion: "Keep moving, steady now, go for the goal." Coaching your child to negotiate the challenges of the outside world, deal with difficulties, and do things independently is the essence of helping your child have wings.

The Job of the Coach

What makes a good coach? There are two brands of coaches. The anti-coach tries to induce motivation by billboarding your worst moments, the coaching-by-humiliation method. The other type of coach is one who believes in you more than you believe in yourself, consistently praises the effort over the outcome, and puts out that positive self-fulfilling prophecy. The best coach for OCD is one who keeps his eye on the goal of freedom and keeps clear that the real opponent is the OCD. This is one of the most difficult things to do with OCD. When a child screams at his parent for moving a pile of papers he had for weeks been protecting from contamination, it's easy for the parent to lose the frame of reference and yell right back. The challenge for parents is to remember that your child isn't the enemy but is trapped in the enemy's web and that your job as coach is to help him free himself. Keeping clear that the OCD is the bad guy allows parents to empower their children to fight back.

Your child starts to scream at you because you made noise during an elaborate nighttime ritual where she needs to recite the Lord's Prayer three times without blinking and without noise, but because you walked through the hallway, she has to start all over again. Okay, quick test—who's the enemy here? Your child clearly thinks it's you, the parent who messed her up. And if your first response is to yell back, "Don't tell me what to do. I'm the parent, this is my house," you have just cast your child as the enemy.

This is the perfect recipe for power struggles. You're assuming that your child is willfully trying to control you. Picture instead the OCD monster with its arms around your child. You're not going to want to get mad at your child because that would be blaming the victim. After all, he's stuck, too. At the same time, picture your child in quicksand: You're not going to want to step over to his side, and tiptoe down the hall, because then you're getting pulled in yourself and nobody will be on solid ground. Relabeling the problem as OCD means saying "Wait a minute, I want to help you not the OCD—what a tyrant it is! Let's put OCD in its place!"

None of us set out to be a "bad" coach, but we all have had our moments. Though you may cringe reading some of the "mistakes," the goal of this section is to spell out the good plays to bear in mind.

Stay Focused on the Immediate Problem at Hand

A good coach doesn't look back and list the litany of failures—"Think of all the soap you've wasted!"—nor does he catastrophize about the future—"How are you ever going to do college if you can't even get out of the bathroom in the morning?" What do these statements do? They might make you feel better for a moment because you've shifted your fear and frustration onto your child's shoulders. How do you prevent this? Stay in the here and now, and avoid generalities like "you're always so slow, you're irresponsible, do you have to be so anal?" Say instead, "It's really got you this morning, but we've got to go. I don't want that obnoxious OCD to make you late for school because you'll suffer the consequences and that's not fair." Because kids are ready to misattribute OCD to their personality; we don't want to encourage that process of condemning themselves.

Remember that OCD is your child's enemy, too. Help motivate him to fight by helping identify what he has to gain from controlling it. In other words, rather than saying "I can't take it another moment—you've got to get better," say, "Hey, I know you want to go to the prom. Let's figure out a way for you to get there."

Let Their Triumph Be Their Triumph

It had been weeks of a nighttime ritual where the litany of questions was staggering—"Am I going to faint? to die? to pass out? to have a heart attack?" Every night, it was the same questions, in the same order, and with the same reply needed—"No, you are fine and nothing bad is going to happen." With behavior therapy, Angela began to fight this worry ritual, reducing the questions nightly till she was able to say, "Nope, no questions tonight." Her mom, so relieved that Angela had gotten to this point blurted out, "Hallelujah, I couldn't have taken it an-other day." The wind totally knocked out of her sails, Angela blew up at her mother, "You don't understand anything. Do you think I want to be doing this?" Let your child savor her triumph. Saying something like, "I'm proud of you. Your hard work is paying off," gives credit where credit is due.

Was It Worth It? Sorting the Pros and Cons of Challenging Activities

All kids need to learn to evaluate their actions, situations, and conse-quences. Children with OCD are more vulnerable to overdoing it. Whether it's a sleepover, a dance, a track meet, or taking an extra class, parents can help children identify the pros and cons of participating in the activity and evaluating whether it was worth it to them. You and your child may not always reach the same conclusions. Camping out for a rock band ticket all night and being a wreck the next day may not seem worth it to you, but being exhausted and sitting in the fifth row may be what it's all about for your child. Ask, "Are there things you would do differently next time to improve the outcome? Were there some things that worked and others that didn't?" Look for partial suc-cesses. Say, "Good for you. You had a few slips, but you worked hard to keep it together." If you approach this process as an experiment to learn from (and resist the urge to say, "I told you so"), your child will be learning an invaluable lesson in pacing and self-regulating, making good decisions for himself, OCD or otherwise.

Whose Wings Are These, Anyway?

Sometimes it will be your wings, sometimes it will be your child's, and sometimes it will be both. Feel free to boss back the OCD yourself if your child is too tired or frightened. When you do, you are modeling how to handle tough moments, demonstrating your belief and investment in your child's treatment, and your willingness to carry the load sometimes.

Devising a Communication System

> The opposite of talking is not listening. The opposite of talking is waiting.
> —*Fran Leibowitz*

We all want to be heard and understood. It's easier to stop and wait your turn when someone is talking than to actually listen. Listening is an effort, but it is worth making. Consider the following dialogue between father and daughter:

Dad: You have to go to your cousins'.
Daughter: I can't go, I can't go.
Dad: You have to go. Stop making this fuss.
Daughter: There's no way I can—you don't get it.
Dad: There's nothing to get—you have to go. Now stop acting like a baby.

What if the following happened instead?

Dad: You have to go to your cousins'.
Daughter: I can't go.
Dad: No, you can't go? Tell me about why you can't go.
Daughter: No one there knows about my problem going to sleep at night. I'm going to be up all night there.
Dad: Okay yeah, well, that would be really unpleasant. What do you think would help?"
Daughter: I don't know—it's hard to be at someone else's house.
Dad: Do you want to tell Aunt Deena about what we do at home with the music, and let her know that you might need her to check on you a few times?
Daughter: Yeah, I guess if she knew, that would be better.

To communicate more effectively with your child, first listen actively. What's the real problem here? Ask for more information. Invite your child to think of solutions and offer some of your own. Keep the communication going both ways.

Relapse Prevention

As we saw in Chapter 4, recurrences of OCD are par for the course. As a parent, you can catch these slips before they turn into "slumps" or even "crashes." You can do this by putting the bad day in its proper perspective. We all seem to be programmed at birth to believe that progress is a steady course upward, yet this couldn't be further from the truth. Expecting life to be full of the unexpected gives kids protective gear for life—like "mental padding." If children walk through expecting some bad days or, glitches—no grape jelly, broken lunch bags, friends leaving you out—they won't be knocked over when this happens.

The Basics of Parenting Style

When you approach your child with the prospect of OCD treatment, you're hardly starting with a clean slate. We all establish parenting styles and a family environment from the get-go. Are you frustrated with lack of compliance? How can you get your child to jump off the cliff of OCD certainty, when you can't even get him not to hit his little sister? How can you increase the odds of having self-reliant, self-controlled, and content children from preschool to postpuberty? According to psychologist Dr. Diana Baumrind, who has been studying child-rearing practices for nearly fifty years, there are some recipes for success.

Dr. Baumrind describes three models of parental authority, each of which is associated with certain child characteristics.

1. *Authoritarian* parents are guided by an absolute standard of conduct and enforce that standard with coercion and threats. Punitive, forceful measures are the norm to curb self-expression that runs counter to parental order. In these families, there is no give and take, no shades of gray; inculcating children with values of obedience is the purpose of parenting interventions. "I am the law" is the operating principle. This parenting style is associated with hostile, oppositional, non-self-directed children.
2. *Permissive* parents are less demanding to responsibility and do not invoke parental power to get compliance. Under the canopy of laissez-faire, children have endless choice and may be in

charge of many of their own activities beyond their grasp. These children may be less assertive and less achievement oriented.

3. *Authoritative* parents are directive with their children, but this is based on rational explanations for their behavior; children are encouraged to participate in reasoning and problem solving and to develop their own navigating system with parental guidance. Authoritative parents are demanding in that they have firm, consistent expectations for their children, but their demands are reasonably made and conformity is expected given mutual respect, not absolute standards. As a result, children raised in authoritative homes may be more active agents, are more self-reliant, achievement oriented, and cooperative. An authoritative parenting style is most successful in general, it is the style of choice in combatting OCD.

Setting a Limit on the OCD versus Lowering the Bar on Your Child's Head

"What's the difference if I yell at her and say, 'that's enough,' or if I tell her it's the OCD? My way gets the job done too, right?" The problem with this approach is that your child is going to take this personally, get the message that she is unacceptable in some way, and eventually feel more stress at home as she turns these expectations back on herself— "I'm a jerk, I'm a troublemaker." When setting limits, be fair. Try not to lay blame for ruining the event—with no reference to the OCD— when the problem is your child feeling like she's going to throw up. Just as you couldn't imagine saying to your child with hemophilia—"Your bleeds are ruining my life," you truly don't want to blame your child. If your patience is thinning and you do explode at your child, remember you can always apologize; parents make mistakes, too. And what are you apologizing for? Not for being fed up with the dinnertime interruptions, who wouldn't be, but for not having the presence of mind to tell your child about it in a more respectful way.

Authoritative Parenting Steps in Making Changes

Asserting Power: Confrontation versus Coercion

Things get messy and conflict is inevitable, but you can get your point across without sacrificing your child's self-esteem. To do this, don't indulge in the absolute power of parenthood—"You will do this or else." Threats make kids feel bad. It's compliance for the wrong reasons because it spotlights the parent's power, not why the request make sense in the situation. While threats and promises work well in the moment, and we've all indulged in them, our children don't internalize a system of right and wrong, don't practice making good choices, and as a result, become dependent on our threatening them in order to act. Instead, model for your children how decisions get made. Explain to your child how things need to be rather than wielding your absolute parental power without reason or discussion. When you're truly in charge, you don't need to remind your children that "I'm your mother, that's why!" In OCD terms, this distinction is critical to helping your child understand why you want him to work on controlling symptoms. Working on his symptoms is going to help him, and while it's difficult for the family, you'll all be on the same team.

Keeping a Watch: Monitoring versus Intrusively Directing

How much privacy and autonomy is too much? The rule of thumb is that you want your children to have as much autonomy and control as they are able to handle. Makes sense, right? If your child is able to do something by himself, let him; otherwise you're sending the message you don't believe he can do it, or you're getting him frustrated because this is about your needs, not his. Your child may actually want your help keeping to a ten-minute shower, asking how you can help is the best way to stay out of the director's chair.

Protecting Your Child from the Overdrive of Everyday Life: How Much Is Too Much?

A 1998 *Time* magazine article heralded the syndrome of the burnt-out nine-year-old, a product of our fast-paced culture. Between soccer, swimming, college-prep tutoring, karate, clubs, and scouting, there's little down time for our children. Maybe you're thinking, *busy is good, what's the problem?* Child experts such as Harvard's Dr. T. Berry Brazelton insist that unscheduled playtime is an essential learning laboratory for developing independent thinking and negotiating relationships with peers, as well as setting the patterns for daily living that children will carry into adulthood. Brazelton warns that if we don't take "fun" seriously, we're going to create "obsessive-compulsive" people. This was the concern of psychologist Dr. David Elkind, when in 1989 he wrote *The Hurried Child.* According to *Time,* kids' free time has significantly decreased— from 40 percent in 1981 to 25 percent as we enter the twenty-first century. Just because we can do something doesn't mean it's good for us. Although your child may be able to survive playing two sports, plus participating in student council and preparing for his Bar Mitzvah, that doesn't mean that's a model lifestyle. Unfortunately, the reality is that colleges are looking for these superkids who have done it all by the time they arrive at the university's doorstep—but truly, it is not healthy. We need to look at the big picture.

Sometimes we protect too much, at other times not enough. "I hate to see her so distressed," lamented one parent, whose eight-year-old had nighttime fears that could be diminished only by elaborate rituals. The rituals included saying increasingly longer prayers for everyone each night, sprinkling water over her bed, lining up her stuffed animals, and turning off and on lights a certain number of times. "It got to the point where we would do it for her just to get her to bed at a reasonable hour. And she would go nuts if we tried to limit it or reason with her." It was of no avail to this family to try and make everything right for their daughter, they were actually helping to entrench her rituals.

Similarly, if you expect your child to be tough and "suck it up," you'll also get frustrated, because your child will get irritated. He may be dealing with the most profound and gripping problems that face mankind, light years beyond what his friends are thinking: "What do you mean asking me to be tough—I'm on the firing line!" Here your role will be for you and your child to get tough on the OCD. Take the example of Peter, a very sharp, quiet eleven-year-old. His mother understood how thoughts got stuck in his head, but his father just saw his son as being too afraid and too sensitive, and dismissed the trouble with an ever-jocular, "Come on, Peter, face it like a man." Peter would sink further into a feeling of awfulness about himself—*I guess this means I'm not tough, I'm a wuss, I can't even control these stupid things in my head. How am I going to be tough with the bullies at school?*

When You Have OCD Yourself: Understanding Without Preventing Your Child's Progress

If you have OCD yourself, you have the added challenge of sorting through your own feelings because you understand only too well what your child is going through. Many parents find it more difficult to set a limit on their child's OCD because they think, *I know she's doing this for a very good reason, I know she would feel awful if she couldn't do that ritual.* What you must keep in mind is that when you don't intervene in an OCD situation, you are really making more room for the OCD.

Lucinda is a ten-year-old whose obsessions about thunderstorms had her constantly watching the weather channel, the news, and the window. Whenever a cloud would cover the sun, no matter how briefly, she would flash on the accidents that could happen if it rained. To counter the risk of an accident, Lucinda would count as high as she could; she thought to herself that if she were on guard counting—not having fun, not doing well in school, if she made that sacrifice—that God would protect her family. Day after day, she counted in her mind, through math, English, and recess. When she couldn't think the numbers, she would trace them with her fingers. She would often cry at her desk, for fear that she wasn't counting well enough or that God knew that she was trying to listen to the teacher as well and therefore that she wasn't really doing it right. She didn't want to tell her parents about this, because it would upset them and then they might get in an accident and it would be her fault. When I told Lucinda about OCD, how this tape recorder in her brain was giving her the wrong message over and over and how she was born with this problem that a million kids have, she agreed to let me tell her parents. I met with Lucinda's parents to share with them what was going on with Lucinda. Her mother, who also suffered from OCD, revealed that she herself prayed throughout the day, in order to protect her family from harm.

Lucinda's mom asked, "How can I tell her not to do this when I have to do it myself? I know how hard it is. Nobody knew about my OCD; I had to hide it and be terrified. I want it to be different for her." I went up to the blackboard, drew a line down the middle and on one side wrote GOOD FOR LUCINDA, on the other GOOD FOR OCD I asked her mom on which side to place allowing Lucinda to miss school in order to ritualize. She hesitated, then said, "I guess I didn't know there was any other way to live." This was a moment of truth for Lucinda's mom. No parent is going to jeopardize her child's happiness; she just hadn't seen it that way.

What Lucinda's mom needed to do first was understand her own OCD, to understand that her prayers were not true prayers, but rather brain tricks and that there is not only another but a better way to live. It was not until she took that risk, that she could begin to help Lucinda—and have the conviction that she was not endangering her child by helping her fight the compulsions. In fact, she was saving her daughter's life.

CHAPTER 7

Good Parenting Skills to Bring to OCD

I'm afraid to discipline Max; I'm afraid of how he'll react, I don't want to set him off.

* * *

Knowing how to respond to my son's behavior has been a constant struggle for me. Many times I was so afraid my response would make his anxiety worse that I decided not to say anything. Many times I wouldn't punish him because I felt sorry for him and thought that his behavior couldn't be helped. In therapy I learned the correct responses to his actions. I learned to recognize when it was OCD and when he was just a normal kid acting up. I know it's painful for him to have so many worries and anxieties at such a young age, but now I know in order to help him I have to stay on top of the problem.

* * *

Sometimes I wonder why we didn't say "no" to Ellie earlier, she wasn't in control of her behavior, why did we let it control us?

—*Parents of children with OCD*

Parents often approach a child with OCD as if he were a bomb ready to detonate; afraid to set him off, parents tiptoe around the danger zone. In fact, parents are situated in a very powerful position to defuse the mine-field. There are thousands of moments in your child's day that are opportunities for her to develop a confident, strategic approach to fearful situations. Coping with anxiety is something that your child can learn how to do, and those lessons will carry her through adulthood. The concepts in this chapter will help you "fear-proof" your home by learning the principles and mechanics of behavior change. Fear-proofing doesn't mean having no fear, rather, it means helping your child face difficult situations one step at a time.

Why don't we get lessons on how to talk to our kids about fear? While fear is less controversial, there are instructions for parents about taboo topics such as sex, drugs, or alcohol. Most parents respond to a child's fear in one of three ways: "Don't worry," "I'll protect you," or "That's silly, there's nothing to be afraid of." None of those responses are of particular use to kids and they all reflect lost opportunities to help kids dismantle their fear. Fear is like a brick wall. You're trapped and you can't see around it. You can break down the fear into a problem to be solved rather than something to escape. Take Margaret who says she is afraid to go to camp. As soon as those words leave her lips, Mom's mind is going a million miles an hour—*How am I going to get her there, she's got to go*—and in the face of catastrophe, Mom's helplessness turns to anger: "Well, you've got to go and that's it." At which point the daughter, scared and now angry with her mom for not understanding, refuses to cooperate. What else might have happened here? What if Margaret's mom could have asked a few key questions:

1. How afraid are you, low, medium, or high?
2. What are your what ifs?
3. What else might happen instead?
4. What do you want to do?

With this information, the two of them could narrow Margaret's fear into specific situations to be tackled. When parents are educated about fear, they can keep their cool and help their children out of their tailspin.

Anxiety: A Part of Life

Fear is a universal biological experience; it represents the triggering of our built-in signal system for danger. It becomes problematic when the alarm is set off where it isn't warranted or is distorted to a degree that is not adaptive. Dr. Aaron Beck, the father of cognitive therapy, defines fear as "the appraisal of danger" and anxiety as the "unpleasant feeling state evoked when fear is stimulated." Children with anxiety disorders have an inborn "will it hurt?" orientation to the world. As a result, they may be more sensitive to their surroundings and less willing to try new things. With such a low threshold on their danger warning system, children with anxiety disorders are very stressed. For them the multitude of trivial or passing threats—a disturbing movie trailer or news item—are registered and need to be dealt with. Take this daily constitutional vulnerability, add a stressor such as a change in routine and this can often tip the scales so that their coping abilities fail them. A child with a combination of stressors, for example, an illness, a change of school, and sleeplessness, will lower his "resistance" to coping with challenges and you may see him unravel under the strain.

Anxiety is not something to cure, but rather a response to learn about and control. When parents don't understand how anxiety works, they often inadvertently help lock in the anxiety in several ways:

- By helping their child completely avoid situations that are difficult.
- By rescuing their child from a scary situation at the height of the child's anxiety.
- By reinforcing the anxiety by paying too much attention to it— either positive or negative.

Therefore, to help your child live and learn with anxiety, learn coping strategies to manage the physical and cognitive (thinking) symptoms of anxiety.

Fast Facts About Anxiety

- Anxiety symptoms such as racing heart and racing thoughts will reset to normal within a given period of time, often fifteen to twenty minutes, if you don't feed the anxiety by hyperventilating and thinking catastrophic thoughts.

This is a safety mechanism for the species that can be thought of as the "what comes up must come down" phenomenon. All these feelings will, like the structure of any good novel, build up, hit the crescendo, then resolve.

Let your child know that the feelings will pass and that his goal is to send a signal to his brain to slow things down. Help your child to do slow breathing, progressive muscle relaxation, and positive self-talk to slow down the anxiety. Try to stay with your child in the situation for about fifteen to twenty minutes until the anxiety diminishes. This will make a good association between the situation and your child's ability to cope with it.

- Anxiety symptoms are diminished by gradual exposure to a scary situation.

Break challenges down into manageable chunks. Set a goal that your child is likely to achieve. Rank the challenges on a ladder; start with the least frightening. Don't advance to the next stage until your child's fear is a 1 or 2 on a scale of 10. So if your child is afraid of the movie theater, first sit in the parking lot, then go up to the door, then go in the lobby, and so on. Always find what your child *can* do that relates to the fear rather than focusing on what your child can't do. This will build in your child a feeling of mastery. It won't work to rush your child to tackle something he's not ready for; in fact, this will undermine progress by leaving your child feeling defeated.

- Frequent practice is much more effective than "spaced" or occasional practice.

Help your child to practice every day so that he has less opportunity to cook up a lot of anticipatory fear. If you practice something once a week, you have a whole week in between for anxiety to build.

- Incompatible emotions such as relaxation, humor, and assertiveness compete with fear and win!

This principle is known as reciprocal inhibition.

Encourage your child to slow things down to increase relaxation. Ask your child what she hates about what the fear is doing. Help her get angry and assertive and "boss back" the fear. Use humor when your child is ready for it. For example, talk to the fear yourself: "Are you going to make us go all over town worrying about this, you're fired!" Take a pretend microphone and interview the sink: "Do you want to have water splashed on you? Do you really need a bath?"

- Avoidance increases anxiety: This principle is known as negative reinforcement.

Escape at the height of fear is extremely reinforcing of the fear and of the coping strategy of avoidance. This is because the relief that your child experiences is commensurate with the intensity of the fear.

Help your child stay in a difficult situation by changing the situation. Stand further back, look in the window, have Mom there. Don't reinforce anxiety by "rescuing" your child from a challenging situation.

- Punishment does not help anxiety—it makes it worse.

Some disorders such as ADHD may respond to reinforcements and punishments. OCD does not. OCD is not about learning impulse control, so punishment will only make your child more upset.

- Even anxious kids need limits and discipline.

"He can't help feeling anxious, so how can I punish him?" While anxiety is a feeling that's not your child's fault, he needs to learn to control it. Anger is a feeling too, but if your daughter is throwing things, you tell her to stop.

When your child is out of control with anxiety, it's not doing anybody any good; she is showing you that she is overwhelmed and that you need to bring her back. It's like taking away the keys—when your child is in that state, she shouldn't be in the driver's seat. Rule of thumb: Accept the feeling while putting limits on the behavior.

How to Increase Your Child's Desired Behavior

Though some children find positive behavior change a reward in itself, if this isn't the case for your child, don't be afraid to sweeten the pot. Children may require incentive systems to take the risk to try a new or difficult behavior. There are two ways to reinforce a desired behavior like doing OCD homework: (1) positive reinforcement—following it with a positive experience such as going for an ice cream cone or getting stickers, or (2) negative reinforcement—removing an unpleasant experience such as reducing chores.

Some parents are concerned that rewards are bribes and that their child should do homework without any special treatment. This is not a helpful attitude because at its root is the assumption that this behavior *should* come naturally. Your child is not being afraid in order to get attention or because he likes it; he is following his constitution. When he tries something new, he is battling the internal messages that say "Don't try, this is too hard, too scary."

The difference between a bribe and a reward is that rewards are given for hard work. When you establish a reward system, you are doing two things. First, you are sending the message to your child that you understand now you are asking him to do something challenging, whether it's taking out the trash, touching his shoes, or going to camp. Second, you are acknowledging his success with the reward you give. Therefore, rewards are the reinforcement for a job well done. On the other hand, bribes have a duplicitous component. When we "bribe" our children, we are essentially tricking them either into doing something wrong or doing something for the wrong reasons. Take the parental ploy "Just behave at this party and I'll give you ten dollars," or

"Go upstairs and get me the remote and you can have ice cream for breakfast." We know at those times that we are asking our kids to do things that we could really do ourselves, or that are really for *our* own good, not necessarily theirs. It is important that rewards are commensurate with the challenge. Just as you wouldn't give yourself a new car for completing a report, you are not going to give your child a trip to Disneyland for petting a dog. What follows are some guidelines for incentive systems:

- *Are you prepared to focus on this project?* Parental participation is at least 50 percent of the success of the program. Take stock of what's going on at home. Is this a good time to embark on a plan? Do you have the time and energy to devote to it? Don't start right before a vacation, in the middle of house renovation, or other high-stress period.
- *Establish a baseline.* Progress happens slowly, and when you're desperate for change, it becomes that watched pot. You can monitor change for yourself by keeping a log of the number of times your child asks you a question, goes in the bathroom, or how long it takes your child to get ready for school in the morning. Working on noticing these changes will keep you from getting discouraged, and help your child feel confident that his hard work is paying off.
- *Choose one or two target behaviors at a time.* Focus on one or two target behaviors at a time. More than two and your child's efforts will be spread too thin and he won't be able to succeed at any of them. More than that and your child will not be able to see his progress, and *seeing is believing!*
- *Let your child choose the target behaviors.* You will get the best cooperation if your child participates in the choosing of the behaviors you want to eliminate. Either your child can generate the list of behaviors, or you can present him with a choice of three behaviors and ask which he is ready to tackle.
- *Let your child choose the reward to make sure it is an incentive.* Your child is not going to work for something he doesn't want. Have your child generate a rewards menu—a list of prizes, experiences she wants—then you can go through and assign point values to the list, so that your child wins a new CD twice a month, not every day.
- *Small, frequent rewards are more effective than large, infrequent ones.* With younger children, rewards can be daily—preferably immediately following the bravery challenge. For example, playing

an extra game or getting an extra story *that* night for meeting the challenge. With older children, small weekly rewards are appropriate; in addition, a monthly reward can be earned for consistent weekly performance.

- *Explain the rules.* "But you didn't say I had to do it without you reminding me, you didn't say I had to do it right away." Such semantic battles can arise over any reward system. It is best to spell out the terms ahead of time. Work out with your child when the challenge time will happen (e.g., after dinner, before television). Be clear. Be specific.

- *Think positively: Use a bravery model.* Rather than telling your child "You have to get over your fears," discuss the incentive system in terms of bravery. "What do you feel bravest to tackle now?" Ask your child to phrase goals positively and in behavioral terms: "I will walk out of the bathroom after washing once," is preferable to "I won't be afraid in the bathroom and I won't wash five times."

- *Behavior changes before feelings.* Look to what your child is doing and focus on the doing rather than the feeling. It is better to make comments like "You did it," rather than "See, that wasn't so bad," since most likely it felt bad for your child, but he did it anyway. That's really the goal—feel the fear and do it anyway. Your child may continue to say, "This is scary," or "I can't do it," even as he is making progress with the behaviors he is targeting.

- *Extinction bursts: What happens when you change the rules.* As we discussed in Chapter 4, an extinction burst describes the initial increase in a behavior when you stop reinforcing it. Your child may initially act up more in an attempt to get things back the old way. If you're prepared for this, you can hold firm, stay calm, and go through the night or two of "bursting" before your child settles into the new behavior. So, for example, if you are working on nighttime fears and your child is used to you running to his room whenever he calls, he may throw a fit when you say, "Now's your time for being brave." He may say, "My stomach is breaking into pieces, you are a terrible mother," and so on. You want to calmly respond and then leave the room, otherwise your child will never have the opportunity to see that he *can* get over this hurdle.

- *Avoid avoidance whenever possible.* Avoidance is when the fear says, "Jump," and you respond, "How high?" Remember that your child may have figured out that avoiding a frightening or difficult situation gets rid of fear temporarily, but you know that in the long run it makes things much harder for your child. Eight-year-old Christina developed a fear of not being able to have access to a bathroom and would constantly ask, "Is there a bathroom there?" Her parents' solution was to map out every route complete with all the bathrooms and reassure her that she could stop at every one. While it was important that Christina's parents took her fear seriously, they shouldn't cement that fear by accommodating it. Christina's parents needed to remember that it wasn't about bathrooms, it was about being sure and having an escape plan for anxiety. Meanwhile, Christina's life was getting more and more confined. So focusing on what Christina wanted—where she wanted to go, instead of how to avoid the fear—was the way out. They could say, "Do you want to be thinking about bathrooms now? Your brain has got a sticky thought about bathrooms, meanwhile, wouldn't you rather be thinking about ballet class? Let's help you be in charge here. Remember, that thought is stuck in a broken record."

- *Keep track of successes, not failures.* Make a chart on which your child can see her progress. Give points for the achievements, but don't mark down the days your child is unable to meet the goal. Your child will feel very encouraged by seeing the points accumulate. You can mark successes with stickers, stars, buttons, or beans. Children like to make their own charts and decorate them with their favorite "boss back" sayings; they can make the charts as ladders helping them see that they're making their way up to the top.

  Likewise with your feedback, focus on the success experiences and ignore the failures, or limit your comments to encouraging ones: "It was tough today, tomorrow's another day, you'll get back on track." Because your attention is the most powerful reinforcement, whatever you pay attention to will happen again. You want to avoid reinforcing a negative behavior by paying too much attention to it by yelling, blaming, or making too much room for it.

- *If your child is not getting a reward within the first week or so, lower the goal.* You want your child to experience success, not frustration. If your child is unable to have some success in the first week, rethink the goal; it was probably too high. You can explain that you were skipping up to the third rung of the ladder, and you've got to start at the first one.

- *When are you pushing too much?* Terry, a mother of a six-year-old with OCD, e-mailed me one day, "How do you know when she's in over her head?" She was referring to her daughter's OCD homework; Michaela was getting more upset each night rather than less. This is a time when we overshot the goal. Though you assess a child's anxiety level and try to start with the least challenging goal, you don't know for sure what it will be like for your child. Again, when you are meeting with difficulty for more than the first couple of days, this may be a time to retreat a step or two to a lower-level challenge.

- *Shaping toward the goal: Use cues and reminders.* New behaviors are acquired in increments. You want to help your child take on more and more of the responsibility for the job, but initially you may be directing the show. This getting closer and closer to the goal is called shaping, where you reinforce behaviors that are on the board not just the ones that hit the bull's-eye. Be flexible initially about what constitutes a success. Even if your child struggles and it gets messy and drawn-out, if he meets the goal, he gets credit. If the goal is for your child to get dressed independently and your baseline is that you have to drag him upstairs, pull out the clothes, and practically dress him, if he goes upstairs on his own or gets out his clothes, reinforce him! He is moving gradually toward the goal. You can congratulate him for being persistent and successful and suggest that he try to make it shorter tomorrow night. If your child forgets to do his challenge, you can remind him, because the overall goal is frequent practice.

  With adolescents, these reminders sometimes become a power struggle; they may choose to wait till you remind them. In these cases, you can do a "sliding scale for points." Points, like bread, are worth more when they are fresh; the longer you wait, the more stale they get and the less they are worth. A child could get three points for complying immediately, two for one reminder, or one point for several reminders.

- *Grandma's Rule: Dinner first, then dessert!* One way of increasing compliance and momentum toward a goal is to take a given—dessert, play time, TV time—and make it contingent on completing the task that you set. Common sense applications of this rule are: "Finish your homework before you can play," or "Watch TV after you clean up your room." The key is to get more mileage out of a given (turning it into a privilege) by placing it after a challenge. So, for example, if your child has a lot of nighttime rituals, but he also likes to get a story at night, arrange that you will come in for stories *after* he has finished his rituals; that way he has incentive to finish them, and finish them quickly in order to have more story time. If your child doesn't want to do his behavior therapy homework, but he does want to play catch with you in the backyard, do the homework first, and then go out to play catch. While this may seem obvious, there are many times when we fail to use this easy, no cost reinforcement method, which is simply a matter of sequencing.

- *It takes about three weeks to establish a new behavior; after that, begin thinning out the reward.* Your child should establish a new behavior pattern within about three weeks, provided that the goal is appropriate. At that point, you can increase the interval between rewards to allow the reward to fade out of the picture and the new accomplishment to remain. So, for example, if your child is getting a Beanie Baby every week for coping with nighttime fears, after three weeks of meeting the goal, you can now give a reward after two weeks of successes and shift to primary verbal reinforcement, or self-reinforcement, saying, "I'm proud of you," or encouraging him to tell a friend. You can explain this switch to your child by saying that that particular battle is over: His bravery won over the fear. Now he doesn't need a reward for that behavior, but he can move on to the next challenge.

- *Model vulnerability, risk taking, and mistake making.* There was a social psychology study conducted by Dr. Stanley Schacter and Dr. Jerome Singer, in 1959 with the take-home message "Misery loves miserable company." In this experiment, anxious participants felt better waiting with people who were also afraid when faced with an anxious situation than with those who were calm and not afraid. It's okay to let your child know that you get afraid sometimes and discuss how you cope with it; this will help your child not feel weird or like he's the only one in the world with this problem. Show him it's okay to take risks and make mistakes; model how you pick yourself up, dust yourself off, and try again.

- *End each day on a high note.* It is more important for your child to learn to manage his anxiety than to complete the task. If a child is struggling with a goal, working at it but not reaching it, the best thing to say is, "I made a mistake, that goal was too high." Help the child end feeling competent with what he could do rather than keep pushing for that one narrow definition of success. At the pool one day, a little girl, not more than five or six, was working very hard at her swimming lesson. During the final exercise, picking up rings, she became very frightened and she swallowed water. She began to scream and cry. It was clear that she was done for the day, but instead of consolidating what she had accomplished, her mother said, "If you pick up the rest of the rings, I'll buy you a Beanie Baby." Unfortunately, this impossible task only emphasized the feeling of failure and distress that the child was already feeling, she was telling Mom she couldn't go any further, but that was just what Mom asked her to do. Why is this a problem? You want your child to carry with him pictures of successful coping, not of ending, literally, in a pool of tears.

When you're trying to help your child change his behavior, it's important to remain calm, firm, and optimistic. Though anxiety is not your child's fault, implementing a program for overcoming fears requires a consistent, authoritative stance. Stay calm when your child is upset or frightened, so your child won't add to his anxiety. Show him you can be afraid yet effective.

Feedback: About Your Child's Goal

Many parents report that their child gets angry with any kind of praise—he hates it!—and they ask me why. Often kids get angry when they're praised, but it's not *because* of the praise, it's because they're being praised for the wrong thing. I learned this lesson from my six-year-old daughter when I asked her to clean up the tornado of toys in her room. After collapsing in a heap and announcing, "It's too hard!" I narrowed her task to putting the stuffed animals in the toy box. When I returned ten minutes later, I said, "Good, you put the toys away—that's great." Taking umbrage with her six-year-old authority, she retorted, "Don't say good, say thank you." It hit me in that moment that one problem with praise is that it's often about what the parents want or what's meaningful to parents. Haven't we all experienced this at work? Someone "makes" us do an unwanted task and then when they thank us, we grumble sarcastically under our breath, "yeah, you're really welcome." So what I should have said to my daughter is, "I know you didn't want to do this, but you did. Thanks." The answer is encouragement and phrasing feedback in terms of the child's own goal for him or herself.

Psychologist Dr. Carol Dweck, who has researched self-esteem in children, emphasizes praising your child's efforts rather than the product. She has found that when children are overly praised for simpler achievements, they may not risk going for tougher challenges for fear that they may fail and then not be praised. However, if you are praising their efforts, children will always be motivated to do more.

Stick to Your Plan: Or, Don't Cave!

Often when behavior plans fail, it's because there isn't follow-through. Don't undermine your own plan. When it comes to homework and laundry, who forces your hand to give in to your child? For example, if your child procrastinates or takes a long time with homework and you set 8:00 as the time when homework clinic is "closed," but if she comes begging for help at 8:30, you help her, you are basically saying: "Here's the loophole! Use it early and often." Like a good swing in tennis, you'll reach your target when you follow through on it. If you set up a plan and then don't keep to the terms, your child will learn not to worry about the plans because they're going to get dropped after a few days anyway. In fact, behavior modification expert Dr. Bobby Newman reminds people that the child's memory of getting a reward through ways that break the behavior therapy "contract" are the strongest and most self-reinforcing, too. His rule: The moment you most want to give in is the worst moment to do so. Your goal is to help your child learn to work within new limits or parameters; if you keep changing them, you can't expect your child to learn. It's not fun being the bad guy, but the sooner you set and stick to the limit, the sooner your child will adapt to the new rules.

Taking Stock: What Kind of Changes Can You Make Now?

We have all had moments as parents when we want our kids to function more like toasters than human beings—I want my toast *now,* I want my child to behave *now!* It's okay to want that, but not okay to expect that. Step back and look at the whole picture; take a reading of what level of change your parent-child relationship can support. If you haven't been successful in getting your child to do the small stuff—listening, waiting, not shouting—you don't have the foundation in place to support the really big changes. If this is the case, you want to first work on establishing those rules. See the resource guide Parenting section for guidelines on the basics.

Maximizing the Success of Your Behavior Plan

Learning How to Set Limits: Dos and Don'ts

- *Telegraph your commands.* Don't blur the message with too many details. Keep your expectation clear and concise. Imagine you're sending a telegraph and have to pay for every word. Be brief. For example, don't engage in a lengthy explanation of why you don't want your daughter to rummage through your purse looking for gum: "it's mine, it will mess up everything and I won't be able to find anything." Just say, "Hey, out of my purse."

- *Stick by what you say.* Don't make a consequence you're not going to keep, and don't make a consequence that punishes you. Don't threaten to remove TV for a week if your child has a TV in his room and you can't keep it from him, and don't threaten to cancel his sleepover at a friend's house if that in turn means that you have to give up your orchestra tickets to stay home with a child who has misbehaved.

- *Stay in charge.* If you let yourself degenerate to your child's level and engage in a "no it isn't" "yes it is" argument, you've lost your authority. Rather than get pulled into a back and forth reparté, snuff it—"This is not a debate; this is not up for discussion; I'm not going to change my mind on this, the more you argue the more irritated I'm going to get."

- *Don't let the tone or words of your message escalate the problem.* Use only as much force and authority as is needed to contain the situation. Use a voice that's calm but firm, not threatening, but be clear that you mean what you are saying. If you scream or yell, you'll bury your message under your threatening tone. Children either get scared or tune parents out when they yell—they don't hear and they don't learn. Use a commanding voice—what would you respond to, a boss who screams or one who gives it to you straight?

- *Don't confuse your message with too many niceties.* I have worked with many families where there is a lack of parental leadership. In these families, parents are looking to their children to give them permission to set limits and the result is chaos. You can hear the ambivalence in the parents' voices, "Come in and clean up this mess, now is that okay honey?" Sometimes parents are trying to be nice and that's why they soften the blow, but your child is asking, "What is Mom trying to tell me?" She thinks, *Mom's being nice, not important.* It's like what happens to adults with speed limits. We see the signs, they aren't menacing, we keep speeding. It's not until we spot the state trooper that it registers that we'd better slow down. You want your message to be clear from the get-go.

- *Don't respond to derailing questions or comments.* Ideally, ignore them. "Why do I have to?" "You never let me get what I want," or "You guys always go out." Stay firmly grounded in the problem at hand: "I know this is important to you and that you want it, but we can't do this now." Or, "I know you wish we would stay home, and that you get upset when we go out, but we have plans to go out—and if we don't, it will be planet of the cranky parents." You can discuss what's "unfair" at another time; now your telling your child what to do.

- *Do practice using your "no" muscle.* Build up your experience and confidence by practicing limit-setting in a non-OCD moment. Your child wants you to buy a new Power Ranger or borrow the car. Don't condemn or comply with your child's complaints. Just listen and repeat your plan. Most parents are shocked at how their children give up the fight very easily when they set a limit. They often think, *I wish I'd tried this earlier.*

- *Don't let your fear run the show.* "I am so frightened for my daughter, I'm so afraid that she won't be able to cope with school." What happens when your fear sets the expectation for your child? As one ad said, fear can be in the car, but don't let it drive! You start making excuses for her and lowering your expectations. Furthermore, it's difficult to keep your fear to yourself— it seeps out. Maybe it's the hesitation in your voice, answering one question too many, the premature offering of "an out" ("You can always call me if you're not having a good time"). This is bad in the short run, handicapping in the long run. What can you do instead? Ask yourself to visualize your child's strength; what do you see? Your child voicing a strong opinion at the dinner table, singing in the choir. Imagine your child's pride, competency, resourcefulness, and that you then imbue that belief into your child. It is on the wind of those wings that your child can soar.

- *Be consistent.* To help your nine-year-old gain control over her reassurance ritual where she asks you every day if she will be picked up from school that day, you have worked out an agreement that she will not ask you but rather look at a preprinted calendar. Some days when she asks you, you remind her to go look at the calendar; other days, you answer the question once or twice. Though in the long run checking the calendar is going to be more helpful, in the short run your child would like to just get the reassurance, so you take the easy out. Remember, when you are inconsistent, you inadvertently reinforce the OCD and send a message to your child, "Try me, I might give you the answer you want." Like playing slot machines, even if the odds of winning are low, because someone hits the jackpot every once in a while, your child is going to take a gamble.

Sometimes the inconsistency arises because mom and dad handle the situation differently. Make sure that your parental plan is airtight. Other times inconsistency comes up if a child shows distress or acts out. I will often ask parents to think about when it will be hard to enforce this plan. Commonly they'll say that if their child starts to cry or get angry, they are likely to dispense with the plan to accommodate the child's OCD. This is a mistake. A better response is to address your child's emotional response but not to drop the plan. Try to soothe your child and then see if she is ready to try again. If not, let the loss go and make a date to try again tomorrow. Whatever you do, don't drop the ball. There are many ways to be flexible with the plan without abandoning it altogether. Keep your authority. The parent of ten-year-old Charlie had difficulty keeping him to a schedule. When Charlie wanted to go out to play even though this was not on the schedule, his mother would step back and let him go. She then concluded, "Charlie doesn't listen." Her behavior reinforced a pattern in which the child called the shots. Even if you agree with the outcome of your child's breaking the rule, be in charge. Say, "You want to go outside even though you're scheduled for homework time. I am going to let you do this because we have time later to do your homework. So when it's time to sit down and do homework at 7:00, I expect cooperation. If not, I will know that you are not ready to handle these changes in the schedule." This way, you are being flexible where you can be, but not sending a message that says, "Here's a rule. Abide by it when you feel like it."

- *Finding time: The things-are-too-hectic phenomenon.* The impact of our stressful, overpacked lives is a national epidemic. For most of us, our lives depend on writing things down on a calendar that is usually so full that the meaning of the phrases "Calgon, take me away" or "Beam me up, Scotty" have proven to be wisdom ahead of their time. Acknowledging the problem will help you limit its effect and prioritize the problem at hand. Look at your schedules. It may be that while no time is a great time to begin a home behavioral plan, there may be some times that are better than others. Jumping on the problem as soon as possible is preferable, although it is not always an option. For an accountant, it's hard to do much of anything but work until after April 15. Families with these types of seasonal time commitments may choose to wait until the busy season is over to launch an active fighting plan, and may instead choose to employ a damage-control plan in the interim. One family found that it was actually easier to implement a behavior plan when Dad was away on a two-week business trip. This allowed Mom and daughter to establish some new rules (without the temptation and interference of getting Dad to do the old rules) and then bring Dad on board after the new patterns were well established.

- *Prioritize your program.* As parents, we send a strong message to our kids about what is important. If we forget about homework assignments and leave tracking sheets in the car, we are sending the message that school is not really important. As a parent who has watched papers from my daughter's school get sucked into the vortex of my house never to be seen again, I can appreciate the challenge of keeping track of behavior plans. This

---

CHECKLIST FOR INCREASING COMPETENCY BEHAVIORS AND DECREASING AVOIDANCE AND SYMPTOMATIC BEHAVIORS

Am I Paying Attention to Positive Behavior?
- Giving verbal praise, hugs, stickers, tangible rewards, or extra social time for my child's successes (touching contaminated objects, refraining from asking questions).
- Praising my child's *attempts* at getting control, not just the successes.
- Not every arrow hits the bull's-eye; praise if it "hits" the board.
- Showing interest and concern for my child's challenges.
- Showing interest in other aspects of my child's life—sports, music, friends.
- Making sure that the behavior goals are within reach.
- Making sure that my child is choosing the target challenges.
- Making sure that my child has chosen the rewards or incentives.

Am I Ignoring and/or Setting Limits on Negative Behaviors?
- Limiting my accommodation of the symptoms: making house rules on not making extra meals, limiting number of towels or utensils used a day, and/or having my child participate in laundry; limiting cleaning supplies and toiletries in house.
- Limiting the number of times I directly participate in a ritual: answering questions, checking the lights or doors.
- Setting limits on my child's avoidance by not "doing for" them: going upstairs for them so they don't do their rituals on the stairs.
- Not getting angry or blaming when I see symptoms.
- Not focusing on the bad days, not catastrophizing about the future.

is why God invented the refrigerator—the family communications center—and magnets. I knew that ten-year-old Margaret was going to get the support of her family for treatment when they came in for the second appointment and told me that they had put a sign on the fridge in bold letters: GO AWAY OCD, YOU ARE NOT THE BOSS OF ME! If your therapist does not provide you with a notebook, buy a bright red or orange one and keep all your child's charts and boss-back work in it. You'll use it now, and you might need it later.

Prioritizing is undermined by procrastination. Procrastination is fueled by beliefs about the difficulty of the task. Undertaking a behavior program to work on OCD is going to be difficult, but it's not going to be impossible. What's more, if you think it's hard now, just know that it will be much harder if you wait—the OCD will likely be more debilitating, and all parties will have to go into battle worn out, running on empty. Remember, you may feel that you need to change things overnight, but you know that lasting change is the product of gradual and consistent change.

CHAPTER 8

The OCD Strategy

A Battle Plan

All parents need to know how to handle the basics with children—discipline, homework, how to cope with a broken leg or broken heart. But with OCD, parents are plunked down in the trenches without a battle plan. Your child has stopped listening to you, and you're at a loss for what to say. With your household turned upside down, how do you pull out of the wreckage?

What looks like controlling behavior from your child is his best effort to cope with this unmerciful tyrant in his ear. This is where you, his parent and teacher, can help your child relabel the voice of OCD and fight back. This chapter outlines the basic training for fighting OCD on the home front. It will take some time and planning to set up your battle plan. OCD won't go away on its own, but your child can retrain his brain to not get stuck on OCD and move on.

This chapter applies the nuts and bolts of behavior therapy described in Chapter 5 to the specific and immediate challenges of OCD at home. To get your child out of the OCD ambush, you need to be able to see it coming: we will first describe some telltale signs. Second, you and your child will need to agree on how and when to talk about OCD,

so we also detail how to develop a language and a communication system to have in place when OCD strikes.

Spotting OCD Moments: The Fork in the Air Is the Fork in the Road

Your child holds up a fork and asks, "Is this clean?" A reasonable question? Maybe if it didn't happen 20 times a day in any number of contexts: towels, chairs, food . . . your hands! How do you answer such a question? If you thought to *reassure,* "Of course it's clean, I promise it is," or to *reason,* "We only have clean silverware in the drawer; think about it, it was in the dishwasher, so it must be clean," or to *appease by avoidance,* "Here, don't use that, I'll wash another for you—see it is clean now," you've fallen into an OCD trap. *Reassurance* isn't a bad thing in and of itself—but with OCD it expires so quickly and it is endless, before you know it you have dug yourself into a black hole. Is there really any way to know 100 percent that something is clean? *Reasoning* with a child is usually a gratifying process; however, in an OCD moment, your child is not available to listen to reason, and will run headlong through any number of airtight explanations. *Accommodating* a situation rather than facing it head on is something we do all the time; however, it's one thing if it's to satisfy a preference and another thing if it's an avoidance out of fear. It's okay to switch that overcooked piece of chicken because your child *prefers* tender meat, but not okay to eat nothing but microwave TV dinners because your child thinks your pans are all contaminated.

All of these solutions are problematic because they've missed the point right from the start: Your child isn't asking you a *question* when he holds up that fork, he's having an *obsession* about contamination. Taking the question at face value is taking a brain hiccup and elevating it to the level of profound thought. Instead, look at the fork in the air as a fork in the road. If you answer, your child is going down the neverending path of pursuing certainty. If instead you label the brain trick that's happening for your child, she's making her way down the path that leads her anywhere she wants to go.

Telltale signs of an OCD moment are when your child:

- Insists on having an answer now.
- Needs to know in more detail than you think is necessary.
- Is awkwardly avoiding something ordinary.
- Is upset that things aren't exactly a certain way.

- Is unable to make a decision or answer a question because there's one *right* answer and he might be wrong.
- Is asking you to repeat phrases over and over again.

Tool Number One: The Framework or How to Explain OCD to Your Child

In Chapter 2, we mentioned how to discuss various aspects of OCD. The following are three more specific scripts to introduce the concept of OCD to your young child or adolescent.

A Script for Explaining OCD to Your Young Child (Ages 4–8)

Do you have bad thoughts that bother you; sticky thoughts that keep playing even though you don't want to listen to them? Maybe they'll say silly things—like numbers or words—or maybe scary things like, "Keep on washing so you don't get germs," or "You better do that again or something bad will happen." Well, that's a brain trick. Sometimes the brain gets stuck on one thought—it's just like when your battery-operated car gets stuck in front of the wall—the wheels are spinning because the battery is on, but it's not going anywhere. So when your brain gets stuck, you've got to pick it up and put it somewhere else just like you do with the car. Is it any fun when the car is stuck spinning its wheels? No, it's boring and it ruins the game. Same thing when your brain gets stuck—it blocks you from having fun. Now, I can help you boss back that brain trick so it doesn't bother you and mess up your fun. First, let's give it a name. Next tell me what you hate about it. Tell me what you want to say when it happens. Tell me what you want to do instead of listening to that brain trick. The neat thing is that the more you fight the brain trick, the weaker and weaker it will get so it doesn't bother you anymore.

A Script for Explaining OCD to Your Older Child* (Ages 9–13)

Some people have thoughts that get stuck in their minds and keep repeating. It's called OCD. If you think of your brain as a computer, then OCD is one small chip that keeps sending out the wrong message to the rest of the computer. So walking in the bathroom all kids might have the passing thought *Ooh gross, it's not that clean in here*, but for kids with OCD, the computer sends out a message on a loud speaker: "Danger!

---

* Adapted with permission from March & Mulle *OCD in Children and Adolescents,* Guilford Press, 1998.

danger! Stop what you are doing and fix this situation, or something terrible will happen!" So it's not that the bathroom *is* actually more dirty, it's just that the brain chip isn't working right and instead of a little whisper of a warning, it registers it as off the charts and sets off all the alarms. When your brain thinks you are in danger, it sends that message to the rest of your body. Then to get rid of the yucky fear feeling, you do things—washing a lot or a magical trick or pattern. But the more that you do that trick, the more it tricks you! It makes more and more things seem dirty or scary, and before you know it, you're feeling bad all the time and having to do more and more tricks to make it go away.

There is another answer. When the fear alarm goes off, you can boss it back and tell it that you are in charge of yourself and you're not going to fall for that brain trick. So you get mad at it, you refuse to listen to it, and you go do what you want to do. At first it's going to be scary to take the risk, but the more you fight the OCD, the stronger you get and the weaker the OCD gets.

Explanation for Teenagers

Imagine that it's a typical day, you're sitting in sixth period Chemistry class and Mr. Gallagher is describing the periodic table of elements— oxygen, hydrogen, nitrogen, helium. All of a sudden out of the clear blue for no reason, he starts to say, "I think we're going to have a fire, do you hear me? It's not safe in here. Fire! Fire! Fire!" At first you think—this is ridiculous, some kind of joke, he's lost it, but he goes on. You look out in the hallway to try to make sense of this, but there's no smoke, no flames, no fire alarm sounding, and no one is running through halls evacuating the building, but Mr. Gallagher is repeating the message—"You can't sit here, it could break out any second, don't you know the danger?" Against your better judgment, though there is no evidence to support what he's saying, you start to get nervous and worried, you want him to stop and you want to get out of there. That's kind of what's happening in your brain in this medical condition called OCD. There's a glitch in the filtering station and your brain sends out these "what if's" or "false alarms" that your body and mind respond to as real. Just because the message keeps repeating doesn't make it any more true. Even if Mr. G. says "fire" a thousand times, it won't cause even a spark, but it will make you feel really anxious like you have to get away from him. Could a fire ever break out? Sure, but you don't need to practice and prepare for it every second. If it's the real thing, you'll know how to respond. Once you know that those messages are due to a brain hiccup, you can start to disregard them, or even get angry at them, call them "bogus" and teach your brain to stop responding to them as if they were real. The more you fight the thoughts the less you have them.

Another way to picture OCD is imagining yourself as a CEO of a company and you have this assistant who keeps barging into your office every 10 minutes telling you exactly how much the company is worth, or which companies are a threat, or when the board of directors meeting is being held. How could you get any work done with these constant interruptions and unnecessary reminders? OCD is like that assistant who keeps reminding you or warning of things. If you were really that CEO, you would say, "Stop interrupting me, I can't think straight, call me only if you have newsworthy information." In essence, you are the CEO of your mind, you are in charge of operations, so that's how you want to respond to your brain when it's bothering you with intrusive thoughts or images—the more you practice this, the more your mind will learn to ignore those unnecessary messages.

Children may fight the notion that their "brain" can do something that is not "their fault," "it is *my* brain, so it must be doing what I want it to be doing." This is a revolutionary idea to your child that may take some time to sink in. Don't engage in a battle over making your child believe that you are right, but keep firm in your belief that OCD is a brain glitch and that you know your child wouldn't be choosing to do these symptoms if it were up to him.

There are several pieces of information that may help. Show your child the PET scan images in Chapter 1. Young children can draw their own pictures of the brain "labeling" the OCD part and the non-OCD part. Older children and teenagers may benefit from a brief explanation of the research. Letting children know that medications help this problem, like other medical problems, may facilitate their putting OCD in a no-fault biological context.

You can show your older child the websites dedicated to OCD and invite them to sit in on the teen chat rooms (see resource guide for site addresses). Finally, explain that children and adults all over the world—in Japan, France, India, and Israel, to name a few, all have the exact same types of OCD symptoms.

Tool Number Two: A Common Language—The Concept of Relabeling: This Changes Everything

Language is power. Think of the times you changed your child's mind about something by teaching her words for the experience. "That's just a bad dream, it didn't happen. That's a shadow, it's not a monster. You just hit a funny bone. That's a nose bleed. That's called *déjà vu*. That's your period. That's panic"—all these words for potentially frightening, albeit common, phenomena contain them, make them more knowable and therefore less frightening. By definition, putting a name on something means that it is describable, that it can be a shared experience. It shows that someone has been here before and that neutralizes the power it held over you when it was still a mystery. This concept of relabeling OCD is the cornerstone of UCLA psychiatrist Dr. Jeffrey Schwartz's *Brain Lock* book. Dr. Schwartz has changed the lives of countless adults with his method of relabeling OCD as brain static, devaluing its repetitive message, and refocusing on preferred non-OCD activities. Why has this intervention been so important? Because for decades, OCD sufferers assumed that their symptoms were in the same category as all the rest of their thoughts, meaningful and important to listen to. They racked their brains to figure out the psychological meaning of their thoughts and urges, a quest that led to more misery, guilt, and frustration. Unfortunately, bound by the limits of our knowledge, mental health professionals often held out the searchlight for patients in these ill-fated journeys.

Labeling the Real Bad Guy

One purpose of language as we've seen is to put a handle on experiences. A second purpose is that putting a name on the OCD (Worrywart, Brainlock, Question Monster) takes the child out of the hot seat and gives parent and child a common enemy. It is through this process of relabeling, as Dr. Schwartz says—"It's not *me*, it's OCD"—that kids can break the binds of OCD. In the highly effective behavior therapy program of child psychiatrist Dr. John March, the "not-me" of OCD is taken one step further by giving the OCD a separate name and character. Located outside the child, it becomes the OCD Monster, Brain Bug, Mr. Mighta, the Worrywart, the Scare Box. The enemy then becomes a character the child can visualize, draw, yell at, sculpt, crush, and ultimately defeat!

Let Your Child Decide How to Refer to OCD

OCD is his monster so it should be his choice. Ask your child how he wants to refer to OCD; note that he may need to switch names frequently so it doesn't become annoying. Many children, even ten- and eleven-year-olds, will enjoy giving the OCD a name, befitting its character—Bathroom Man, Disaster Man, The Picker, Checking Man. Younger children can use dramatic flair and name the OCD something relating to its preoccupation. Middle schoolers sometimes prefer naming it after its process: Junk Mail, Broken Record, Brain Hiccup,

Brain Trick. Adolescents may prefer to simply refer to it as OCD. You can get as creative as your child likes. The important thing is that you are making a distinction between OCD hiccups of the brain and the spontaneous, rational thoughts of your child's mind.

My colleague Dr. D'Arcy Lyness and I have found that having children "illustrate" the story of OCD by drawing pictures of the OCD monster or even making three-dimensional statues can be extremely

Portrait Gallery

Checker Man

Certainty Critter

Even Steven

Mr. Perfect

therapeutic. Putting a name to OCD nails down the elusive; visualizing and then creating the OCD with your own two hands enhances the transformation from something unknowable and frightening into something tangible and controllable. On page 182 are some sample portraits. Ask your child to draw and label his own. Use the empty frames below if it helps.

Name and Draw Your OCD Characters

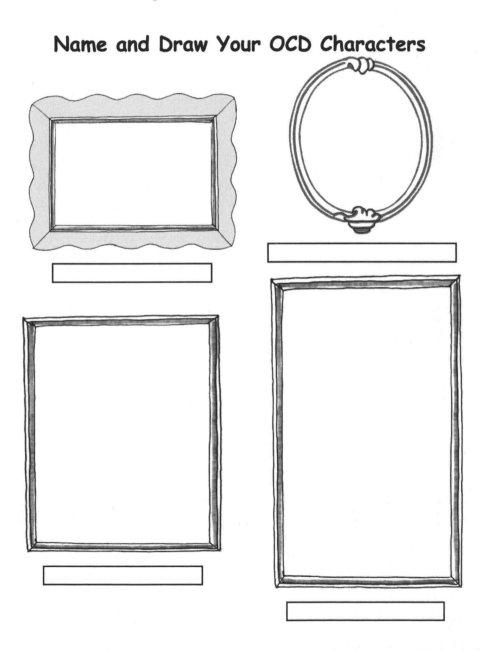

Tool Number Three: A Communication System

What is so frightening and frustrating to children with OCD is that they are having this intense experience of intrusive thoughts and urges, but they can't communicate about it. They don't really understand it themselves, and they have no language or metaphors to hook on to. So it's like having really big news—a really bad experience that you can't tell anyone about. What a recipe for stress, moodiness, anger, frustration, and isolation!

The most important intervention for parents is to give your child a language to communicate these strange experiences. It will help you externalize the OCD and not confuse it with your child. Then he can start to put things in perspective and regain executive control over his brain.

What Do You Say to the Enemy?

Some children have difficulty warming up to this exercise because it seems weird to "talk to yourself." The idea is that you are not locked into listening to what a bully (in this case, your brain) is telling you. Instead, you can break free—bust out and defend your territory. Asking your child what she says to a sibling when he's bothering her, or to a kid at school who is a pain, can help rally the "Knock it off, leave me alone" data bank. With younger children, you can ask them to imagine what a superhero like a Power Ranger or Batman would say if he were fighting off a bad guy.

The following questions can be helpful to build up your child's boss-back arsenal:

1. What makes you the most mad about OCD?
2. What do you want to say to the OCD?
3. What do you say to a bully who is bossing you around?
4. What would you rather be doing than listening to the OCD?
5. How do you want to be treated by your brain?

After compiling the list, your child can decide how to display it. You can make a colorful poster with markers, make "boss-back" stickers on the computer, or record a tape. One family made boss-back cards and whenever their child was struggling, he would choose a card from the deck. The cards had different boss-back calls: "You Don't Have to Do This!" "This Is Brain Lock," "Fight Hard, Be Free," and so on.

Then ask your child to make a list of what he wants to say back to his "fear" loudspeaker. Here are some samples from my patients:

Go away, meany, leave me alone!

Die, dread disease!

You need to go to bathroom school!

You are not my friend—you scare me and you don't tell the truth.

You are lame, you can only think about one thing.

Be gone, thou villainous rump-fed toad!

I've had enough of this stuff.

This isn't real.

It's not going to happen.

I'm the boss of me; I'm doing what I want.

Get a life OCD; you can't have mine!

It is important to establish with your child why she wants to get better. In that way, your child is asking you to help with *her* goals, as opposed to you bugging her about what you want. It's a very different dynamic. Gathering information about the goal can be accomplished in several ways. The exercise "On the Horizon" (see below) helps your child define the specific goals of what he wants to do—be able to touch

a soccer ball, stay at a sleepover, and so on. You can also get this information by completing this list with your child:

What do you hate about OCD?

What would you rather be doing instead?

When and How Much Help Does Your Child Need?

Some parents can read fear on their child's face. Still, it's important to quantify the fear with your child. This will help your child begin to see the variations in his fear level, to understand that not all fears are off the charts, and to graph his progress over time. Teach your child how to answer these questions (page 187) or use the fear thermometer from Chapter 5.

What Do You Want Us to Say to Help?

Every parent knows what happens when you say the wrong thing to your child. Here's an opportunity to enlist your child's help to provide

---

Fear-Meter • Help-Meter

1. How afraid are you?

   Low   Medium   High

   0   5   10

2. How much help do you want?

   Red Light   Yellow Light   Green Light

   Stay away, I'm okay   Stand by   Come in, I need you

---

suggestions for how you can talk about OCD with him. This doesn't guarantee that your child will cheerfully accept your help in the heat of the moment, but it does give you guidelines that you can refer to.

One child told me that her mother's saying "I understand" made her mad. What she wanted her mother to say is, "I'm on your side." Some children prefer that the parents get mad at the OCD for them; some children don't go for dramatic role play and prefer that you just relabel—"That's this OCD junk again, we don't have to do this." Of greatest importance is that you discuss with your child how to talk about this.

For some children the help they need from parents is less talk and more action. There are several jobs parents can have. Show this list to your child and ask for any given symptoms they are tackling, "what's my job?"

- Being a time keeper if for example your child is keeping washing to 1 minute.
- Physically moving your child through an exposure—walking him away from the sink, or out of the bathroom.
- Doing an activity such as playing cards or riding bikes as they are "waiting out" the anxiety after doing ritual prevention.

Putting the Pieces Together: The Action Plan for OCD Moments

The stage is now set. You have made all the preparations to battle OCD head on. The plan is as follows:

1. Reflect what your child is feeling.
2. Relabel the problem as OCD.
3. Resist OCD rules with show and tell.
4. Refocus on a preferred activity.
5. Reinforce your child's efforts at fighting.

1. Reflect What Your Child Is Feeling

Although you want to stop what your child is doing, it's best not to come across like that to your child. If you don't empathize, your child will feel that you just want him to stop what he's doing because it's bothering you. When you empathize, your child knows you know that he's in a predicament, not that he's choosing to engage in the behavior, so he doesn't have to feel blamed or ashamed for being afraid. Remember, don't respond to the specific content of your child's behavior, because that will distract both of you from the fact that your child is stuck in a trap. Bottom line: Empathize with your child, don't engage with the OCD.

So, first and foremost, reflect the situation. Try using the following communications. Say them definitively, simply, and genuinely. Be prepared to be shot down. Think of empathy as taking a step toward your child; you can also do this nonverbally, for instance by assuming an open posture and tone of voice to express warmth and acceptance. With teenagers it can help to use slang, it is disarming in the best sense; they may even laugh at your bumbling effort to be "hip" and this may lower the temperature on the moment.

> It feels so scary to take this risk.
>
> You are stuck.
>
> You are scared.
>
> You feel like you can't.
>
> This is so hard.
>
> You are really struggling.
>
> It feels dangerous to you.

2. Relabel the Problem as OCD

Your child needs reminders that this is a brain trick happening for no good reason, because the OCD is making him feel like there is a reason to be scared. Here's where you draw on the words you've agreed upon to discuss this:

This is a brain glitch.

This is OCD.

Your brain is getting stuck in a trap.

The worry wart is bossing you around.

I hear the buzzing of brain bug.

It's that trickster OCD.

That sounds like something OCD would say.

It's a false alarm.

3. Resist OCD Rules with Show and Tell

The OCD won't let your child get through the normal tasks of the day. This is where you help your child remember what he *wants* to be doing and help him jump the groove of the broken record of OCD. By shifting the emphasis from the content of the symptoms ("Is it clean?" "Is it safe?") to the crux of your child's life ("What do you want to be doing now?"), you are conveying your confidence that your child can do this challenge and that he deserves to have his life! This is pointing to the fork in the road. You want to help your child see that going down the road of OCD only leads to more OCD, whereas taking the risk to fight the OCD leads to freedom, fun, life!

Now encourage your child to take the risk of fighting the OCD. Drawing on answers to the questions "What do I hate about OCD" and "What's on the Horizon?" you can coach your child to refrain from engaging in the ritual or to do the ritual wrong. Use the ten-minute rule to fight the ritual for ten-minute blocks, tracking your child's fear temperature so that you can both watch it drop. If your child is still anxious at the end of ten minutes, encourage him to try for another ten; if he can't fight any longer and engages in the ritual, he has still succeeded in regaining some control. A successful exposure is when your child's anxiety drops at least 2 points on his fear thermometer (scale of 1–10), so try to help your child keep fighting until this drop. For many children using this method, their anxiety will completely resolve within the ten minutes, they will have "forgotten" about the OCD and be ready to move on.

Show OCD Who Is Boss

- "Do you want to be doing this now?"
- "What would you rather do instead of having to worry?"

- "Let's Show this OCD who is in charge."
- "You don't have to be a robot, you can do what you want."
- "How do you want to break OCD's rules?"
- "Do the ritual wrong."
- "Do it shorter."
- "Refuse to do it and walk away."
- "Do it while singing a song."

Tell the OCD Who's the Boss

Here is where you draw on your child's "boss back talk" lines. If he can't boss back the OCD himself, boss it back for him: "OCD leave my son alone, he has better stuff to do than to be dealing with you, you are a troublemaker and we're not going to listen to you."

- Tell the OCD what you think of it.
- Tell OCD it's not your job to worry!
- Tell OCD that you aren't going to follow its rules!
- Tell OCD you have better things to do.

To help your child get mad at the tricks OCD is trying to pull you can use the Old Tape/New Tape exercise. Your child first says what OCD is saying and then can "argue with OCD" and make a new tape of what he wants to hear instead. So if OCD is saying, "You might have bumped into that person's private parts," the new message would be, "If I bumped into someone I would know it! And even if I did bump, so what? That doesn't make me a bad person." Or, for a child whose OCD says, "You better check the lights because there could be a fire and it will be your fault!" She can say instead, "I know what's safe enough. It's not my job to go overboard."

4. Refocus on a Preferred Activity

Your child has bossed back OCD with show and tell. Now he needs to *pick up his brain* and put it where *he* wants it to be. You are moving your child out of the OCD moment and focusing instead on the big picture—being free, being in charge. Remember that your child will feel anxiety now from breaking the ritual, but that anxiety will pass if he is not engaging in obsessing or doing rituals. Rather than waiting for the feeling to pass, get busy with something else.

Dr. Schwartz writes in *Brain Lock* that OCD is powerful but it's also limited, well frankly, "stupid" because it can only do one thing—

Old Tape
What the OCD says:

New Tape
What you want to hear instead:

put doubts in your mind. The way you outwit it is by refocusing; "if you stand right in front of this stupid but powerful opponent, it will knock you right over." Get moving is what Dr. Schwartz advocates. Walk away from the OCD situation and do something else that is enjoyable and functional. Remember that when your child shifts brain gears to an activity that he likes and wants to do, in effect he is changing his brain chemistry, and retraining his brain to shift out of OCD mode. Take another look at the PET scans from Chapter 1 to see this effect in black and white.

- Let's keep moving; let's pick up your brain and put it where you want it to be.
- OCD doesn't deserve your time, let's do what you want to do.
- The bad feelings will go away if we keep moving.
- Let's do those brain teaser questions; let's go biking, let's shoot some hoops.

5. Reinforce Your Child's Efforts at Fighting

Freeing your child of OCD is a battle won one step at a time. You want to reinforce any effort that your child makes at distinguishing himself from the OCD and breaking its rules. For example, if your child fights the rituals or curtails them but ends up going back and doing them, focus on the success, "You bossed that back," or "You saw that it was OCD and you knew how to fight," rather than focusing on the loss.

The main message here is: "Good for you, you're teaching your brain a lesson. Rather than have those OCD thoughts race around and around like a hamster running in a wheel, you're teaching your brain a new way out of that loop. The more you fight it, the faster your brain will learn!

In Chapter 7 we discussed the ins and outs of reward systems. In addition to verbal praise, the key with a tangible reward is that your child should feel acknowledged for his hard work, and that the reward should be something he likes. For older children this may be a new CD, stretching a curfew, or even cash. For younger children, celebratory ice cream outings, a movie, or an extra bedtime story can work. One idea contributed by Kristine Fruehling is to put small prizes under your child's pillow from the "Bravery Fairy." This may be especially appropriate for younger children who can't wait it out for stickers or points.

Pounce on every positive result of your child's efforts. Look for opportunities to praise her hard work, even if she isn't 100 percent successful. The language of progress is praise:

I am proud of you.

You are going to win this battle.

You are a real fighter.

You handled that situation really well.

Wow, I'd be afraid of you if I were OCD!

You are one tough kid.

It must feel good to be in charge, good going!

Check back with your child to see how he felt about handling an OCD moment. What worked best? Encourage him to reflect on his strategies and their effectiveness. The language of progress is strategy:

How did it feel to boss back OCD?

What kind of trouble was it making for you—how did it try to ruin things?

How did you say "No" to OCD—what did you think to yourself?

What helped you to fight back?

OCD Situations: Types of Intervention— Accommodation and Active Challenges

Accommodation: A Necessary Interim Solution

Accommodating? Isn't that enabling, isn't that giving in to the OCD? Many parents have been accused of "enabling" their child, a term borrowed from the Alcoholics Anonymous nomenclature, meaning that your actions are allowing your child to manipulate you and dig deeper into the problem. What's wrong with this formulation is that it casts the child in the role of "wanting to" manipulate his parents; turning OCD into the child's "bad behavior" that kids should stop on their own. OCD is not bad behavior. Everyone wants to dig out of the OCD—your child most of all; your role is to empower your child to do so.

To many, *accommodating* is a dirty word. It's what you don't want to do with OCD. While it is true that you don't want to go out of your way to make room for OCD, you cannot expect it to disappear immediately when you begin addressing it. Just as Rome wasn't built in a day, winning over OCD is going to take time, planning, and perseverance. To maintain a winning edge on the home front, it is as important to keep your child fighting the OCD in the situations within his reach as it is to accommodate those that are not. Your child's therapist can help you sort this out. There will be compromises. When your child has not yet tackled a problem in behavioral therapy, you have to make alternate arrangements to live with the symptom. It may be necessary to comply with the OCD conditionally in the interim. For example, if your child seeks reassurance through repeated questions, you can limit the number of questions or answers in a day. Some families use question coupons, with which the child can budget himself, while others have a two-time repeat limit.

A second type of accommodation is when you make a change in the environment to avoid a potential OCD situation. For example, eight-year-old Becky has trouble choosing underwear each day because it has to fit just right. Every morning she picks through the many pairs in her drawer, trying them on to find the one pair that fits just right on the first try. This ritual could take half an hour. Because not finding the perfect fit was a 10 on her fear ladder, Becky was not ready to fight the Perfect Underwear Monster. To lower the bar, we limited the pairs of underwear in her drawer to five, cutting the time on this ritual to about five minutes.

For twelve-year-old Peter, his OCD makes it very difficult to make decisions—each choice of clothing, food, movies, and so on, is monumental and creates much anguish, for if he makes the "wrong" decision, he fears something bad will happen. Lowering the bar for Peter meant taking many decisions out of his hands. For example, his parents made out a menu for the week and posted movie time and play time.

Active Challenges: Focus on What Your Child Can Do

Your child will get homework for daily challenges from his behavior therapist. For a compulsive hand washer, the homework might be to touch the floor and not wash your hands. Hitting the bull's-eye for that assignment would be not to do the ritual (for example, touch the floor and walk away). Occasionally your child will hit the bull's-eye; more often, your child will at least hit the board. These are not "failures" but the moments you want to capitalize on. Focus on what your child can do, not what he can't. Remember that the idea is to encourage the spirit of breaking the rules of the OCD, and there are many ways to do this. Whenever your child is showing you that he can't do the homework or is saying that it is too hard, you can help him find what he can do. Here is a list of ways you can help:

- Have your child do the OCD wrong—do the ritual backward, change the "magic" word, do the ritual the "wrong" number of times.
- Suggest your child sing the ritual instead of saying it.
- Say, "See how long you can fight doing the ritual, one minute? five minutes?"
- "Pretend you are your superhero—Elvis, Superman, Super Mario—how would you fight the OCD?"
- Do the boss back talk for your child.
- Write lower-level challenges on slips of paper, put them in a jar, and have your child pick an easier challenge to do.

Use flexibility when your child gets stuck: break down the task into smaller manageable chunks. If your child has a counting ritual and was supposed to fight it on a reading assignment, do it for half the assignment or every other page. Have her fight it every other page and switch off with you reading every other page. If your child can't meet his goal of using a towel from the bottom of the pile (contaminated) instead of from the top, compromise: let him use one from the middle. If he is afraid to look out the window with the shade up, how about the shade half way down? If a young child is struggling to brush his teeth without rituals, split the job with him: you brush the top half and he'll brush the bottom. If you can find a middle ground on a "too difficult" exposure, your child will get more confident *during* the task and may actually be able to go on to do the intended goal. If you don't break things down, your child may give up and be even more anxious next time.

Creativity helps, too—not the artistic kind, but in having the flexibility to open up the solutions that are not immediately obvious. Bring your family into the process. Siblings and even the family dog make for great co-therapists. "Rover, what do you think Mary wants to do more, wash or take you for a walk?" Talk to your imaginary audience. "Get a load of this, I can't get him to do his chores, and I pay him allowance; OCD is getting him to do all these jumping jacks and steals his time to boot!" Or, "hmm, she's asking me if the shirt is clean, I don't know, let me pose that question to the shirt, 'Excuse me shirt, would you say that you are clean enough?'"

The Strategy in Action

Case One: Parent Isn't Directly Part of the Ritual

Mara's mother had had it. "I'm a prisoner in my own home, I have to be quiet all the time so Mara can do her prayer rituals. Why do I have to tiptoe?" "Because you're messing everything up, I have to start all over again," Mara cries back. "You don't care—you don't care what happens to me." Who's the bad guy here? Mara and her mom are pointing fingers at each other. This is a perfect recipe for a power struggle as well as fertile ground for the OCD to grow.

Using the strategy, Mara has given her mom permission to help her fight one nighttime prayer ritual—to limit it from thirty minutes to ten. Here are the steps they now use when Mara gets upset:

Reflect: "Mara, I know you are trying so hard, and it's just not easy work."

Relabel: "This is not you—it's the brain trap. You're going to get out of it, and I'll help you."

Resist the OCD with Show and Tell: "I know you don't want to be doing this now, you want to get a good night's sleep before that algebra quiz," "It's not fair that the OCD is making you worry now, you want to be refreshed for tomorrow," "How long do you want this prayer to be?" You show the OCD that you are in charge—you know how you want to pray." "Let's boss it back—tell the OCD to take a hike—you can sing the prayer—instead of repeating it." "Can you tell the OCD to leave you alone, that you've got important things to do in your life and you're not going to waste your energy on this."

Redirect: "OK, now that you shortened the ritual we've got time to snuggle—let's get a book and read before bed."

Reinforce: "I'm proud of you—you are really working hard at this. I think your conviction about what's important is really going to help you. You sounded really strong when you said that part about OCD not knowing what a prayer really is."

Case Two: Example of the Parents' Role When They Are Part of the Ritual

For Fannie, going to bed at night was something she dreaded—her OCD, "Mistake Man" would bother her every night with all the bad things she'd done since she was a small child, the time she threw carrots at a party, in kindergarten when she scratched a classmate, the time she took money from her mother's wallet, she couldn't get it out of her head. Fannie's mom had been hearing "confession" for months until they learned another way.

At bedtime, when Fannie says, "Mom, I'm really feeling bad about the bad things I've done," Fannie and her mom have found a creative way to boss it back.

Reflect: "Fannie, I know this makes you feel really bad."

Relabel: "Those old thoughts are getting stuck again. It sounds like Mistake Man is trying to trick you into thinking that you are a bad person, that just because you've made a few mistakes, you're bad. I think *he's* the one making a big mistake!"

Resist the OCD with Show and Tell: Let's show Mistake Man that you know that it's okay to make mistakes, that people learn by making mistakes. Why don't you sing me all the bad things you've done, and the chorus can be, "We're bad, we're bad, we're really,

really bad." Yeh, let's do a rap song, I think Mistake Man will really enjoy that. You see if we show him that you're not afraid of being "bad" then he won't be able to scare you anymore.

Redirect (after several inspired verses of "we're bad"): That was really fun, I don't think Mistake Man has a chance now, let's do some more singing, how about "My Favorite Things" from the *Sound of Music?*

Reinforce: Good for you, I'm proud of you! You are teaching your brain a good lesson. It's bedtime, and you don't have to be stuck with those thoughts in the net, you're breaking free!

While this five-step system may seem cumbersome at first, over time you will learn from your child what steps you can "skip" because she is already doing them and which steps you need to emphasize because she is having trouble accomplishing the goal of that step. As you read over the list and think about what steps you are already doing, look at what you need to practice. This will help narrow your task. Write out cue cards for yourself. It's not cheating, and it may help your child feel like she's got company in learning a new way of handling OCD moments.

GUIDELINES FOR COACHES

- Do listen seriously to your child's fears, frustration, and distress. Remember that it has to feel very scary in order for your child to believe it.
- Accept that fears are real to your child.
- Acknowledge what you hear.
- Don't try to talk your child out of his fears.
- Don't make fun of your child for his fears.
- Don't compare your child's reactions to others'.
- Let your child choose the goal for the week.
- Freedom comes from untangling step by step, not by obliterating the enemy.
- Freedom comes from pointing out the other path.
- Make a distinction between your child and the symptoms.
- Distinguish OCD symptoms from your child's thoughts.
- Externalize the OCD by giving it a name.
- Help your child relabel what's going on as an OCD moment with choices.
- Don't work out a plan in the moment.

CHAPTER 9

Pressure Points in OCD

I'm in Kmart and my daughter is screaming at the top of her lungs. It was supposed to be a reward, but none of the dolls are just right. We're madly rooting through to find a box that's not nicked or dented. I know she shouldn't be screaming; my heart is going a mile a minute trying to settle her. I know I've just got to get her out of there. I've got a kid who's losing it, but the looks I get from people . . . then some guy mumbles something about Child Protective Services. If he even had a clue about what was really going on.

—*Mother of six-year-old with OCD*

There are times when OCD launches a horrific disturbance in your family. Moments like these touch down like a tornado in your living room, leaving you to wade through the wreckage. For some families these notorious scenes are a daily reality, while for others they happen only occasionally when, for example, sleep deprivation tips the scales and your child "loses his cool." This chapter details how to handle moments when things teeter on the edge of explosion and how to set up daily life to run smoothly to put more of a buffer between you and that edge.

Trigger Points: Trouble Shooting in the Heat of the Moment

Crises can escalate in the blink of an eye for a child with OCD; even quicker if other neurobiological challenges such as wired-in impulsivity, inflexibility, sensory integration deficits, or learning disabilities are stirred into the mix. Parents struggle not only with how to set a limit, but *whether* to do it at all; maybe it's better to stay out of harm's way. The key is knowing when and how to set limits that don't escalate the situation, which may involve modifying your parenting approach and objectives for now.

Parenting is a top-down endeavor; in order for parents to help children be more flexible and nonexplosive, they need to make sure to have those departments covered themselves. In his book, *The Explosive Child,* Dr. Ross Greene captures this idea with the following equation:

$$\text{Inflexibility} + \text{Inflexibility} = \text{Meltdown}$$

Here is a quick checklist of Dos and Don'ts for parents to monitor their own degree of self-control in the heat of the moment:

- Don't dig in to prove a point—your power is in being flexible enough to walk away—after all isn't that what you are asking your child to do?
- Don't get louder when your child isn't listening—re-evaluate his readiness to listen at that moment.
- Don't threaten specific consequences in the middle of an argument—you may not want to enforce them later and that will teach your child not to take you seriously.
- Don't name call or be verbally aggressive or abusive.
- Don't use physical aggression.
- Do apologize if you "lose it" with your child.
- Do learn the early warning signs for your losing control.
- Do learn anger management strategies such as walking away, counting, punching pillows.

It's Not Their Fault: Why Children with OCD "Lose It"

When parents understand that children with OCD explode not to manipulate or because they are bad kids, but rather because their brain circuits are overloaded, they can approach their children with compassionate guidance. In their book, *Teaching the Tiger,* an excellent resource addressing the educational needs of children with OCD, ADHD, and TS, authors Dr. Marilyn Dornbush and Sheryl Pruitt describe how children with neurobiological disorders experience "storms" with over-arousal. When stress increases, children feel more and more on edge, the feeling of being out of control enters and then the pressure builds up and explodes. Their ability to comprehend consequences of actions is impaired, and any additional input—visual, verbal and tactile—increases the storm and may contribute to a more violent outburst. Afterwards these children may be surprised and feel remorse—they had no idea what they did or why.

Dr. Ratey and Dr. Johnson in *Shadow Syndromes* present a surprising explanation for why this may occur. Children with OCD have "noisy brains"; the constant din of "what ifs, oh no's, watchouts" is a sort of mental static that creates stress just like standing next to a jackhammer or being at a Rock concert. However, unlike OCD, the noise in those situations is short-lived and escapable. Drs. Ratey and Johnson describe how sometimes rage or outbursts—intense and blaring—are the antidotes to brain noise and have an organizing effect on the mind. Like blowing a whistle at a schoolyard full of buzzing children, everything comes to a halt. Melting down and blowing up are not adaptive solutions, but neither are they "bad behavior"; rather, they may be a child's attempt to force a crescendo to an otherwise relentless drone of irritating brain noise.

When your child is struggling in an OCD moment, it's as if he's in a fight with someone. Proceed as you would if you were walking in on a fight. You don't immediately start by listening to each side of the argument. You divide and conquer. Separate the two parties—in this case your child and the OCD—to help your child calm down. If you immediately begin to engage with your child around the OCD, you will be escalating the battle. If he were able to say it wasn't important to get all his shoes lined up perfectly, then he wouldn't have needed you in the first place. So inflammatory is the situation already, that trying to reason at this point is like throwing gasoline on the fire. Your child will be forced to argue with you, or at least respond to your input. He is not ready for input.

Picture that in an OCD moment, all circuits are busy, so laden with conflicting messages—*this is crazy, I'm such a jerk, I'll never be clean, it's in me*—if your child hears any more of almost anything, he will combust. He is only ready for containment. You want to stay calm yourself, moving your child out of the situation and helping him calm down: "We will deal with that, you are out of control now. We need to slow it down now; we can't get this sorted out like this." Trying to talk plain *sense* only prolongs his negative experience of being out of control. It's not his fault that it happened, but it is his job to learn to control it. This will help him be more sturdy even in his weakest moments and it will help him to not feel guilty for beating up on you. You've cared enough to say *Stop*.

Encouraging Self-Control and Responsibility, Not Blame

How do you handle these outbursts? Though OCD is not your child's fault, he needs your help in setting limits on this problem in his life. This is one place where OCD is no different from other parenting challenges.

When your child is escalating, the goal is:

- Not to stop the outburst.
- To slow it down.
- Not to add fuel to the fire.

Children need help with limits for two primary reasons. First, they need help limiting the territory the OCD is claiming in their lives; it's not really a fair fight otherwise. Second, all children need practice learning tolerance for frustration. Though it is often tempting for parents to accommodate the OCD by complying with rituals, or accommodating a child's wishes because of the difficult life he has, accommodation deprives the child of important opportunities to practice tolerating frustration. Over time, it can also create a reverse hierarchy, in which the child senses that he or she can call the shots. While on the surface this may seem like every child's dream, in reality it is overwhelming because he's in way over his head. Also, it puts your child at a disadvantage because being out of control isn't an effective strategy in most situations. Granted, the "practicing" of tolerance for frustration is often unpleasant, too, and may even get downright ugly, but remember that this can happen even if your child doesn't have OCD. It is one of the necessary evils of life. Is it better to practice and get competent at something difficult than to avoid it altogether and cross your fingers it doesn't happen. All of us have witnessed or starred in our own variation of parent contortionist, coaxing a screaming child out of a store—"It's not fair!" or "I wanted the big one" or even, "You're a jerk" echoing in the air like the stroke of Big Ben. Kids get frustrated. They have to learn frustration tolerance and limits. The stakes are made higher by OCD, but the answer is the same. You need to give your child practice at dealing with frustration and discomfort in small doses so that she can build up her security in knowing that she can cope and survive. The goal is not stopping the outburst, but rather managing it by not adding to it, by containing it, and by discussing it afterward so that your child can learn how to handle the feelings without major unpleasantness.

While you can't live your life watching every step, it is important to know that just having OCD is so stressful that your child may be more reactive and have difficulty rallying his resources to cope with relatively benign interactions. Start small.

Many parents wonder, *How much of what I'm seeing is in fact OCD? Is this a temper tantrum? fatigue? Just what is going on with my child?* Assume that all factors are operating at all times, and the bottom line is that your child's doing the best he can with what he's got. In the meantime, you have a crisis on your hands, and your main job is to slow it all down. Here are some basic guidelines for dealing with crisis moments:

Managing an Escalation/Managing OCD Moments

DOS
- Stop. Pull back, breathe, don't go with your first reaction.
- Approach calmly, proceed with caution.
- Contain. Stop, drop, and roll. Don't deal with the cause/source of the fire. Reestablish safety either by setting a limit or removing your child from the situation.
- Talk slowly and calmly.
- Label what's going on: "It looks like you are stuck. You are really having a hard time now."
- Give feedback—later. Once the calm has been restored—whether it's in five minutes or the next day—process what happened, get your child to reflect on it, get the appropriate response from your child for next time.

DON'TS
- Don't wait until you have an unavoidable eruption—nip it in the bud.
- Don't panic. If you are out of control, leave the room briefly until you are ready to go in calmly. Would you want a frenzied fire-fighter trying to rescue your loved ones?
- Don't take this opportunity to criticize or correct your child.
- Don't use threats: "Now you've done it, you're in for it now."
- Don't try to reason with your child about the situation.
- Don't discuss the what or why until your child is calm enough to hear you.

An Ounce of Prevention: Fostering Constructive Approaches to Frustration and Anger

Encourage your child to talk about his feelings rather than acting them out.

We expect children to know how to handle anger, but we send them to school to learn how to multiply and divide. Teaching a child to express his feeling in words rather than actions gives your child more control over himself and his environment; it increases his chances of being understood rather than reprimanded. "I'm getting frustrated; this is too hard; I'm getting angry; I don't understand, I need to be alone; I can't talk now," are examples of what children can be encouraged to say. When you discuss managing anger with your child, make clear that *feeling* angry is always valid and important but there are ways to express it that are appropriate or not. Children can also be encouraged to take a few minutes to cool down so that they don't say or do something that they regret; this is how you can prevent a little anger from turning into a big storm. Reinforce your child for expressing anger appropriately and showing self-control.

The following suggestions can be used to redirect or slow down the storms when things are heating up for your child.

YOUNG CHILD
- I can't hear you when you are shouting.
- When you can talk to me in a regular voice then I can help you figure this out.
- You need to stop shouting now and then I can help you.

To create a teaching moment with a young child, share one of your own experiences of anger. Young children love to hear stories about their parents; Share a story of when you were young and got angry and what happened, or even a recent anecdote of how you handled your anger (or didn't handle it).

MIDDLE SCHOOLER
- Slow down so we can talk this out.
- I know you don't want to lose your cool.
- Is this worth losing privileges over?

Middle schoolers want to understand feelings and have a heightened sensitivity to interpersonal relationships; all of this is fascinating to them. With these children, it is most fruitful to let them talk it out: "What happened, let's figure out what you want to do about it." Because managing feelings is something children this age are trying to be expert at, even though it is new to them, they may easily feel evaluated for not being successful enough or doing it wrong. Make sure to be encouraging of their efforts.

TEENAGERS
- Hey, I want to know what's going on but slow down so I can hear you.

- Taking the car without asking means that is a punishable crime, we'll talk about that later, let's talk about what happened.

Be matter of fact; teenagers are only too ready to tune parents out for "wigging out" at them. State things plainly and calmly. Talk in the third person and follow your child's lead when he's telling you something about himself by talking about a friend: don't push for a confession.

Strategies to Cool Down a Hot Moment

COGNITIVE: COOL DOWN TALK
- You've got ice in your veins.
- Slow it down.
- My power is in staying in control.
- Put on the brakes.
- Count to 10.
- Keep your cool.
- Don't blow up it's not worth it.
- Breathe.
- Focus.
- This isn't a big deal, I can handle it.
- I am in control.

BEHAVIORAL
- Walk away.
- Take deep breaths.
- Squeeze your hands and release.
- Count to 10.

Generate alternative responses through problem solving. Go through the following steps:

1. Identify the problem.
2. Think about the consequences of an inappropriate response.
3. Identify your goal.
4. Generate solutions to meeting that goal.
5. Evaluate and choose the best solution.
6. Evaluate the results of that solution.

When your child erupts in anger, it's of no use to ask your child why: if they had the presence of mind to explain it, they wouldn't have done it. If a child has broken a house rule (shouting, hitting, etc) you need to re-establish the limits. Give your child a chance to tell you the rule he broke rather than you telling him; this allows him to "get an answer right" and rather than be lectured at, become a more active participant in the process. Then restate his answer and reinforce, "Right, we don't hit and we use words because hitting hurts others," or with a teenager, "Yes, destroying property is unacceptable and it doesn't solve the problem." Review with your child how she will handle the situation next time and whether there are signals that you can give to help prevent your child from escalating; for example, "The temperatures rising, I see a storm brewing, the volcano is starting to smoke, time to get a grip, we've got to slow things down." Finally, have the child make reparations—apologize, repair damage, chip in with allowance money, write an apology letter. Resist forcing an apology; it is better belated and from the heart than instantaneous and not genuine. If there is an extreme situation (screaming in public, hitting, breaking property), give a consequence such as the removal of a privilege (no TV, or car, one less bedtime story). Don't feel pressured to decide on the consequence at the moment; often the consequences parents say in the heat of the moment are the ones they will never keep. Wait until you've calmed down enough to give a consequence that you will stick to and that is appropriate to the transgression. Make it clear that you know that it is not your child's fault that he gets into his temper, but that he is responsible for his actions.

Looking at Early Storm Warnings: Examples of Hope

The following anecdotes illustrate first what happens when children are in charge, and second what happens when parents reclaim authority and direction.

Six-year-old Hope has had OCD since she was three years old. It began with perseverations about certain cartoon characters, leading to contamination fears and a multitude of just-so patterns that seemed to be increasing by the second. Every moment of life seemed to be regimented by a certain sequence, a particular placement, an exact wording. If these conditions were not met, Hope would become instantly distressed and would go on a rampage—crying, screaming, sometimes even hitting. Hope's parents watched with terror as their little daughter deteriorated so rapidly and dramatically. The red cup was on the left—it was always on the right, the juice had to be exactly even in each cup. She would shake, moan, and scream at her parents.

Hope's parents became well-trained in avoiding the explosive stage; as soon as Hope began moaning and pacing, they would race around to fix whatever was wrong, if they could. That was impossible, of course.

There was always that unforeseen situation. One afternoon Hope was in the backyard playing under the hose. She had just been to a store, a frustrating and overstimulating environment for her. On a whim, her younger sister borrowed one of Hope's old bathing suits. Hope took one look at her and acting as if she were possessed, started screaming at the top of her lungs, pulling at her skin. She couldn't stop screaming. Her mother, desperate to stop the screaming and calm Hope down, immediately took the suit off Hope's sister. Here is a child whose OCD and the added challenge of sensory integration deficits made her vulnerable to experiencing more frustration; her response was so powerful that she never really had the chance to learn normal developmental frustration tolerance. Importantly, there may be days like this even if your child is better prepared to handle herself emotionally. The maxim, "Today was bad (awful), tomorrow will be better" applies here.

While not an easy situation for any parent, what's missing here is that the parents do not have a handle on Hope's behavior; they don't understand what's happening, and they don't have the words or ideas to redirect it. Instead, Hope's OCD and six-year-old entitlement is at the wheel and she is careening out of control. Let's now look at Hope a few months later, after her parents have been doing behavior therapy for OCD.

The focus of Hope's OCD is now evenness. From the braids in her hair to the tension in her shoelaces, everything has to be even. One afternoon the family was driving Hope's older sister back from a birthday party. As soon as her sister got into the car with goody bag in hand, Hope began, "It's not fair," and within seconds she was shouting, crying, and kicking her feet. Fairness is a big issue for six-year-olds, but for Hope it is exacerbated by the OCD. She began to moan and scream, "Where's my bag? I have to have my bag! Go get my bag! It's not right, I need to have my bag to make it right." Mom and Dad took a spontaneous risk and began role playing "Even Steven (their name for OCD)." "You are not my friend, Even Steven, all you do is make me feel bad and sad. You are not nice, it doesn't have to be even—I wasn't invited to the party." "Steven" (played by Dad) replies: "Nah uh, you should have a bag, you want a bag, you didn't get one." Mom comes back with, "You make me so mad. Stop teasing me. You're not my friend, you are mean!" Hope's parents could see in the rearview mirror that her scowl was turning into a look of bewilderment: Mom and Dad didn't escalate and neither did Hope. They all did better having someone else to blame.

In this scenario, Hope's parents were successful in defusing an explosion without directly confronting Hope. Later they discussed the situation with her. They empathized that it was hard not to get a goody bag, how tough it was that Even Steven really bothers her about fairness, and then asked her how she could boss him back. Hope said, "I would tell him he's mean and bossy to me." After reinforcing Hope's solution, her parents reiterated that the way to handle herself the next time she's upset is to "tell, don't yell."

Preventing Eruptions: Know Your Child's Triggers

"How can I tell when my child is in over his head?" "What can my child deal with at any given moment?" "It's like she's a bomb, and I'm walking through a minefield." It's like sensing the weather. You want to begin to be able to predict the storm patterns and intervene as early as possible when you see the storm starting to brew. Stress accretes, so you don't want to add to it when your child is already heading toward meltdown. Take five-year-old Mark. He is angry because his mother would not re-make the macaroni and cheese that his babysitter made, and he believes that the babysitter's food is contaminated. His mother, setting a limit, says that she will not remake the macaroni, so off he storms to the couch. Brooding, his world not right, the anguish of the imperfection eating away at him; it's like completing a 2,000-piece jigsaw puzzle only to find the last piece is gone, irretrievable. Mark is overstimulated by this frustration—all circuits busy. Then Dad walks in to see how he's doing, notices that he has flour in his hair, and thinks that Mark must have leaned on the table where Mom was making pizza. Thinking that it might cheer him up to joke with him, Dad says, "Mark, is it snowing in the kitchen? What's all this white stuff in your hair?" Kaboom! Incredulous, Mark's dad watches in surrealistic slow motion as the flames, the smoke, the bomb go off. He sees the mistake he made, but it's too late with Mark, who's screaming and running around the house, shaking his head, and pulling at his hair. What caused this? Just an ordinary day's collections of events and one straw that broke the camel's back.

Parents may be very familiar with what sets off their child, if not, track your child's meltdowns for a few weeks writing down (a) the antecedent, (b) the problem behavior, and (c) the consequence. Not only will you identify triggering situations, but you may learn that you are reacting to your child's behavior in ways that are reinforcing it. Here are some tips:

- Avoid your child's triggering situations (when possible) until they are ready to handle them: If your child gets crazed every time she's in a department store . . . don't take her until she has more control.

- Be mindful to not overschedule your child's day: many children need down time between activities.
- If your child has trouble with transitions, keep them to a minimum; give them reminders before: you need to turn off the TV in 5 minutes, 2 minutes, now!
- If your child has trouble making decisions, take many decisions out of her hands. Rather than do you want to take the bus today or drive, make a chart for bus days and driving days.
- If your child gets bored easily, brainstorm a list of activities that he can always do if he's at a loss.

When Should Parents Make an "Issue" of Something

Discipline used to be about stopping a behavior, in any manner possible at any cost. The result was that kids got yelled at when they were least able to hear, felt resentment and humiliation, and plotted their retaliation. Discipline is now understood as an essential piece of a child's ability to regulate him- or herself. The parents' efforts at discipline should be directed at galvanizing self-control rather than insisting on submissiveness. How do you know when to put your foot down? What is a battle worth fighting?

Dr. Greene in the *Explosive Child* has a system to help parents "choose their battles." This book is an excellent guide to the ins and outs of managing explosive children, a quick summary follows, but readers are encouraged to get the book and live by it! First write out the top ten issues that bother you and sort them in three baskets. Basket A is best kept fairly empty except for the essential safety issues: no harming others or destroying of property. These issues are important enough that parents would do anything to enforce, even endure a meltdown over. For Basket A issues there is no negotiation. Basket B is where the action is; it contains those issues that are important, currently unattainable but that your child is ready to learn new skills to handle. Basket B identifies the skills your child needs to practice, the sorting through process itself reinforces several key interpersonal skills: learning to listen, compromise, and work things out. In Basket C place issues that are not important enough to discuss further—so you don't! Your child's behavior in Basket C is not your preference, but is tolerable. Filling up Basket C gives children enough of a sense of autonomy and control and increases the chances that they will participate and cooperate with the meat of this program—Basket B. This prioritizing that Dr. Greene advocates is essential for parenting. Reserving execution of unilateral parental authority for only those situations where it is needed maintains order and gives a sense of responsibility and respect. By prioritizing your issues, you can deliver an authoritative loud and clear message without turning into white noise to your child.

When OCD Escalates to Crisis

As hard as everyone may be working to help your child break free from his OCD, there may be times when eruptions occur. All children get frustrated and angry; OCD creates additional stress, fear, and frustration, and this has to go somewhere. Some kids talk about it a lot; for other kids it seems to gain on them, overtake them, and prompt fits or explosions. Keeping people safe during this time is paramount. Don't be afraid to stop your child if he is getting wound up. Staying calm but firm, tell him that he is out of control and needs to slow it down. Tell him that if he is not able to do that for himself, you will help him. It is important to set limits on how this frustration is expressed. You want to join with your child's frustration and be empathic, but there are still limits to what's acceptable. Whatever the infraction, after the dust has settled, you want to let your child know that she has every right to feel mad or frustrated, but that it's not okay to hit, scratch, or break things. It's not your child's fault that she has this problem, but it is important that she obey house rules for safety and conduct. The fact is that it's not good for your child to be out of control. There is no evidence that releasing frustration by exploding is helpful to anyone, in fact it often makes people feel worse. Because there are not a lot of places where she can release frustration, it puts your child in a bind either to not express her problems or to do it in an inappropriate way. If you teach your child an acceptable way to get upset, it will give her the freedom to do so as needed.

In some cases, OCD erupts into violence. Violence in any circumstance is a very serious matter. Generally violence does not come out of the blue; signs of frustration such as verbal violence may precede a physical showdown. In these situations, you should be getting professional help. Your child's therapist can guide you preventively to get extra in-house support if you need it, such as having a mental health technician in your home a certain number of hours per week to help maintain safety and teach safety measures. A safety plan may include learning passive restraint and being prepared to call 911 if you or your family is at risk. When there is violence, it is generally not from the OCD alone. People with OCD may have violent obsessions but they do not generally act on them. The violence described here is violence due to the presence of another disorder such as oppositional defiant disorder, an agitated depression, or ADHD.

With younger children, these crises are generally manageable at home using passive restraint, such as a tight hug or wrapping your child in a blanket. These situations require professional consultation to evaluate the risk level and to provide appropriate crisis-intervention services. Although parents often report that after the storm passes, their child is oblivious of what just happened, it's important to talk about it. For instance, "You were really upset and you hit her, that is not okay, I know it's your OCD, but look what it did here. We have to teach that it is *never* okay to hit." With older adolescents where there is greater physical risk, it is important to have professional advice to ensure everyone's safety. There may be times when families cannot establish safety on their own and a temporary residential placement is the best solution to move ahead.

Turning Down the Heat in Daily Life

While we can't have a 100 percent foolproof plan to prevent crises, we can reduce our chances by taking the steps described above to teach children about how to handle anger and frustration. Setting up routines that decompress the pressure points of daily life is another way to stop crises before they start.

General Pressure Points

For many children with OCD, mornings and evenings are very difficult times. For some children there's pressure to get their rituals just right to start or end the day right. For other children, it is the time when they are home, where their rituals take place. For those with contamination fears, it may be about decontaminating from the outside world or protecting oneself from recontamination when they venture out again. It is important to appreciate these pressure points and work out systems with your child to make these times more manageable. Imagine if you were a traffic engineer—you would not want to do construction (extra activities) during rush hours, so the key is not to overload high-stress transition times such as morning and bedtime.

Mornings

It was a Monday morning to remember. I walked into Julie's room to wake her up, braced for a struggle, but wasn't prepared for the sniper that hit me. "You touched my bed last night and now it is ruined. Stay away from me, you're dirty, get away." At this point, Julie is hovered in the corner of her bed, physically impossible to reach. Her face is red with tears, and she is paralyzed. I'm scared, it's all dirty. I can't move. My heart is pumping adrenaline so fast. It's an emergency but I can't get to the victim.

—Mother of ten-year-old with OCD

Morning sets the tone for the day. For all children morning is a time of racing around to brush, wash, eat, finish one last drop of homework, and still beat the school bell. Kids don't want to start off the day on the wrong foot; children with OCD, have this and more. If Mary didn't do her compulsions just right in the morning, she would have bad luck all day; Charlie would have to wake up at 5:00 A.M. to make sure he could fit in all his praying to keep his family safe; Joseph had to do everything with his right hand and foot first—that was the good side. Many children with OCD are kept so busy by their rituals that they don't make it to school with the burden of their OCD, there isn't time.

Your child's therapist should work out a plan with you that accommodates the symptoms your child is not yet ready to fight and includes challenges that he is up for. For example, eight-year-old Nina had washing and dressing rituals that not only took over an hour each morning but also included a panic scene. Her morning survival plan was to have her mother coach her before going into the bathroom so that she could "get out of there alive" (i.e., not get stuck counting the tiles). Normally, she could spend twenty minutes counting the tiles in sets of 12 until she got to 144. It just felt right. Instead she put up a sign on the mirror that read: *Numbers don't count—so I don't have to either!* If she was stuck in the bathroom longer than five minutes, her mom would knock and walk her out. Getting dressed was much more challenging for Nina because she would rebutton her clothes—it had to be twice, even numbers were good, 12 was best, 144 was perfect. If she buttoned only once or any odd number, Nina became very uneasy and nervous; even though she thought it was so embarrassing to count, she had to do it. *Something bad will happen today, I know it.* Because Nina's typical morning was to rebutton four or six times, we limited her to twice. Later in Nina's treatment, she was able to target the rebuttoning and get rid of that ritual, but prior to this, it was too overwhelming to consider giving that up.

Ways to Take the Stress Out of Mornings
- Help your child get up on time: use "dueling alarm clocks" one by the bed, one across the room with about fifteen to thirty

minutes of hitting the snooze button before the one across the room sounds and your child has to get up.

- Do as much preparation as possible at night—set out clothes, make lunches, pack book bag, leave it by the door.
- Don't leave tomorrow's decisions until tomorrow morning—deal with after school plans, permission slips, and so on the night before.
- Work out a plan to limit ritualizing time in the morning—use a timer, the length of a song on a CD, or something similar.
- Don't do other non-kid things in the morning such as taking a call or reading the mail. Stay focused on your child.
- Establish an acceptable "reminder" system with your child (e.g., we need to be in the car in ten minutes, five minutes).
- Have breakfast bars or other quick food to eat on the bus if necessary.

Bedtime

Bedtime is another typical trouble spot for kids. With all the distractions of the day muffled, there is nothing to come between your child and her thoughts. What can you do to make nighttime easier?

WAYS TO TAKE THE STRESS OUT OF BEDTIME
- Make sure your child is tired and not wired: eliminate caffeine especially after school, build in physical activity daily (exercise, kickball, walking the dog) in the afternoon.
- Have a consistent nighttime routine that allows for a wind-down period before your child gets into bed. Make the routine the same every night, it will help your child begin to anticipate bedtime and move into relaxation mode by the time she gets to bed.
- Older children need to unwind too—encourage them to read magazines, catalogs, or a novel before bed, shower (if not ritual-laden), or listen to soothing music.
- Identify and address specific fears that may interfere with your child's sleep (e.g., fear of the dark, recurrent nightmares, separation anxiety).
- See appendix for specific relaxation strategies to use at bedtime.

Twelve-year-old Max was very frightened about going to bed. He didn't want to tell his mother why, he would procrastinate as long as he could, and then when he finally *had* to go to bed, he would sneak back into his parents' room and fall asleep on their bed. Max was having intrusive images at night: He saw disgusting monsters and creatures with evil, contorted faces, and he couldn't get rid of them. He knew that monsters weren't real, but he was completely terrified by the pictures that seemed etched in his memory. The only thing he knew to do was to run away, so he would go find his mom. I explained that this was OCD, that in this case the slide projector in his brain was stuck on "gruesome" and the more that he got frightened, the more the slides would stick. I told him that he was in charge of his brain, and he could look at what he wanted to look at. He could then get angry that his brain was showing him this stuff, rather than get scared. His boss-back talk sounded like this: "You picture factory, you better do better than this, I'm going to fire you, you are going to be out of a job, this is not what I have to look at, I don't like it, and it's up to me. You can keep flashing me these stupid pictures, but I know they aren't real, and I know that they can't hurt me." Max's father, a sports fan, got involved in nighttime coaching that sounded like a pregame football huddle. He would say, "Max—who's in charge?" "Me," Max would respond, "Who is?" "ME!!" "Okay, now if your brain pulls any of that garbage on ya, what are you going to do?" "I'm going to stare it down till it runs away from me!"

For months six-year-old Jessica was in a ritual where her handwriting had to be perfect. Laboriously and with hands shaking, she would copy each letter first on scratch then on her good copy. Every move was calculated with the determination and precision of a diamond cutter. One false move and she lost it. Many a day Jessica had run through the house screaming out of control. Nerves frayed, evenings ruined, Jessica's parents would go back and fix the problem for her. One night Jessica sat down to do her homework and began showing the early signs of her frustration. Her parents encouraged her to sit down and keep working but, within a few minutes, Jessica had hit her limit and was jumping around on the furniture screaming that she couldn't do it, her parents had to do it for her. In the past, her parents had been so upset by Jessica's distress that they felt they had to do what she wanted to put her out of her pain. On this particular night, Jessica's parents looked at each other and silently agreed that they were not going to give in. First they coaxed her, "You write so nicely, come on"—to no avail and then they ignored her. A few minutes later, Jessica turned to her parents and said proudly, "Look, I did it!"

Is This Distress or . . . Manipulation?

Is she really struggling or does she just know how to get me? Many parents get caught on the thorns of this question. The answer is, it depends. Children with OCD are struggling with problems that are very real and that they would never make up in a million years—there are so many less painful ways to get attention. When you look at the problem solely as manipulation, you overlook how much children suffer with OCD. Also when you see a child's behavior as manipulative, you are assuming that they have the presence of mind to plan, coordinate, and execute. Keep in mind that we are all doing the best we can at any given time. But kids with OCD are still kids, and so from time to time if there's a way to get more of something good (like time with mom) or less of something bad (challenges or chores), all kids will give it their best shot. Children may occasionally blame it on OCD, "use" it to avoid something more unpleasant. Again, don't invest too much time figuring out which is which. Instead keep focused on the goal. For example the child who says, "I can't put my laundry in the hamper because of OCD." Recall the guiding principles from Chapter 7: Focus on what your child *can* do; Don't give excessive amounts of attention to what your child can't do. You might excuse her from touching the laundry, but find some other way for her to get her laundry to the washing machine or substitute another household chore instead. Parents can anchor themselves with the questions: What needs to be done: What can she do? What am I willing to do? This is accommodating what your child can't do but not letting them off the hook.

None of us would knowingly let a drunk driver behind the wheel, but when a child is out of control with OCD and making reckless demands, and we meet them, we are basically taking our lives in our own hands. You may think to yourself, well if I just do what she's asking, as outrageous as it is, she'll calm down, and a couple of times you may even be right, but in the long run it's not a reliable way to parent and it's not worth it.

Daryl was afraid to go to sleep because of separation anxiety and OCD fears, but what he told his mother is that he "has to watch cartoons at night or else something bad will happen," he would become very insistent about *needing* to watch television and would even sneak back in his mother's room at night. So frazzled by the scenes he would make if she pressed him to go to bed, she would quickly back off not wanting to escalate the situation. But whether a child is kept up late by OCD or by a ploy, he still needs a good night's sleep! When Daryl's mom realized that she knew best (not her son, and certainly not OCD) she was able to set a firm limit: no television at bedtime (she substituted a story) and was coached on how to "return" Daryl to sleeping in his own bed.

About Avoidance: Using OCD as an Excuse

"I can't go; it's my OCD." Whether it's avoidance of something your child wants to do like a sleepover or doesn't want to do like a school trip, the bottom line is that you don't want fear making the decision for your child. The solution is to break down the fear and challenge it one step at a time. Maybe sometimes you will be taken for a ride and your child will be using the OCD to get out of an obligation, but that is preferable to sitting on your child to find out *for sure* whether he is *really* afraid or just pulling your leg. Refer back to Chapter 7 for steps on tackling your child's fears.

Summary

Our discussion of pressure points has focused on both anticipating disasters and troubleshooting when they hit. Prevention means becoming familiar with your child's triggers or pressure points during the day, and where possible orchestrating things to turn down the intensity of daily life. Your child can do his part too by learning constructive ways to express his feelings and therefore defuse things on a daily basis. Even with the best-laid plans, unforeseen things happen. Remember that responding successfully to a flare doesn't mean "stopping" your child at any cost, but rather containing the moment and not adding fuel to the fire.

CHAPTER 10

Coping with the Diagnosis of OCD
Taking Care of Yourself

Some days I feel like it takes every ounce of energy I've got to deal with OCD, and there's no way I'm giving up. But after I finish getting Steven out the door in the morning—negotiating the traps of showers, food, shoelaces, light switches, his book bag—I am exhausted. And then I need to start my day: work, school, siblings, the mail, the dishes. It is ludicrous. I don't think I can handle it all.

* * *

I don't know if anyone can understand the isolation I feel—unless they have a child with OCD. If my child had diabetes or even ADHD, people would know what it's like; they've read about it, seen it on TV, it's "normal." But it's impossible to explain OCD to people. Maybe if I said Jeff was possessed, that would capture the experience of his obsessions, but then I would seem crazy. I feel very alone.

* * *

I walk around with the weight on my neck—I am a bad parent. I know it couldn't be true, I work so hard. But no matter what I do, the problem is there staring me in the face.

* * *

As strange as it sounds, when my child has a "normal problem" I am so relieved—I can handle it. He broke his leg once, it was so easy, I was familiar with the problem, I knew it could be fixed and he would be better. Over. OCD is so murky and tough.

* * *

I know now that the more I stay calm, the more my daughter stays calm; if not, we're like this combustion machine.

—*Parents of children with OCD*

Parenting from the Top Down

There is a Buddhist saying that if your compassion does not include yourself, it is incomplete. It happens far too quickly that you fall into managing your child's OCD full-time and lose touch with yourself. And yet you are the glue that's holding it all together. Just getting your child with OCD through a single day can demand more micromanagement than most other parents face in a year. In this hectic climate, finding ways of taking care of yourself is a necessary prescription. And while we all long for the Bermuda getaway, the strategies in this chapter will provide you with restorative moments that are free and that you don't have to pack for. In this chapter, I will present: (1) a rationale for why you need to take care of yourself now, (2) how to act in ways that are self-conserving and refueling, and (3) strategies for keeping your thinking realistic and sorting out priorities.

Your Sanity: An Essential
Resource for Your Child

Taking care of yourself may have come to sound like another unwanted job, but without you, your child may not achieve recovery. Parents play the role that no one else can play for a child. And while that may be the very thought that keeps you in the fray too long, let it now be the one that helps you step out from time to time to recharge. You are reminded on a daily basis that you are irreplaceable. You need to be preserved, tended to. The importance and hazards of your role have been overlooked too long.

For many parents, the idea of taking care of themselves seems as remote and absurd as asking soldiers in midbattle to stop for a game of tennis. When you are dealing with active OCD, you feel your head is spinning. You don't know where to begin—everything is wrong, your child is freaking out, your house is a mess, and you feel about two weeks past combustion point. It may feel indulgent to take a break, close the door to your room, take a swim, or go out for a kid-free dinner. It's not. The parenting rule of thumb to wait till the coast is clear to take a break is one that has its place, but not with OCD. If you wait for a relatively calmer moment, you may be waiting a long time. But if you take a short get-away, you'll have immediate results. It doesn't help your child if you are miserable and stressed out, so rather than staying in the game for the sake of being there, practice stepping out and see how differently you feel—refreshed and renewed—when you step back in.

Who benefits from your taking care of yourself? Everyone. When you step out of the fray, you recharge and come back seeing the light at the end of the tunnel that was eclipsed by the heat of the moment. The fact is that you must be an executive parent. This is a term that Dr. Russell Barkley coined for parents of children with ADHD who must take charge of their child's welfare and keep charge longer than most parents do. Your child doesn't know how to get out of the OCD on his own; if he did, he would have, and it wouldn't exist. When you are in charge, there is a positive trickle-down effect: You are calmer, your household is calmer, and you can be more deliberate and effective in your moves. The reverse is also true: When you are stressed and combustible, it spreads like a contagion. When you are angry, even the air molecules around you are bristling.

The Importance of Acknowledging Negative Feelings

With OCD you are beleaguered with so much to do that you probably have stopped asking yourself what this is like for you. It has become the air you breathe. It is important to acknowledge how it is to be coping with a child with OCD. It's not fun. It's not fair. Some days you want to run away from home, or just tell your child to just stop it, or worse! Of course, you love your child, but if you didn't have these other feelings, you wouldn't be human. Many of us are afraid to admit negative feelings about our children—there is a temptation to avoid these unpleasant thoughts—but holding them in is toxic to us. These unexpressed negative emotions leave us vulnerable to anxiety and depression; they accrete and weigh us down. We become irritable because we are not being true to ourselves. When parents don't admit that a situation is difficult, they start to accuse themselves when they are stressed: *I should want to be doing this, a loving parent would make any sacrifice, maybe this is my fault.*

When you talk about angry or sad feelings, you can feel the burden lift from you. These feelings lose their power to frighten you when they are uttered. The fact is that we are safe in our thoughts and feelings; there is a world of difference between having a thought and acting on it. There are many ways to acknowledge negative feelings. Some parents write poetry, others join support groups, get counseling themselves, or plan venting sessions with their spouse. The important thing is to know that these thoughts and feelings don't make you a bad parent, they make you human.

Accepting Anger and Planning for It

How many times have we said or done things in the heat of the moment that we later regret? It takes practice to observe and not react under stress. It goes against our nature. When you are late for work and your child has been scrubbing his hands for half an hour, you feel the tension rising in your body—you're worried about your son, you're angry that nothing you've said has worked, you know just how late you're going to be and how it's going to throw your whole day off. Stress. If you can walk out of the room, count to ten, or splash water on your face, incredible things can happen in those seconds. You may think, *Okay, so I'm late, I'll work it out*, or you may think, *We've got to go. I'll have to leave without him*, or *I will calmly but firmly tell him that we are going now*. The late international child expert Dr. Haim Ginott, author of *Between Parent & Child*, said "Anger, like a hurricane, is a fact of life to be acknowledged and prepared for." When a parent gets angry with a child, it communicates that there are limits to his patience. Which is true, so it's okay. The point is not to make the delivery of that message worse than whatever inspired it. The three steps to survival offered by Dr. Ginott are (1) accepting that you will get angry with your child; (2) feeling angry without guilt or shame; and (3) expressing the anger safely without attacking the child's personality or character. So saying, "I'm angry and I'm tired and I need a break" will allow you to exhale and it will get your point across to your child. Beyond the immediate situation, your admission of anger also gives your child an opportunity to learn how to express anger safely.

Sadness: Coping with the Loss

Another difficult feeling parents have is acknowledging that there is loss when you have a child with a medical condition. It takes great courage to admit this, for you may fear that it will be mistaken for not loving your child, for not seeing what a gift it is to have a child when others are not so fortunate. You may even feel superstitious that somehow if you don't accept this, if you are ungrateful, that something worse will happen—a punishment for the mother or father who dared to want more. But only you know what it's like to be in your shoes. This was not how things were supposed to be, and you have every right to wish things had been different. You could have done without the anguish or expending the time and the resources that it takes to manage OCD. Your frustration and disappointment is *not* at your child. It is at the predicament, at how things are not as you thought they would be.

Acknowledging the loss enables you to see the gain. As one mother wrote, "I never wanted my daughter to have to go through this, but I have never been more proud. She has overcome so much. She did the work, but I was a part of it too. I feel proud of all of us."

Guilt: Getting It off Your Shoulders

Elizabeth, mother of twelve-year-old Melinda, who has been OCD-free for two years, told me that she opened up a book on OCD that said it was caused by underparenting. "It made me furious! How could they print that? At least I knew it was wrong because we went through behavior therapy, but think of all the parents out there who are already dealing with the stress of OCD day-to-day, and then on top of that they read it's their fault!"

So many parents naturally feel guilty; just as children blame themselves for OCD, parents do the same. When something is wrong with your child, you search yourself for a reason: *Should I have stayed home with him more? Was I too demanding? We shouldn't have moved, it was too much for him.* Guilt can proliferate into so many unhealthy directions. When you feel guilty, you can become irritable and impatient, or, conversely, you can try to make up for it by being overly indulgent. In addition, it will be obvious to your child and she might begin to hide her symptoms to protect you from feeling guilty. Guilt is a very destructive emotion. The facts are that OCD is nobody's fault. Shift focus instead to all you have done for your child—the hours of nurturing, helping with homework, car-pooling, anguishing, and taking in the wonder of your child.

Shame

Some shame comes from the fact that we live in a world of stigma. You coach your children not to listen to those who tease, but it is hard to buffer yourself from the comments of those who don't understand. Many parents have war stories about the profound disappointment they have felt in the support—or lack thereof—from their relatives. Comments that invalidate the seriousness of the problem, "He'll grow out of it. Uncle Joe was the same way. Don't make such a fuss about it," or invalidate your efforts, "You indulge that child too much!" can feel like a slap in the face. Many parents feel ashamed and may begin to make up excuses for their child's behavior, ducking out of social obligations to avoid the disapproving looks from family members.

This is especially difficult at holidays and other family gatherings. Breaking tradition and choosing to do small family gatherings can be tough, though that may be the best option for averting these painful encounters and preserving a sense of a holiday. Another strategy is to prepare family for what to expect. One mother described how she informed her extended family that her daughter would be vacuuming immediately after the meal and to just ignore it—though it was a little awkward when it happened, because they had been warned, there were no questions asked.

If it's not an option to go head-to-head with family members or friends who are meddling unhelpfully, you can respectfully close things by saying "I can't go there now."

Getting Off the Hook with Your Thoughts

Some of what wears on parents of children with OCD is their thoughts and beliefs about the situation. OCD can be likened to getting "stuck on hooks"—certainty, cleanliness, orderliness. The hook parents get stuck on are often their dysfunctional thoughts about their role in OCD. Guilt, sadness, and anger are feelings parents commonly experience. These negative thoughts interfere with good parenting by clouding the issues and sometimes adding "fix Mom's guilt" to the child's "to do" list. Most parents have thought *It's my fault, if I'm a good parent I could make my child feel better. I have to protect my child from pain at all costs. I can't make my child do something if it's hard for him.*

Overcoming Your Own Dysfunctional Beliefs

A dysfunctional belief is an automatic thought that has no basis in reality. It colors the way we feel about a situation and undermines our ability to take action. Generally, these are negative to the extreme. These are the hooks that get you stuck and begin to unravel your life.

For example, Janice watched her seven-year-old daughter get so frustrated that she had temper tantrums when she was around other children. But it was Janice herself who froze up unable to help when this happened. In recreating this scene in therapy, Janice was able to identify her dysfunctional thought as a fear that her daughter would be schizophrenic. She was catastrophizing, jumping ahead to the worst future she could imagine, and it paralyzed her. When we talked about how unrealistic that fear was, Janice was able to let go of it and help her daughter learn to better manage her frustration.

Dr. Aaron Beck identified several key dysfunctional thinking patterns in which the underlying belief is: "something terrible will happen and I won't be able to handle it." Examples include: *catastrophizing:* predicting negative results to the extreme, the worst case scenario is the one you are planning on; *black-and-white thinking:* seeing a situation or person as all good or completely disastrous; *overgeneralizing:* taking one negative event and adding always or never, rather than seeing something as the result of the situation at hand, it's a lifetime trend; *discounting:* devaluing personal accomplishments because "anybody could do that." In his book, *Anxiety Disorders and Phobias* co-written with Dr. Gary Emery, Dr. Beck delineates the three questions for challenging dysfunctional automatic thoughts:

1. What's the evidence? Typically anxious thinking means jumping to conclusions that would never "hold up in court." Write out your evidence for the thought, and then identify the errors.
2. What's another way of looking at the situation? What are the alternative possibilities for outcome in this situation? What is most likely to happen?
3. So what if it happens? Often what locks in fear is when we block-out and keep safe the idea that the situation is impossible to survive. If instead we say, "so what if that actually happened?" that allows us to see what resources and strategies we could draw on in order to cope.

In order to get control over this kind of thinking, it helps to look into that dark abyss of worry about your child. Don't be afraid to hold up the fears that you find there, because then and only then can you evaluate and correct them.

The following are several examples of how to reframe common dysfunctional thoughts. The more that you actively practice seeing experiences in a different light, the more you can buffer yourself from discouragement.

- *Dysfunctional Belief:* It's my fault. I did this to my child, I should have known, I should have seen a genetic counselor, maybe I shouldn't have married my husband. He has had those tics, and we never talked about what they were. How could I have done this to my child?

  Reframe: It's not my fault. This could have happened to anybody. I can help my son, I care.

- *Dysfunctional Belief:* I'm being mean if I say no to my child. If I accommodate my child's requests, the rituals will be shorter; if I don't accommodate, my child will get so angry and make a scene.

Reframe: I need to be strong enough to help my child learn that she can cope without doing rituals. I want her to grow up healthy, not a prisoner of OCD.

- *Dysfunctional Belief:* I need to know where the OCD is in order to control it. The monster has invaded my house. It's terrible, it feels like when we had mice. I need to know where they are; I check every day to see if we are getting them back. So I ask David every day, "Is this OCD, is that a ritual, are you stressed, was it bad today? Why were you in the bathroom so long?"

Reframe: The way to fight OCD is one step at a time; I can't let my worry rule my child's life. Especially since things are so stressful, I need to make home a nuclear-free zone as much as possible. I don't want to be adding fuel to the fire. That's the last thing I want to do.

- *Dysfunctional Belief:* Symptoms mean that I have failed as a parent. I should be able to get rid of this. I see it crop up again. We had gotten through the hair checking and now I see her stop at every mirror, flip the vanity mirror down in the car. Maybe all teenagers do that, but to me all I think is OCD and I can feel that brain path wearing down more and more. I feel like I have to stop this to save her.

Reframe: It is the nature of OCD for symptoms to come and go. I can help her cope with this, I should expect this so that I can help her manage this when it happens. I don't want to send the message that my child should hide her OCD, or to make her nervous like she's getting worse. I want to be informed and aware. New rituals don't necessarily mean that she's getting worse.

- *Dysfunctional Belief:* I don't know what to do; we'll never get out of this mess! This is impossible, it will never change.

Reframe: I am overwhelmed; I can deal with this one step at a time. Doubt in OCD is contagious, it's okay not to know what to do, but don't panic. That will be a better answer for my child than to get angry or to acquiesce to the OCD demands. Kids don't break. If I convey that this is dangerous and needs to be stopped right away, she gets nervous and thinks, Wow, I guess I am really bad off. Or, she may get angry and feel that I am ashamed of her, that she embarrasses me and that's why I want her to fix it.

- *Dysfunctional Belief:* This is so hard for my child, I've got to do everything I can. He's got such a burden—I'll be a super parent—I can run to the grocery every day for the right food, do his laundry separately, cook a different meal—he needs that and how can I complain, look what he's dealing with.

Reframe: This is hard, but my child is strong and can fight this with my support. If I do everything for him, I'm going to run myself ragged and he'll see himself as more disabled than he is. I will do what I can and help him see what he can do for himself.

- *Dysfunctional Belief:* If my child won't let me help, he doesn't want to get better. He's fighting me, he must not care about himself.

   Reframe: All kids want to get better; I can ask him how I can help. I might want him to show 100 percent enthusiasm 100 percent of the time, but he's a kid. I don't want to pressure him, all I can do is let him know I'm there. If I don't push, he'll come to me when he really needs me.

You can get the upper hand on your thinking errors if you identify them, find alternatives, and then be on the look out for them in times of stress. To help you, take a piece of paper and list three of your dysfunctional thoughts about OCD, now challenge them using the questions on page 222, then write out your alternative thoughts on brightly colored index cards and keep them on your mirror, the fridge, on the dashboard, so that you can practice working in new messages to your brain that are true and self-preserving rather than self-destructing.

Finding Outlets for the Isolation You Feel

Many parents cope with OCD alone. You may feel isolated because few people know about your child's condition. To the common observer your child may look normal, healthy, and bright; only you know how she suffers inside. To protect your family's privacy, you may be reluctant to confide in others. Even if parents tell friends or relatives, this may create stress, not alleviate it. Because others may not understand, they may look at you differently—"oh, a psychological problem." In that moment of judgment, you understand firsthand what your child is battling.

Parents struggle with their mixed feelings about how to balance their needs and the needs of their child. You must look at your situation and identify your bottom-line requirements, what you will fight for, and what you will negotiate. Attending a support group can provide an excellent sounding board for such decisions as well as an opportunity to learn strategies from other parents who are dealing with similar issues. In addition, group members can share information about therapists, schools, pediatricians, and so on. There are many online support group options as well, see the resource guide for more information. It

---

EXERCISE

List three of your dysfunctional thoughts about OCD.
1.

2.

3.

Review them and challenge the logic. Now list three alternatives that you will practice saying to yourself.
1.

2.

3.

---

can be discouraging if you compare yourself only to your friends whose children do not have such problems. But it's comparing apples to oranges. Your children are different. It's not fair, but it is what it is. This is a time to reach out and connect to other parents in the same boat.

Stress: Locating It and Lowering It

Life doesn't stop just because your child has OCD. OCD is only one issue nested in a matrix of other demands in your life. After battling the invisible monsters that keep your child chained to the sink, tortured by thoughts of sin, or paralyzed at the threshold of the door, you finally get your child off to school and then, only then, your day begins.

Stress management happens on two levels. The first is the macro level: the game plan for your life right now. This involves prioritizing your child's treatment, cutting back on other commitments, scheduling stress-busting activities, bringing in people to relieve you from parenting, and allowing yourself the convenience shortcuts (don't cook, use paper plates, don't clean).

The second level of stress reduction is the micro—the moments that refresh. Make sure that you have some decompressing activities in your daily repertoire such as rigging your life for humor (read the comics), rent Robin Williams videos, practicing counting to ten before jumping into a situation, take brief time-outs, walk the dog, read, or call a friend, play with your children when you can, sing at dinner, play ping pong, put up reminders to smile and breathe.

Knowing Your Limits: There Are Some Things You Can't Do

Heidi, a tall, strong woman, tells me that her ten-year-old son Andy can't walk on the floor because it's dirty, and sometimes he also can't put his shoes on because they are dirty too. Yet her son Andy gets around the house and gets into the car. When I ask her how they function this way, she describes how she carries her son up to bed then out to the car. I look at Heidi, young and attractive, on whose face the shadow of exhaustion falls. She won't be able to carry Andy for long, or worse, she will become injured from the strain. While this is an extreme example, it is clear that it is physically impossible for Heidi to continue this way for long, and for the sake of being there for the long haul for her child, she will have to work out an alternative. Maybe you aren't literally carrying the weight of your child on your back, but you're probably carrying him in ways that are debilitating, and because you are essential equipment for your child, we must preserve you. This is your ongoing challenge. Your child will want many things from you to which you'll need to say no.

Realistic Expectations for This Time

These are extraordinary times; OCD creates crisis in your home. OCD is painfully time-consuming. Tally up the time it takes doing rituals, fighting rituals, calming down your child, going to doctor's appointments, doing the extras your child needs to get through the day, all this on top of the standard fare—getting out of the house, going to school, homework, friends, soccer practice. Redefine your expectations for yourself and your family by acknowledging that this is not business as usual for anyone. This is a time to conserve energy and perhaps adopt a "just say no" policy to any extra time commitments with which you may be faced (e.g., volunteering for PTA). Don't fall into the trap of the "shoulds"—I should be getting more done, I should have more energy, I should have a cleaner house, I should be doing volunteer work, and so on.

When you are feeling overwhelmed, it is also harder to see your child's ability to cope. Your view colors everything.

At the same time, make sure that you keep in some things that matter to you—whether it's hobbies, volunteer work, or music. Being happy will help you do what needs to be done for your child. Not surprisingly, Dr. Judith Rapoport and her colleagues at NIMH reported in *The Journal of Clinical Psychiatry* in 1993 that family involvement in community activities predicted improved outcome of OCD treatment; social isolation and negative overinvolvement, which may result from the family closing in on itself under the pressure of OCD, predicted poor outcome.

The Lean Years

Some periods in our lives call for living down to the bare bones—no extras. This is one of those times. Your mantra can be "I am doing what I need to survive." I can remember a period in my own life, when as a sleep-deprived new mother, who was also interning and finishing a dissertation, my heart sank when a colleague told me that she just didn't feel right unless she hung up her clothes neatly in the closet, set out her clothes for the next day, and flossed her teeth every night. I flashed to my nighttime routine—which on a good night meant I actually got out of my clothes and turned off the lights before I collapsed into bed, only to get up and start all over again. I had to consciously remind myself that these were not stellar conditions, and *my* goal was getting through.

Pacing Yourself

To cope with a child with OCD, you need the patience and pacing of a marathon runner. Instead, many exhausted parents keep dashing for the finish line. Even marathon runners have to slow down sometimes. Don't try to fix the whole problem every day. Rather, try to live every day. See the triumphs and celebrate them, brush yourself off from the tough days, and know that you and your child have tomorrow.

Dismantling the Dragon for Yourself

The treatment advocated in this book is one that externalizes the OCD and makes it the villain. This helps children recover because the enemy is a concrete entity outside of them, not an intangible process inside of them. Parents also need to get power over the OCD themselves. It may be this elusive monster that tricks you, goads you, makes you become superstitious and doubting. Was it the medication I took before I got pregnant? Did I not spend enough time with him when he was little? Okay, I'll do anything—I will quit my job, just make my child better.

To come to grips with the condition, you have to look the devil straight in the eye and begin to see that you are stronger than it is.

This was the case with Beverly, who had been traumatized by the ordeal of her daughter Kelly's first PANDAS episode. For two years, the image that haunted Beverly was of Kelly neck twisting and head bobbing during their summer vacation. She felt sick thinking about it. Her daughter was not her daughter, it was somebody else—someone she'd seen in a movie who was extremely impaired. Beverly came to me for help because she realized that her fears and distress about her daughter's condition were getting harder to hide and were interfering with her ability to help and to enjoy her daughter. Through a treatment called EMDR (eye movement desensitization and reprocessing) developed by Dr. Francis Shapiro, in the 1980s, a fast-track treatment for anxiety and posttraumatic stress disorder, I helped Beverly look closely at those pictures of Kelly and describe them to me. Beverly saw her daughter becoming someone else, though her terror grew, she stayed with those images, and then a new thought came to her: she remembered a severely brain-injured child she'd met once, and realized that was who she had been seeing in the picture, not her daughter. Like tectonic plates shifting, the dreadful feelings began to split off from the picture of her daughter that day. Over minutes, the tears flowed, the pictures began to dissolve, and now she could see her beautiful daughter. Little by little, Beverly was able to not flash back on those images when Kelly was having a setback. Instead, new pictures flooded in, she could see her daughter as strong—her strong body, her assertive spirit, her beautiful dark hair, the graceful way she moved. Beverly was dividing up the territory for herself, looking right at the OCD and splitting it off from her daughter. She felt a heaviness lifted from her heart. She had her daughter back. You can have your child back, too.

Know Your Own Strengths

Often when we identify with our children's experiences, what we feel is the vulnerability, the worst moments and what we forget is *how* we got through—the first day of school, being on the school bus, exams, a first date—or even, *that* we got through.

Think about a time when you were anxious. How *did* you get through? When you tap into strategies—what you said to yourself or what you did—you have a starting point for ideas about helping your child. More importantly, you will have the idea that the situation is highly survivable, you will convey that essential message to your child. The more you are afraid of your child's discomfort, the more your child will confuse what is uncomfortable with what is unbearable.

PART THREE

TURNING POINTS AND BREAKTHROUGH MOMENTS

Solutions for Managing Daily Life

The fact that OCD seems to pop up in so many different forms leaves parents feeling greatly outnumbered. Though OCD may be clever at metamorphosis, it is a one-trick pony. Underneath, it plays the same song making children doubt and have sticky thoughts about contamination, mistakes, bad thoughts, or order, every time. In time, parents and children can become expert detectives in recognizing OCD despite its many masks and close the curtains on OCD's show before it even gets started. Over the years, children have described their symptoms to me, sure that I will think theirs are the strangest I have ever heard. But they always make "OCD sense." They are always new twists on the same themes—certainty, safety, and "just rightness." Knowing that even the most bizarre symptoms fall under some OCD category can be very reassuring to children: It helps them say "that's not me, that's OCD."

A comprehensive presentation of all OCD symptoms is impossible, since there are as many variations on a theme as there are people suffering from the disorder. Therefore, this chapter presents only the major themes of OCD. Don't get alarmed if you can't find your child's specific symptoms here. Every research study I've reviewed has an "Other" category into which many cases will fall. In other words, it is normal to have "weird" OCD symptoms that don't fit neatly into a category. Things like mundane sounds and images, or avoidance of the pronunciation of a particular letter, represent as much as 50 percent of symptoms in a sample of children with OCD. Consider these the random workings of the OCD net—who can account for where it goes—but what OCD does with the contents of that net is always the same.

This section deals with the nitty-gritty of OCD symptoms and how to treat them successfully. Organized in a user-friendly format by theme, each of the following chapters will describe through illustrative vignettes what these symptoms are like for your child, the key behavior therapy intervention, and how it translates to the home front.

All of the suggestions in these chapters identify the problem as OCD and then fight it as laid out in the five steps described in Chapter 8. To recapitulate, the steps are:

1. Reflect what your child is feeling.
2. Relabel the problem as OCD.
3. Resist OCD rules with show and tell.
4. Refocus on a preferred activity.
5. Reinforce your child's efforts at fighting.

There is no "right" way to apply these steps. It is best to be flexible with these principles and know that sometimes you will use all five steps; at other times, you may just empathize or relabel, or help your child get involved in something else; still other times you may do nothing but be understanding from a distance. Above all, remember that *most* children know that their fears are unreasonable and make no sense. The key in intervening is showing them the fork in the road—helping them act on what they want to be doing, rather than getting stuck on the endless path of what *might be true*.

Recall that the way to do this is not by reassuring them that it's okay, but by setting out a few questions as stepping stones so that they can come to that conclusion on their own. "What is OCD telling you will happen if you don't listen?" "Would you give that advice to a friend?" "How far out did OCD go this time?" and then reminding your child that he has every right to "disobey" OCD and follow his own rules and beliefs.

You and your child need to work as a team in winning the battle against OCD. Your child should be in charge of choosing goals, because he knows how difficult each symptom is to tackle. Keep the goals small, gradually extending the periods of time he is tolerating ritual prevention. If you are struggling with how or when to help your child, ask him. Often children can be very clear about what they need from parents when fighting their OCD symptoms. But also be prepared that your child is going to fight *you* from time to time when you are helping him; know that it's because he's having a hard time, and it really isn't personal. Take this opportunity to explain that you are on his side and ready to help in whatever way you can. In the end, your child will appreciate how you believed in him enough to set him free.

Treatment is going to be very hard work for your child and for you. Before learning about OCD, you and your child were struggling just to run in place. Now armed with the diagnosis and treatment, your hard work will bring you down the road of freedom. Progress may be slow; on average an active phase of behavior therapy takes approximately four to six months. As with many skills, speed is never the critical factor. What is critical is that the child is progressing through his goals and understanding the techniques so that eventually he doesn't need a therapist to tell him what to do. He will know how to break the rules of OCD on his own. And he will carry that knowledge throughout his life. OCD expert Dr. Martin Franklin, tells his young patients, "My job is to help you not need me anymore—to help you put me out of a job." By following the suggestions outlined here, you are helping train children to be their own therapists—to spot and outsmart the tricks of OCD, to prevent relapses, and allow themselves to be "in life" rather than "in therapy."

The excerpts in this part illustrate the moments of truth in therapy when a child sees OCD for what it is. Following these turning points, there will be battles won and battles lost, but most important, children experience in these moments the fork in the road. They learn that there is a choice. They have a new roadmap, an alternate route other than to the dead end of OCD.

Progress is messy, and it is ongoing. Though as parents we may prefer to think of our jobs as more finite—like cooking, it is really more like renovating a house: You use supplies, you run out, sawdust gets everywhere, there's lots of clean-up, and there's always more to be done.

CHAPTER 11

Contamination Fears

A Parent's View: Before Treatment

I walk in the bathroom and the lump in my throat drops to my stomach. There are towels all over the floor—dirty ones that she can't pick up because they've been used. There is water everywhere—she's got to wash without touching anything—the faucets, the soap. She splashes soapy water on everything before she uses it—it's flooded. There are trails of toothpaste by the drain, rejected because they weren't in the clean middle part, toilet paper wasted. I feel my pulse throbbing in my head because I don't even know where to begin to clean up the place, but that's the easy part. What's harder is seeing these concrete signs of my daughter's entrapment. I want to be mad at her, because I want it to stop. At the same time, I feel so bad for her and I know this is serious. I want to chase this OCD away, but I don't know how to get at it.

After Treatment

Our lives have changed completely. I have my daughter back. I could always read it in her face when OCD was stressing her out, now I see her smiling. She's not being careful all the time, trying to inconspicuously avoid people and things. She's just being herself. Though sometimes it's hard for me to relax when thinking about her future, the relief I feel for her now is indescribable.

Theme and Variation

Contamination is the most common OCD theme; it is estimated that as many as 85 percent of children with OCD have some kind of washing compulsion during the course of the disorder. For children with contamination OCD, their fears go far beyond the rules of good hygiene. They are not following the rules that parents teach them. Instead, they are in the grips of the OCD monster Mr. Clean, who frightens them with threats of dreadful consequences if they do not keep scrubbing away at invisible dirt or constantly avoid contact with harmful objects as mundane as a doorknob or as profound as a parent's hug. These rules of OCD do not keep children safe: They make them late for school and unable to sleep at night. They may result in chronic cuts and abrasions from using harsh chemicals or even dehydration and life-threatening weight loss when food becomes the carrier of pollution.

Contamination obsessions are of two major types: (1) concerns about contact, either with objects or people which are disgusting in and of themselves, or about germs that could lead to infections such as AIDS, rabies, or stomach viruses; and (2) concerns about symbolic contamination, wherein a place, color, or word is considered bad or unclean and anything associated with it must be avoided. For younger children who don't understand about chemicals or germs, contamination fears may present more directly in terms of their experience—that they have lipstick on them, that they have eaten their Chapstick, that the floor is dirty, or that spots or old stains are bad or dangerous. One young child had to hold her breath in the bathroom so that the smell would not go in her mouth and get her dirty; another would only "air dry," refusing to use towels because of their potential for harm.

Identifying Contamination Symptoms

RED FLAGS
- Long trips to the bathroom
- Multiple and/or long showers
- Excessive use of soap, toothpaste, toilet paper, towels
- Squeezing out toothpaste, rolling out toilet paper to get to the "clean part"
- Avoidance of doorknobs, light switches, furniture
- Refusing to wipe after toileting
- Insisting that no one else use his bathroom
- Keeping food or silverware separate from family's
- Inspecting silverware to make sure it's clean
- Multiple questions about cleanliness or freshness of food
- Avoidance of the floor or things on the floor—shoes, book bag, trashcan
- Avoidance of stained clothes, furniture, sidewalk
- Concern about germs, ickiness, illness
- Avoidance of physical contact, especially with hands

- Asking family members if they've washed after toileting
- Refusal to share supplies—scissors, pencils, or rulers that someone else has touched
- Chapped or bleeding skin
- Inspecting food for discoloration or food packaging to make sure it's not bent, dented, or scratched for fear of poisoning
- Checking furniture for stains, gum, sticky spots
- Refusing to handle tissues (even own)

Some cleaning compulsions are obvious: Your child spends inordinate amounts of time washing his hands or refuses to touch the doorknob. Sometimes children are better at hiding their contamination symptoms, and the condition may be flagged by things such as high utility bills (from long showers or extra laundry); rapid depletion of cleaning supplies, soap, or toothpaste; sudden refusal to wear favorite clothing or to sit on a certain piece of furniture. Some children fear being contaminated by the food they eat. For example, they won't eat at a restaurant—because there's too much they can't monitor—but even at home, they may watch if Mom has washed her hands or if the pan is clean; they won't eat if the babysitter cooks, they'll use only plastic disposable plates and forks. Even food color can be a source of contamination. For example, red foods such as licorice, "M&Ms" or spaghetti sauce may be avoided because they are the color of blood.

Ultimately, fear of contamination may leave a long trail of clues—an invisible web—because children with OCD have to vigilantly track the crisscross of imagined contacts that an object might encounter. Sometimes it is the child's own hands that become the enemy to be avoided. An obsession attacks: "What if that towel is dirty? What if the person before didn't really wash their hands and now the germs are on the towel? I better put it in the laundry or someone else will touch it and they'll have germs and then who knows what they could touch. I better not touch anything or anyone." In the blink of an eye, the danger zone has extended to encompass the entire world. While it's bad enough for a child to have to observe this endless chain of possibilities all day long, there is also another track running simultaneously that says, "This is crazy. You know this is unnecessary. Why are you doing this?"

How can these thoughts be so powerful? Because physiologically they strike like your worst image of disgust—it is the combination of hair and soap scum in your shower drain, the runny consistency of vegetables that have spoiled, the wretched smell coming from a dumpster in August. As you read this, notice what happens to you when you first imagine those things. You may start to grimace and a feeling of disgust may rise from your stomach. Now observe how quickly those pictures and feelings leave you. Imagine if you couldn't shake them, that they grew more vivid and palpable with each passing moment, and the more you tried to get rid of them, the more they grew until they completely overtook you. These images stick like "tar on your brain" as one sixteen-year-old described it. Surrounded by inescapable feelings of dirt and disgust, this is the unique torment of the child with contamination fears. From the outside, these children often look like they are being perfectionists, as if they are making a rational choice to wash this much or getting some kind of satisfaction out of their excessive behavior. Truly they are trapped. There is no joy, no feeling of clean, there is only washing and more washing.

Breaking Free:
Two Cases of Contamination

Imagine if the very food you eat could be contaminated by the words spoken around you. Katie, who has had OCD since she was five, thought that bathroom talk, a burp at the table, or even her own thoughts anticipating a disgusting event could do just that. She would have to cover her mouth to prevent the germs from getting in, and shake her food and blow on it to get the germs off. If what was said was so gross that the food was not "salvageable," she would have to throw the food out. Meals were so stressful, according to Katie's mother, with her shaking and blowing, and throwing out food, that sometimes she couldn't eat at all and was losing weight.

At her school cafeteria, Katie sits across from a boy who has come to be known as The Burper. This youngster has earned the distinction of burping louder than anyone in school. While his daily performances amused his classmates, for Katie, they meant racing to eat as much lunch as she could before he struck, for at that point, her food was ruined, and she would have to throw it away. Even dessert.

To tackle this problem, the first step was to relabel these warnings of contamination as an OCD brain trick. Even though bathroom talk is arguably kind of gross, it can't pollute her food; the invisible pee, poop, and burps can't fly into her mouth or her food. Next we established the motivation for taking on the challenges: "I don't want to have to blow and shake, I don't want to have to throw out my favorite foods just because someone burped around them or said bathroom talk. . . . I don't want to have OCD!" We then made a hierarchy of gross situations:

bathroom talk, burps, thinking of poop, going in the bathroom with food. Without further ado, we set out for "show and tell" of ritual prevention. Putting discretion aside, I did my part of burping and then singing the Alka-Seltzer song over a plate of pretzels, which Katie and I then ate, coaching her to boss back the "shake and blow monster." Next we brought in Katie's eleven-year-old brother who was only too happy to oblige us with his burping and bathroom talking talents. Katie did very well with the exposure, which she then practiced for homework, with her brother chiming in during specified times only. It was hard at first, and she needed coaxing from her mom to keep eating; the more she worked on it, the easier it got. Her favorite boss-back talk is, "Poop poop, who cares?" Two weeks later, Katie reported, "I feel like OCD is going away. When my brother started saying gross things while I ate and I didn't shake off my food or blow out air, I felt really excited and proud. I can even bring food into the bathroom now—before I'd have to throw it out." At lunch, she can laugh now when The Burper strikes. "Burp, burp, who cares?"

For fifteen-year-old Patrick, OCD began when a woman who was HIV-positive came to speak to his class about AIDS. After this visit, he began to wash his hands constantly for fear of contracting the disease, and although he felt silly doing this, he quarantined the clothes he wore that day. Soon after, the OCD really took hold during a class trip to Canada. Standing in a cathedral—surrounded by the crutches, casts, and canes left behind by the ailing who had come to be healed— Patrick began to feel very afraid that he was going to get sick because he was in that church. "I didn't know what to trust, I felt so contaminated that I tried not to breathe in that church. I thought I would become injured or sick, too. I didn't want to put anything in my body. I know that sounds crazy, but I thought that if I ate anything on that trip, I would become sick or die. I was a slave to my thoughts, my mind wouldn't let me eat anything. I was terrified. I looked at my friends, there they were eating away, laughing, having fun and I thought, *This is so unfair. I can't believe they're having such a good time and here I am with these crazy thoughts—don't walk that way, don't stand here, you'll be contaminated.* I was starving. Finally after not eating one whole day and a morning, we went to a McDonald's and I wolfed down french fries and a Coke. When I got home, the first thing I ate was cereal—after that I felt like I couldn't eat cereal anymore, like all of the disease was in cereal so if I ate it—even a different brand, in a different box, I would get sick. I couldn't wear any of the clothes from that trip, couldn't even think about anything Canadian. If we passed a car with a Canadian license plate, I would have to wash. One time when we parked next to a car from Montreal, and I was trying to convince my dad to park somewhere else but couldn't tell him why, he got mad at me. I was so desperate. I love hockey, but since so many of the players are Canadian, I couldn't go to hockey games. When my dad asked, I know he thought I was avoiding him. I wasn't. So many times I wished I could have explained the weird things I was doing, but I was too afraid. I really thought I was crazy."

When I met Patrick he had been on medication for approximately nine months, and although to all appearances he was functioning—going to school, doing sports, playing with friends—internally he was just barely scraping by. His avoidance of things Canadian and religious was spreading: He couldn't cross t's because they resembled the Cross, his Latin books had to be kept separate from all the rest because that was the language of the Church, and he began to wash his hands between classes. He was feeling crazier and was getting more desperate. When I told Patrick that this was a contamination fear, the most common type of OCD, he was relieved. He always thought he was different because he didn't care about dirt—it was all this other weird stuff. I explained that it was symbolic contamination, and it's just as treatable as the more typical contamination fears.

Patrick and I then developed this boss-back talk: "This is dumb, I'm tired of taking time out of my day to do this stupid stuff. It's just where my brain got stuck, I don't have to do this." We began to work on dealing with the issue of the clothes from his trip. He brought shirts from his trip to the office. Within a month, Patrick was grabbing clothes out of his clothes basket and saying, "I'm over this." I went to his house to help him open the taboo drawers that he hadn't touched since the trip. Patrick was smart, determined, and solid. There was nothing below a 5 on his fear ladder (page 241), but he worked his way up, and was so pleased to be able to wear some of his favorite clothes again before he outgrew them.

The pinnacle of our work was the day that Patrick and I looked at a AAA guidebook for Canada together, toasting his progress with, what else, Canada Dry ginger ale. For weeks Patrick knew that I had the book and he wasn't ready to look at it. "I know this is crazy," he said, "but I think that if I see the pictures, it will all come back and I'll mess up everything I've done." A few weeks later, with the total concentration of an Olympic weightlifter, Patrick looked at the book—the cathedrals, Montreal—and in a moment that I will never forget, he said, "Wow, Canada is a really cool place, you know, I didn't really get to see it, with all the OCD. I've got to go back there someday."

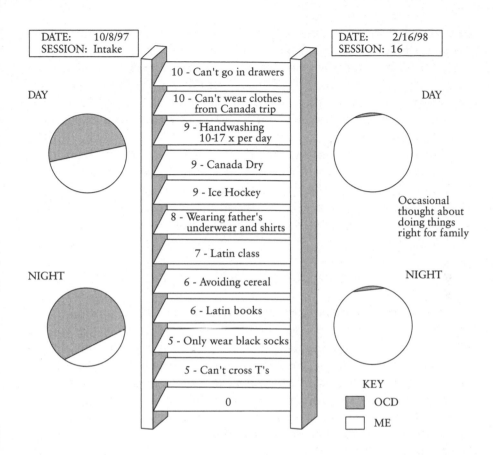

DATE: 10/8/97
SESSION: Intake

DAY

NIGHT

10 - Can't go in drawers

10 - Can't wear clothes from Canada trip

9 - Handwashing 10-17 x per day

9 - Canada Dry

9 - Ice Hockey

8 - Wearing father's underwear and shirts

7 - Latin class

6 - Avoiding cereal

6 - Latin books

5 - Only wear black socks

5 - Can't cross T's

0

DATE: 2/16/98
SESSION: 16

DAY

Occasional thought about doing things right for family

NIGHT

KEY

OCD

ME

Key Intervention: It's Not About Being Clean, It's About Being Sure (Enough)

Take one look at a child whose hands are cracked and bleeding from hours of washing, and it's clear that OCD is not about being clean, but about being certain. What makes it impossible to escape the feeling of contamination is the equally unbearable feeling of being uncertain. Though most children know in reality these fears are not founded, the OCD tugs at them with the trick—"Well, if you're thinking that you can catch AIDS from touching the sink handles, then it could be true, better not take a chance."

Doubt weighs heavily on the child and ultimately wins out. OCD wins until the child becomes familiar with "the fork in the road." He could spend his whole life making sure that things are safe but because of that one brain glitch in OCD, which is the inability to register completion, the all-clear signal will never come. Like a leaky bathtub that can't fill with water, the brain with OCD can't register a task as complete, can see no end to the task before it. So waiting for "clean" is an endless prospect. The other road the child can take is freedom—paying attention to what he cares about more than cleanliness, while being clean and sure "enough."

The question during behavior therapy exposure is not, Do you *feel* clean? We've already established that the brain gauge is "out of order" for that one. On the contrary, in order to reset the gauge, *the purpose of the exposure is to feel the discomfort about not being sure if you're clean,* and see that you can survive it without washing.

Is Your Freedom Worth Ten Minutes?

When you are in search of dirt and germs, the world is your oyster. From the shoes on your feet to the public telephone around the corner, and every square inch of sidewalk in between, there is no shortage of material. In therapy with my patients, I start at the bottom rung of each child's contamination ladder, then lead that child through exposure and ritual prevention experiments. Taking the child's fear temperature at regular intervals ("On a scale from 1 to 10; how afraid are you?") and using the ten-minute rule as a guide (almost all anxiety in kids ebbs within that time limit) children are able to see for the first time that their anxiety will diminish over time without doing the ritual washing. In those ten minutes, an incredible transformation occurs: A child starts off incredulous, gripped by worry, a 10 on their fear thermometer; then show and tell begins. They are grabbing the doorknob, the dollar bill, the telephone, and the toilet seat with boss-back battle cries such as "Life isn't about clean. It's not my job to worry. I want to have fun!" We play cards for about five minutes—temperature now down to 6—then do more boss-back talk. I may goad them by saying that OCD wants them to go wash—it's telling them that their freedom isn't important, it's all about being clean: "Don't listen to Dr. Chansky, she can't protect you like I can." "Yeah," I continue, "OCD is really your friend, it knows how to take care of you—so what if the rules are different for you. So what if you can't have fun like the other kids—you don't mind, do you?" Then, with five minutes of success under their belts, children are free to be red-hot mad, "NO! I'm not going to listen to this stupid stuff!" A few minutes later and after three games of spit, they've made it through, saying, "That wasn't as bad as I thought—how could something so hard, be so simple too?" Practice at home following this session is essential for the child to master the skill, so that later he can't chalk up the success to beginner's luck and return to ritualizing. Be forewarned: practice at home may be more anxiety producing than in the safety of the office, so your child may have more difficulty completing the exposure. Your child's therapist should prepare you for this by reminding you of the exposure one rung lower (less anxiety-provoking) on the ladder so this can be practiced instead if necessary.

Behavior Therapy, Not Behavior Scare-apy

Some people think that going to behavior therapy means they'll be forced to stick their hands in toilets and contaminate their clothes with the "stuff"—and all in the first session. In fact, behavior therapy was never meant to be about forcing people to do anything. If it were, it would be no different from OCD's reign of terror. Behavior therapy is about helping children regain control and take on challenges that are holding them back from freedom. It is not a prepackaged, one-size-fits-all therapy. The child chooses the challenge he is ready for, and that's how therapy progresses. Any step can be divided into smaller ones so there is always a challenge that is the right "size" for a child.

Is it safe to expose kids to germs? I would never ask a child to do something I was not willing to do myself—and I've got my hand on (not in!) the toilet right along with them. In these sessions, I am modeling reasonable risk taking. There are no guarantees of safety, but the contrived exposures are actually simulations of what people do all the time, just without knowing it: You pet your cats good-bye, take out the garbage, stop and pump gas in the car, maybe even thinking, *Ooh, I better wash my hands when I get to work.* But by the time you get to work and stop to chat with the secretary, you can't resist the chocolate-glazed donut on her desk. Into your mouth it goes, not another thought. No one gets hurt. Park yourself inside a public bathroom for a day and try counting the number of people who don't wash their hands, yet our hospitals aren't filled with forgetful hand washers.

The purpose of these exposures is not to make children careless or sloppy, but to return the *choice* of washing back to its rightful owner—the child, not his stymied brain.

Some kids with OCD know what "normal" washing consists of and may even do it from time to time. Others know that their washing is excessive, but they've done it for so long that they have lost the schema or picture for what's okay to do. You can teach them how to wash once and done, but they might think, *Well, it was okay this time because my hands weren't really that dirty because I scrubbed before I came to the appointment, and I was careful not to touch anything in my therapist's office.* It is for this reason that we need to be more extreme in our contamination exposures.

Breaking the Rules: Turning the Trick Back on OCD

Thoughts would just stick to me. There was a boy in my grade who used to pick his nose. It was really gross—everybody thought so—but I know that nobody thought about it as much as I did. I couldn't get near him in the hallway, touch his locker. Whenever I sat at a desk, I would think, *I wonder if Peter sat here,* and then I would start getting really sick, and I couldn't touch anything on the desk. I kept one folder that was dirty, and I would lay it down on the desk and put the other stuff on top of it. Instead of making it better, it just got worse—then I had to watch everywhere the folder went. Lying in bed at night, I would picture Peter and I'd have to get up and wash my hands to get rid of the feeling. I couldn't get away from it. I thought about those stupid experiments they have where kids carry around a sack of flour to learn about the responsibility of having a baby—they should see what it's like to have OCD. When Dr. T. told me to intentionally bump into this kid Peter, like get behind in line at the drinking fountain, I thought she was nuts. But I did it—I kind of just made myself do it, and it wasn't so bad. Then I wiped his desk with a tissue and then wiped the tissue all over me—at first I was freaked, but as time went on, I thought, *So what if he picks his nose, I'm not going to catch anything*—it's just gross, it's not contagious."

—*Twelve-year-old boy*

Taking It to the Home Front: What You Can Do to Help

Your child's therapist together with your child can help determine how to use your help to hasten the recovery process. When in doubt, ask. Ask your child what help he needs and how to say it, ask the therapist how to handle the tough moments you are facing. Don't get stuck thinking that you *should* know, because there are no hard-and-fast rules and your role will change depending on what your child is tackling. What follows are general guidelines and specific interventions.

Talking the Talk

Overcoming contamination fears means two things: (1) learning to live with the thoughts and feelings of being unclean, and (2) not avoiding situations that are perceived as contaminated. Therefore, the overall strategy for parents is to relabel the situation as an OCD moment, rather than as a legitimate question about cleanliness or safety. Then show children the fork in the road: "You are asking me whether the cheese is safe. That sounds like OCD to me. Let's look at the fork in the road; there are two ways we can go here. If you follow the OCD path, it's saying make sure it is 100 percent safe. Do you want to have that job? Do you think this is dangerous, or does part of you know that it is *probably* okay to eat that cheese? OCD is going to keep scaring you into making you follow its rules. Is OCD really helping you here, or is it scaring you and bossing you around? Let's look at the other road you could take. What would you rather be doing instead? If you were free and following your own rules, what would you want to do now? Would you rather turn off that broken record of OCD and do things *your* way? Let's show and tell OCD who's the boss and take a risk to put you back in charge." Differentiate your child from the OCD: "Do *you* want to be washing now? Can you tell me what else you'd rather be doing besides worrying about cleanliness now?"

- Relabel the situation as OCD by identifying the brain trick: "Your brain isn't sending you the right message about that— we've got to teach it."
- Help your child fight the symptoms with show and tell: "Let's break the rules and do it *your* way."
- Help redirect your child: "Remember your goal is being free. You want to be clean enough. Can I help you get out of here? I know you don't want to be doing this."

Cognitive-Behavioral Interventions

Help your child distinguish between the feeling of being dirty and the facts. The facts are that he is no dirtier than anyone else, but his OCD is going to make him *feel* dirtier. Remind him that feeling dirty or anxious means he is doing the right thing. The feeling will pass—that's the point. Remember that behavior changes first, then feelings, then thoughts.

Shorten your child's washing time: Don't let him wait for the "it's clean" feeling. He should practice the agreed amount of time by using a timer or arranging that you'll knock on the door when time's up.

Don't let your child avoid things that could be dirty. Encourage him to gradually make contact with the untouchables—not a one-second touch, but significant contact. Your child must feel the anxiety in order for the exposure to be successful. The point is for him to learn to tolerate that feeling and see that it diminishes *on its own* without washing.

Sometimes it's easier to determine when your child should wash, rather than when he shouldn't. In *Getting Control,* Dr. Lee Baer offers the following rules for washing:

1. It's okay to wash after going to the bathroom.
2. It's okay to wash before eating.
3. It's okay to wash when you can *see* something dirty on your body.
4. It's okay to wash when you have touched something *labeled* poisonous.

Use a "challenge jar." Have your child write out ten or fifteen challenges that are just within her reach on slips of paper and put them in a "challenge jar"; your child can then pull out a challenge every day and earn points toward a chosen reward. For example, touching the kitchen door, the refrigerator door, using the same towel two days in a row. Once your child has completed those challenges, put in new challenges that are more difficult. Keep the old challenges on hand, so that when your child is having a tough day and is unable to tackle the new challenges, she can do some "drills" practicing with the "old."

Setting Limits on the OCD (Not on Your Child)

How and when to set limits are best decided in a collaborative fashion with your child and therapist. All the while, remember that the reason for doing so is to help your child win against the common enemy OCD.

Limiting time: washing, showering. Limits should be set gradually in order to increase your child's chance of success. Take the example of a child with showering rituals. On the bottom of a piece of paper write down how long your child is showering each day. Then ask your child what his goal is; in other words, how many minutes would he spend showering if he were free from OCD. Write this goal on the top of the page. If he is having trouble determining how long his shower should be, he can ask siblings, parents, or even friends and take an average of the answers. Then ask your child by how many minutes he wants to reduce his showering this week; say, five or seven minutes. Each step he takes brings him closer to his goal at the top of the page. If your child meets with less than 50 percent success the first week (at least every other day), it probably was set too high. Reduce the difficulty of the goal for now. Determine how your child wants this system to be enforced. Does he want to use a timer, a knock on the door, sending in the family dog?

Limiting supplies: number of towels, toothpaste, and so on. Open up a discussion with your child by saying you know it's not his fault, but that you need to help him work on limiting the amount of towels or laundry done each week, or the amount of cleaning supplies used. If your child is having difficulties with multiple supplies, write down each supply (toothpaste, mouthwash, shampoo, soap, et cetera), write down how much he is using now, how much most people use in a week, and rank the materials by how hard it would be to cut back on them. Then beginning with the "easiest" to limit item, help your child set a goal for the week.

Limiting participation in OCD and/or avoidance. If you are answering questions about cleanliness many times a day, set a goal on how often you will answer them. Or help your child set a goal for how many times a day she wants to be worrying about cleanliness and determine question coupons. Decide with your child how many question coupons per day she can spend worrying about cleanliness. Make sure to set a reasonable goal; you're not going to go from fifty times a day to three in one week. Don't engage in discussions about whether something is actually clean. If you have answered the question before, kindly relabel: "This sounds like something OCD would want to know. Remember, my job is to help you, not OCD. It's not letting you believe what you want to; it's a brain trick. Let's not fall for it." Or you could address your answer to the OCD, "There you go again, OCD, don't you get it, you're a brain hiccup, I'm sorry but we don't take advice from hiccups!"

If you are washing extra dishes for your child who is afraid that the dishwasher detergent is contaminating the food, see if she will wash them herself, or limit the number of times a day you will be dishwasher. If you are picking up laundry off your child's floor because he can't touch "dirty clothes," see if he will kick them to the hamper, or make sure he keeps them in one area of the room. Find out if there is an aspect of the laundry process he can be involved in, such as putting away the clean clothes. Your child's behavior therapist should teach your child how to wash—how much soap to use, how long to rinse, and so on. Learn the technique yourself so you can help your child stick to it at home.

Boss-Back Talk in a Nutshell

"Feeling clean shouldn't feel bad—this is not going to take over my life."

"I am clean enough. My brain just won't shut the gate on 'you're dirty.'"

"You need to go to bathroom school. I'm doing things my way!"

"I'm going to say 'no' to my brain. I'm in charge."

"Clean is not the most important thing in the world—it's not my job to worry about it."

"I'm going to be firm with the scaries. They are not going to boss me around anymore!"

Flashes of Hope

Maxwell struggled with hand washing and avoidance of disgusting objects like tissues, furniture where any sniffling person had sat, shoes, doorknobs, or anything that touched the floor. With intensive behavior therapy he faced his fears and learned to not let the "gross" alarm rule his life. Even after he appeared to have conquered most of this, I often found myself watching (anxiously, of course) for things to reappear. My flash of hope came in the lobby of K-mart when looking around for my son, I saw him—fourteen-years-old—slithering across the floor trying to outsmart the electronic-eye door opener, by getting to the door on his stomach before it opened automatically. Then I knew I had my son back.

*   *   *

While we are still in the midst of our nine-year-old Brianna's OCD, there are times that give me encouragement that this will someday all be history. Early on, she was avoiding foods due to possible ink contamination from wrappers. One evening we were passing out Dove ice cream bars and Brianna was worried that it wouldn't be safe to eat. "It might be poisoned from the ink of the wrapper." Rather than responding in the usual OCD-boss-it-back way, we all offered to eat it for her. She quickly decided to chance it and happily ate it herself.

*   *   *

Twelve-year-old Bob became alarmed after learning in a drug abuse prevention class that certain chemicals, if inhaled, could cause brain damage. After this he was petrified of volatile fumes and would barricade himself in his room with towels under his door whenever his mom was cleaning or using nail polish or hair spray. He wouldn't use white-out or magic markers or even spray deodorant. He refused to go to the gas station or be around paint. OCD had taught him that if he smelled certain things he would lose his memory and get brain damaged. To reassure himself, in addition to covering his nose, or staying in his room he would repeatedly ask his mother if he has lost his memory and would have her run through a series of questions: what's your name, the date, what's 100×100? Just to make sure that he hadn't suffered brain damage. Bob named his OCD "George," after a guy he thought was sort of a bully. He set out to teach George a lesson about the difference between using chemicals as they were intended and intentionally putting your nose right up to them and sniffing them to get high. "Why would people be advertising these products on TV if they were dangerous to use?" "You've got the wrong guy George, I don't want to get high!" Within a couple of months of exposures to these contraband substances, Bob was back in charge, working with glue and wite-out, helping his dad pump the gas, watching TV when his mom did her nails, and even helping her with windexing which, prior to "George's" arrival, had been fun for Bob. When Bob wrote me a thank you card at the end of treatment, he signed it in blue permanent marker—the icing on the cake!

*   *   *

At age sixteen, Tara's life turned upside down. The focus of her life, which used to be filled with friends, school, family, narrowed down to her two hands. She couldn't touch anything, and no one could touch her. Her shoes, keys, the bathroom, laundry basket, dirty clothes, even her family was off limits to Tara. She would try to fix all the contamination of the day with half-hour showers at night. Once she had showered, no one and nothing was allowed into her room. Then, more careful than a diamond thief, Tara would move through her house, dodging doors, keys, shoes, money, papers that anyone had held. Tara describes her recovery:

I learned to throw myself into situations that are tough—just like when Dr. T. came to my house and we wiped our shoes, the ground, the toilet seats, and then contaminated my room—there was no turning back, it was too big. It got easier and easier as time went on. I told myself that my brain was mixed up and what I was feeling was not right and I could fix it. What I learned is that sometimes the way to fix a problem is to make it too big to fix. Going to college helped me to get farther away from my OCD. College is so big, everything is new, I don't know what's clean anymore, and I can't—and I don't want to—spend my time figuring it out. It was kind of liberating to me. I just watched myself doing what everyone else did: touching people, touching money, doorknobs, grabbing silverware out of a pile that other people touched. It dawned on me: *I'm living in a place where I don't know what's clean, and I can't know.* It's really been great.

CHAPTER 12

Checking/Repeating/Redoing

Doubting Your Own Senses

In the Thick of It

Anthony, age six, had always been a bright, verbal child, with a twinkle in his eye and a million questions on his mind. Anthony's mother explained, "We were very proud of our inquisitive child. Now that's all changed. I feel like the inquisitor has become the enemy. I first noticed a problem when I walked past a bush while heading out of the schoolyard. Anthony said, 'Mom, I touched that poison ivy. I might have put it in my mouth.' 'Of course you didn't Anthony—that's silly,' I replied. 'Mom, but I'm afraid, I ate a leaf—it's poisonous, I'll die.' 'Anthony, listen to me—you didn't eat the leaf, you didn't even touch it. I was watching you and you didn't. Now come on.' 'But what if you didn't see me, and I ate it, Mom look in my mouth, is it green?' We stood there in front of that bush arguing until I yelled, 'Anthony, you didn't eat the leaf and that's it—end of discussion—we're going!' Anthony started to cry and obediently followed me to the car. I felt terrible yelling at him, but there seemed no way out. After that, it mushroomed. At the dinner table Anthony asked me if the juice had poison in it. 'No, of course it isn't poison. Now knock it off.' 'But what if it is poison? You have to try it first.' Well, I agreed, and that was a huge mistake. Now for weeks Anthony won't eat anything unless I try it first. I feel like I have to ask permission before I can do anything in my own house. I have lost all leverage. And the poison ivy is still stuck in his mind. He has us telling him all day 'No your mouth isn't green,' when we refuse to answer, he runs to check in the mirror. How do you reassure someone who can't be reassured?"

Another View

Bob, who we met in Chapter 11, with OCD named George, also had checking rituals, his homework would take hours, because not only would he recheck his math problems by working them out again by hand, but he would check his work on the calculator and actually recheck the calculator's answer two, three, sometimes five times. He knew it didn't make sense, but there was always a shadow of doubt, maybe he had punched in the wrong numbers, maybe the calculator made a mistake. Bob also had a ritual where he would have to check to make sure his shirt was tucked in. Though the small thread of reality in this fear was from the dress code at his school, it went far beyond that to the point where Bob thought that if his shirt wasn't tucked in that he would do poorly in school. Over and over throughout the day, Bob would run his hand over the top of his pants to make sure his shirt was tucked, he tried to be subtle about it, but that wasn't easy. When Bob realized that this was George doing his "overdrive" trick, he began to tackle the symptom. First he refrained from checking his shirt, but to take it a step further and "spit in the eye of OCD" he wore his shirt untucked. Returning triumphant, Bob came into session and summed up what he had learned from this exposure with the following proclamation: "I can tuck the shirt in, I can leave it untucked, I could go to school naked, I'm still going to do well in school!" Bob had definitely set the record straight about who's the boss.

Feeling uncertain can be excruciating for your child. It's a physiological jolt to the doubt center; for parents it can be maddening. After washing, checking and rechecking is the second most common type of OCD symptom. Anything in a child's experience can be grist for the checking mill. For many children, it manifests in the betrayal of the most basic trust of senses of sight or sound: "Did I really lock the door or window? Did I hear the teacher right? Am I reading the board right? Did I unplug my curling iron? Did I close the drawer? Is the water faucet off? So an obsessive thought, "What if I pressed the wrong numbers on the calculator?" can make a child spend an hour recalculating a problem 5, 10, even 50 times. While it seems hard to understand to those who are not in OCD's grips, imagine how you feel when you are closing up the house before leaving for vacation. You run around closing windows, unplugging computers, turning on timers, making sure passports and tickets are packed. You've already checked, but since you're going to be gone a while, you give it a second look just to make sure, preparing for all the what-ifs that could occur in your absence.

Later in the airport, you check again, "Do I have my plane tickets and passport? Did I unplug the coffeemaker?" Or, think back to your wedding day, how you had to keep going over lists of tasks so that every detail would run smoothly, demanding that florists, best man, and caterers swear on their firstborn child that they would be there when they said they would. These are fairly universal experiences of anxiety under extraordinary circumstances. When you multiply that feeling of uncertainty and need for guarantees by infinity and imagine living like that every minute of your day, you begin to comprehend the world of the child with checking OCD.

For other children, checking may relate to a chance occurrence or thought. Someone at school rips his pants, and this spawns your child's ten-minute ritual in the morning of testing the security of each seam. A case of Lyme disease leads to your daughter's nightly methodical checking to make sure each freckle and mole isn't "moving." A passing "what if" thought watching Mom wash the counter with Comet—*Gee, it looks like flour*—led one teenager to repeatedly check that the cabinet under the sink was closed any time she was cooking. It got to the point where she would only eat sealed, prepared food because the fear was so strong.

When children don't get the "all clear" signal in their brains, they are seized by a gnawing fear that a task is not complete. Stuck in a vicious cycle of uncertainty, they go back and check again, or ask a parent to check or reassure. Recall from Chapter 2 that this behavior does not come from a willful lack of trust; rather, it is the brain circuit of "unfinished business" that activates itself. In order to shut down that circuit, a child feels he needs to know beyond a shadow of a doubt—for sure, absolutely, 100 percent.

Parents may react the first few times by reassuring their child, but when it doesn't work this quickly turns to frustration and indignation. On the other hand, parents may acquiesce to their child's concerns against their better judgment, by running around the house, checking doors, windows, the faucets, checking the smoke detectors daily. In desperation parents can do very irrational things! One mother confessed after being asked so many times by her five-year-old if he was going to die, that she told her son, "No, you're never going to die." Parents don't like to lie, but reassurance *is a trap!* While reassurance is not dangerous in and of itself, in an OCD moment, children can't process it properly: It's dangerous, like sugar to a diabetic, and useless, like trying to put out a four-alarm fire with a squirt gun.

Checking rituals are time-consuming, and the ripple effect is that getting to school and home is often difficult: Kids miss the bus, families miss events, and so on. Parents may get pulled into checking for their child in order to avoid being late. Parents feel resentful at being "enablers" of their children's OCD but don't know what else to do, because they don't want to be late again, or they hate to see their child so upset. Children don't want to ask or check over and over, but just as soap and water is a quick fix for a contamination fear, asking repeatedly for reassurance gets the doubt off a child's mind—temporarily.

Parents can resist getting pulled into their child's OCD—and still "throw their child a rope"—by staying kindly but firmly grounded in reality and pointing to the fork in the road. "If you want to be 100 percent sure, then for the rest of your life you are going to have to keep asking, checking, and redoing things. If, on the other hand, you want to be free to do things once and done, you can trade in your job as a worrier for a regular life as a kid."

RED FLAGS
- Checking or changing underwear to make sure they're dry.
- Repeatedly checking calendar or day planner to make sure events are not forgotten.
- Repeatedly calling and leaving messages for fear that it didn't work the first time.
- Checking the doors, windows, locks, smoke detectors.
- Checking to make sure the faucets, television, and light switches are off.
- Checking the contents of the book bag.
- Checking that no furniture or papers are close to electrical outlets.
- Checking for papers on the ground; rug edges flat to prevent tripping.
- Re-asking questions such as: "Are you going to get divorced? Is the water supply going to run out? Did I copy the assignment down right? Did I hear you right, can you repeat that? Is the match really out? Are the lids really closed on the cleaners, poisons?"

Key Intervention in Behavior Therapy

In behavior therapy, children with checking or repeating rituals are taught that their senses are giving them the wrong message. Instead of heeding the call to double- and quadruple-check, they are coached to break the ritual by *doing it wrong* or not at all, by feeling the doubt and uncertainty of whether something is done or right, and then walking away. By not checking the book bag, or leaving a closet door wide open, they will see their awful feeling pass, giving them a lot more time and freedom. They won't feel like robots or like they are controlled by Checker Man. They will be confident that they know *well enough* that something is finished.

To accomplish this, we go back to our pie charts. Using the example of Janice, a child who checks the lock on the door, we ask her, "How much of you fears the door is still unlocked? Is there another part of you that knows pretty well that it's closed?" Looking at Janice's chart, we see that she is more certain that the door is closed, and therefore she can be encouraged to fight by applying the Umbrella Rule. "It looks like there's a 5 percent chance that the door is open, right? On a perfectly sunny day when there's a 5 percent chance of rain, will you carry an umbrella? No. Right, that's good thinking!" Therefore, we can approach this situation by saying, "Janice, the OCD is bossing you around a lot, even though it has no right to because it's *wrong* about judging risk. We want you to be more and more in charge of yourself, and we want OCD to be less bossy.

How much of you thinks the door is open if you don't check it?

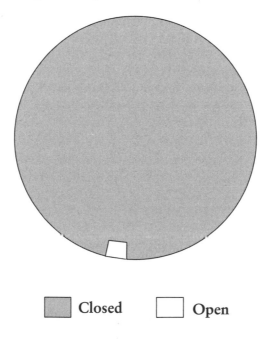

■ Closed   □ Open

How do you want to *show* OCD you are in charge? How can you break the checking rules? And how do you want to *tell* it to leave you alone? Well, you can say to yourself, 'It's the brain trick again. It's not worry time now. I think the door is locked because I locked it. I'd rather take a tiny risk of not knowing rather than interrupting what I'm doing every two minutes to go back and check.'"

At first Janice decides that she is not going to ask her parents if the door is locked anymore; next she cuts her checking from five times a night down to two; then she begins to move more s-l-o-w-l-y when locking the door, so she can say, "Okay, brain, here's your chance, pay attention, no repeat performances! Do you see me locking the door? Take notice now, because I'm not going to do it again." Finally, Janice goes to bed without checking the doors at all. She knows it's her parents' job to keep the house safe, that her urges to check are false alarms from her brain, and she's not giving in to them.

Strategies on the Home Front

First Ask: Who Wants to Know?

Encouraging your child's curiosity doesn't mean it's always good to answer all of her questions. Both for you and your child, step one in managing OCD at home is distinguishing between a "real" question and an obsession. How can you tell the difference? By asking the following questions: "Do you want to be asking me this now? Is OCD sending you junk mail again? Which mailbox does this go in, "want to" or "have to?" Do you want to be worrying about this? Or do you feel like you have to?" Questions that your child feels desperate to ask even though he doesn't want to (as evidenced sometimes by the fact he's asked it five hundred times before) are clearly OCD. Parents may initially perceive this as a child's inability to trust them, when it's actually the brain that won't let him trust himself to believe what he knows. Following the relabeling strategies in this book, your reply should be neither yes nor no when your child asks, "Are my pants ripped?" Instead, say, "Oh boy, here comes that Disaster Man again. Do you want to be asking me this, do you know the answer? He just doesn't get it. He's wasting your time, that's not fair, he's making you ask the question anyway. Let's fight him and tell him to leave you alone, let's rip him in half!" Sometimes it's not the same question over and over again, but rather it is an attack of the "how do you knows," "I might have," or the "what ifs": "How do you know if I'm not going to die in my sleep?

How do you know if Grammy and Grandpa are okay? How do you know the house won't catch fire? How do you know there are no bugs in my bed?" In these cases, parents need to quickly relabel the litany of questions as OCD: "I think OCD thinks this is danger quiz show time, making you ask all these questions. Did anyone invite OCD here? Do we want to hear what it has to say? Do you want to be thinking about these things? Let's tell OCD that you know when enough is enough!"

Then Ask: What Do You Think?

Once you have established that your child is having an OCD moment, being bossed to ask questions or check when he doesn't want to, step two is helping your child determine what *he* or *she* thinks about the situation. For example, if your child worries every time a candle or a match is lit and keeps going back even hours later to make sure the candle is out and keeps submerging the matches in water, you can ask, "How dangerous do you think it is?" Have him either give a percentage between 0 and 100, or a simple low, medium, or high. Then use the Umbrella Rule discussed with Janice above to establish *what your child would want to do if he were in charge.* Then ask him what OCD is telling him about the risks, what fears it is playing on the loudspeaker in his brain. You can also ask him if he would advise a friend to take the same precautions. Finally, encourage your child to act on what he believes is *likely* to happen rather than what OCD is threatening *could* happen.

In summary, the answer isn't more answers, because your child is stuck in question-and-answer mode. The answer is getting your child unstuck. This is really no different from your child being stuck at the sink asking, "Are my hands clean enough? How do I know if my hands are clean enough?" You are not going to tell him to keep washing until they are clean enough, because his own brain isn't letting him know what "clean enough" is. Likewise, his brain isn't letting him know that an action has been completed the first time through, so you want to help him: "Your brain can't close the gate on the 'what ifs,' I see how upset this is making you, we need to boss it back." The way out of the endless maze of back-and-forth questions is to focus on the process (the child is stuck with an obsessive thought) more than the content (what the child is asking). The parent calls attention to the third party—the OCD—and joins the child in fighting back the "doubting dragon." For example, "It sounds like the doubting dragon has got you—you're getting so upset, and it's getting late. If we can tell the dragon to buzz off and leave you alone, then we can still have our bedtime stories." This way the parent offers the child a way out, rather than helping him to dig himself in deeper with the OCD.

Successful management of this type of symptom involves a cooperative system in which the child's limitations and the family's needs are both taken into account. In this system, parents coach a child either with a timer ("two minutes of checking, then we go"), coaching phrases ("fight this thing, it's getting you stuck"), or using incentives ("if you can get in the car on time, we'll have time to stop for donuts"). See box below for ideas to limit checking.

IDEA BOX FOR REDUCING CHECKING

Identify the danger zones for checking (doors, outlets, book bag, light switch). Don't go in those areas without a plan:

- Establish your purpose for being in those areas: to *look* (because you want to) or to *check* (because OCD is telling you to)
- Decide how many times you are going to check, reducing the number gradually from your baseline
- Put up signs to remind you of your goal: No checking here! Check-free Zone!
- Bring a helper with you to make sure you keep to your goal.

Making a checking budget. Decide how many situations you are going to check in a day. Give yourself checking coupons to spend.

- Post checking coupons on site. To limit checking to 3 times, put three coupons (brightly colored index cards) in an envelope by the sink, door, or bookbag, then behind those put one more card that says, "Danger Zone: Go get a helper." If you've done your three checks and go back for more, the danger card will remind you that you need more folks on your team to win the battle.

Establish check-free zones and expand them as you progress:
- If you check doors, choose a door you will not check
- If you check homework, choose a subject you will not check
- If you check your watch, cover it for certain periods each day

Do anti-checking maneuvers to see that you can survive:
- Leave the door open
- Leave a schoolbook at home
- Load up your bookbag with your eyes closed
- Cover up your mirror

Handling Reassurance Questions:
Once and Done

When your child asks you a question, the ultimate goal is to use the Once and Done Rule: Answering the question just once. If, however, your child is repeating the same questions, the key is to relabel this as OCD. "That's not *your* question, that's an obsession. I want to talk with you, not the OCD." Then point to the fork in the road. "The OCD wants you to keep asking to be 100 percent certain. It's not very smart, is it? It can do only one thing; it keeps repeating the same question like a broken record. How do you want to do things? What would you do if you were boss? Do you want to be asking that? Does part of you already know the answer to that question? How big is that part? Let's make that part even stronger by bossing back the OCD. The doubt has got you. Let's fight it together. Let's show your brain who is in charge by not asking that question—ask me a question you want to ask instead. Now let's tell OCD to take a hike, go fly out the window, we don't want it here." Then after relabeling and fighting OCD with show and tell, help your child "pick up his brain" and put it where he wants it to be by engaging in a more desirable activity. Getting the questions down from twenty times to once and done is a gradual process. See Idea Box below for guidelines.

IDEA BOX

To reduce the number of times your child asks reassurance questions:

- Establish periods of the day when your child will practice *not* asking the questions with "it's not checking time now"; gradually increase these blocks of time as your child successfully resists asking.
- Have your child write down the "answer" on a card rather than asking you—this is *less* reassuring and brings your child one step closer to independence.
- Make question coupons for the number of times your child may ask a question each day. Reduce the number of coupons each week that your child has met his goal.
- Give your child points for each hour she doesn't ask for reassurance, or asks and then relabels the question as OCD for herself.
- Encourage your child to change the question: Ask it wrong, sing it, say it backward, or replace it with a nonsense phrase "Are the aliens landing on earth today?"

Sometimes, rather than asking for reassurance or checking himself, a child will ask a parent to check for him. While you may be tempted to take this personally and angrily say, "I'm not your servant, I'm not going to do your dirty work," it is best in these moments to remember that your child is being bossed around too! Instead, use the same strategies as above. Relabel: "That is an obsession, it's a brain trick. Your brain is telling you that the water might be on, but your brain is sending you the wrong message—it's giving you the wrong information." Show and Tell: say to OCD, "Knock it off. You are interrupting my movie, I'm not going to listen to you. You're wasting my time."

Flashes of Hope

I started to feel better when I could say to my six-year-old, "That's the Checker, you don't have to check." Before that I would get so upset when he would run back upstairs to make sure his books or his Legos were still in the same place—even though he'd just spent ten minutes checking it. Initially I would get so upset because I was so afraid for him. I would get angry, get hysterical, or try to convince him it was fine. Then he would get furious, and we would both end up crying. He's been free of symptoms for nearly a year now. I do worry that it will come back, but I know that if I can keep my fears under control, then I can really help him cope.

—Mother of six-year-old

* * *

After months of practicing, the first time when I left the house without actually checking the water and the stove and the locks, I felt one hundred times lighter, I couldn't imagine that I could go to school without worrying about all the bad things that could happen. I just kept thinking, *It's not my job, it's not real, I'm allowed to be free and happy. The more I fight this, the more I'll be free.* And I just pushed myself through that one day—after that it got a lot easier.

—Ian, fifteen-year-old

Megan's mother writes:

Every night we would argue with Megan to go to bed, some nights until midnight. She would not settle down, kept jumping out of bed and checking the windows. She had to sleep with the shades up, the door wide open, and the light on. She kept asking about burglars; she wanted us to say good night in a certain way. It seemed like she was manipulating us, but she was also scared. It was confusing, but she couldn't explain what was happening to her. We didn't know about OCD; at first we would try to reassure her, but then we would yell—we thought she was acting up.

Megan, age thirteen, writes:

> I used to sit on my steps crying to my parents because I thought I was going to stop breathing and die or that someone would come murder my family and I, or just me, or that they would kidnap me.

Now, after a year of treatment, Megan's mom writes:

> Megan did most of the treatment herself, but just knowing what the problem was and reminding her, "No, that's just OCD" helped us to help her. I knew how far we had come the night Megan went to bed with the shade down in her room and her bedroom door almost completely closed, no jumping out of bed to check, no questions asked. She just went to bed like any other child. We get along so much better now—our house is no longer a battle zone. She can even watch scary movies and that doesn't set her off.

Megan writes:

> I'll tell you the truth. I thought telling my OCD to go away wouldn't help me and was stupid. But it really makes a difference. Now I can go to bed without any worries. I can go to sleepovers without being scared. I had to work on each problem one step at a time, but I got so far! We called OCD The Scare Box, like it was this box in my brain that just said scary things—that didn't make it real, it was just like a tape recorder. I told it, "Listen or else; I'm the boss, you're not, OCD. Leave me alone. This is my brain, and you're not taking control of it. Knock it off! I'm in charge. I know I'm going to be safe." It was really hard work and not fun to deal with, but it really did work. I'm not a scaredy cat—it was not me, it's just a part of my brain. Whenever I slip, I just say those things each night and it really helps, believe me!

Fourteen-year-old Justin has been a checker since he was eleven, unable to settle in at night, seized by the idea that the doors are unlocked. His parents would tell him to just forget about it, do something else, and Justin would try to explain he could think of nothing else but the doors. One day he came in to the session and said, "You won't believe what I did today—it was kind of amazing. . . . You know I told you kids at school see me go back to check if I've locked my locker. Sometimes it's two or three times, sometimes it's more. Most kids don't care, like it's just something I do, but today I had gone back two times and I was doing okay I felt like it was okay to leave, it wasn't going to be one of those days when I feel like I'll never leave the building. And these jerk loudmouths called me down the hall just as I was at the door and said, 'Yo, Justin, you left your locker open.' I turned around, my face turned beet red, I was furious—I was trapped, like I knew either if I went back and checked I'd look like a fool, but if I didn't I'd be obsessing all night. It's exactly what goes on in my head—they were doing what the OCD does to me, it makes me furious. It's like they see me choke, and I hate that, I feel like such a jerk—I'm this robot, this lame robot and I hate it. I was so mad like they knew they had me."

Justin: I just thought about how you said "throw yourself out of the bathroom—like when I was checking that the faucets were off—and before I knew it, I was just throwing myself out the door. I felt like there were these chains on me, but I was breaking out of them. I couldn't believe it. I felt kind of bad, but I kept thinking, *I'm not going to choke. This is stupid, if it's unlocked. I'll deal—I can get new books, new pencils, but you are stealing my free will, and I'm not going to let you.* I felt kind of good too like, I'm bigger than this—I felt big."

Me: Wow, Justin, that is so excellent—what a victory for you. You faced the fear and you pushed back—right out of the building. In charge! How do you feel now?

Justin: You know, it was easier than I thought, I thought I'd feel horrible, but it wasn't that bad—and I felt good like, I went to the mat a total KO.

Me: You sound really confident there. Are you ready to reclaim your locker for good?

Justin: Yep, I'm sick of wasting time.

Me: Okay, we can start slow—having you walk out without checking, or you can go for broke and shut your eyes when you lock it, or—

Justin: I know—or just go right to leaving it open.

CHAPTER 13

Just Right

*Evenness, Ordering, Symmetry,
Numbers, and Hoarding*

"I have to see it right, and it's wrong!" screamed fourteen-year-old Noah, his parents wrestling him to the ground. "It's okay, you look fine, you are fine, calm down." Noah was flailing as if trying to shake off a scorpion. His assailant was a pattern of thinking that demanded he be able to see his face "right." For several months Noah and his family were at the mercy of this pattern that he needed to see in his own face: His eyes had to look a certain way to him—the "good look"—or he couldn't go on. He would go back and forth between the mirror and his family until he felt that the good look had returned to his face. His family was afraid that he was psychotic: They couldn't see what he was talking about, but they knew it was serious.

Noah explained how all this started when his art class was studying portraits. His teacher explained that the two sides of many portraits' faces often bear a different "look," which Noah found unsettling, because he wanted both sides to have the same look. Then, on a trip to the art museum, he glanced at the portrait of a man and felt the subject's eyes following him. At that moment, he had a bad feeling—that was the look of evil to Noah. In the bathroom mirror that night Noah caught a glimpse of the same look in his eyes and had a sick feeling that he was evil, too. From then on, whenever he looked in the mirror, he would have to stare at himself so that he could recapture the "good" look on both sides of his face.

His parents were at their wits' end; they kept trying to reassure him that he looked fine. They even suggested covering up all the mirrors. Noah knew that it wouldn't help, though he didn't understand why. He just knew the bad picture would be stuck in his mind. Noah had handwashing rituals when he was eleven but had been able to stop them with some encouragement from his parents. While with hand washing, he could walk away from the sink and say, "enough," this obsession was always with him. It was more personal; it attacked his confidence, made him doubt who he was: "I am nuts to be staring at myself in the mirror. I am crazy to be thinking I can fix a picture by looking at it a certain way."

Noah needed to know that this "just right" symptom was really no different from hand washing. His brain was stuck on doing things a certain way that made no sense, but unless he did it that way, he felt a terrible dread in the pit of his stomach. To help Noah conquer this symptom, he had to see the bad look and not fix it. Looking first at an imaginary mirror Noah drew on the blackboard, we practiced other ways of responding to his reflection. Within two weeks, he was ready to face the mirror. This time, he realized that there's no such thing as seeing yourself "right," that anyone who looks closely enough can see many different looks in his face. "The mirror is a piece of glass—it's not going to run my life. Okay, so I see that look, so what, keep looking at it, what else do I see? It's me—it's just me. Yeah, could I do something wrong today? Sure, anybody could, but that has nothing to do with the look on my face. I'd rather not know for sure than stand here looking in the mirror for hours to try to prevent it."

Coaching Noah through this, I could see his anxiety break like a fever. His body was tense and pained as he first looked in the mirror, but then he turned a corner. "This wasn't bad. I thought it would be horrible, like maybe if I didn't fix it by seeing it the right way, the evil would get me. How dumb. I guess that's what OCD is all about. Looking evil doesn't mean being evil." To galvanize his confidence, I asked Noah if he could take it one step further, by trying to make his worst evil faces in the mirror to see that he could tolerate even that. We summoned the most hateful, evil images from movies that we could recall, practiced the expressions of chainsaw murderers doing grizzly deeds. Humor can erupt in the strangest of places. As we both began to laugh at the absurdity of the exercise, it was clear that Noah not only had "won" back the mirror from OCD, but he was well on his way to winning back himself.

Just Right

The category of evenness or "just right" OCD encompasses many different symptoms:

- Ordering objects: Lining up dolls exactly by height or straightening papers on the desk.

- Repeating the same mundane action: Walking in and out of a doorway several times.
- Touching certain objects in a certain way.
- Making things symmetrical: Footsteps, chewing, touching one side of the face and then the other.
- Counting: Floor tiles, syllables.
- Perfectionism: Rewriting a letter ten times or more until it is perfectly formed.

What unifies these different behaviors is a sense of precision; for some children that precision means that they feel uncomfortable until something is done the right way or the right number of times; for others it is a pursuit of perfection.

While this may look to the outsider as rigidity or inflexibility by choice, generally these children are not in control of where they are headed, and the results are often disastrous. Take for example the child who keeps sharpening a new pencil down to a stub because the point never felt sharp enough, or the child who turns in homework glopped-up with white-out and tattered with holes from erasing because one letter was always slightly flawed. While these children know that their actions are going against their every intention, they don't see a choice. As with the child trying to get through a doorway who has to cross the threshold ten times, they can't move on. Sometimes children do the compulsions to avoid a feared consequence, such as a fatal car accident or illness to a family member; for other children it's simply because *not* doing it just right would feel impossibly uncomfortable.

In the past, these children were seen as rigid by choice. Worse still, some psychoanalytic thinkers hypothesized that this was a compensation for a sadistic desire to control and dominate others. It is hard to imagine this shoe fitting when one considers the unhappiness of the child who is chronically missing recess to finish her work or the child who misses softball practice because he can't get his cap on exactly straight. As we saw in Chapter 2, current thinkers hypothesize a brain glitch: The "it's done" or completion message is not available. As Dr. William Hewlett describes, the "dreadful uncertainty" or "incomplete" circuits continue to fire—even after the job is done. The physiologically triggered feeling of satisfaction that normally follows a completed action never comes. Children repeat, count, fix, and "even out" with a physical urgency in an attempt to evoke that elusive feeling of completion. The sense of completion most of us get by clicking the last piece of a jigsaw puzzle into place never registers, not through some flaw in personality or compensatory maneuver, but rather a wiring glitch.

The Crack of the Bat

Unlike compulsive washing or checking, which are loosely purposeful though excessive, "just right" OCD can appear bizarre and robotic. What is it like for these children? How can that need for completion be so strong?

There are subtle parallels in our daily lives—like the click of your seatbelt—that signal to us clear as a bell, done! Imagine if you needed to have that feeling in many mundane situations throughout the day. Most people have experienced the auditory delight at a baseball game when bat meets ball just right and there is a crack that is like nothing else in the world. Now imagine a game where you saw the bat hit the ball . . . but there was no sound. The stadium would be in an uproar. Fans would be jumping up and down for a replay until that crack of the bat was heard—such is the world of a "just right" kid.

What children need to know about just-right is that it's like waiting for a sneeze to happen. You think you *have* to sneeze, feel like you can't think of anything else *but* sneezing . . . and then you don't! It's not finished, almost unbearably, but then your brain ultimately moves on. That comparable physical sensation of awaiting the anticipated just-rightness will pass if you take a different action.

What to Look For

RED FLAGS
- Patterns: Walking a certain way, going up the stairs by ones or twos, or going up and down repeatedly
- Tapping on objects, walls, or banisters in a certain cadence
- Bad luck and good luck numbers
- Excessive slowness because of precision or redoing many times
- Evening things out: Scratching one arm, having to scratch the other
- Lining up objects in rows, making ends even
- Classifying and categorizing with great precision, sorting objects
- Counting, repeating actions a certain number of times
- Rewriting assignments, using white-out, refolding or rebuttoning clothes, retying shoes, re-cuffing socks
- Walking through the door in a certain way
- Leaving a room through the same door entered
- Getting up and down from the chair a certain number of times

- Holding the edges of a book or paper exactly evenly
- Brushing teeth or hair excessively or too hard

Primary Intervention in Behavior Therapy—
Just Right? Not So

Children with just-right OCD have become slaves to fixing things or redoing them in order to get that "okay feeling." The first intervention is to explain to your child that the brain center that sends out the "okay feeling" isn't working, and instead the "it's not right yet" or "incomplete" button is stuck. In other words, relabel the rule of just-right as a brain trick—a broken record, junk mail, or a bossy boss who says, "Do it again, it's got to be my way or the highway, make it even!" Next, you'll work with your child's therapist, using exposure and ritual prevention techniques, to help your child use Show and Tell to see that she can break the rules of just-right and survive, that the bad or incomplete feeling *will* pass without her evening-out or fixing. Armed with boss-back talk, and using the ten-minute rule, your child will set out on behavioral experiments, trying things she's never done before.

These experiments are of two kinds. The first type is breaking the rules—intentionally doing the opposite of the OCD commands. Those whose compulsion is to order will instead "mess it up," counters will name colors to prevent themselves from counting or do things the *wrong* number of times; those with strong superstitions will "step on the cracks," and kids with symmetry compulsions will make things "lopsided." The second type of experiment will be to get your child to resist fixing things: If he makes a mistake, he leaves it; if the picture is crooked, he walks away.

For most children, this may be the first time they've ever tried to do things differently, not because they *believe* in the necessity of their counting or ordering (they don't!), but because they're frightened about taking a risk. Many kids think it's just faster to fix or even things out. They need to be reminded that OCD is like the greedy monster depicted in Chapter 2: The more you feed it, the more it wants. What seems like a quick solution—giving in just this once—becomes instead a whole way of life. By contrast, the relief they feel from being released from their robotic actions is nothing less than sublime. As one child described, "Though these patterns are so dumb, I didn't think I'd ever be able to change them, when I broke them, I was surprised at how much easier it was than I thought it would be."

Boss-Back Talk in a Nutshell

"This isn't Simon Says, I'm doing it my way."

"Life isn't math class, I'm not counting."

"Don't fix it, be free."

"I don't need to hear the crack of the bat."

"Just-right isn't as important as being free."

"OCD doesn't know how to finish things, but I do."

"Perfect is a trap, good enough is something I can live with!"

"My freedom is worth ten minutes!"

"You can keep going OCD, but I'm stopping here!"

"You're not going to make me a robot, I'm in charge!"

"I'm not going to listen to this—I know it's not necessary."

"You are a brain hiccup, you're not smart enough to tell me what to do."

In therapy, your child will make a hierarchy of rituals and avoidances and work his way up by doing experiments in session and practicing at home. You'll learn ritual breaking for several subtypes of just-right OCD. Your child's therapist can help you determine how to best support your child. Later in the chapter, I'll offer some suggestions for how you can help.

Subtypes of Just-Right

Patterns and Symmetry: Surviving Just-Wrong

Dylan, age fifteen, had to walk in patterns, making sure that there were an even number of steps in each sidewalk square—grass was easier, cobblestones were hell. He counted his steps so carefully in order to prevent harm to his family. Even was safe, odd meant danger and that he'd have to go back and do it again. Though he hated it and knew that it was crazy, he thought he better not take a risk and break the pattern, given that he wanted his family to be safe.

When starting out with Dylan, I asked him how I would get from our chairs over to the window directly in front of us. He replied, "Just get up and walk to it—is this a trick question?" "What if I thought I had to get up and walk around the table six times before I could proceed to the window or I might die?" "That would be a waste—what does the table have to do with it?" "But what if I didn't want to take the chance to find out if just walking was safe?" "Okay, I get it. You'd be wasting a lot of time . . . just like me." I told Dylan that right now he could kind of hide the patterns, but what if OCD asked him to stand up and do jumping jacks every three steps to make sure everyone was safe, would he go for that? "This really is ridiculous—I've had enough of this crap." Now, Dylan was ready to begin messing up his steps in earnest. Hopping, walking with eyes closed, or walking while singing the words to "The Three Stooges" theme song, Dylan began to "find his feet" and reclaim his walking territory from OCD.

The parents of Jenn, age ten, explained: "At dinner we could see Jenn's hands were under the table, but we didn't have to look to know what she was doing. 'Thumb-pinky, thumb-pinky, right hand, left hand'—there was a certain pattern she would do with her hands, usually two times, sometimes four, sometimes ten, but always an even number and always till it felt done. Sometimes it would be her feet too. Toes up then down, up then down, till it felt right. It wasn't as conspicuous as some of her other symptoms, but when we saw it, we knew she was tense and we wanted her to stop. It was upsetting to see a visible reminder of her problem. We wanted her OCD to leave her alone."

In session with Jenn, we worked on breaking the rules and changing the pattern—doing it on one hand or foot only. "At first I felt like I was going to explode," said Jenn, "not evening things out. But I knew that I hated OCD and that really I was in charge. I knew I wasn't a robot and that OCD couldn't force me to do things. There's nothing physically making me do it, so I did my boss-back talk and then I fought the urge to even. Sometimes I would mess it up on purpose. I imagined that I was a powerful boss in an office, and I was telling OCD what to do, and saying, 'Now I'm the boss, I'm the grown-up. I boss you, you listen to me, I'm in charge here.' My parents helped me, too—instead of getting mad, they learned to say, 'Jenn, it's not your fault, we'll get through this. I'm not going to let the OCD win, we're going to boss it back!'"

Counting Rituals

Some children may need to repeat an action a certain number of times to feel "just right," while others, like Dylan above, have rules about numbers to avoid—such as odd, even, or certain numbers and all their multiples. The fear associated with the "bad" numbers can be so strong that kids may write the wrong answer to a math problem, or only do the even-numbered problems, or may even stop doing math altogether to not take any chances. For other children, counting itself is the ritual.

HOW TO BREAK THE ASSOCIATION
BETWEEN A SITUATION AND COUNTING

- *Gradually reduce the number of times an action is performed.* If a child has to brush hair one hundred strokes, reduce it to fifty, twenty, and ten; then help her brush without any counting.
- *Change the way the counting is done.* Say it in a French accent, sing it, say it faster or slower, count backwards.
- *Refrain from counting.* Instead, engage in conversation or list colors, months of the year, favorite musicians.
- *If a child is counting to a particular number, count to the "wrong" number.* If he avoids certain numbers, such as 13 or 6, do exposure to those numbers; for example, have "13 Day," turn the TV or radio dial to 13, put up posters of 13, write 13 on a piece of paper as many times as possible without doing anything to "undo" the bad luck.

In order to concentrate on keeping an accurate count, children may ignore conversation or isolate themselves from others so that they are not distracted. This may look like rude or inattentive behavior—children blatantly ignoring friends, parents, or teachers—but they are actually focusing very intently on counting exactly right to ward off an imagined catastrophe such as a parent's death or a fire.

Perfectionism: Cultivating Excellence, Not Perfection—Entering the World of "Good Enough"

We think of a perfectionist as one who indulges *his* own need for precision and demands the ultimate in exactness. When children are getting only five hours of sleep because they were up forming their letters just right or rereading each sentence ten times to make sure they understood it right, "indulgent" and "demanding" are hardly accurate descriptions. The brain trick here is that "good enough" doesn't exist. Like a relentless tyrant, OCD keeps saying, "It could be better, more even, more perfect." Unfortunately, often in the process of redoing, things deteriorate; a teenager cutting her bangs evenly ends up with no bangs, or a paper erased so many times ends up illegible. Some children with perfectionism OCD may procrastinate. Rather than being sucked in for hours in pursuit of the elusive just right, they put off work or sometimes stop doing work altogether in anticipation of defeat.

For this type of OCD, we ask children, "Is there a way to do it well enough and also get the other things that you want?" When you're in the perfection tunnel, all you can see is what's wrong—there's no light at the end of that tunnel. As Dr. David Burns points out in *Feeling Good Therapy,* "Perfection is the world's greatest con game . . . everything can be improved." The answer is not more perfection and fixing; rather, it's finding the fork in the road, knowing that you don't have to go into that tunnel. When you step out of the pursuit of perfection tunnel you see the other things you want to achieve—time, fun, relaxation—and you break its spell. Putting words to the voice that drives the perfection machine—let's call it Mr. Perfect—a child can see and become angered by how it is robbing him of his time and be determined to stop his campaign. "Mr. Perfect says, 'This is the most important thing—you know you can make it perfect if you keep doing it, so what if other kids are playing and having fun, you're different, this is more important than anything in your life.' Do you agree with that? What do you want to tell Mr. Perfect?"

OCD has left eight-year-old Susanna frustrated and behind in her work. Her parents and teachers were urging her to work faster, with reassurances that it didn't matter how it looks. However, these words didn't even reach Susanna's processing board. They buzzed like static, because she was already engaged in a brainwashing voice, hearing on the loudspeaker in her brain, "It's not right, it should be better, it can be better, do it again!"

During a session with Susanna, I made the distinction between working hard by choice—when you want to—and doing it for Mr. Perfect—when you feel like you have to. We talked about how satisfying it is to do things a certain way, to make a report cover really beautiful, coloring in every feather of the peacock until it's just the way you want it. "But there are probably other times it isn't so fun to have to do it just right. For example, if you're finishing up a worksheet in math class and the 7 doesn't look right, and you have to keep erasing it and fixing it until it is perfect. Meanwhile, the bell rings, the teacher is waiting, your friends are standing over your shoulder, and you're getting more and more nervous and tense about making the 7 just right." "That happens all the time. I want to leave it, but I can't." I explained why Susanna can't leave—"because Mr. Just Right is saying that nothing is more important on earth than getting the 7 perfect. Do you agree with Mr. Just Right that nothing else matters? Maybe it's just making you feel like you're going to die or something bad is going to happen unless you get it right. It's like there's a battle going on in your head between Just Right and Good Enough, who says, 'Sure you want to do your best, but don't waste time on it and mess it up more.'"

We practiced "good enough" by going to the extreme first. We drew pictures with our eyes closed and wrote words with our eyes closed. We tried to write things at lightening speed. Then we imagined being in school and practiced bossing back Mr. Just Right.

Obsessive Slowness

Some children with OCD feel they are moving slowly, like moving through Jello. This may be abundantly clear to an observer—it can take hours to eat a meal or to get into a car. In some cases, however, there is no hint of it from the outside, while inside the child's mind The Rusher is badgering them: Why are you taking so long? Hurry up! Can't you get things done faster?" Against this backdrop of haste, they are caught in a web. They move more slowly to make sure they are not messing up. You can address this with young children by helping them see that they can function in different speeds—turtle speed is super slow, cheetah speed is super fast. You can practice this with talking, drawing, or walking. Once children have practiced turtle and cheetah speed (i.e., slow and fast), then you can encourage them to find an animal they want to be in between—for example, a horse. Then whatever activity they are doing—homework, teeth brushing, or eating—they can decide what speed they want to go. Older children can experiment with operating in different gears, or simply choose between slow, medium, or fast.

Hoarding and Collecting

Some children collect items for fear that they will need them someday or that something bad will happen if they throw them out. One child could not throw out birthday cards because she had an obsession that this would mean she was going to die. Another child believed that if he threw something out, something bad would happen to the person who gave it to him. Sometimes, there is no feared consequence associated with throwing things out, but there is a need to pick up items—bottle caps, papers, rocks—because it wouldn't feel right not picking them up. Feel right, that is, in crack-of-the-bat sense. To the outside observer, this situation looks highly solvable—just throw the stuff out or don't pick it up to begin with. To the sufferer, this triggers doubt and dread and the thoughts, *I could never, I might need it, or if I don't pick it up someone could trip on it and get hurt, I can't throw it out.* Approach this one step at a time, throwing out little things first, less important things. Encourage your child to fill up a bag with old toys to give away so that she can get new toys.

Children with hoarding behavior may have difficulty spending money, but unlike someone who is stingy and finds pleasure in saving money, the child with OCD feels anxiety about spending money, fears that spending money will bring bad luck or that he will run out of money. Some children may actually keep tabs on parents' money, worrying that it will run out. The approach here is to help your child spend some money and save some, beginning with a small amount—Show and Tell. Show the OCD that it is okay to spend money, that people need to do so, because it is necessary for life and also because it can be fun to spend money on something you like. For example, if a child gets $5 a week allowance, a challenge could be to spend $2 and save the other $3, and then increase it until he can spend the whole amount. Remember, the point is not to change your child into someone who spends all of his money, but rather to give him back the power to choose when and how he does spend rather than letting OCD fears make the decision for him.

Psychologists Dr. Gail Steketee and Dr. Randy Frost emphasize how hoarding represents a cognitive blindspot wherein the person focuses on the "what if" of *needing* the object, which eclipses the real consequences of not throwing things out—being overrun and encumbered by mountains of belongings.

Redoing: If at First You Don't Succeed, Don't Try Again!

Will had just-right compulsions about light switches, his clothing, and shutting doors. Nothing felt right the first time, and he would have to repeat an action until it did. His symptoms were mostly a problem at home. His family came to ignore the lights flicking on and off, the sounds of doors and cabinets opening and closing. At school his greatest challenge was changing clothes after gym class. He had to retie his shoes till the tension was exactly the same in both shoes and rebutton his shirt so that each button felt just right or he'd have to do it over again. Sometimes he would go into the bathroom to redo his shirt; t-shirts weren't an option because his school uniform was a button-down shirt. Through behavior therapy exposures to "not fixing" his clothes and shoes, Will was able to overcome this symptom. He wrote: "Actually, after I had that awful feeling of not fixing things, I thought to myself, *This is totally unnecessary. Mankind could never survive if everyone did this stuff—therefore there is no reason for me to do it. I'm fighting this till I win.* Incredibly, I felt the bad feeling pass—I never thought it would—I felt like I burst out of a bubble or something. I felt better than okay because I felt free."

Parents' Intervention for "Just Right"

As described in the behavior therapy section, there are two key interventions. The first is relabeling: "The feeling of just-right is your brain getting sticky—not letting you feel done until you've done something a certain number of times." The second is knowing that the uncomfortable feeling that comes from breaking OCD's rules really will go away without doing rituals and your child will feel much better. When working with your child on breaking free from these symptoms, ask him the following questions:

"How is OCD bossing you around?"

"What is it telling you to do?"

"What do you want to do instead?"

"What is the guarantee that OCD is offering?"

"Do you believe it?"

"Is it worth the price you're paying?"

"Could you 'sell' that guarantee to a friend?"

"How do you want to break OCD's rules?"

Here are some examples of breaking the rules of Just Right. Enlist your child's creativity and imagination to generate other ways to launch a mission against Just Right. Remember to have your child rate the difficulty level of the experiments from 0 to 10 or low, medium, high. Begin with easier challenges and work your way up the ladder. You can vary the degree of difficulty by adjusting the amount of time the child does the challenge. In general, it is most effective to designate "practice" periods—specific days or parts of a day, where your child is going to concentrate on doing things "her way," not "OCD's way."

- *Rewriting:* Limit the number of erasures, have him make "mistakes" on purpose; for example, don't cross one "t" or dot one "i"; have your child write with eyes closed. Choose one homework subject each night that is going to be OCD-free.
- *Rereading:* Ask your child to read out loud, read with a brightly colored card covering what he's already read (so he can't reread) and keep moving the card down as he finishes a line. Xerox the material and have your child cross out the words with a thick marker as he reads; that way he can't go back.

- *Ordering:* Have your child put objects in the wrong order; for example, not arranged by height or color, mix the objects up haphazardly; or leave objects out (don't put them where they belong).
- *Symmetry:* Have window shades at different heights; have your child wear different-color socks or two different earrings.
- *Hoarding:* Keep a basket at your front door for your child to deposit the day's collected items. Your child can then sort for a minute or two at regular daily or weekly intervals, discarding all but the essential. In your child's room have her sort belongings into three piles and mark three boxes or grocery store bags with the following three categories: keep, maybe keep, and give away. As they are sorting a drawer, alternate placing items in every category—otherwise everything will be "keep." Give away the "don't needs" and put the "maybes" in storage for a period of three to six months. If your child doesn't use the items during that time period, then those are ready to be given away.

Relabeling Reassurance Questions

Your child may ask for reassurance: "Is that letter right? Are my pigtails perfectly even? Are my pant seams perfectly straight?" Rather than getting pulled into the black hole of certainty, point to the fork in the road: "Who wants to know? Sounds like Mr. Perfect again. Do you want to keep thinking about this? Or do you want to be having fun? Let's boss it back."

Set Time Limits for Rituals

If your child is getting stuck because of just-right rituals—whether in the morning preparing for school or at night doing homework and getting to bed—you can help him set a time limit and provide incentives for meeting it. Decide on a reasonable amount of time for individual tasks or for groups of related tasks, such as bedtime or before-school preparations. Then set a timer or be a human time keeper—checking in with your child at regular intervals to see how he's keeping to *his* schedule. Incentives for a young child could be watching cartoons before school or a special breakfast, or extra stories at bedtime for getting in bed on time. For older children, earning extra computer time or watching a TV show during the week could be helpful. It's best to make the incentive immediate, as your child's motivation to get to that preferred activity will carry him through the targeted task.

Supporting Your Child in Limiting Rituals

Whatever your child's goal—whether it's closing the drawers once, not shuffling on the stairs to keep a right-left pattern, not re-rewriting a homework—you can be there as needed to help your child with the "pick up your brain" part of the ritual prevention. Ask your child how to help: Does she want you to say something encouraging ("That's junk mail, you can fight this," or "Don't let it scare you; you know what's important") or would she rather you be available to help her walk away from the scene and get busy with something else while she's trying to fight ritual?

Flashes of Hope

Bedtime was always a special time for me and Carolyn, but OCD really ruined that. It started out with little things. Her dresser had to be arranged a certain way; she had to close drawers; the curtains had to be exactly even. Eventually, I wasn't allowed to say anything—all my lines were scripted—questions had to be answered precisely the same way every night. Rituals for putting on pajamas, arranging the pillows in the bed were executed with such stress. I began to dread bedtime, probably Carolyn did too. It was like an army obstacle course or something. I always felt we were both walking on the edge of a cliff. For a while, we tried doing everything "right" but things got worse instead of better—each night there were more rituals and so many nights she was so stressed she'd end up on the floor in our room. With behavior therapy we both learned how to get mad at OCD for stealing our special time, ordering us around, so little by little, ritual by ritual, Carolyn began to fight the OCD. It wasn't easy—some nights we fought each other instead—she'd feel like I was making her change. I would try to remind her about why we were doing this. The other night we were having a bedtime chat and we started giggling about something together just like we used to do. I felt the tears of relief. It hit me how far we'd come.

*   *   *

Watching Adrienne do her homework was exasperating. What we didn't know was how painful it was for her. All we knew was that it would take hours longer than it should. A twenty-minute vocabulary assignment could take three hours, and she needed help with every step. She would ask, "What's the right way to do this?" not just with math, although those she would need us to check, but with essays, creative writing, even vocabulary definitions. We would try to turn it back on her because we didn't want to hand-hold, and we thought she was being too dependent or perfectionistic. She would get frustrated, then desperate, then cry hysterically. Before we knew it, it was 11:30 at night and she had only finished half of her homework. What was so difficult for us was that Adrienne has always been good at everything—everything was always so effortless—but suddenly there was something to worry about. It made us afraid for her future. We feel fortunate that we had her diagnosed with OCD and found help for her; we only wish we had identified the problem sooner. Now she is able to work independently and the distress is gone. The weight has been lifted and she can just work.

—Mother of thirteen-year-old Adrienne

Adrienne writes: "I still get straight A's but I don't have to fight with myself for them—there's less work and suffering."

Chapter 14

Intrusive Thoughts and Imagined Impulses

Harm, Scrupulosity, and Sexual Thoughts

When fifteen-year-old Haley came into my office, she wanted to meet with me alone. She was too ashamed for her mother to hear the thoughts she had been contemplating for the past month. "I just want to be normal, I don't want to be a bad person." Through her tears, Haley's story unraveled in a torrent of words. "You're going to think I'm crazy, but it all got really bad with the TV show *Ellen,* the episode where she said she was gay. I'd been having these weird thoughts that I wasn't praying right, that I was praying to the devil and that I was going to be gay . . . but it's not about being gay, 'cause that would be okay. It's more like, it's not going to end there, it's that I'm going to have to pay, because I don't want to worship the devil, I'm going to be in purgatory—like if I do something, get a part in a play, I got it because I prayed to the devil . . . but I don't. I'm a practicing Catholic, but I'm not sure anymore. I can't tell if maybe I want to be praying to the devil because I thought of it, and, I can't *feel* my faith now. When I try I just keep thinking, *You want to be praying to the devil.* I think I'm going to be punished by being miserable. I'm going to have a have a sex-change operation. And even then I'm not going to be happy, like it's going to be wrong then. So it's like I'm damned; it's basically that if I fight praying to the devil, then I'm going to have to pay with my happiness. Now I'm afraid to save money because I think that I'm saving it for a sex-change operation—and so that means this whole thing is going to come true."

She continued: "I dread waking up in the morning. The thoughts are waiting for me, then the bargaining starts: 'Do you want to do well on your test today or not get cancer when you're older? Do well in the dance performance today or find a husband when you're older?' It is impossible. Every day I have these impossible bargains, like I have to choose, and then I feel selfish if I choose having fun and then worry that the bad thing would come true in the future."

Haley had come in to be treated for depression; she'd never even heard of OCD. When I told her that she had a treatable medical condition called OCD, she was silent for a moment and then exhaled slowly; the relief was palpable. It was as if she had been given a second chance at life. She said, "You mean I'm not crazy; I'm not going to have to throw myself off a bridge to get away from this?" I told her that for her, OCD is a fine net on a long pole catching outrageously far-out thoughts. Within two weeks of getting the diagnosis, Haley was hard at work relabeling OCD as chemicals running through her brain. She liked to picture OCD as a pushy reporter at a press conference, issuing ultimatums—either betray God or never dance again, pray to the devil or fail tests, give up your faith or your mother will get sick. Her boss-back talk was, "No comment, I don't respond to threats, I don't do deals." Through exposure to the worst that OCD could pitch at her, Haley regained control over her life and quickly became proficient at identifying moments where OCD was at it again, but now from the perspective of a spectator rather than that of a target. When doing the exposures with the Deal Maker, we did our own version of *Let's Make a Deal,* calling it *Let's Make . . . It Worse:* I would read out Haley's obsessive thoughts, then she would have to take it one step further, make it even more horrible, so that she could test her mettle at OCD's game.

"I just doubted my thoughts of turning away from God and doing something totally opposite—because I'm a practicing faithful Catholic. I thought my life was going to totally change because I had OCD, but now I know it was totally untrue, and that my life will get better because I know how to fight it."

"Bad Thought" OCD

Praying to the devil, stepping on the gas instead of the brakes, a flash of a dismembered limb, a fear of killing people by looking at them—these are but a few examples of what children with "bad thought" OCD encounter. Such OCD symptoms, which are by nature invisible, are most confusing to parents. When a child is washing her hands or turning the light off and on, it is a clearly visible and familiar behavior, albeit in overdrive. However, when children are having distressing, intrusive thoughts, images, and impulses, parents have no clues about what to target, because so much of the process is internal for the child. Unfortunately, parents' distress about these symptoms is contagious and signals to the child "Uh, oh . . . this is really bad, I am really crazy." To stop the contagion of anxiety, parents need to be prepared to respond appropriately to OCD symptoms that may be bizarre or distressing. You don't want to inadvertently pull your child in more by asking, "Why would you ever think that?" The important factor here for parents is to remember that the explanation is the same: The OCD part of their child's brain is locking them into something unpleasant—but unreal—and they need to boss it back to regain control. This chapter will describe several types of "bad thought" OCD and guide parents to dealing with the process of the OCD instead of being frightened by its content.

For children like Haley, profound distress is created by the intrusion of OCD because by just being there, they pose a challenge to what the child wants to be thinking. But once they attack, the thoughts and images are so compelling that they redefine the child himself on contact, eroding his sense of who he is. It's like having walked into a movie theater expecting to see a comedy only to find yourself watching violent pornography, and even though it was a mistake, unbidden, and you walk out, you can't shake the idea that you've seen it and it has changed you. To make things more unsettling, the thoughts and images are often diametrically opposed to how the child actually feels. For example, a devout Christian believes he is praying to the devil; a happy child has an intrusive thought of suicide; a peaceful daughter lives with graphic pictures of poking out her parents' eyes with knives. What is a child to conclude about these horrific experiences that come out of nowhere? Children turn these thoughts back on themselves—older kids think *I am horrible, I am appalling, I am really sick.* Young children think they are very bad boys or girls. Take fifteen-year-old David's words: "I don't want to be having these thoughts—are they mine? Who else could they belong to? I must be thinking them for a reason. Maybe I really want to do those horrible things. I guess I have to face up to the fact that this is me, I am this terrible person, otherwise I wouldn't be thinking these awful thoughts."

With this subtype of OCD, children experience intrusive thoughts that don't politely knock on the door of the mind, but rather barge in, make demands, and refuse to leave. "If I wake up in the middle of the night, I'm sunk, I try not to wake up too much—it's like I'm sneaking around from myself, it's there waiting for me: 'I see your eyes cracked, I'm here, you have to deal with me—think of the horror—the Holocaust.' And then it's over, I'm up for hours. It's horrible, I ask myself, *Why are you showing me this now?*"

This type of OCD, though not how OCD is typically portrayed in the media, is very common. There is great variability in how the symptoms present. Some children have clear behavioral rituals to undo a bad thought or image—praying, counting, or confessing. Others have mental rituals: invisible compulsions of fixing thoughts internally by saying a word or prayer, executing a counting ritual, or changing the picture in their mind. OCD expert Dr. Ian Osborn, in his book *Tormenting Thoughts and Secret Rituals,* describes the "counterimage" in which an intrusive picture—for example, stabbing your mother—is neutralized by picturing the opposite—hugging your mother. Children can pass hours, trying in desperation to conjure the opposite picture. "I have to see it right," I've heard many a child say. It's so hard to do this because the bad pictures keeps on flashing, taunting, saying, "This is really what you want to see—you know it." At these times children's frustration tolerance plummets and their irritability soars. While they may look like they're sitting doing nothing, it's like they're cutting diamonds, and just asking them a question is akin to bumping the jeweler's elbow. Or, if someone says the word "cake," and the child thinks "knife," her work will be ruined and the whole process must begin again until the good picture has been safely achieved. Finally, many children with "bad thought" OCD have no visible symptoms other than distress and avoidance. They may have bouts of crying, appear irritable, or feel generally troubled because the thoughts are grabbing at their core, making them doubt their very soul. They may not have any rituals, they may hide them from you, or they may have only mental rituals—for example, praying or visualizing a counterimage. In the example above, Haley had no compulsions, but under OCD's covert attack, her distress was relentless.

As we will see below, there are different treatment strategies depending on how the OCD manifests. When there are rituals present, whether internal or observable, the treatment will consist of exposure and ritual prevention using the child's fear hierarchy as a guide. When there are obsessions only—endless loops of fears and images without compulsions—the treatment consists of flooding: prolonged exposure to the feared stimuli until the child no longer responds to it with fear.

RED FLAGS
- Urgency about prayers
- Fearing that he said a curse word or put up the middle finger
- Lengthy prayers
- Excessive apologizing for "no good reason"
- Seeking reassurance that he didn't hurt someone or commit a sin
- Avoidance of others for fear of hurting them; avoiding riding a bike, walking on grass, driving a car for fear of hurting a person or animal
- Refusing toys or gifts for fear of ruining them
- Saying "I'm a bad person"

- Talking about bad thoughts
- Needing to confess minor transgressions—thoughts, actions
- Constantly asking "Are you okay?"
- Indecisiveness, fear of terrible consequences for making the "wrong choice"
- Looking in the newspaper to make sure he did not commit a crime; feeling like he cheated on a test or game
- Confessing to crimes or misdeeds that he did not do because he could imagine doing them
- Inconsolable when you reassure that they didn't do anything wrong

Common Examples of Bad Thought OCD

HARM TO SELF OR OTHERS
- I'm going to poke or kill myself.
- Someone is going to come and murder my family.
- Aliens will possess me.
- I might jump out the window.
- I might cut myself with a knife or razor.
- Seeing people dying, bodies burning, death

AGGRESSIVE THOUGHTS
- Killing bugs when walking
- Killing animals on bike, people in the car
- Stabbing or kicking someone
- Thoughts of hating a loved one

SCRUPULOSITY
- Needing to pray because of bad act or sin
- Praying to the devil
- Needing to pray repeatedly to prevent harm
- Confessing or apologizing for small, insignificant mistakes
- Extensive, specific prayer rituals
- Feeling unable to believe or have faith
- Needing to prove the existence of God
- Blasphemous thoughts: *I hate God; God is bad*
- Refusing to answer questions for fear they may be telling a lie

SEXUAL THOUGHTS
- Thoughts or images of sex or incest
- Thoughts of touching or looking at others "private parts"

- Images of genitals
- Intrusive thoughts about sexual orientation
- Repetitive thoughts of being bad, perverted, or inappropriate

Primary Interventions in Behavior Therapy

Relabeling: You Are Not Weird; OCD Is Weird

> The hardest part has been wondering whether I was crazy or not—whether I would lose control and do something horrible.
>
> —Eighteen-year-old girl

Job one in conducting behavior therapy for this type of OCD is distinguishing between a real thought and an obsession. If this difference is not clearly established from the outset, a child will continue to wonder and doubt himself and therefore continue to fall prey to OCD's tricks. Ask your child, "Do you want to be thinking these thoughts, or seeing these images?" If the answer is no, it's clearly OCD. Usually children can answer these questions quickly and definitively. If the child is confused about the answer, it's also probably OCD. Confusion itself is a red flag of OCD. There are two ways you can help children out of this jam. First, you can establish with the child that when she is truly having fun, at a movie or a baseball game, she doesn't wonder if it's what she wants to be doing, she knows it for sure. If she's confused about whether the OCD is *really* what she wants to be thinking about, it's because she's making room for the OCD. OCD is mixing her up. When in doubt—witness the "doubting disease," as the French call OCD—assume it's OCD. Second, if she persists in being confused, you can ask her, "Well, if this *is* what you want to be doing, would you recommend it to a friend?" Put that way, most children are clearly convinced that the awful, nasty thoughts or the incessant confessions are not there by choice. They are OCD. Children need to hear, calmly and plainly, that while such thoughts may be bizarre, they are still rooted in a medical condition: "I know you don't want to be thinking these obsessions. If you truly were evil, these thoughts wouldn't bother you. But they do upset you. They don't make you weird or a pervert. Don't take credit for OCD's dirty work. Put it out there—it's the long pole—the OCD really went flying today, you should hear what far-fetched thought it pulled in this morning. That sounds like something OCD would say, but it doesn't sound like you."

The next step is distinguishing between an impulse or intrusion and a wish or plan. Children become very frightened when the obsessions picture them actively hurting someone or engaged in something equally unacceptable. It is crucial at this point to clarify the difference between the pictures we see and the actions we want to take or will take. Have a child experiment with this. Ask him to *think* of something horrific that is not part of his OCD repertoire—perhaps smashing a car window— then ask him to estimate the likelihood that he would actually do that on a scale of 1 to 10. Next ask him to *picture himself* smashing the car window. Afterward, check in on his 1 to 10 scale and see if it has changed. The lesson here is that because a child has the ability to picture something, no matter how awful, does not mean he's going to do that. It can be very reassuring to children to know that people with OCD don't act on the obsessions they have. Furthermore, if children were truly as evil as these obsessions suggest, they'd be fascinated and bragging about them. The therapeutic response to these symptoms is to say: "It's an obsessive image, it's just a picture, it's not real. It's not true and it's not what you want to be true. It's not the movie you want to be seeing, but better keep playing it so that it will go away. If you try to stop it, it will be like pushing the pause button at the worst part. Throw it back at the OCD. Okay, big deal, that's a body, that's sex, that's a knife. It's just a picture."

There are two primary techniques employed to address this type of OCD. Exposure and ritual prevention are used when kids have rituals such as prayers to neutralize the bad thoughts or pictures. In these cases, a child changes the ritual or refrains from doing it altogether in order to break the connection between rituals and anxiety reduction. If, on the other hand, the child has no rituals, but only intrusive thoughts, images, or impulses, we use the technique of flooding illustrated in the case of Haley—continuous exposure to the feared situation until the anxiety reduces through habituation. Because avoidance of the obsessions is what locks in the symptom, the primary intervention with obsessions is flooding, not fighting or fleeing the thought but exposing your child to it until he habituates to it much the same way your body adjusts to the temperature of a cold pool.

Think of flooding as "wearing" out OCD's scare tape. When you keep replaying the scary message, it gets more worn out, and eventually it doesn't even sound like anything, it might even start to sound silly to your child, but you've got to keep repeating it until the fear temperature comes down.

The important paradox in therapy we discussed in Chapter 2 is that the more we suppress a thought, the more we bring it on. Instead, you want to look your enemy squarely in the eye, ask it to shell out its worst to you, and know there's nothing it can do to you because it isn't real. By changing your actions with an obsession, you change your emotional reaction. You're not afraid, you're not at OCD's mercy, you are in charge, and you begin to break free. This technique is executed with the therapist or child describing the worst of the symptoms. Often this is audiotaped on a "loop tape" made on a five-minute repeating tape (the kind used for phone answering machines) so that the child listens to the message repeatedly until the anxiety reduces.

Limiting Participation in OCD and/or Avoidance

Limit your child's time praying or hearing confession: If you're involved in a long prayer ritual, remove yourself from the situation and return when the ritual is over. If your child is not agreeable to this, limit the amount of time you are there for the ritual. Always put special time with your child *after* his ritual time; he will be motivated to complete his rituals quickly if he knows that he can spend time with you or watch TV after he finishes his rituals (see Chapter 7 for description of Grandma's rule).

If your child asks questions, such as: "Mom, do you think it's bad if someone thinks about hurting God?" Say, "Is that a question from you or OCD? It sounds like one of those way out what ifs. Let's remember who you are first. You are you—and no thought, no matter how 'bad' is going to turn you into someone else. Anyone can have a bad thought, but yours is getting caught in your net. Shake it out, throw it back, you don't want it. Do you want to be worrying about this now? I bet there are one hundred things you'd rather be thinking about now. Let's pick up your brain and put it where you want it to be."

If your child asks you numerous questions during the day, you can set a question time at night or whenever it's "worry time." Designate a period of five to fifteen minutes each day when the child can worry, pray, or focus on the unpleasant thoughts. This intervention serves two purposes. First, it helps your child's mind shift out of worry mode; second, it helps postpone the worrying, which may often be forgotten later in the day, so your child won't need to "do" worry time, because he's not having obsessions then. Therefore it's good for now and for later. The child implements this play by saying to the OCD, "It's not worry time now, it's my time. You'll have your time later, you'll just have to wait. Don't mess up my schedule."

Help limit your child's apologies: "One apology is yours; the rest belong to OCD, and I'm not taking any of its apologies." Practice saying "not sorry" or substituting another word, for example, "spinach" when OCD forces an unnecessary "sorry."

Interventions in Action

Here are some turning points in behavior therapy—at home or in the office—for several themes of Intrusive Thoughts and Images OCD.

Aggression and Aggressive Thoughts

It was December, and I had been working with ten-year-old Jenn for about two months, when she came in and announced, "New problem; the kids at school are talking about whether they believe in Santa, and now my OCD is saying really bad things about Santa, telling me not to believe in him, but I want to." Jenn was mortified to tell me the details because she thought I would think badly of her. I assured her that her discomfort told me that she wasn't a "bad person"; if she felt okay about this stuff, she'd probably be bragging about it instead of dreading telling me. Jenn's intrusive thought was "fuck Santa." Deathly afraid of having the thought—what kind of strange person would shout obscenities at such a beloved figure?—she was terrified that she would say it. Every time she had the thought, she tried to push it out of her mind, but it kept coming back stronger and stronger.

The solution was to let the catastrophe happen, expose her to the thought without her trying to avoid it. I told Jenn that she was going to need to face the fear, to say, "fuck Santa"—not one time, timidly whispering—but many times. She wasn't ready to try it—it was too high on her fear thermometer—so instead we wrote it out on a piece of paper as many times as we could in two minutes.

We were able to write the word "fuck" many times in two minutes; in fact, we filled up several sheets of paper. Next up, Jenn was ready to say the bad word out loud, for two minutes. Initially hesitant and visibly uncomfortable, as much as this exercise might delight any teenager, it was dead serious for Jenn. As we continued, Jenn gained the confidence that ironically saying the *bad* thing was the right thing to do. Eventually when the anxiety broke, Jenn began to loosen up and say it "once more with feeling." We both began to laugh at the absurdity of trying to say anything for two minutes, let alone an obscenity, and through our giggling, our lines deteriorated into hilarity. "I guess I'm not afraid of this anymore," she said. "Nope, I guess not," I replied. Jenn felt much better after the exposure, and we both laughed about how the janitor would be shocked when he came across those papers in the trash. This is a quintessential example of what OCD expert Dr. Edna Foa calls changing the emotional reaction to an obsessive thought.

Worries About Harm

When thirteen-year-old Sarah's family came to me, they were at a loss. Faced with the most frightening of OCD symptoms, Sarah's obsessive thought was that she wanted to kill herself. They had been to several doctors previously with many emergency calls and didn't know what they were doing wrong that Sarah was not getting better. Sarah's mother recounted one terrifying afternoon when Sarah's elderly grandparents were downstairs in the living room, spaghetti water boiling on the stove, and Sarah had the ghost-white look that her mother had come to know as a sign of "the thought." She told me, "Sarah grabbed my arm and screamed, 'Mom, I think I want to kill myself, I really do, I think I'm going to jump out the window! Mom, this is it—don't leave me, it's got me, I think I have to jump! Mom, help me, I can't stop it!' I was panicked, but I knew I had to be calm. I'm trying to think, *What's the right thing to say here?* I forced out the words, 'No, you're not going to kill yourself, of course you don't want to do that,' but then Sarah got really mad and screamed at the top of her lungs, 'Mom, you don't get it! I can't take it, it won't stop! You don't know, I'm going to kill myself and you don't care!' Sarah burst into tears and her whole body was shaking from fear. As I held her and rocked her I felt surreal. I thought of my parents downstairs and the pot on the stove and thought the whole house might burn down, but the real emergency was here with my daughter on this ordinary afternoon."

The intervention that worked best was helping Sarah's parents to confidently but firmly relabel these thoughts as brain noise so that she could separate herself from the hell of those thoughts. Teetering on the edge, Sarah was more terrified when her parents reassured her about the thoughts; it made them too real, too meaningful. She would think, *Well, maybe I am really contemplating killing myself.* A year later, Sarah's parents told me, "Sarah, the child who clung to us for dear life in the middle of the night, who couldn't stay alone in her room for the terror of her own thoughts, now asks us if she can go stay with a friend who is freaking out about being alone! We just sit and watch her leave, and think, *There she goes . . .*"

I am just learning how to drive, and as I'm driving past this pile of leaves, I have the thought *What if there was a kid in those leaves, and I ran over him?*

And I start to get really nervous like I don't want to drive the car. I can't tell my friends that I want to go back and check; they'll think I'm totally crazy. I think this is OCD, 'cause it is far out there and made me really nervous, but it kind of took me by surprise. I don't usually have thoughts about hurting others. At one point I was entertaining the OC thought of going back to all the houses of the people's leaves and asking them if they had kids injured by a car in the leaves. Guess that sounds pretty OC!

—*Nicole, sixteen-year-old with OCD*

The issue about running over someone is a very common OCD thought. Many adults (before treatment) stop and go back and look many times to make sure no one was hit. Every real or imagined bump in the road, every creak they hear, signals to them they need to turn around and search for dead bodies. Any of us might have the passing thought of *Hmm, was that a squirrel? Was there something in there?* but we quickly dismiss it. For people with OCD, the sensor on the harm alarm is set too low. Relabel the thought as OCD for your child and immediately devalue it: "That's OCD, I'm not going there. Throw some water on the OCD fire, stomp it out, deprive it oxygen, because it doesn't deserve it—it's of no use to you."

For Nicole, merely relabeling the thought OCD is sufficient, as she has mastered the practice of shooting down OCD thoughts. Also, because she identified the thought as an obsession early on, she hadn't developed the learned response of needing to do the compulsion (turning around and driving back to the scene of the potential crime) in order to reduce anxiety.

It takes one minute to listen to Disaster Man and three hundred hours to get it out of my head!

—*Ten-year-old Maria*

Maria named her OCD Disaster Man for his great knack at ruining any good time by broadcasting all the terrible things that could happen—tidal waves during summer vacation, tornadoes, car accidents, unemployment, and threatening retribution for all the "bad things" she has ever done or thought. This left Maria worrying endlessly about everyone's safety and unable to relax and enjoy herself at all. What added to her distress was that her parents, frustrated by the onslaught of questions and reassurance needs, were often impatient with her and tried to shrug off her fears with "you'll live." Maria had been to two doctors prior to seeing me, but OCD had never been mentioned. "Being one minute late to pick her up could cause me such anguish because I feared the state in which I would find her," said

Maria's mom. "Now that she has OCD under control, I can leave her home alone, and she'll smile and say, 'I'll be fine, Mom!' I have to pinch myself and say, 'Is this for real?'"

Maria, who is a talented young actress, benefited most from role-playing how she was planning to respond to Disaster Man when he hit. Her mother would play Disaster Man and say, "Oooh, you've got to get scared, start worrying, don't have fun, come on, it's your job." To which Maria would reply, "Stop making me think about this. If you want to worry, that's fine, but leave me out of it. Stop 'what if'-ing me. It's not my job to worry." As Maria put it, "As I kept saying it, I got stronger."

Importantly, rather than responding with "We're *not* getting into that," her parents were coached to relabel these moments for Maria: "Maria, you're in the worry tunnel—I can't get in there, or we'll both be stuck. It seems like the walls are made of steel, but if you boss it back, they will melt away. So Maria, let's help *you* be in charge now. Do you want to be asking me about this, or do you want to be doing something else?"

Scrupulosity

One's religious beliefs are such a private matter. Whether we pray alone or in an organized setting, each of us has our own unique relationship between ourselves and the greater out there. With something so rooted in faith, there is plenty of room for doubt to enter in. "Am I right for believing in God, or am I wrong? If I'm going to be wrong, I should not believe in God now. What if I think I'm praying to God, but I'm really praying to the devil?"

Many families encourage children to pray, perhaps before dinner or at bedtime. But when supper is stone cold because your child is repeatedly thanking the Lord for the food or is staying up until 1:00 A.M. making sure that she hasn't missed anyone in her nighttime prayers, even the most devout family would be concerned.

Again, the most important intervention is helping your child distinguish this brain garbage from the sacred and private beliefs she has. To do so, the question is, do they want to be praying this way? Does it make them feel at peace? Then it's prayer by choice. If it is fraught with fear and feels more like a test they have to take, then it is OCD.

"Am I forgetting anybody? And if I did, something bad is going to happen to them and it will be all my fault." That was Sally Ann's fear. From age seven, Sally Ann's prayer ritual got longer as she would go through the litany of people in her family, her extended family, her friends, her teachers, people at church, and in Brownies. Suddenly she would jolt up in bed and remember that she had forgotten someone—the bus driver—and she would call her mom and dad in and begin from the very beginning the recital of all those that she believed she had to protect. Her parents felt torn between exasperation at this apparent need for control and a sorrow in seeing the weight of the world placed on the narrow shoulders of their seven-year-old daughter. The net result was sheer frustration. They couldn't say, "Stop praying!" That wasn't the message they wanted to send. We had a family meeting and talked about what Sally Ann and her family think are the differences between prayer and what Sally Ann was doing at night. Prayer is a quiet time to thank the Lord, they told me. Then we talked about what this nighttime ritual was about: tension, responsibility, and fear. Sally Ann nicknamed her OCD The Trickster, and over the course of a few weeks she bossed The Trickster out of her nighttime prayers. She said, "This is my prayer time and you are ruining it. You don't understand what prayer is. God watches over everyone even if I don't mention them." Occasionally Sally Ann would be hit with a wave of panic and run into her parent's room pale-faced— "What if this isn't true? What if I really should have prayed for everyone? What if something does happen?" At those times, her parents would help her relabel these doubts as OCD, and ask her, "What do you want to do? How do you want to pray? It sounds like The Trickster is trying to get you to follow his rules again!"

Another example of scrupulosity is the compulsion of having to undo every "bad" thought with a prayer. A bad thought could be as benign as thinking the word *bad*, or seeing the word *bad*, or it could actually be thinking, *I hate my mom* or *I want to hurt my brother*. Often there is an internal goading process fueled by uncertainty and uneasiness, the way that OCD yanks the rug of certainty right out from under you. *Maybe I don't know myself, maybe I am a murderer, maybe I'm a sinner. I wondered about it, so it must be true.* Take Christina, who would have to ask God to forgive her for any bad thought she had. The problem grew throughout the day as she kept up an internal dialogue in which her OCD would torment her: "You have more bad thoughts, you're just not thinking them so you won't have to pray more, but that makes you bad. You're bad for not wanting to admit your bad thoughts." Christina would pray for forgiveness. As soon as she turned her head, got off her mental watch, the thoughts would inch back in. She would just start crying during the day from the stress of being cornered by these thoughts. She felt like she was stuck in a boxing ring. Through relabeling and ritual prevention, Christina practiced refraining from prayer. She let the bad feeling happen and could boss it back.

290 FREEING YOUR CHILD FROM OBSESSIVE-COMPULSIVE DISORDER

The Boss-Back Talk

"Religion isn't a math problem—I'm not going to figure this out."

"My faith is my own. I worked for it and it's mine."

"The minister doesn't pray as long as I do. Why am I doing this?"

"Prayer comes from your heart, not from worrying."

"I am a good person, no matter what I do, even if I forget someone in my prayers."

"Prayers aren't about lists."

"I don't have to figure this out."

"I want to believe, so I'm going to."

"Not all questions have answers."

"God does not want me to suffer."

"This isn't prayer, this is OCD."

Another less obvious manifestation of scrupulosity is children who apologize profusely, or are vigilant about not telling lies, or about not letting anyone else tell a lie. One child was so worried about someone getting hurt by her "misdeeds" that she would tearfully recite for her parents all her "transgressions" every night; for example, "I used a Kleenex at Susan's house and I didn't ask her, I think my piece of cake was bigger than Steven's at the party, I stuck out my tongue at Rita. I had a bad thought of throwing the cat when she jumped up on my lap."

Some children may be so afraid of telling a lie, that rather than risk it, they stop answering questions and may routinely say, "I don't know." Here the task is to remind children that "not knowing for sure" is very different from "lying on purpose." A child can be encouraged to take risks by answering factual or opinion question such as "what's the weather going to be like tomorrow?" or "what's your favorite flavor of ice cream?" without knowing 100 percent what the answer is. Introducing phrases like, "It's my opinion . . ." or, "I believe that . . ." and asking the child to use them everyday for homework is a way of exposing them to the risk that they might be telling a lie. One child was so afraid of telling a lie that when phone solicitors would call for his parents he refused to say, "they're not home right now" even though that's what his parents, seated right next to him at the dinner table, wanted him to say! Given the abundance of opportunities that tele-marketers gave him to work on that exposure, the child was able to quickly overcome that symptom.

Make flash cards with different topics on them and have your child choose a card and practice answering that type of question each day.

Categories could include "opinion," "yes/no," "factual," or "lie on purpose." If they are struggling with the OCD mumbles "I mighta, maybe, sort of, kind of" qualifiers that help OCD win the certainty tug of war, ask your child, "Is that your final answer?" Mimicking the popular game show host, this question gives your child a second chance to take a risk.

Another example of "extra good" behavior is children who are afraid that if they don't say "please," "thank you," or "I'm sorry" all the time that something bad will happen. Ask them, "are you using good manners because you want to, or because OCD is telling you something bad will happen if you don't?" Remind them those good manners are their choice, that they should feel good when they are polite, not frightened that they've just warded off a disaster. Because children with this type of symptom are at no risk of becoming rude, practicing "bad manners" is the exposure and ritual prevention intervention here. A child can be encouraged to not say "please," "thank you," or "I'm sorry" for periods of each day, so that they can take back those words from OCD. It may be easier initially to substitute a word when the child slips and says sorry, "Oops, I meant to say 'broccoli.'" This will help her get through the distress of not saying the safe word. While at first these exposures are very difficult for the child, in time, parents and children alike have come to enjoy the irony in the comment, "Hey, good job being rude today, keep it up!"

Sexual Thoughts

At age five, Peter began to have strange ideas, "Mom, I just touched that girl's arm, am I going to turn into a girl?" or "If I look at that girl, will I be her, will it rub off on me?" Then whenever he bumped into a girl, he would have to think of a boy or touch a boy to "undo" the girl thought. Initially Peter's mom would get upset and frantic about these behaviors. Fearing that her child was psychotic or sexually obsessed, she tried to talk him out of his symptoms, and this quickly turned into a frenzied shouting match where both mother and son would end up in tears. Peter did not want any part of behavior therapy, but Peter's mom went instead and learned not to be afraid of his thoughts. This allowed her to stay calm, soothe him, and relabel. They called it "The Problem," and Peter's mom could redirect him not to listen to The Problem rather than trying to convince him that the thoughts weren't true. Now Peter is a happy, carefree child.

Having intrusive thoughts or images of genitals or sexual acts, which happens even in young children, can be very disturbing to a child: *Why am I thinking that? What's wrong with me?* It can be even more frightening to a parent. They may worry that their child has been sexually abused or somehow exposed to inappropriate material, truly they are often beside themselves trying to understand how their child could be struggling with such explicit thoughts. Parents (and children) are relieved to hear that these thoughts are just one more way that OCD presents. Intrusive sexual thoughts are very common in children with OCD, in fact in one study, they were present in 25 percent of the sample, equal to the number of children who had a magic number to which they needed to count. Remember: Job one is distinguishing between an obsession and your child's desired thoughts. This process may require a discussion about sex education. The technical information side will be tailored to your child's age level, but the take home message for all children is that sexual feelings are normal and are built-in responses from our bodies. Those feelings don't make you "bad" they make you human, and in fact if we didn't have those feelings, the species wouldn't last. Sexuality is a matter of personal, willful expression about special, private feelings that are pleasurable. If these pictures or thoughts feel more like a jolt, an assault, like they hit with great urgency or importance and feel disgusting or shameful to your child, then in our Brain Post Office, those thoughts and images need to go in the OCD Junk Mail slot. The question again is, "Do you want to be thinking about this, or is this something that you have to think about it because you can't get it out of your head?" Next, help your child relabel as follows: "This is an obsession, this is a chemical glitch—the brain lab came up with that one, not me. It's a picture, it's not true." It's important for parents to remember that, although it's normal to feel alarmed and uncomfortable with the content of these thoughts, they are no different in process from contamination obsessions. Although your child's natural impulse is to suppress or avoid such thoughts or images, in behavior therapy your child will be coached to "keep looking" until he habituates to the pictures and they no longer evoke distress.

Some children with intrusive sexual thoughts have difficulty handling any age-appropriate sexual material. For example, seeing a couple on television kissing, or lying in bed, or listening to suggestive song lyrics may trigger obsessions and feelings of self-disgust. These activities then become grist for the behavior therapy mill. Rather than running away from those thoughts or images, because they'll chase you, you want to keep looking at them until the message "You're bad, you're perverted, you want that" wears out. You can spur a child to fight OCD by framing this situation as OCD not letting the child do what regular kids his age do—watch TV, listen to music he likes. This helps move the symptom out of the uncomfortable realm of sexuality, to the familiar formula: OCD is making the rules for the child and that's not fair! OCD is overreacting saying you are bad or perverted because you want to listen to the music you like. As one ten-year-old girl said, "If listening to Ricky Martin makes me bad, well I don't think so because everyone else likes him, but even if it does, then I'd rather be "bad" than waste my time worrying about OCD!"

Flashes of Hope

Haley writes: When I hear things, stuff that would be against my morals, it doesn't mean I have to think about it—it's like my radar is always on. Some thought will come in like a teacher will talk about suicide and even though there's no way I want to do that, the thought just sits there and goads me . . . *How do you know you won't, you're thinking about it, aren't you. If you're thinking about it, you must want to do it.* Before, I would get really scared, like, wow what if I wanted to, maybe I do, how do I know for sure that I won't, then I'd start to sweat and feel sick. Then I realized it was the butterfly net, I had one of those OCD thoughts in my net, and I'd start to get mad. I'd think, *I'm not making room for this garbage.* I'd say, "Okay, OCD, thanks for bothering me again, what else do you want to pile on that sandcastle, how about a little icing on that cake, yeah, you really know who I am, yeah, you know that even though I love my life, I'm seriously going to think about this baloney, you're really stretching it this time."

When it's quiet, when I start to thinking, I'm pretty relaxed, my mind starts to fish for something—it's like when you're trying to put a baby to sleep and finally he is and you start to creep out of the room, it's like it senses it and wakes up. Well, OCD notices when I'm calm, and it comes back with, "What about murder? What about rape? What about suicide? How can you sleep? Listen to those things!" But now I know what to do: They are words, not destiny. Even if you can see it, it doesn't make it real. They are just pictures, not magic. Because you can see it doesn't mean it's going to happen.

Gabrielle's mother writes: Not only was Gabrielle afraid of a cloudy day, but every day, she would rush to the window, regardless of the weather, and make me promise her it was not going to rain. It wasn't about the rain itself—it meant danger. She didn't want to go to school, she was afraid of going to friends' houses, the fear was that something bad would happen to one of us if it rained.

Gabrielle is now free! She once in a great while feels the haunting trying to take control, but she is mentally in control, nipping it in the bud. We watch her walk into school without us, waving, smiling. I am so proud of her victory. Gabrielle writes, two years after termination of treatment: To be honest, I don't remember what it was like to live in fear. But I don't want people to think I had a mild case, I didn't; it was awful, all the time. But when I started to talk about it and know it was OCD, it helped. It wasn't always easy to boss back my fear. I was so scared that my mind wouldn't think logically enough to say, "It's just my broken record." But that was the perfect description, and when I did say it, it helped. Now I actually like thunderstorms—they are relaxing to me—and I can even do sleepovers. Bottom line is I can do what I want now: I am free of OCD!

* * *

The mother of six-year-old Elizabeth writes: This morning we were having breakfast and Elizabeth was looking out the window at our new pool. She said to me, "Mommy, you don't know this, but I got up in the middle of the night and came downstairs and there was a boy in our backyard staring at the pool." So I asked her why she didn't come get me and Kelly, Elizabeth's sister, said, "Yeah right, what color hair did he have?" Elizabeth dropped her head and said angrily to Kelly, "I don't know." So I asked her if she was having an unwanted thought, a stuck tape. She said with her eyes down, "Yes." I asked, "Did it repeat itself over in your head?" She said yes. I asked how much. She held both hands up. I said, "Ten times—wow!" She said that she kept thinking that a boy would fall into our pool and crack his head open. I said, "See, Elizabeth, that's what OCD does. It gives you a thought you don't want and it doesn't stop till you tell it." I explained how everyone in my family and lots of other people have that. Then I asked her, "Now what does Dr. Chansky say you have to do to your unwanted thoughts?" Everyone responded in chorus, "Boss it out." I asked how she bossed out the thought. Elizabeth said, "I told it to stop, and then my brain got real sleepy and I went back to sleep." Then feeling proud and back on her game, "See, Kelly, I didn't come downstairs, I saw it in my head and, oh yeah," she added with all of her six-year-old moxy, "the color of the boy's hair in my head . . . it was black!"

CHAPTER 15

Managing OCD in the Larger Context

The impact of OCD is felt everywhere in a child's life. The home front may be the hardest hit, but OCD is not something your child can leave at the door. The demands spill over into every arena—friendships, sports, school, and religion. As parents, you want to make the world right for your child. With OCD, the challenge is balancing the accommodations your family needs to function against the need for privacy about the disorder. A further complication is the fact that even if you choose to share information about your child's diagnosis, you aren't guaranteed the understanding of others. Often pushing against a wall of ignorance—or worse, stigma—parents find themselves pioneering in what author and OCD advocate Connie Foster has called the "political movement to change people's minds about OCD." This chapter provides a framework for when and how to extend intervention to other contexts, using the child's needs as a guide.

The Family: Siblings' Role

At first my siblings didn't understand what was going on, so they would make comments that would hurt my feelings. I wish that for just one day they could experience what I was feeling.

—Sixteen-year-old with OCD

*   *   *

I wish my siblings knew that I was struggling with some things and that was the reason for me acting so weird.

—Fourteen-year-old with OCD

*   *   *

Gina's brother is six years older than she is so we could explain the OCD in detail. He was very patient with her and often helped to calm her down when my husband and I were almost over the edge.

—*Mother of a twelve-year-old with OCD*

What is a family? For young children, family is virtually the air they breathe; it is their world. Everything that happens, happens to all: Every move sends shock waves through the system. Even teenagers, while more physically independent, are active participants in the family drama: a missing paper or a "bad hair day," and everyone can suffer. Simply put, OCD is a family disorder. It takes teamwork to conquer it, and every family member plays a role. For some, that may be an active coaching role, while for others it may be the important cooperation of steering clear of the conflagration and not fueling the fires. Every job is significant. Throughout this book, we've explored both the hardships for parents—the guilt, loss, frustration, fear, anger, and exhaustion, as well as the steps to cope—keeping stress low and using the five steps (Reflect, Relabel, Resist, Redirect, Reinforce) to turn a moment of chaos into an opportunity to break free. In this section, our focus on family shifts from parents to siblings.

Siblings often experience conflicting feelings about their brother or sister with OCD. Feeling guilt, concern, and love all at once, they can at times display acts of great altruism and sacrifice; however, at other times the hatred they feel for their sibling is explosive. As one parent told me,

At times, eight-year-old Anna would do anything to help her six-year-old sister Hope, who suffers from OCD. When Hope began screaming in the car that her hair ribbon fell out and it wasn't even, Anna, who had carefully styled her own hair with two ribbon ponytail holders that morning, ripped the ribbons from her hair and gave them to Hope with the speed of an EMT rescuing a victim from the jaws of death. Often, however, Anna hates that she can't bring a friend home because of her sister's volatile behavior and can't go out in public without being humiliated by the scenes her sister creates. Sometimes Anna screams, "I hate you" at Hope—which only fuels the fire.

FEELINGS SIBLINGS MAY HAVE
- Anger at their sibling for their symptoms
- Anger at their parents that there is a double standard for behavior, that their sibling doesn't get punished for making a scene, but if they forget homework one day, they're in trouble
- Frustration at their parents for not putting their foot down and for being controlled by their sibling

- Confusion: *If I can stop myself from doing things, why can't he?*
- Guilt that they don't have problems, that they are not suffering, when their sibling suffers so much: *It should have been me.*
- Lack of entitlement to complain about things that are bothering them, since their problems are "insignificant" in comparison to their sibling's difficulties
- Resentment that their sibling is "hogging" their parents' attention
- Pressure to be the "model child" to make up for their sibling's behavior
- Embarrassment that their sibling is "weird" or "different"
- Loyalty in protecting the sibling from teasing by other children
- Fear that they may develop this problem, too
- Love for their sibling who is so close to them
- Responsibility to rescue their sibling from this problem and fix everything
- Frustration about having to tiptoe around the sibling and compromise all the time when he gets to have everything his own way
- Feeling put upon by their parents who may actually ask and expect more of them because they don't have a "problem"

Given the array of feelings that siblings may have, their needs in the recovery process cannot be overlooked. As in other family crises, siblings of OCD sufferers need to talk to their parents because they understand it firsthand. However, those are often the very people who may be too overwhelmed or busy to discuss it. The alternative of going outside the family circle may mean breaching trusts and bearing shame to try to explain what has been going on.

A good first step is to have a family meeting with your child's therapist. This is an opportunity for the entire family to (a) get accurate information about OCD and (b) get support for the fact that they are all dealing with something they didn't ask for. During these meetings, family members can share ways that OCD is impacting their life. Once these issues have been raised, the therapist can help process siblings' feelings, as well as determine to what degree there are specific behavioral changes your child is ready to make to improve the quality of life for all. Very often families find themselves in the situation where a symptom has become unbearable to the family but is out of the child's reach to tackle. At those times, the therapist can help brainstorm interim solutions using "house rules" as described in Chapter 5. Whether it's managing a messy bathroom with "untouchable" towels strewn across the floor or not having to let your child with OCD win every fight against his sibling to prevent frustration, solutions can be worked out that are agreeable to all parties. Sometimes, a second family meeting without the child with OCD will allow siblings a chance to air negative feelings freely, help them get validation for their worst feelings (i.e., find out that it's normal to feel that way), and move forward by tapping into other, more positive feelings.

Many parents have expressed the wish that they had explained the facts about OCD to their other children earlier. There are several videos and children's books available in the resource guide that you can watch or read as a family and then discuss. Through the prism of other children's lives affected by OCD, siblings may be able to gain perspective on how this really is a medical condition and not something "weird that my brother does." Other parents wished they had let their other children vent frustration about the OCD, rather than making them feel guilty for horrible feelings.

One mother described how she felt she had no room for her kids' frustration about the OCD because she was up to her ears with her own: "Don't even go there" had become her pat response to complaints. One day when her daughter launched into "I can't take the bus with her anymore—it's too embarrassing, I hate this problem," instead of getting angry, she replied, "You know, I hate this too, I wish it would go away too." To her surprise both she and her daughter felt better. They didn't feel guilty, and they had a powerful, shared moment where they affirmed that they were not going to let this disorder get the better of them.

WHAT TO DO TO HELP
- Educate your other children that OCD is nobody's fault.
- Give them the facts about OCD being a biological condition, just the same as asthma or diabetes.
- Help them see that everyone is mad at the OCD, including their sibling who has it.
- Let them know that while it may seem like their sibling is getting lots of "breaks," he doesn't want to have OCD.
- Normalize for them that it's okay to hate their brother sometimes, that love and hate are both strong emotions that we feel about those who are close to us.
- Let them know they are not a bad person for being angry.
- Validate their feelings of frustration and unfairness: Be honest when you are being "unfair"—they will appreciate your honesty even if they are unhappy with the outcome.
- Give them a role to help: Siblings can be good time keepers during time limits, they can help boss back the OCD, distract your child with games, activities, and conversation.

- Let them know that you know they are doing the best they can at any given moment.
- Allow them time away from the problem. They don't always need to be actively helping; sometimes steering clear of the situation or not fueling the fire by getting angry is help enough.

"It's Not Fair!"

Getting your family through the crisis of OCD means validating each person's feeling about the experience. Researchers studying trauma have found that what buffers us from trauma following a crisis is having the experience of trauma validated. What makes a crisis a trauma is not only the event itself, but also the frame we put on it. For example, self-blaming explanations such as, "I'm a jerk for having this problem," or "I'm selfish and bad for hating that my brother has OCD" generate guilt and shame, which are destructive to self-esteem. Self-preserving thoughts such as "It's normal to feel angry, this is making life really hard," or "Anyone would want this to go away—it isn't fair" are validating and help guard against negative emotions.

Sometimes things have to be unfair. For example, if you know that your child's OCD or tics get worse when she is tired, getting enough sleep is going to become a household priority. It's one variable in your child's illness that you can potentially control, and you would be remiss not to. That may mean a change in your other children's nighttime patterns to help the house shut down at a reasonable hour. But remember, even if you decide to keep things "unfair," what you can do is to validate your child's perception of unfairness. If your child complains that something is unfair and is told "You're wrong," or to "suck it up," it will lead to bad feelings. It will help if you can admit that you are making things unfair and listen to your child's unhappiness about it. Take the following examples:

Child:	I hate Maria. She takes up all our time. Her OCD is all we ever talk about.
Parent's Invalidating Response:	Don't say you hate your sister. We are a family who sticks together.
Parent's Validating Response:	I know you're frustrated with how much time these problems take. I feel that way too sometimes. But remember, it's not Maria's fault— it's just something we all have to

	deal with. It doesn't have to take up all of our time; let's make a plan to do something together.
Child:	Knock it off, Aaron—everybody's looking at you, you're being a jerk.
Parent's Invalidating Response:	How dare you say that about your brother! You're grounded.
Parent's Validating Response:	I know this is hard for you, and it is embarrassing, but name-calling is not okay, and it's not going to help the situation. You can wait in the car if you want.

The ultimate unfairness is having OCD, and at times you may need to remind your other children of this. As one mother put it, "We explained that as hard as it is for us to deal with, it is a thousand times harder for Peter. We never tried to hide OCD or make it sound like an incurable disease. We all became more understanding and supportive."

Use "Scenes" as a Measure of What's Doable

Remember that if something is embarrassing for the siblings, it's probably also difficult for your child with OCD, and that may be a cue to rethink your expectations about what your child is able to handle. For example, it may be too much to try for a family vacation now if OCD is going to create more problems than it's worth. This year may be the year to take separate vacations or settle on day trips that may be less stressful for everyone. Family dinners out, attendance at religious services—all of these issues should be carefully considered to try to maximize the good experiences you are having as a family and minimize the disasters. Even if your family value is togetherness, you may need to define this more flexibly until your child's OCD is under control. You are not making permanent changes, only adapting to the limitations at hand. Remember that you would do the same if your child had a broken leg or needed surgery.

Even through the darkness in sibling relationships, there are times when the beauty of family teamwork is revealed.

Helen, mother of a six-year-old with OCD, tells of a disastrous day in which her older daughter, Kelly, after being screamed at by her sister during an OCD rage, lost it herself. Hitting and throwing things ensued, and finally when the girls were separated, Kelly screamed, "I hate her, you have to stop her! You are not doing anything to fix this! Why was she born? This is terrible for our family," stormed off to her room, and refused to talk. The next morning, Helen, shell-shocked, was walking around the kitchen saying, "What am I going to do about Kelly, how can I help her?" Her three-year-old daughter, Jenna, looked up at her mom and said, "Mom, you've got to love Kelly, give her hugs and love her." That night Helen approached Kelly, held her, and told her she loved her; Kelly's anger melted away and she let her mom talk it through with her. Though certain corrective messages needed to be delivered about not hurting each other with words or objects, the first message that Helen communicated with the skillful guidance of her three-year-old therapist Jenna, was to show that she still accepts her child even though she disapproves of her behavior.

OCD is confusing for adults to grasp. It can drive even the most patient parent to the edge of insanity. So it's easy to see how siblings— much less practiced at empathy and self-control—are going to need a lot of latitude to get through.

A Word About Grandparents and Extended Family

Experiences with extended family can vary greatly. One mother described what a godsend her parents have been to her daughter's recovery. The daily phone conversations between Maria and her grandparents were a treat, and a welcome break from the heat of the power struggles that were happening as they tried to wrestle free from OCD. Other moms and dads have described feeling judged and abandoned by their parents who just don't "get it." As we discussed in Chapter 6, a lack of accurate information about OCD can spawn hurtful, unsolicited, or unhelpful advice. When relatives don't see that your family is in crisis or offer simplistic solutions "just be more strict" or "she'll outgrow it, stop worrying," it's hard to find common ground. While being in the middle of a crisis is not a good place to reroute family dynamics, you may want to take stock of your relatives and consider who might be most open to learning about OCD. For these relatives, seize the opportunity to educate them by sharing books, videos, and the OCF website. With their newfound understanding these relatives may be able to spell you for a few hours or maybe even a weekend, or be an extra support person for your child. Just a knowing comment like, "this is hard" may be a breath of fresh air for you. For the relatives who don't understand, do damage control for yourself and pull back from contact for a while. Think about what things these relatives can do for you that doesn't involve "understanding" the situation. For example, doing an errand for you, or taking your other children to see a movie so that they are getting some good attention. This could give you and your child with OCD some special time as well.

Peer Relations

Next to family, friendships have long been recognized as a fundamental element of growth and adjustment in children. This sentiment was voiced cogently by Dr. David W. Johnson writing in 1980 in a collected volume entitled *Social Psychology of School Learning*: "Experiences with peers are not superficial luxuries to be enjoyed by some students and not by others. Student-student relationships are an absolute necessity for healthy cognitive and social development and socialization." Several studies have documented the social vulnerabilities of children with anxiety disorders. These children may perceive themselves as less socially competent, have lower self-esteem, and report more depression; they may be viewed by their peers as being more shy and withdrawn.

While all children want to be liked, or not disliked, anxious children's fears about this are especially primed. They are typically concerned about being perceived negatively or of disappointing others. When this is combined with a medical condition that makes them feel different from others, they may pull back further, having gotten confirmation that they don't belong or are too weird to be liked. In fact, if a child has had OCD for several years without diagnosis or treatment, a second order of business after getting the OCD under control is doing catch-up work on the social practicing that they've missed out on because the OCD has taken them out of circulation for so long. One issue is correcting the misperceptions they may have about themselves in relation to others; another issue is teaching them the social skills they've missed. For example, one young man who had OCD since age eight began treatment at age sixteen and within six months had completed active OCD treatment. However, at that point it was as if his life was just beginning—girls, managing increased school demands—so the treatment switched focus to accelerated catching up on social skills. As in the popular movie *Blast from the Past*—in which a family retreats to their basement in an atomic bomb scare and reemerges thirty years later to find a world that they don't understand—it was as if Andrew had reentered the world, only to find that all his friends had raced ahead.

Children with OCD often avoid social contact because it's too hard to explain what's going on for them, or too embarrassing if, for example, they have to do certain rituals getting in and out of the car, and so on. While you don't want to force your child to socialize, as you will be guaranteed a miserable life, you can help your child identify the people and activities that he or she enjoys.

Many children with OCD have an additional strike against them as a result of other conditions they are battling, such as ADHD and/or learning disabilities, which may interfere with social expression and comprehension, cause difficulty reading social cues accurately, and create struggles with impulse control. Social skills groups can offer a unique opportunity for children to be with other children for whom this is not easy and learn and practice communication strategies in an actual social situation. These groups are often organized by psychologists, social workers, or occupational therapists. Most groups are run for boys and girls separately. Ask the leader about the age range and approximate skill level of participants to make sure the group is well matched to your child's needs. See the resource guide for more information on social skills.

Talking to Friends: Kid's Perspectives

At first I didn't want my friends to know. But whenever I was sad, they always made me smile (or tried to). Three years later, I'm thirteen and in "Truth or Dare," this is my biggest and most common truth. My friends have been totally great.

*   *   *

My friends don't know that I have OCD. I keep it a secret because I'm afraid they will laugh at me.

*   *   *

I wanted my friends to know I had OCD; they didn't need to know much more.

*   *   *

At first I was too embarrassed to tell my friends, then one night, I got so upset I just started to cry, then the whole thing came out. They have been great—they always ask me to choose the movie because they know that some movies are hard for me to see—but it's no big deal, we're friends, we accept each other.

Secrets

Everybody has them; when and who you tell is one of the lessons you learn on life's long road. Even in a trusting friendship where lots of secrets are shared, the decision to tell a friend about OCD often feels very risky. "Are people going to think I'm crazy, are they going to blab it all over school?" A child's fear of being met by disapproval or hurtful confusion is not unfounded, and depending on how confident your child is feeling about his control over OCD, he may choose not to share this information. There is no right or wrong answer here; helping your child make this decision may involve a discussion about how to assess the level of trust in a relationship. Ask questions such as: Is the friend accepting? Does he tease? Will he keep things private? Does he tend to gossip? Has he shared personal information with you? Rehearsing different scenarios through role-playing with your child will help him identify the reaction he wants from his friends and prepare him for other possible responses. Your child may choose to test the waters by sharing a less personal piece of information first—a test grade, a girlfriend, a family secret—and based on your child's comfort level, he can decide whether to reveal more information about himself.

Children and adults understandably get stymied by how to explain OCD to others who are not familiar with it. Some sample explanations of OCD with varying degrees of specificity are given below:

"Sometimes I feel afraid a lot."

"I have a lot of fears, and they interfere with me doing regular stuff."

"Sometimes my brain doesn't work right, and I get stuck on certain thoughts."

"Sometimes my brain plays tricks on me, and I think I have to do rituals to get rid of bad thoughts."

"It's like the computer in my brain can't switch out of gear and it gets stuck on certain thoughts and fears."

"It's like a brain hiccup; my brain gets stuck on certain thoughts."

"It's a wiring problem, sometimes fearful thoughts get stuck in my mind."

"It's a physical problem, just like diabetes. My brain keeps repeating scary thoughts and pictures, so that's why I can't watch scary movies now—they stay with me for weeks."

"I have fears that are difficult to control. They don't just come and go—they stick."

"It's like having this broken record in your ear all the time telling you scary stuff. It's a real pain, but I'm working on controlling it."

Some children want their friends to know but not ask about it all the time. One thirteen-year-old explained to a friend that he got scared by thoughts like "Am I going to die?" and the friend began to harass him by asking, "Are you afraid now? Now? Now?" Most likely, talking about OCD will not make or break a friendship; rather, it can be one more brick in a solid foundation or one more unbalanced weight in a shaky one. Once sixteen-year-old Leah was able to get out from under her OCD and not view it as a personal weakness, she could tell her friends about what was hard for her. In the pure gold of what can happen in friendships, Leah's friends pulled together and began to take care of her and look out for things that might upset her. Twelve-year-old Jody was very happy when she was able to tell her friends that she could see the popular movie *Titanic,* because she wasn't afraid anymore.

Power in Numbers

It takes knowing just one other person with OCD to make a world of difference to a child with OCD. Even hearing that there are over a million children with OCD in the United States doesn't seem to have the impact of knowing about one real person like themselves—a mirror of their own struggles. Many children express great relief to see a person like them with OCD, fighting the same battles: "He's so smart, she's so athletic . . . and they have OCD, too!" Your child doesn't have to jump on a bandwagon and talk to twenty other children with OCD, but be aware of opportunities to connect to others with OCD. There are several websites for children and adolescents with OCD, the OCF has a newsletter for children called *Kidscope,* and there are activities for children at the yearly OCF conference. Aside from OCD-related activities, sometimes non-school socialization opportunities such as theater, dance, music, religious organizations or camp can be a fresh start for kids who either feel different or whose symptoms have made them too high-profile at school.

School

Getting There

Taking a look at Joe and Charlie getting ready for school in the morning, we see the burden that OCD places on the shoulders of children. Joe does not have OCD. After hitting the snooze button on his alarm clock several times and hearing his mom shout from downstairs, Joe finally rolls out of bed and into the shower, throws on the jeans from the floor, pulls out a reasonably clean t-shirt, grabs his book bag, and heads for the door. Mom throws him a breakfast bar, he says, "See you tonight," and off to school he goes. This happens all across America.

In Charlie's house it's a different scene. Before he can get out of bed, he precisely touches each of the four corners of the bed, in clockwise order. Then out of bed, he's careful not to let his body bump into anything as he moves. The shower is a black hole for Charlie; he hopes that this morning won't be a tough one where he has to stay for a half hour washing and rewashing. His mom's going to kill him, he's going to be late again. Getting dressed—a trap—"Can I get away this morning with only doing things twice? Please don't let it be more." He puts on his clothes, has to pull his pants up and down twice—good bad, good bad. Now the shirt—all those buttons—if he doesn't get it buttoned exactly right on the first try, he has to start all over again. Breakfast—what if he has a bad thought while he's eating, he's going to have to ask his mother to say something to undo it . . . "Not this morning, I'm already late, forget breakfast." The book bag—"I checked it last night, but I better do it again." Now the good-bye ritual. Charlie has to say good-bye to mom without having a bad thought or something could happen—ready go! "Bye, Mom, I love you"—*fire*—"Bye, Mom, I love you"—*murder*—"Bye, Mom, I love you, and I'll see you tonight." *Made it!*

Getting Through the Day

Children spend more than eleven hundred hours a year in school-related activities. We know that how a child walks through those doors directly affects how his day will go. A child who is hungry, tired, worried, or depressed will be hindered in his efforts to participate and learn in school. When children are barraged by frightening thoughts or trapped in endless rituals, there are tremendous ramifications on their availability to listen and pay attention in class, complete assignments, and socialize with peers. In her booklet, *School Personnel: A Critical Link,* educational psychologist Dr. Gail Adams describes the predicament for the child with OCD:

> Although the large majority of children and adolescents with OCD have average to above-average intelligence levels, OCD can exact a heavy toll on students' academic performance . . . If the majority of one's attention and working memory is devoted to obsessional thoughts, and in some cases, mental compulsions, few, if any, mental resources will be available to allocate to academic assignments.

Even if schoolwork itself is spared, OCD symptoms related to negotiating bathrooms, hallways, and the cafeteria, avoiding contact with pencils and chalk, can be a constant challenge. For example, when trying to explain why he was refusing to attend school, Jordan confessed that all he could think about in school was whether he might be sitting at the desk of a boy who picks his nose, and the disgust he felt engulfed him.

Some children may manage to keep OCD symptoms out of school; however, even in these rare situations, OCD has repercussions. The child may be tired from staying up into the night with rituals, he may be depressed, or he may be generally stressed from contending with the battle. Imagine a coworker who often makes mistakes or is jumpy or withdrawn; you can't understand why until you find out that he has two jobs, that he works the night shift, and then comes into work. Knowing this isn't going to change his predicament, but you are likely to be more understanding and not blame him now that you understand the reason.

Involving the School: If, When, How, Who?

There is great variability in the educational needs of a child with OCD ranging from needing no additional support at school to requiring a residential therapeutic school out of state. Likewise, individual schools vary tremendously in their responsiveness to children's needs and to what extent these are carried out with or without red tape. I have worked in some schools where significant changes in a child's schedule, homework assignments, and staffing were swiftly implemented without any formal paperwork. On the other hand, I have worked in schools where arranging for an psychoeducational evaluation and meeting for an Individualized Educational Plan (IEP) takes months, meanwhile the child is suffering terribly from his symptoms in class.

In addition to the variability of children's needs and school's services, there is a continuum of parent readiness to extend the scope of intervention beyond the realm of home base and the therapist's office. Some parents see the educational piece as a matter of fact issue of access, others are contending with the stigma of a psychiatric diagnosis, for others merely adjusting to their child's diagnosis gives them more than they can handle at the moment. Wherever you may be now, and you can only be where you are, know that you are in good company.

My goal in this section is to inform parents of their rights for ensuring that their child's educational needs are met. In theory, the laws that protect your child's educational rights bring with them significant benefits, but in practice their implementation is not always a straightforward matter. According to a recent report from the Department of Education, the majority of school districts, 90 percent in fact, are not in compliance.

GOALS OF SCHOOL COLLABORATION:
- Limiting the negative effect of OCD
- Accommodating situations over which your child has no control

When Daniel allowed us to tell his teachers about his OCD, we were met with blank stares and disbelief. Some teachers thought this was an excuse for Daniel not completing assignments. He was an honor roll student! That really burned me.

—Mother of a fourteen-year-old with OCD

After I explained to my daughter's teacher about using "turtle" and "rabbit" speeds to help her with her obsessive slowness, it worked so well that the teacher decided to use that system for the whole class.

—Mother of an eight-year-old with OCD

Schools are entrusted with the task of educating, socializing, and protecting our children for the six to eight hours a day they are there for thirteen years. Within the classroom every aspect of the child's world intersects: cognitive, emotional, social, and artistic. While there are always exceptions, teachers try to facilitate the child's growth in each of these dimensions. Therefore, they need to understand that kids with OCD are "normal" kids with specific types of problems. One courageous mother who spoke with her daughter's school found that they really didn't understand OCD. When Mom explained that her daughter keeps her work very neat and organized, the teacher asked, "But if she sees that the desk next to hers is messy, will she run screaming down the hallway?" This example illustrates the need for sharing accurate information with school personnel.

For many families, the decision to include the school in a child's treatment is fraught with uncertainty: "Will my child be labeled? Will this make things worse?" Sometimes it is the parents who hesitate to take this step, but many times it is the child who doesn't want to be singled out or get any special treatment for fear that teachers will resent having to make that extra effort. Kids worry that teachers won't believe them, and some have even expressed a wish that their problem were more visible—being in a wheelchair, for instance—so that people would clearly know there are going to be things they can't do.

The fact is, there is no universal prescription for when to inform school personnel of your child's OCD. In evaluating the need for school involvement, the pivotal issue is to what degree the OCD is disrupting either your child's educational experience or the classroom. Take the examples of Sherrie and Margot. Sherrie, ten years old, has had OCD since age seven. Sherrie explains that her mind is constantly giving her puzzles to do—thinking of words, spelling them forward and backward, making sure that each word she says can reduce to the number 7, her lucky number. Sherrie has to fight this on the bus, at recess, and when she's going to bed at night. Class time is a relief to Sherrie; her mind is kept busy and the OCD doesn't break through. At this point, her family has decided that there's no need to inform the school about Sherrie's OCD, because there is nothing she needs from her teachers.

On the other hand, Margot's OCD occurs almost exclusively in relation to schoolwork. Perfectionism is at the center of Margot's OCD: Her uncertainty about the right way of doing an assignment leads to studying four hours for a quiz and staying up till 1:00 A.M. checking and rechecking her homework. In this case, it was essential to involve Margot's teachers in her treatment. They suspected that Margot—a straight-A student who was too tense—was having difficulties and were glad to learn what was going on and how they could help. Shorter assignments, setting clear time limits for assignments, and encouraging Margot to risk turning in mistakes were critical interventions that the school implemented under the direction of a behavior therapist.

Some parents wait until their child is in jeopardy of failing or getting detentions for tardiness. This is one approach. On the other hand, you may try to work preventively by approaching the school before there is a crisis. An older child can be included in this process because he can best report what is difficult for him, while with younger children the adults generally meet first, and then include the child in the implementation of the plan as needed.

Approaching the School, What Are My Rights, What Are the Options?

When children require only minor adaptations in the school environment for example, those that are free and require minimal staff time to implement, it is possible that no formal special education services be required (examples of these are described on pages 316–321). In these cases, approaching your child's teacher or guidance counselor may be sufficient to move forward. However, because school districts vary widely, parents may discover that even in these situations, schools require that their child must go through a special education procedure.

Do Children with OCD Need to Be Classified?

The answer is in some cases. For children with more severe cases of OCD, they may qualify for services under the Individuals with Disabilities Education Act (IDEA). This is a federal law that governs and funds special education. In order for children to qualify for services under IDEA, they must be evaluated to document the adverse effects of their OCD-related symptoms. Alternatively, children who either do not qualify for IDEA, or if families do not wish to have their child go through the special education classification process, may be eligible for services under Section 504 of the Rehabilitation Act of 1973, a civil rights statute that protects the rights of children with disabilities from discrimination and makes provision of reasonable accommodations. There are many important differences between IDEA and a 504 plan. The chart below highlights some differences and is adapted from an article by Matthew D. Cohen, J.D., which appeared in ATTENTION!, the newsletter of CHADD, Summer 1997.

In summary, a 504 plan offers a faster, more flexible, less potentially stigmatizing conduit for getting your child needed services; it is especially helpful for children with less severe disabilities. There are times when 504 plans work beautifully for a child. Typically this occurs when you have enthusiastic, flexible teachers who welcome parent and/or therapist's input, and follow through on plans. However, given the fact that parents can technically be excluded from the formulation of the 504 plan, you may end up with a plan with "no teeth" and no recourse. Ultimately the success of a 504 plan depends on the goodwill of the teachers and staff to follow through.

IDEA	Section 504
Provide remedial or additional services	Eliminate barriers, establish "level playing field"
Funding for special education services	No funding of its own
Requires Special Eduction classification	Does not require Special Education classification
Eligibility based on a disabling condition that adversely affects educational performance	Eligibility based on physical or mental condition that substantially limits learning
Multidisciplinary evaluation required every three years	Nondiscriminatory testing, no frequency of testing indicated
Parental consent required for testing	Parental consent not required
Entitled to Individualized Educational Plan (IEP) with measurable objectives to be reviewed annually	Entitled to 504 plan, no frequency indicated
Parents must participate in development of IEP	Parents do not have specific rights in the development of the plan

In contrast, IDEA offers more accountability and safeguarding. Should you feel that your child's IEP is not being followed, you have the right to appeal via an impartial hearing where it is determined whether the child is receiving the necessary help.

If you are facing these complex issues, it is important to become well informed about how these processes play out in your school district (other parents at a local support group may be a good resource), you can also contact your local special education Parent-Teacher Association (PTA). Professionals such as special education advocates and attorneys bring not only expertise, but help you advocate for your child's rights because they are not emotionally involved. In addition there are many excellent books and websites on this topic, see the resource guide for more information. Parents need to make their own decision about which route is most appropriate for their child.

How Do I Get My Child Evaluated for IDEA?

A parent or the school's Child Study Team (CST) can make the referral for an assessment. Normally, evaluations are provided by the school, however parents do have the right to an independent evaluation if they do not agree with the tests provided or conclusions of the school's evaluation. Note that this evaluation can also be used to assess for a learning disability which may coexist with the OCD.

What Is the Classification for Children with OCD?

To be eligible for special education services under IDEA, a child must meet criteria for one of the eligibility categories specified in the law. Traditionally children with OCD have qualified under Seriously Emotionally Disturbed (SED), this classification is given if a child is found to have (1) an inability to learn, (2) an inability to maintain interpersonal relationships, (3) consistent inappropriate behaviors under normal circumstances, (4) pervasive unhappiness or depression, or (5) physical symptoms or fears related to school or personal problems. There has been considerable controversy surrounding the question of how OCD should be classified. Recently education and mental health professionals have advocated classifying OCD under the Other Health Impaired (OHI) category as it is used for children with other neurobiological disorders such as Tourette's syndrome and ADHD. To meet criteria for OHI, the child needs to have an evaluation documenting a deficit in academic, social/behavioral and/or communication or motor development resulting from the health impairment. He is then entitled to receive special education services.

The SED versus OHI debate is being played out in schools across the country. To advocate for this issue, it may be helpful to bring to your child's IEP meeting *Teaching the Tiger,* by Dr. Marilyn Dornbush and Sheryl K. Pruitt where, on page 177, the "Other Health Impairment" category is defined, and it is stated, "OCD is also considered a chronic health problem."

Special education services can encompass a wide variety of interventions including, an additional aide in the classroom designated for your child, occupational therapy services for children with sensory integration deficits which interfere with their educational experience, a behavior therapy specialist working with staff to make necessary accommodations, home tutoring if the child is unable to remain at school, or in some cases a private school if there are no public education resources that are appropriate to meet your child's educational needs.

It is important to know that a special education classification is confidential information and can be withheld from transcripts to college on request if a child is declassified or chooses to forego special help later on.

Occasionally children's school difficulties become so severe and disabling that they are unable to function in a traditional school setting. At these times, alternative schools can be considered; for some children, residential schools may be necessary. At this writing, there are no residential schools specifically for children with OCD. However, schools vary in their familiarity with OCD and their capacity to address the special needs of children with OCD. For more information about residential schools that may be familiar with OCD, contact the OC Foundation.

Spirit of Collaboration

When you're worried about your child's welfare, it is easy to feel that others don't care or aren't helping enough. In addition, it can be awkward to collaborate with schools, when there's tension around who's in charge or who knows best. You can help diffuse that tension and build bridges with statements such as "I want to share information that I think will be helpful for you to understand what is going on with Johnny," and "We need your help because he is really struggling with math." Though you may be feeling stressed and angry, you will do best to leave that outside the schoolhouse doors. What unites parents and teachers is their concern for children, and while one can meet with resistance in any situation, there are many school personnel who are hungry for information about anxiety and OCD. One way to look at this is that information about OCD may help the teacher unlock the enigma of your child.

According to Dr. Gail Adams, school personnel are uniquely positioned to be a consistent presence for children. As she wrote in a 1996 *Obsessive-Compulsive Foundation Newsletter,* "with appropriate training, school personnel can play a crucial role in identifying, assessing, and treating childhood OCD." In fact, in many cases, it is the teacher who recognizes a problem with a child in school and brings it to the attention of the parents.

Parents may work with the school on their own. However, if your child is in behavior therapy, it can be helpful for his therapist to approach the school with your consent. The therapist can educate all parties on OCD, do team building, devise interventions that are appropriate for your child's place in therapy, as well as be a liaison between home and school. In approaching the school, there are three main goals:

1. Providing correct information about your child's difficulties;
2. Working out a system to support your child; and
3. Establishing a communication system to share information and monitor both your child's symptoms and the effectiveness of the plan.

With children in elementary school, starting with the classroom teacher is a good first step; he or she may then suggest including the guidance counselor. With a high schooler, it may be preferable to start with the guidance counselor or advisor, who can coordinate with the various teachers in your child's day.

Give the Facts: General Information

With children with minimal difficulties not requiring special education classification, parents may prefer to talk about their child's problem as anxiety instead of OCD, or may begin by talking about anxiety and later, when they feel more comfortable, will broach the OCD issue. There are pros and cons to this approach. While on the one hand this may preserve your family's privacy, it may send a confusing message to your child about what it means to have this diagnosis. If you choose not to share the information with school, it is important to explain to your child your reasons why so that he understands that this is due to widespread misunderstanding of the diagnosis, not a reflection on him. Each family must make the decision that is right for them, though their stance with the school may need to change in response to their child's changing needs. Here are some useful phrases to explain your child's condition to school personnel:

"My child has anxieties and fears that are hard to control, and sometimes has to do things in a certain way to get rid of the fear."

"He has chemically driven behavior that gets set off in certain situations."

"He knows that the fears make no sense, so it doesn't help to reason with him, but there's a brain glitch where the fear is wired-in and makes it hard to move forward."

"This is not a discipline problem, because he is not doing this willfully."

If you do choose to discuss OCD specifically with the school, find out what the teacher already knows; this will give you a starting point. In addition, bring pamphlets and resource information. There are several excellent resources available specifically for school personnel, which you may choose to tell them about or purchase for them. See the resource guide for information.

General Interventions: Safety and Accommodations

The single most valuable thing a teacher can do for a child is to believe that the child is not crazy for having these fears and doubts and convey that belief to the child. Taking this as the starting point will naturally lead to a child feeling safe to be himself. He'll understand that the teacher is setting limits on the OCD rather than setting limits on him. A second key issue is keeping the classroom free from stigma and ridicule. Because teasing is a universal phenomenon, maintaining a safe classroom is a perennial challenge for schoolteachers. There are many strategies that work, and ones that clearly don't. If a teacher singles out your child, saying, "Everybody leave Sally alone, she has a problem, I don't want to see anybody teasing Sally," it's a near guarantee that Sally will be teased, albeit more covertly, with the additional labels of "tattletale" or "teacher's pet." Both Dr. Gail Adams and Connie Foster recommend an innovative approach to this crucial issue of peer teasing that involves making an example of mental health awareness.

A unit on "Good Health Intervention," takes a broader look at the body and the problems it can encounter. A "Bodies, Head to Toe" curriculum presents different organs and how they can malfunction, covering everything from brain disorders—OCD, tics, trichotillomania, headaches, and seizures—to cancer, heart disease, diabetes, allergies, depression, alcoholism, and arthritis. In this way, nearly every child will be able to relate to the experience of having or knowing someone who has suffered with a disabling condition. This will facilitate the child's identification with the idea that it's not his fault and how he would not want to be teased about it. The power of this intervention is that it targets the empathy of the "how would you like it if somebody did that to you" lesson without attaching shame about it. Also by thinking about others in the child's community (family, neighborhood, church, or synagogue), we mesh with what parents have taught their children about caring for others. In other words, this is not a school issue, or a kid issue, it's a life issue.

To preserve the child's privacy when managing symptoms day to day, it can help the teacher to have a code word or hand signal to refer to the OCD or anxiety. In this way the teacher can redirect the child— "It's getting sticky, I'll write it down for you instead"—or the child can use the system to signal the teacher that he needs a break.

It's also important to designate a "safe" school employee or location where a child can go to cool down or get brief, on-the-spot help if she is struggling. Often this intervention can prevent the child from developing a school-avoidance problem. There is widespread professional support for the idea that it is preferable for a child with OCD to stay in school rather than having to leave daily, and eventually be home schooled. That can only happen if the child has a safe person and/or place where he can go to clear his head and refuel. Whether it is a guidance counselor, nurse, or art teacher, it's crucial to have someone who is accepting of the child and a place that is accessible—if only for ten minutes—so that the child can regroup and return to his class.

The designated staff person can get materials from the behavior therapist, such as a relaxation tape or the child's "cue card" of boss-back talk to help the child cope with the situation. Many children have expressed the need to get up and walk around to "get away from" or "shut off" obsessions. A hall pass to get a drink of water or run an errand to the office can serve this purpose. It's best if this pass doesn't have to be negotiated each time, because if a child has to explain every time, he won't use it. Some teachers have used a brightly colored index card as a signal that the child needs a break: The child simply shows the orange card to the teacher and the situation is understood.

Other general recommendations identified by Dr. Adams:

- Focus on the child's strengths to combat feelings of low self-esteem.
- Structure class activities to facilitate inclusion of students who may be socially isolated.

- Consider assigning the student to a teacher who is more empathic to the child's needs.

Identifying Specific Problem Areas

You and your child can inform the teacher of specific areas of difficulty—for example, fear of contamination by brushing up against a classmate while changing classes, or rewriting handwritten work to make it perfect. The teacher may have observed other times when your child struggled and can add these to the list of situations to be addressed.

> IMPACT OF OCD ON SCHOOL PERFORMANCE*
> - Interference with normal thinking process
> - Distraction from tasks/assignments
> - Decrease in work production
> - Drop in grades
> - Appearance of poor attention, noncompliance, daydreaming, lack of motivation, laziness
> - Tardiness, school absenteeism
> - Interference with social functioning

Solutions to Commonly Encountered School Problems

Contamination

Contamination may involve books, papers, chalk, and so on. Many children divide their book bag into bad parts and good parts because of symbolic contamination. They may keep all materials away from the science books because of a bad thought they have during science, or because a child in that class represents the contamination fear. Getting an extra few minutes to pack up at the end of class may help. Teachers can:

- Allow a child to leave class five minutes early to switch to the next class without having to contend with the busy hallways;
- Give the child a separate set of books for home if he is unable to bring school materials into the home for fear of contamination;

---

* Used by permission of the author, Dr. Gail Adams, copyright © 1997.

- Allow the child to be the first to hand out tests or materials, so that he only has the teacher's "germs" to contend with rather than those of each child.

Bathroom Trips

Restricting bathroom time is generally helpful with the following caveats. Ask the child to estimate how many times she needs to go to the bathroom each day. Once the goal has been generated, it is preferable for children not to have to ask to go to the bathroom, because anticipating the teacher's reaction can become a stumbling block. A child may sit for an hour, anguishing over whether they can or can't go to the bathroom—not an ideal educational mindset. The teacher can dismiss younger children to the bathroom and remind them of their goal: "I know you can do it, you can fight the Fear Monster so you don't get stuck in the bathroom." Teachers can help in other ways:

- Initially, it can help to give a child free reign to go to the bathroom for hand washing. Paradoxically, a child may feel less need to go to the bathroom when he doesn't have to worry about asking to go or being punished.
- When a child is ready to limit his trips, giving a certain number of passes—three a day, for example—will help.

Slow Work/Perfectionism

While symptoms vary, the unifying thread is that all OCD symptoms are time-consuming, and so problems with lateness and slowness are universal. Children's work can be slowed down because of intrusive thoughts and rituals; other times it can be that they need to move extremely slowly so that they don't make any mistakes, or so that the cadence of their movements is exactly even, or so they don't actually bump an elbow, catch a nail, or move a paper when they didn't want to. As discussed in Chapter 13, one effective intervention is helping the child learn to work at different speeds. For each assignment, the teacher can let the child know which "speed" using animals or gears as a reference point to work at, thereby informing the child of how precisely or quickly the work needs to be done. For example, "the math sheet needs to be done at rabbit speed, but you can go turtle for your art project." Teachers can also:

- Reduce the amount of work to be completed,
- Set a time limit and have children work until time's up.

Handwriting Difficulties

Many children with OCD struggle with writing, as this is a place when perfection and evenness can attack. Teachers can:

- Offer alternatives to handwriting (for example, using a laptop computer, photocopying notes from another student, or using the teacher's master notes along with a highlighter pen to actively follow the lecture),
- Reduce the amount of writing the child has to do, for example, writing out definitions for ten vocabulary words instead of twenty; or writing one instead of three pages of an essay.

Creative Writing

Many children with OCD have difficulty with open-ended assignments because there are just too many choices! "What topic should I choose? What are the most important things to write about? What's the best way to say it? What should my first sentence be? How do I know I'm being clear?" The child most likely has the answers to these questions, but the barricade of doubt makes them inaccessible. Teachers can offer the following suggestions to help them break through:

- Have the child tell you the most interesting or important facts about the topic.
- Ask the child to pretend he is describing the information to a friend rather than thinking of it as an assignment in which he will be graded.
- Ask the child what questions he has about the topic; these can then become areas to pursue.
- Set a time limit of one minute and have the child scribble down the most important points to cover. Once the material is out, in whatever form, have the child circle the most important ideas, and then number them. It can then be organized into an outline which the child can begin to fill out. If the child gets stuck again, the teacher can repeat the time limit intervention.

Reading Difficulties

Most of us have sat for a half an hour in front of a book and then realized that we haven't gotten anywhere because we've been drifting off in a pleasant daydream. For children with reading rituals, reading is torture. Recall the myth of Sisyphus, who was doomed to roll a huge stone up a hill repeatedly, only to be sent back to the bottom when he neared the top. These children may have to reread a sentence many times, either because they didn't hear it just right, or they messed up a word and have to start over, or because they're not sure they "got it." Perhaps they hit a trigger word, such as "bad" or "death," and then have to do a ritual to undo the bad luck of that word. Still other children may need to count up the letters in each word and find a way for it to be divisible by 2, or to end up an even number. Teachers can:

- Suggest the child read aloud; or listen to the book on tape,
- Use a colored card to cover lines already read,
- Shorten the reading assignment,
- Make a photocopy of the reading assignment and have the child cross out the words as he goes with a black marker so that he can't go back and reread.

Test Taking

Take the average child's nervousness about a test and add to that the anxiety that a child with OCD carries—"What if I have a bad thought? What if I get stuck? What if it's multiple choice, and the answer is an odd number? I can't circle it, someone will get hurt; I need to color in the circles till they're completely black." Teachers can:

- Use untimed tests. Children tend to feel less stressed when they don't feel the pressure of time, and typically they do not need much extra time, but simply knowing that they could have it allows them to work more effectively.
- Allow the child to take the test in a quiet area away from the other children. This may reduce the child's anxiety by not having to see other children racing ahead, working more quickly. Sometimes children will be able to cope better if they are able to take the test in a separate room away from the distractions of other kids.
- Change the format of the test. Have the child take the test orally if rewriting is a problem; complete the test on the computer or dictate answers on a tape recorder.
- Allow the child to answer multiple choice questions using a letter (a, b, or c), or a short-answer format if number rituals make choices difficult.
- Allow the child to check off the correct answer instead of getting stuck having to fill in circles perfectly on a computerized answer sheet.

Homework

Homework presents problems for many children with OCD. Kids with perfectionism OCD may not be able to complete the work in the time given, or avoid it altogether because they can't do it just right, or they may be so spent from dealing with the school day that they have little energy left once they get home. In addition to reducing homework assignments, teachers can help by:

- Giving a time limit for each assignment and accepting whatever work the child completes during that time.
- For subjects such as math or science, allowing the child to do every other problem, so that all content areas are covered but without as much repetition.
- For long-term assignments, breaking down the project into parts each with a due date and a time estimate, and meeting regularly with the child to help him stay on track.

Reassurance Seeking

"Can you repeat that?" Children may doubt that they've heard the assignment correctly or read it correctly when it is written on the board. They may persist in asking the same question to make sure they have it right. If teachers are unaware of the OCD, this may be perceived as being oppositional or acting out. If a child is asking fifty questions a day, the "once and done" guideline is going to be an unreachable goal, and gradual reduction of the number of questions is needed. Teachers can:

- Limit the number of questions by using tokens or points so that a finite number of questions can be asked during each class.
- Differentiate between questions the child wants to ask and certainty questions. If the child repeats the question, the teacher can say reassuringly, "You've got it, and I know you don't want to ask anymore, we need to move on."

Dealing with Lateness

Initially accommodating the child's situation, the teacher may allow lateness; later in treatment as the child is actively fighting OCD, incentive systems that reward success (arriving on time) but do not punish failure (arriving late) can be helpful. For middle school and high school students who have rotating schedules, they may benefit from having first period free every day so they are not missing a class if because of rituals or medication-related sleep issues they can't start the day at 8:00 A.M.

For most children, implementing these interventions, which improve their quality of life, will be enough incentive to keep working in school. Some children will need incentive programs that reward success and compliance with in-school treatment plans in order to keep moving forward. Eleven-year-old Stefan's contamination fears were sending him to the bathroom as often as ten times a day for as long as fifteen minutes at a time. A careful assessment of his day revealed that the majority of the trips were in the morning, before lunch; after lunch he was better able to resist washing because he knew he was going home soon and could shower there. We instituted a plan where Stefan had four passes to the bathroom each day, and each trip was brief—five minutes maximum, except for the trip right before lunch, which could be a maximum of seven. Stefan received points each day for meeting his goal; if he succeeded 75 percent of the time, as defined by either meeting the daily goal four out of five days or only extending one bathroom trip each day, he could trade in his points for a compact disc. After meeting his goal for two weeks in a row, we decreased the frequency of trips to three. One week into this plan, Stefan was ready to limit bathroom trips for hand washing to lunch time. Within a few weeks, Stefan was able not to wash before lunch, which even his mother was happy about! Stefan had several exposures in behavior therapy to not washing before eating, and then saw how none of his friends washed up before lunch and decided he could live with that, too.

Medication Monitoring

It is good, safe practice to let the school nurse know of any medication your child may be taking in case there is an emergency. The teacher can also be helpful in keeping track of symptoms when dosage or side effects are in question. By providing the teacher with a checklist of three or four symptoms to be tracked, she can note, for example, the number of times the child asks to go to the bathroom or asks questions, and the speed of transitions between subjects.

How Should the Teacher Communicate with Your Child?

Many children I've worked with have been hesitant to let teachers in on their problem. They fear the teacher will either think they are "faking" or will start to treat them as "fragile," like they're going to crack. It is important that the child feel there's an open door with the teacher if there are problems and that the teacher will respect his privacy. Determine at a meeting outside of class how this communication will occur. Does your child want to meet regularly with the teacher? Or would he prefer to talk about it only when he brings it up?

Home-School Connections

There's nothing worse than feeling dumped on. Parents don't like it, and teachers don't either. Good fences make good neighbors. It is important for parents and teachers to feel that they are sharing the work, and the responsibilities for the child are divided appropriately and not dumped on one or the other side of the fence. Fostering good communication includes setting up a workable system, determining as a team how frequently that communication should occur and by what means. Some parents get a weekly fax or phone call from the teacher; some parents even communicate by e-mail with the school.

Summary

In this chapter, we have looked at the other dimensions of life that are impacted by OCD: siblings, peers, and school. These arenas may fade in and out of center stage through your child's life. For some, these may be the very issues that you are losing sleep over now, keeping family peace, or negotiating a workable educational setting for your child. For others, you may be exhaling with relief that this is not on your plate right now. Wherever you may be in this process, the message of this chapter is that while managing OCD is not something that you can do alone, the other systems in your child's life can become part of the solution, rather than being part of the problem.

CHAPTER 16

Seeing Your Child Through OCD

Life is what happened to you while you were making other plans.

—*Anonymous*

* * *

Dear Mom and Dad,

I'm afraid to tell you how bad I felt before I knew about OCD. I used to feel like I wasn't normal, like I just wanted to be normal and not weird—not to have this obnoxious cough that I hate that I have to do over and over, or to have to ask you about the weather, because I knew that you couldn't tell me for sure if there was going to be a thunderstorm, or to have these bad thoughts about God. But now I know I am normal, I just have OCD. I like myself; in fact, I think I'm pretty neat. I don't like the OCD, but I'm moving on. If it wants to worry, that's fine, but I've got better things to do. I don't know what I would have done if you hadn't believed me and taken me seriously. It doesn't matter, you did.

Love,

Tracy

In his book *OCD: New Help for the Family,* Dr. Herbert Gravitz discusses how getting the diagnosis of OCD—having a name to put on this dizzying set of experiences—can set families free, because only then, with clear problem in hand, can you go about getting the solution. Dr. Gravitz reminds his readers of philosopher Jean-Paul Sartre's definition of freedom: "Freedom is what we do with what's been done to us."

OCD fits this model of something that's been done to us, and nowhere is it clearer than in children with OCD—bright, caring, imaginative children who are also saddled with this frightening condition. How can it be that these young minds can be so heavily burdened? While this contradiction weighs on the heart, this is why we have two hands. In one hand you carry your fear, sadness, and anger that your child and family are forced to contend with this condition. In the other hand you carry your conviction, courage, and belief in your child. The fact is that parenting a child with OCD requires you to lead a "double life." Truthfully there is no contradiction; you will always carry both.

Having a child with a chronic condition means facing your own uncertainty. While no child comes with a life-time guarantee, parenting a child with OCD requires you to face with courage such questions as, "Will my child make it through school, marry, get a job? Will she be plagued with this condition as an adult?" Just as we ask children battling OCD to live with uncertainty—to turn away from the prison of needing to know for sure and turn toward the freedom of living day to day—you too need to do so as parents.

Out of Darkness

Hope's mother, Aliza, writes about her experience with her daughter, now six, who has had OCD since age three:

> Our daughter has the prettiest almond brown eyes in the world. We can look into those eyes and melt with such an overflow of love, and we can look into those eyes and feel a pain so deep as we watch her eyes mirror her *mind*, not her heart. For years, her eyes were so sad, terrified with tears, darting, searching, staring, and so lost. I remember crying to my older sister that she is too young to be so sad. For years, she ran around our house, trying to control everything and everyone with all her fears—and her eyes—well, they were so scared and lost. Then one day last summer, my husband and I were in the kitchen and while looking outside there was Hope, all by herself, swinging on her swing set. Swinging with eyes that danced and sparkled and laughed so free. I guess we thought we would never see her happy. Her face was radiant. What a beautiful sight! Then there was the day driving home from school, and she spoke the words to me that I have never heard from her, "Mom, isn't it a great day!" Big smile and laughing eyes. That's what we hold onto—we have Hope, we've seen it in her eyes.

When I first began working with anxious children as a graduate student at Temple University, my heart went out to these burdened children, and I had a strong urge to rescue them. I can still picture a nine-year-old boy, short, compact, and serious, with an overlay of unshakeable concern across his sweet young face. He was like a miniature seventy-year-old, very concerned about weather phenomenon, the safety of buildings in case of an earthquake or hurricane; every inch of the world presented this youngster with more grist for his worry mill. What I did was to help him slow down his thinking and test out the likelihood of his fears. But I didn't understand OCD back then, and while I gave him some tools with which to sort through the products of his mind, I didn't help him to step outside of this worry process. I needed to show him what his brain was doing and help him to see there was another way, that he could step back and say, "Something is wrong with this machine, and I don't have to listen to it."

Now that I've been working with anxious children and their families for over ten years, I *still* want to make it all better. However, I have come to trust that as much as kids want it all taken away with the wave of a magic wand, they really want to understand how their anxieties work so they can fix it for themselves. I have had the privilege of being let inside the most frightening, bizarre, horrific recesses of kids' minds, and have been struck each time by their courage to share with me their dark secrets so that they may be dispelled.

I have been equally struck by the courage of the parents I have worked with, who grapple with the fear, isolation, and physical and mental exertion of OCD on a daily basis. For many parents, helping their child with OCD was one among many other jobs juggled—other children, a career, and caring for aging parents. They've had to endure comparisons made over the backyard fence—watching families functioning apparently seamlessly while they live trying to keep the lid on a cauldron, hearing other parents complain about not being able to find the right size soccer shoes while they are reeling from another sleepless night filled wrestling with their child's demons. Witnessing their child's vulnerability—and moving from a helpless bystander to an active advocate—has meant a sea change for many parents as well. One mother needed to overcome her own social anxiety in order to step forward and speak with school personnel on her son's behalf. Supermarkets, department stores, and church became places where she would no longer apologize for her children's behavior, but rather where she educated other children and adults about acceptance. Thus life presents us with these moments that shape us.

Often parents remark about the strength of their children. One mother wrote, "It's strange, but at the same time that I think of Mimi as so vulnerable, she is the strongest person I've ever known. She has endured so much hardship for her fourteen years, and yet she bounces back from episodes that send me into a tailspin for days."

In preparing to write this book, I asked many of my "graduates" to complete questionnaires about their experiences with OCD. It was with awe and delight that I read of so many children who could barely remember their symptoms. OCD had become something they had conquered, and when it did return, they felt prepared to fight it back. I read of the relief that so many parents described of having their child back—rescuing him from the darkness of OCD and marvelling at how normal life had become.

One mother shared such a moment when OCD had fallen off her radar screen for a while.

> It was a snow day, big storm, school was cancelled and my seven-year-old came inside after being out for a few hours and announced, "Mom, I picked up trash outside on our block to help the elderly and the ill, a whole bag-full." I guess I didn't give her the response she was looking for, I said, "That's great, you picked up trash on the very coldest day of the year. I'm proud of you." "No, mom," she said, "You don't get it, hello, it's me, your daughter, Elizabeth, you know how I feel about trash—it's yucky—you know, before I couldn't even touch my own Kleenex, now look what I did!" I got zapped back to reality, and the full impact of that moment hit me. I gave Elizabeth a big hug. Trash, I thought to myself, just one more way that life can be beautiful.

I was once asked whether working with OCD has made me more fearful of the world. The answer is no. In fact, I have perhaps overcorrected for fear in testing that my family and I can live with uncertainty. Walking around New York City one sunny Saturday, we stopped in at a deli and got my daughter a yogurt for a snack. She carried the yogurt and a spoon till we found a place to sit down and eat. Then she dropped the spoon, and I picked it up, wiped it off, and gave it back to her. My husband was horrified: These were, after all, the grubby streets of New York. "How many times do you think the clerk dropped it?" I asked. In moments like these, I have felt flexible, at peace with my vulnerability, and only a smidge self-righteous. But about a year later, the tables were turned, and I got my just desserts. My daughter and I were eating sandwiches at the hairdresser's while my husband was getting his hair cut. The meat fell out of my daughter's sandwich and onto the floor; she reached down to pick it up—to throw it out, I assumed—but instead popped it in her mouth. My jaw dropped. Flexibility or no, that meat was destined for the trash. I said, "Meredith!" She said proudly and loudly, "Mom, you taught me this. You told me it's okay to lick my shoes." Everyone in the salon turned and looked at me and said, "What?" "It's a long story," I explained and kept on eating.

In the last weeks of working on this book, Rayne, a fourteen-year-old whose OCD was wreaking havoc with her faith and spirituality, came to therapy three days into a setback. Rayne, who has had OCD symptoms since she was age seven, had been in behavior therapy for only two months when she had gone on a church retreat—three full days of Bible study, discussion, and affirmation of faith. When the pastor asked for anyone who was doubting their faith to come up to the pulpit, Rayne had burst into tears. She so much wanted to be a Christian, to move forward with her beliefs, but OCD has turned this into a Herculean task by refusing to allow her to feel her faith—and she had been in training for only two months. I explained to her during our session that this was like making a child with contamination fears go to a three-day lecture on germs and antibacterial solutions.

As I sat looking at Rayne, wrung-out and unsure, I felt the lump in my throat too. She told me, "All I want is this solid faith that other people just take for granted. They may never even think about it. All I can think about is life and how I understand nothing about it. I question everything, and it is so scary. It is tormenting me. I reach no answers, so it's like I'm condemned to go on with unimaginable fear and sense of alienation from everything I ever believed in or had faith in."

"There is no question this is unfair," I told her. "This was to be your weekend, and OCD took it away from you." Quoting nineteenth-century French author Comtesse Catherine de Gasparin—"Doubt is hell in the human soul"—I told her that she had spent the weekend in hell. I knew that the way to help her back on track was to flood her with the fears and doubts so that she could move past them. Part of me—the mother in me, the kindred spirit—did not want to. I felt awful having to put this vulnerable soul through boot camp, again. At the same time, I knew I had to. I started, "So what if life is meaningless, there is no purpose, we are a failed experiment, nothing holy, there is no God, it's all a sham, no master plan . . . you have to figure it out for sure."

Rayne began to respond. She said, "Figuring it out is like living in the matrix, there's no escape."

"That's right," I said. "If we had to prove anything 100 percent—even the fact that we actually are sitting here in this room—it would be never-ending. That's OCD, that's the chemical that knows no reason; how about the fork in the road?"

Rayne knew her fork. "I know I will climb out of this because I want to believe, it's my choice to believe, it is my right to believe. Not even the pastor has to prove his faith the way I am. I have faith that I will resolve this. A year ago an experience like this would have slid me into a dark hole for weeks. And today I'm already fifty times better than I was yesterday."

I reminded Rayne of the territory she'd already won back. Just days before the retreat, she told me that when she was listening to her ten-minute flooding tape, which contained her worst fears about spirituality, she began to think, *I know what's important to me, no one can know for sure, why should I try. Even if I am wrong, and there is no God, I've lived a happier life by not having to prove it. I trust in myself. This isn't a mathematical problem, this is my life. I am optimistic that I can separate the OCD me from the real me. One day I know I won't be scared and I know that I can deal with things until that day comes. Beginning the journey is the hardest part, I think, so I'm well on my way already.*

Witnessing this experience, I think of Shakespeare's lines from *Hamlet:* "What [a] piece of work is a man, how noble in reason, how infinite in faculties, in form, and moving, how express and admirable in action, how like an angel in apprehension, how like a god!" and I am filled with awe at the integrity and fortitude of these young warriors.

Children of the Revolution

Steve, age twenty-six, has been dealing with OCD and depression since age eight, but he hid it well. Because he succeeded in school, his misery stayed under the radar of the adults around him. Steve didn't know that his intrusive thoughts, his inability to fit in, and the weight of his sadness were the symptoms of a medical problem. He just thought that life was like that. By increasing public awareness about OCD, the lives of people like Steve—young enough to benefit from recent advances in treatment—might be greatly changed.

Connie Foster, OCD advocate and educator wrote in a 1996 *Obsessive Compulsive Foundation Newsletter,* "I truly believe that what is needed in the mental-health field today is nothing short of a full-scale revolution. The sad truth is that even on the very threshold of the twenty-first century, the world is still rampant with stigmas, myths, and misconceptions regarding OCD and like illnesses . . . illnesses that are caused by physiological—not psychological—conditions. As always in a revolution, the children are the best people with whom to inaugurate these needed changes." From the mom who enlightens that neighbor over that backyard fence, to the legislator who fights for nondiscrimination, each one of us can move this revolution one step further.

The history of OCD has been one of toxic darkness, of countless lifetimes lost to this disorder, first through misunderstanding and then misinformation and needless blame. This is the past. Our children are our future. The world they enter is one of light and life. We cannot cure OCD, but we are no longer fumbling in the dark. With effective treatments being continuously refined and improved, as parents you can feel competent as you take swift, decisive action in response to OCD and guide your child on the road to recovery. The hope is back in your hands.

PART FOUR

APPENDICES

*Resources Including Books,
Videos, and Organizations*

Organizations for OCD and Related Issues

Obsessive-Compulsive Foundation
 (OCF)
337 Notch Hill Road
North Branford, CT 06971
(203) 315-2190
http://www.ocfoundation.org

Obsessive Compulsive Information
 Center (OCIC)
Madison Institute of Medicine
7617 Mineral Point Road, Suite 300
Madison, WI 53717
(608) 827-2470
*http://www.healthtechsys.com/mim
 .html*

National Institute of Mental Health
 (NIMH), PANDAS Program
Pediatrics and Developmental
 Neuropsychiatry Branch
NIMH
Building 10, Room 4N 208
Bethesda, MD 20892-1255
(301) 496-5323
*http://www.intramural.nimh.nih.gov/
 pds/web.htm*

OC & Spectrum Disorders Association
 (OCSDA)
18653 Ventura Boulevard
Suite 414
Tarzana, CA 91356
(818) 990-4830
http://www.ocdhelp.org

OCD and Parenting On-line Support
Louis Harkins, owner
*http://www.onelist.com/subscribe
 /ocdandparenting*

Genetics Studies in Obsessive
 Compulsive Disorder—The
 Rockefeller University
Toll-free (888) 920-9100
Contact: Maude Blundell,
 blundem@rockvax.rockefeller.edu

Anxiety Disorders Association of
 America
11900 Parklawn Drive, Suite 100
Rockville, MD 20852-2624
(301) 231-9350
http://www.adaa.org

The Association for the Advancement
    of Behavior Therapy
305 7th Avenue, 16th Floor
New York, NY 10001-6008
(212) 647-1890
http://www.aabt.org/aabt

The Tourette Syndrome Association
42-40 Bell Boulevard
Bayside, NY 11361-2874
(800) 237-0717
http://tsa.mgh.harvard.edu

Children and Adults with Attention
    Deficit Disorders (CHADD)
499 NW 70th Avenue, Suite 101
Plantation, FL 33317
(800) 233-4050
http://www.chadd.org

Trichotillomania Learning Center
    (TLC)
1215 Mission Street, Suite 2
Santa Cruz, CA 95060
(831) 457-1004
http://www.trich.org

Pioneer Clinic for Trichotillomania
2550 University Avenue West, Suite
    229-N
St. Paul, MN 55114
(612) 649-1105

Learning Disabilities Association of
    America (LDAA)
4156 Library Road
Pittsburgh, PA 15234
(888) 300-6710
http://www.ldanatl.org

National Information Center for
    Children and Youth with
    Disabilities (NICHCY)
Box 1492
Washington, DC 20013
(800) 695-0285
http://www.nichy.org

American Occupational Therapy
    Association, Inc.
P.O. Box 31220
Bethesda, MD 20824-1220
http://www.aota.org

National Alliance for the Mentally Ill,
    Child and Adolescent Network
    (NAMI-CAN)
200 North Glebe Road, Suite 1015
Arlington, VA 22203-3754
(800) 950-6264

Books About OCD

Baer, Lee. *Getting Control: Overcoming Your Obsessions and Compulsions.* New York: Plume. Penguin Books, 1992.

Ciarrocchi, Joseph W. *The Doubting Disease: Help for Scrupulosity and Religious Compulsions.* New York: Paulist Press, 1995.

Foa, Edna B., and Reid Wilson. *Stop Obsessing!: How to Overcome Your Obsessions and Compulsions.* New York: Bantam Books, 1991.

Gravitz, Herbert L. *Obsessive Compulsive Disorder: New Help for the Family.* Santa Barbara, CA: Healing Visions Press, 1998.

Greist, John. *Obsessive Compulsive Disorder: A Guide,* 2d ed. Madison, WI: Obsessive Compulsive Information Center, 1994.

Jenike, Michael A., Lee Baer, and William E. Minichiello. *Obsessive-Compulsive Disorders: Practical Management.* 3rd ed. St. Louis, MO: Mosby-Year Book, 1998.

Johnston, Hugh F. *Obsessive Compulsive Disorder in Children and Adolescents: A Guide.* Madison, WI: Child Psychopharmacology Information Center, University of Wisconsin, 1993.

March, John and Karen Mulle. *OCD in Children and Adolescents: A Cognitive-Behavioral Treatment Manual.* New York: Guilford Press, 1998.

Neziroglu, F., and J.A. Yaryura-Tobias. *Over and Over Again: Understanding Obsessive-Compulsive Disorder,* 2nd ed. New York: Lexington Books, 1995.

Osborn, Ian. *Tormenting Thoughts and Secret Rituals.* New York: Dell, 1998.

Rapoport, Judith. *The Boy Who Couldn't Stop Washing.* New York: Penguin Books, 1991.

Schwartz, Jeffrey M. *Brain Lock.* New York: Regan Books, HarperCollins, 1996.

Steketee, Gail S. *Overcoming Obsessive-Compulsive Disorder—Client Manual, Best Practices Series.* Oakland, CA: New Harbinger Publications, 1999.

Steketee, Gail S. and Kerrin White. *When Once Is Not Enough: Help for Obsessive Compulsives.* Oakland, CA: New Harbinger Publications, 1990.

VanNoppen, Barbara L., Michele Tortora Pato, and Steven Rasmussen. *Learning to Live with OCD: Obsessive Compulsive Disorder,* 4th ed. Milford, CT: OC Foundation, 1997.

Books for Children and Adolescents on OCD

Colas, Emily. *Just Checking: Scenes from the Life of an Obsessive-Compulsive.* New York: Pocket Books, 1999. (Adolescent-Adult)

Foster, Constance H. *Polly's Magic Games.* Ellsworth, ME: Dilligaf Publishing, 1994. (Child)

_____ *Kids Like Me.* Solvay Pharmaceuticals. Ellsworth, ME: Dilligaf Publishing, 1997. (Child)

Hesser, Terry Spencer. *Kissing Doorknobs.* New York: Bantam Books, 1999. (Adolescent)

McDowell, Jake. *A Kid's Guide to OCD and The Locked Box.* Milford, CT: OC Foundation, 1996. (Child)

Moritz, E. Katia, and Jennifer Jablonsky. *Blink, Blink, Clop, Clop: Why Do We Do Things We Can't Stop: An OCD Storybook.* Secaucus, NJ: Childswork/Childsplay, 1998.

Summers, Marc, and Eric Hollander. *Everything in Its Place: My Trials and Triumphs with Obsessive Compulsive Disorder.* New York: Putnam Publishing Group, 1999. (Adolescent-Adult)

Wilensky, Amy. *Passing for Normal: A Memoir of Compulsion.* New York: Broadway Books, 1999. (Adolescent-Adult)

Books About OCD and Education

Adams, Gail B., and Marcia Torchia. *School Personnel: A Critical Link in the Identification, Treatment, and Management of OCD in Children and Adolescents.* (Available from the OCF)

Dornbush, Marilyn P., and Sheryl K. Pruitt. *Teaching the Tiger: A Handbook for Individuals Involved in the Education of Students with Attention Deficit Disorders, Tourette Syndrome or Obsessive-Compulsive Disorder.* Duarte, CA: Hope Press, 1995.

Videos About OCD and Education

Obsessive-Compulsive Disorder in School Age Children. An educational package for teachers which includes three educational videotapes and informative booklets on childhood OCD. Obsessive Compulsive Foundation, 1998.

Books About Psychopharmacology

Fruehling, J. Jay. *Drug Treatment of OCD in Children and Adolescents.* Milford, CT: Obsessive Compulsive Foundation, 1997.

Wilens, Timothy E. *Straight Talk About Psychiatric Drugs for Kids.* New York: Guilford Press, 1998.

Books About Anxiety Disorders in Children

Kendall, Philip C., T.E. Chansky, M.T. Kane, R.S. Kim, E. Kortlander, K.R. Ronan, F.M. Sessa, and L. Siqueland. *Anxiety Disorders in Youth: Cognitive-Behavioral Interventions.* Needham Heights, MA: Allyn and Bacon, 1992.

Manassis, Katharina. *Keys to Parenting Your Anxious Child.* New York: Barron's Educational Series, 1996.

Books About Body Dysmorphic Disorder

Phillips, Katharine A. *The Broken Mirror: Understanding and Treating Body Dysmorphic Disorder.* New York: Oxford University Press, 1996.

Books About ADHD

Barkeley, Russell. *Taking Charge of ADHD: The Complete, Authoritative Guide for Parents.* New York: Guilford Press, 1995.

Books About Parenting

Faber, Adele, and Elaine Mazlish. *How to Talk So Kids Will Listen and Listen So Kids Will Talk.* New York: Avon Books, 1980.

Ginott, Haim G. *Between Parent and Child: New Solutions to Old Problems.* New York: Avon Books, 1965.

Greene, Ross W. *The Explosive Child.* New York: HarperCollins Publishers, 1998.

Hallowell, Edward. *When You Worry about the Child You Love: A Reassuring Guide to Solving Your Child's Emotional and Learning Problems.* New York: Fireside, 1997.

Koplewicz, Harold W. *It's Nobody's Fault: New Hope and Help for Difficult Children and Their Parents.* New York: Times Books, 1996.

Kurcinka, Mary Sheedy. *Raising Your Spirited Child.* New York: HarperCollins Publishers, 1991.

Swedo, Susan Anderson, and Henrietta L. Leonard, *Is It "Just a Phase"?: How to Tell Common Childhood Phases from More Serious Problems.* New York: Golden Books, 1998.

Turecki, Stanley. *The Difficult Child.* New York: Bantam, 1989.

Turecki, Stanley and Sarah Wernick. *The Emotional Problems of Normal Children.* New York: Bantam Books, 1994.

Wenning, Kenneth. *Winning Cooperation from Your Child!: A Comprehensive Method to Stop Defiant and Aggressive Behavior in Children.* Northvale, NJ: Jason Aronson, Inc., 1996.

Whitman, Cynthia. *Win the Whining War and Other Skirmishes: A Family Peace Plan.* Los Angeles: Perspective Publishing, 1991.

Books on Mental Health

Burns, David D. *The Feeling Good Handbook.* New York: Plume, 1990.

Hallowell, Edward. *Worry: Hope and Help for a Common Condition.* New York: Ballantine Books, 1997.

Ratey, John J., and Catherine Johnson. *Shadow Syndromes: Recognizing and Coping with the Hidden Psychological Disorders That Can Influence Your Behavior and Silently Determine the Course of Your Life.* New York: Pantheon Books, 1997.

Books About Social Skills

Nowicki, Stephen, and Marshall Duke. *Helping the Child Who Doesn't Fit In.* Atlanta, GA: Peachtree Publishers, 1992.

Books About Tourette's Syndrome

Bruun, Ruth Dowling, and Bertel Bruun. *A Mind of Its Own: Tourette's Syndrome: A Story and a Guide.* New York: Oxford University Press, 1994.

Haerle, Tracy. *Children with Tourette's Syndrome: A Parents' Guide.* Rockville, MD: Woodbine House, 1992.

Shimberg, Elaine F., Oliver Sacks, and Elaine Shapiro. *Living with Tourette's Syndrome.* New York: Fireside, 1995.

Books About Legal Issues for Children with Disabilities

Lathan, Peter S., and Patricia H. Latham. *Learning Disabilities and the Law.* Washington, DC: JKL Communications, 1993.

Books About Sensory Integration Deficits

Kranowitz, Carol Stock. *The Out-of-Sync Child: Recognizing and Coping with Sensory Integration Dysfunction.* New York: Perigee Publishing, 1998.

Books About Trichotillomania

Anders, Jeffrey L., and James W. Jefferson. *Trichotillomania: A Guide.* Madison, WI: Obsessive Compulsive Information Center, Dean Foundation for Health, Research and Education, 1994.

Books About Sleep Problems

Mindell, Jodi. *Sleeping Through the Night: How Infants, Toddlers and Their Parents Can Get a Good Night's Sleep.* New York: HarperCollins, 1997.

Cuthbertson, Joanne, and Susie Schevill. *Helping Your Child Sleep Through the Night.* New York: Doubleday and Company, 1985.

Videos About OCD

Callner, Jim. *The Touching Tree*. Awareness Films, distributed by the OC Foundation.

Hope and Solutions for OCD. Awareness Foundation for OCD and Related Disorders, 1999. Available from Dr. Gail Adams: *GBAdams@aol.com* or (630) 513-9234.

Assistance with Medication Costs

The pharmaceutical companies listed below have special programs to provide free medications for patients who can't afford them. You or your doctor can contact the companies directly:

Ciba-Geigy Patient Support Program: Anafranil	(800) 257-3273
Lilly Cares Program: Prozac	(800) 545-6962
Pfizer Prescription Assistance: Zoloft	(800) 646-4455
SmithKline Paxil Access to Care Program: Paxil	(800) 546-0420: patient requests (215) 751-5722: physician requests
Solvay Patient Assistance Program: Luvox	(800) 788-9277

Sample Assessment Instruments for OCD

Sample questions from the CY-BOCS interview. Note the CY-BOCS should be administered by a trained professional. Excerpts are presented for illustrative purposes only.

CY-BOCS OBSESSIONS CHECKLIST

Your name: _____   Date: _____

Check all symptoms that apply. (Items marked "*" may or may not be OCD phenomena.)

CURRENT   PAST
_____

Contamination Obsessions
Concern with dirt, germs, certain illnesses (e.g., AIDS)
Concerns or disgust with bodily waste or secretions (e.g., urine, feces, saliva)
Excessive concern with environmental contaminants (e.g., asbestos, radiation, toxic waste)
Excessive concern with household items (e.g., cleaners, solvents)
Excessive concern about animals/insects
Excessively bothered by sticky substances or residues
Concerned will get ill because of contaminant
Concerned will get others ill by spreading contaminant (aggressive)
No concern with consequences of contamination other than how it might feel*
Other (describe): _____

Aggressive Obsessions
Fear might harm self
Fear might harm others

Fear harm will come to self

Fear harm will come to others (may be because of something child did or did not do)

violent or horrific images

Fear of blurting out obscenities or insults

Fear of doing something else embarrassing*

Fear will act on unwanted impulses (e.g., to stab a family member)

Fear will steal things

Fear will be responsible for something else terrible happening (e.g., fire, burglary, flood)

Other (describe): _____

Sexual Obsessions

(Are you having any sexual thoughts? If yes, are they routine or are they repetitive thoughts that you would rather not have or find disturbing? If yes, are they:)

Forbidden or perverse sexual thoughts, images, impulses

Sexual behavior towards others (aggressive)

Other (describe): _____

Hoarding/Saving Obsessions

Fear of losing things

Other (describe): _____

Magical Thoughts/Superstitious Obsessions

Lucky/unlucky numbers, colors, words

Other (describe): _____

Somatic Obsessions

Excessive concern with illness or disease*

Excessive concern with body part or aspect of appearance (e.g., dysmorphophobia)

Other (describe): _____

Religious Obsessions (Scrupulosity)

Excessive concern or fear of offending religious objects (God)

Excessive concern with right/wrong, morality

Miscellaneous Obsessions

The need to know or remember

Fear of saying certain things

Fear of not saying just the right thing

Intrusive (nonviolent) images

Intrusive sounds, words, music, or numbers

CY-BOCS COMPULSIONS CHECKLIST

Your name: ————————————————— Date: ——————————

Check all symptoms that apply. (Items marked "*" may or may not be OCD phenomena.)

CURRENT PAST

Washing/Cleaning Compulsions

Excessive or ritualized hand washing

Excessive or ritualized showering, bathing, toothbrushing, grooming, toilet routine

Excessive cleaning of items; such as personal clothes or important objects

Other measures to prevent or remove contact with contaminants

Other (describe): ————————————————————

Checking Compulsions

Checking locks, toys, schoolbooks/items, etc.

Checking associated with getting washed, dressed, and undressed

Checking that did not/will not harm others

Checking that did not/will not harm self

Checking that nothing terrible did/will happen

Checking that did not make mistake

Checking tied to somatic obsessions

Other (describe): ————————————————————

Repeating Rituals

Rereading, erasing, or rewriting

Need to repeat routine activities (e.g., in/out of doorway, up/down from chair)

Other (describe): ————————————————————

Counting Compulsions

Objects, certain numbers, words, etc.

Other (describe): ———————— ——————————

Ordering/Arranging

Need for symmetry/evening up (e.g., lining items up in a certain way or arranging personal items in specific patterns)

Other (describe): ————————————————————

Hoarding/Saving Compulsions

(distinguish from hobbies and concern with objects of monetary or sentimental value)

Difficulty throwing things away, saving bits of paper, string, etc.

Other (describe): _____

Excessive Games/Superstitious Behaviors

(distinguish from age-appropriate magical games)

(e.g., array of behavior, such as stepping over certain spots on a floor, touching an object/self certain number of times as a routine game to avoid something bad from happening.)

Other (describe): _____

Rituals Involving Other Persons

The need to involve another person (usually a parent) in ritual (e.g., asking a parent to repeatedly answer the same question, making mother perform certain mealtime rituals involving specific utensils).*

Other (describe): _____

Miscellaneous Compulsions

Mental rituals (other than checking/counting)

Need to tell, ask, or confess

Measures (not checking) to prevent harm to self _____; harm to other _____; terrible consequences _____

Ritualized eating behaviors*

Excessive list making*

Need to touch, tap, rub*

Need to do things (e.g., touch or arrange) until it *feels* just right

Rituals involving blinking or staring*

Other self-damaging or self-mutilating behaviors*

Other (describe): _____

To order a complete copy of the CY-BOCS write:

Wayne K. Goodman, M.D.
c/o Tomasina Gray
University of Florida, College of Medicine
Department of Psychiatry
100 Newell Drive, Building 59, Suite 14-100
Gainesville, FL 32611

Leyton Obsessional Inventory

Your name: _____   Date: _____

Instructions: Please place a check in the appropriate box for each question. If answer is yes:

0—This habit does not stop me from doing other things I want to do.

1—This stops me a little or wastes a little of my time.

2—This stops me from doing other things or wastes some of my time.

3—This stops me from doing a lot of things and wastes a lot of my time.

1. Do you often feel like you have to do certain things even though you know you don't really have to? ☐ ____

2. Do thoughts or words ever keep going over and over in your mind? ☐ ____

3. Do you have to check things several times? ☐ ____

4. Do you hate dirt and dirty things? ☐ ____

5. Do you ever feel that if something has been used or touched by someone else it is spoiled for you? ☐ ____

6. Do you ever worry about being clean enough? ☐ ____

7. Are you fussy about keeping your hands clean? ☐ ____

8. When you put things away at night, do they have to be put away just right? ☐ ____

9. Do you ever get angry if other students mess up your desk? ☐ ____

10. Do you spend a lot of extra time checking your homework to make sure it is just right? ☐ ____

11. Do you ever have to do things over and over a certain number of times before they seem quite right? ☐ ____

12. Do you ever have to count several times or go through numbers in your head? ☐ ____

13. Do you ever have trouble finishing your schoolwork or chores because you have to do something over and over again? ☐ ____

14. Do you have a favorite or special number that you like to count up to a lot or do things just that number of times? ☐ ____

15. Do you often have a bad conscience because you've done something even though no one else thinks it's bad? ☐ ____

16. Do you worry a lot if you've done something not exactly the way you like? ☐ ____

17. Do you have trouble making up your mind? ☐ ____

18. Do you go over things a lot that you have done because you aren't sure that they were the right things to do? ☐ ____

19. Do you move or talk in just a special way to avoid bad luck? ☐ ____

20. Do you have special numbers or words you say, just because it keeps bad luck away or bad things away? ☐ ____

APPENDIX C

Ideas for Encouraging Sleep in Children

Setting the Tone: Talking to Your Brain About Sleep

- Tell your brain that it's not worry time, it's sleeping time, and that it needs to wait until morning to tell you things. You can imagine a box with a great lock on it to keep the thoughts "safe" until the morning.
- When thoughts do come into your mind, imagine that there is a boat gliding along the water on the horizon, put the thoughts on the boat and let them pass on by. Or imagine a train moving in front of you, place the thoughts on the train and let the train take them away. You can pick up the thoughts at the station in the morning.
- Listen to quiet music such as classical music lullabies.
- Keep to a consistent schedule, so your body and mind learn to anticipate sleeping time.
- Have neutral expectations: Don't say, "I'll never sleep tonight," or "I have to sleep tonight." The task is to focus on relaxing not on sleeping. The expectation of needing to sleep can place tremendous pressure on a child, further reducing the chances that she will sleep. Say instead, "I am learning how to relax. My body knows how to go to sleep. It will do that when it's ready. I can help it by breathing and relaxing." "Sleep comes to me when I'm ready."

Diaphragmatic Breathing

Lie on your stomach, chest flat against the floor. Breathe in and out, slow and low. In this position you will be doing belly breathing, which is the kind of breathing we do when we are relaxed. Some children can picture a pleasant place while they are breathing—for example, the beach, a stream, a field of flowers, a beautiful snow-covered mountain. While they are doing the breathing exercise, they can imagine the sights, sounds, smells, and textures of that scene. This focusing on the present enhances relaxation and reduces distraction. Other children may need a more cognitively active exercise. In bed, start your breathing and imagine that with each breath you are blowing up a balloon, then track the flight of the balloon, watch it fly up above the treetops, above the buildings, into the clouds. Then "blow up" another balloon and track its ascent. Watch as the sky fills up with colorful balloons, which you are blowing up one by one.

Progressive Muscle Relaxation

Begin with your toes. First stretch your toes, feel the tension, give it a color of tension, hold the tension to a count of 3, then let the tension go—feel the relaxation in your feet and give it a new color. Say, "toes, relax." Continue up the body and repeat this sequence. Calves, knees, whole leg, legs, pelvis, stomach, back, chest, shoulders, arms, fingers, neck, face, eyes, mouth, and, finally, head. For younger children it may help them to picture a fairy sprinkling magic dust on each body part to make them relax, or the friendly king of "Sleepland" who leads the relaxation exercise by pointing his scepter, or the child can picture himself as an animal such as a cat to help enhance the connection with relaxation.

INDEX

academic difficulties, 26
see also school issues
accommodation interventions, 193–94, 314–16
action plan, *see* parental action plan
ADHD, *see* attention deficit hyperactivity disorder (ADHD)
adolescents/teenagers, 179–80, 333–34
age of onset, OCD, 33
aggression/aggressive thoughts, 281, 285–86
anger, accepting/planning for, 219
antidepressant medication, common side effects, 126–28
see also medications
anxiety, 25–26, 47, 52, 112–13, 138, 160–63, 313–14, 334
avoidance increasing (negative reinforcement), 162
books about anxiety disorders in children, 334
diminished by gradual exposure, 161–62
discipline/limits needed, 163
facts about, 161–63
management techniques, 112–13
OCD *vs.*, 313–14
punishment increasing, 162
reciprocal inhibition, 162
relieving—by negative reinforcement, 47
resetting to normal, 25–26, 52, 161
uncomfortable *vs.* unbearable, 138
assessment:
CY-BOCS Compulsions Checklist, 340–41
CY-BOCS Obsessions checklist, 338–39
CY-BOCS ordering information, 341
Leyton Obsessional Inventory, 342
sample instruments, 338–42
seeking out expert for formal, 61–64

associations/foundations/organizations for OCD, 61, 331–32
attention deficit hyperactivity disorder (ADHD), 56, 74, 76, 124, 126, 162, 209, 311, 335
authoritative parenting style:
asserting power (confrontation *vs.* coercion), 155–56
defined, 154, 155
keeping watch (monitoring *vs.* intrusively directing), 156
steps in making changes, 155–56
autoimmune disorder, *see* PANDAS (pediatric autoimmune neurological disorders associated with strep)
avoidance, 165–66, 247, 284–85
increasing anxiety (negative reinforcement), 162
using OCD as excuse, 215

"bad thought" OCD, 43, 44, 278–94
aggression and aggressive thoughts, 281, 285–86
behavior therapy interventions, 282–84
boss-back talk, 290–91
common examples, 281–82
exposure and ritual prevention, 283
flooding, 283
harm to self or others, 21, 281, 286–88
limiting participation in OCD and/or avoidance, 284–85
red flags, 280–81
relabeling, 282–84
scrupulosity, 21, 281, 288–91
sexual thoughts, 21, 281–82, 291–93
baseline, 164
bathroom trips (school), 317
bedtime/sleep:
diaphragmatic breathing, 343
ideas for encouraging in children, 343–44